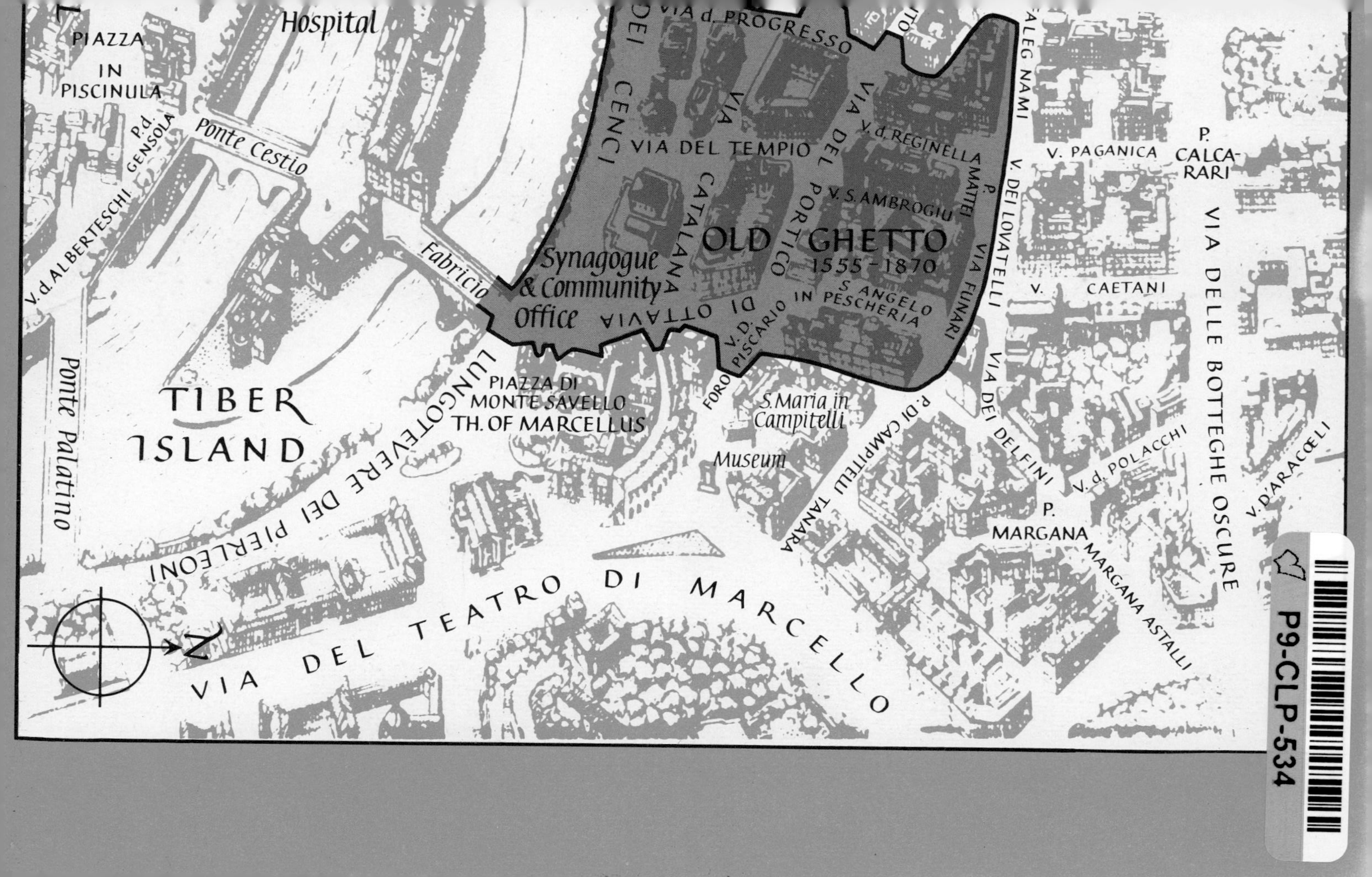

Hospital
PIAZZA IN PISCINULA
P. d. GENSOLA
Ponte Cestio
V. d. ALBERTESCHI
Fabricio
Ponte Palatino
TIBER ISLAND
VIA d. PROGRESSO
DEI CENCI
VIA CATALANA
VIA DEL TEMPIO
VIA DEL PORTICO DI OTTAVIA
V. d. REGINELLA
P. MATTEI
V. S. AMBROGIO
OLD GHETTO 1555-1870
S. ANGELO IN PESCHERIA
VIA FUNARI
V. D. PISCARIO
Synagogue & Community Office
FALEGNAMI
V. DEI LOVATELLI
V. PAGANICA
P. CALCARARI
V. CAETANI
VIA DELLE BOTTEGHE OSCURE
V. D'ARACOELI
V. d. POLACCHI
VIA DEI DELFINI
P. MARGANA
MARGANA ASTALLI
P. DI CAMPITELLI
TANARA
FORO
S. Maria in Campitelli
Museum
PIAZZA DI MONTE SAVELLO
TH. OF MARCELLUS
LUNGOTEVERE DEI PIERLEONI
VIA DEL TEATRO DI MARCELLO
N

Black Sabbath

ALSO BY Robert Katz

Death in Rome

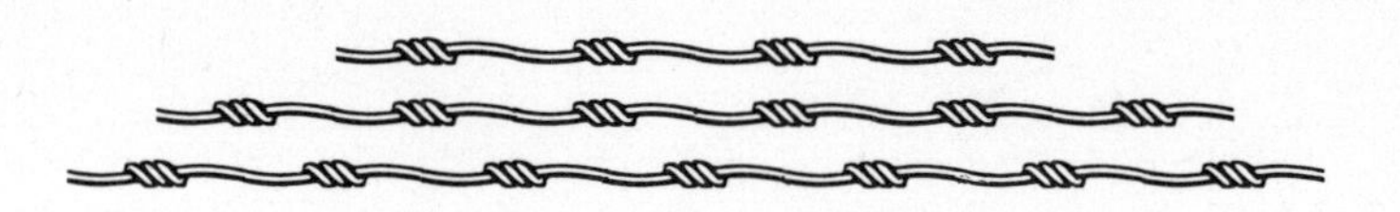

Black Sabbath

A Journey Through a Crime Against Humanity

Robert Katz

THE MACMILLAN COMPANY

Library of Congress Catalog Card Number: 69-10503

FIRST PRINTING

The Macmillan Company
Collier-Macmillan Canada Ltd., Toronto, Ontario

Printed in the United States of America

This book is dedicated

to the people of the ghettos,

who suffer an oppression

that knows no racial or religious bounds,

only masters and slaves

CONTENTS

FOREWORD

VERY EARLY IN the morning on an autumn Saturday in 1943 a group of more than one thousand men, women, and children were taken by force from the warmth of their homes and sent on a long journey to Auschwitz. Only fourteen men and one woman ever returned.

It seemed to have happened very suddenly. One moment they lay fast asleep in their beds. The following Saturday, driven hard on a train for a thousand miles, almost all of them were dead.

During the years 1940 to 1945 such events took place so many times no one has been able to count them. On the surface there was nothing especially different about this one, although it was unique in the place from which they came. Nor were the people whose fate is related in this book readily distinguishable in any particular way.

There was one woman among them who was already five years old the year Abraham Lincoln was elected to his first term as President of the United States. There was a man who owned one of the biggest stores in town, a well-to-do benefactress of local charities, and an admiral—the elderly father-in-law of a world-renowned American nuclear scientist. But most of them were ordinary people: babies who cried for their mother's milk, teen-aged youths with secret loves, fathers and sons who labored without respite in the foundry of an unjust world.

The majority were poor and lived in a ghetto. Others were

middle class and a few were rich, or were so regarded by their closest contemporaries. Like most of the civilians sent to Auschwitz and the other extermination centers operated in Poland by the German government of those days, they were Jewish—in their case, Jews from Rome. As individuals they lived and died much like the millions of other Jews who shared their final destiny.

If, however, such similarities did not somewhere break off sharply; if indeed there did not exist some most unusual aspects to this affair, an account of what had taken place would by now be superfluous, especially in a book. In the first place, while much of what follows in these pages is now being made known for the first time, the main outlines of the roundup of the Jews of Rome have been public knowledge since the day it happened, with additional information having been subsequently added.

More important, in the past quarter of a century the story of the slaughter of the Jews of Europe has been told an infinite number of times in an infinite number of ways. A whole circle of of theories has been advanced to explain the phenomenon. They range from the supernatural and from simplistic notions about good and evil to highly sophisticated ideas about the sociology of mass murder. Though the world appears to have learned nothing positive from its first experience with institutionalized genocide, most people have accepted one or another of the theories explaining it, and even the vast majority of the injured parties—that is, the Jews themselves—seem quite willing to put the matter to rest, if not forget. At this late date, in fact, any mere retelling of the story to the present generation of adults has only the effect of anesthetizing the audience to the horror of the past and as a consequence the horrors of present and future.

The pressure of so many terrifying images over such a long period of time has generated a powerful field of desensitivity. It rings and shields us from further intrusions on our conscience. It has moved into a position of prominence in the whole system of "protective" devices, which in truth serve only to wall in our ability to act as free individuals to prevent new crimes against humanity, including—it has become necessary to say so—ourselves. Only by becoming conscious of this barrier can we begin to deenergize it. Only by disassembling the old images with an opposite charge of that which they have obscured can we hope to pass through.

I began looking into this story in 1964. I was working on another book, which required some research on the Jews of Rome, a number of whom entered into the subject with which I was then dealing.[1] This work was being done at the same time an international controversy was unfolding over a series of articles that had appeared a year earlier in the *New Yorker* magazine. The articles, written by Hannah Arendt, had been collected and published in a book entitled *Eichmann in Jerusalem* (New York: The Viking Press, Inc., 1963, rev. ed. 1965). The fury it had aroused centered around Arendt's challenge to the version of the Nazi assault on European Jewry, as told by what she called the Jewish "Establishment," that is, the ruling class of Israel and the major Zionist and other Jewish philanthropic and service organizations in the United States and Europe.[2] She had suggested, without actually saying so, that the "Establishment" had helped to create a myth about the Nazi period, one in which cunning monsters had through diabolical means assaulted an innocent, God-fearing people, who, according to one Jewish authority, "had succeeded in creating . . . an exceptionally moral society."[3]

Arendt instead sought to demonstrate that on the one hand the German most directly responsible for the deportations of Jews to the death centers, Adolf Eichmann, was a rather ordinary bureaucrat—a man like countless other men who were to be found in any group, including Jews. Implicitly rejecting the monster theory, she held that Eichmann had carried out the duties of a law-abiding citizen as demanded of him by an apparently legal government. That his acts were criminal revealed more about the nature of an ordinary man in a totalitarian state than the nature of an inhuman murderer. On the other hand,

Arendt tried to show that the Jews, or at least their leaders, were not as innocent as they had been portrayed. More than merely comply with Eichmann's demands, she said, Jewish leaders actively cooperated and consequently, since they were conscious of what the end result of their labors would be, were guilty of participating "in the destruction of their own people."[4]

Arendt had arrived at this interpretation, as she herself advised her readers, not from research at the primary sources, but as a result of her coverage of the 1961 Eichmann trial in Jerusalem. In writing her articles she had used trial documents and secondary sources, notably Raul Hilberg's exhaustive study, *The Destruction of the European Jews* (Chicago: Quadrangle Books, 1961).

Hilberg, whose work agrees with at least the second part of Arendt's thesis, had used primary sources, but only on the German side. As he stipulated in the preface to his book, its scope was inclusive only of seeing the Jews and their institutions through German eyes. His study, he said, "does not encompass the internal developments of Jewish organization and Jewish social structure."[5]

Hilberg's self-imposed limitation and Arendt's heavy reliance on his work was pointed out as a fundamental flaw by her more discerning critics, who were to be found both inside and outside of the "Establishment." They asked, quite convincingly many thought, how she could possibly draw conclusions about that which had never been properly and fully studied, and not at all at its primary sources—namely, internal Jewish documents and other direct evidence on the Jewish side.

As these arguments were being developed in public debate, in the press and other media throughout the U.S., Europe, and Israel, my own researches were leading me to just such material, in connection with the Jewish community of Rome. One document, for example, was a report written during the German occupation of the city by the president of the community, in which he described extensively how his organization had acted during the first two months of the Nazi takeover of the city. Another was a personal diary kept in the same period by one of his assistants (which, I discovered three years later, had been "edited" by others to conceal certain information).[6]

While such documents were virtually irrelevant to the work I was doing then, and in the end were put aside, I continued to pursue them out of curiosity evoked by the controversy described above. The more I searched, the more apparent it became that if Rome were any example, Hannah Arendt had, it seemed to me, turned the principal issue on its head, and her serious-minded critics had seen it inside out.

This was the issue of Jewish cooperation. It was key because no one disputed it, and to the extent that it had taken place for reasons that were not wholly altruistic, the entire myth was undermined.

From the material at my disposal, it appeared quite clear that although the end result of course remained unchanged, the Jewish leaders had to be viewed as having cooperated not in the *destruction* of their people but in their *salvation.*

This is what the critics were saying, but they had, quite understandably, put forward the elements of the idea in an inverse order. As one professor of international law wrote in an "Establishment" journal: " . . . this 'collaboration' was designed to salvage Jewish property and to organize emigration of those threatened with physical destruction . . . said contacts were essential for the work of rescue."[7] In other words, according to this and other critics of Arendt, the Jewish leaders had cooperated with the Germans to save their institutions—*i.e.,* property, organizations, their position of leadership; in short, their entire social structure—in order that their people might survive.

But on the basis of my evidence, which at the time was admittedly far from exhaustive, it had actually happened the other way around: the Jewish leaders had cooperated with the Germans to save their people *in order that their institutions might survive.*

There is a world of difference between the two. Most people can survive very well were they to lose one or another highly parochial social structure into which they happened to be born.

The larger social system, in which we all live, offers a wide variety of such substructures of equal spiritual and material value from which to choose, should one of them disappear. Or, they can build a new one. But the same cannot be said of the threatened social structure. Organized Jewry could have survived if it had rescued only one fertile Jewish couple, but if it had not saved its institutions, it would have sunk into the quicksand of history like the guilds, the czardom, and vaudeville.

If the Rome case were any guide it would help to answer a number of questions raised but undealt with by the controversy.

For one thing, to speak of the Jewish leaders as participating in the destruction of their own people is to create, however unintentionally, a monster theory on the Jewish side. It is simply impossible that there could have been so much bad faith and so much self-serving behavior among the thousands of Jewish leaders functioning more or less independently throughout Europe. But once the issue is reflected and stood down side down, we see the same Jewish leaders, acting almost always in absolute good faith, engaged in the "noble" work of assuring the survival of organized Jewry, its whole gown and train, here splendid, there a little shabby, but always of the fabric of social stratification and the lace of power and privilege.

We can then begin to understand why it was "essential" for, say Rudolf Kastner, the Hungarian Jewish leader, to cooperate with Eichmann in order to save 1,700 "biologically valuable" Jews in exchange for nearly half-a-million passengers for the death train to Auschwitz.[8]

If it can be shown that in general the Jewish leaders were nothing more than servants of their institutions, ordinary functionaries, and finally ordinary human beings, who had been no more successful than any of us in creating "an exceptionally moral society," the Germans could then be put to the same test. For that matter, so could whoever else who entered into the period in question, such as the Americans, the British, the French, the Italians, the Church, and the much debated members of the Resistance—Jewish or otherwise. In the end, it seemed to me, something could be learned about the men and the institutions of all of these groups. Thus could the myths begin to fall.

Two questions remained, however: Would the full weight of the evidence support the view of the issue that had emerged from the preliminary research? Was the Rome case relevant to the period as a whole? At this point I decided to look further.

The answer to the second question came first. The roundup and deportation of the Jews of Rome, it did not take very long to determine, was a special case. That it had happened at all was its most apparently singular quality. That it had taken place more or less like every other deportation in Europe and with the same result seemed astounding.

The Jews of Rome who were seized that Saturday morning had lived in a world of superlatives. They had been torn from the oldest and most stable Jewish community in the Western world, with 2,000 years of direct experience in dealing with persecution. They had been cut from the heart of an "Eternal" and "Holy" city, most sacred to all mankind and especially to Christians, and from a universally recognized center of civilization. Yet none of this did anything to make their suffering any lighter than that of Jews who had been taken from even the remotest mud flat *shtetls* of eastern Europe.

Further, the Jews of Rome were Italians, an integral part of a people whose government had been the closest ally, not an enemy, of Germany; part of an old and highly cultured nation, of which its then living members knew almost nothing of anti-semitism; residents of the city of the Pope and an "open city," which had been politically neutralized by agreement between the Italians and the Germans. But again, in Auschwitz all of this counted for nothing.

While this tells us a great deal about the real worth of that which was valued in Rome, clearly it also speaks for the mud flats and everything between. No one in Europe, Jew and non-Jew alike, lived outside the system of values created or transmitted by twentieth-century Western society. The moment the Jews of Rome disappeared in Auschwitz, just like anyone else, the event became a workable model of all the others.*

At the same time the distinguishing qualities of the Rome

* Comparative research with regard to other European Jewish communities, as will be seen in the last section of this book, offered confirmation of this.

case, which arose from its geopolitical condition, make it an especially rewarding one to study. The further one moves from a center such as Rome, the more difficult it becomes to detect the shading and the detail necessary for an accurate reconstruction of experiences worn thin by time. Moreover, events that were never visible in other places can be viewed through the prism of Rome.

The Germans, for example, scarcely deliberated at all before rounding up and finally exterminating the Jews of, say Katowice, Poland. But they debated among themselves for almost two years before going after the Jews of Rome. The reasons for the delay concerned foreign policy considerations: Nazi relations with friendly and neutral states, especially Italy and the Vatican. Obviously, then, the destruction of Jews anywhere had an effect in one degree or another on foreign policy, and therefore—like the ripples from the pebble thrown in the pond—on the entire system. But in places like Katowice it was too slight to have even been articulated, much less would it later be detectable. In Rome, however, we have a nearly complete record of the whole complex affair.

Here another uncommon feature of the Rome episode played a crucial role. Unlike many of the millions who died in the death camps leaving nothing behind, not even their names, the Jews of Rome and the community they came from have left a rich legacy of information, without which a large and important part of the story could never have been known. They furnished unique material from which a kind of rope ladder could be built for a deep descent beneath the surface of events.

The parts of the story, though they had never been isolated and put together, lay in documents, trial records, books, private papers, and in the minds of the men and women involved and still alive. They were scattered for the most part throughout Europe, particularly in the big cities of Italy and Germany. But they were also to be found in the suburban home of a former diplomat of the Third Reich and at the end of the now rusty tracks that lead into Auschwitz as it is today. Important pieces had traveled as far as Montreal, Canada, Ithaca, New York, and a kibbutz in the foothills of Mount Carmel. Some parts of course were irrevocably lost in death and destruction; still others, as will be noted below, are as yet irretrievable, buried in the memories of fearful men and files of timid and self-protective bureaucracies.

A great deal has been recovered. All of the available material that a considerable amount of research can uncover has been examined by me. Almost in its entirety it represents primary and unpublished sources. I have been fortunate in having also had access to privileged documents and information never before revealed.

I have interviewed many people. They included: leaders and officials of the Jewish community of Rome during the occupation as well as now, German officers and diplomats who held high positions in the wartime city, eyewitnesses and survivors of the roundup and deportation, Jews of the ghetto, those who fought in the Resistance, and many others—Jews and non-Jews—who lived in occupied Rome.

The pieces I have gathered have here been joined together. The source of each of them has been recorded, including all of the interviewees I have cited. Where accounts have conflicted, I have related all sides. Nothing has been invested with my imagination, although I alone am responsible for the manner of presentation. As to the question whether the evidence supports the views expressed, my answer is this book.

One thing is certain: The social system that created Rome as a capital of humanism and civilization at one end and Auschwitz as the capital of inhumanity at the other lives on in other forms. To observe the movement of a group of citizens of this world from one capital to the other is to make a journey through that society and an exploration of our own. It is a journey down.

PART ONE

The Gold of Rome

The laws of the country, even if wrong, must be obeyed.

— THE TALMUD[1]

1943

SEPTEMBER

SUN.	MON.	TUES.	WED.	THURS.	FRI.	SAT.
			1	2	3	4
5	6	7	8	9	10	11
12	13	14	15	16	17	18
19	20	21	22	23	24	25
26	27	28	29	30		

OCTOBER

					1	2
3	4	5	6	7	8	9
10	11	12	13	14	15	16
17	18	19	20	21	22	23

I

It was a hot September. The days dawned stifling, and the city lay for endless hours in robes of motionless heat. All the stones of Rome, the amber surfaces, the grey, diamond-shaped cobbles, and the domes of bluish silver glittered mockingly in the sun. At dusk old shadows rushed in. They flooded the city canyons first and rose to cap the Seven Hills, but without relief. Not even night brought a turn in the inexplicable weather. At the time, 1943, it seemed so unnecessary, cruel.

On Saturday morning, the 11th, Rome was lifeless. The shops were closed, the streets empty, and vacant trams stood motionless in their tracks as if entrapped in a photograph. There were signs that fighting had taken place in the streets.

In Via Gioberti, which runs from Termini train station to the Church of Saint Mary Major, a raw hole about the size of a window had been blown out of the side of the building at the height of the third story. A few blocks north, near the Hotel Continental in Via Cavour, discarded shells and grenade shrapnel lay scattered on the sidewalks.

Just outside the Aurelian wall, at Porta San Paolo, the 2,000-year-old Pyramid of Cestius had been freshly chipped and riddled by machine-gun fire. A huge piece of artillery equipment lay abandoned on the cobblestones. Puddles of blood, unhosed and unswept, had blackened in the hot sun, staining the pavement.

On the inside of the same wall stores had been looted. Splinters of glass, the dust of broken plaster, and empty, doubled-up tin cans were strewn along the tree-lined boulevard that led from the Pyramid to the Circus Maximus. Rubbish and litter violated anew that which had been desecrated only a few years before.

Here on Aventine hill there had been an ancient Jewish cemetery. Mussolini, the Duce, had wanted to open a wide avenue from the entrance to Porta San Paolo to the Via dei Trionfi, or the Street of Triumphs. The soldiers of the nascent Fascist empire had had need of a worthy, unfettered road, along which they might return under the shade of cypresses from their wars of conquest. But the Jewish burial grounds had stood in the way, and the Duce ordered them destroyed.

When the Jews of Rome learned of this decision, one among them went to the chief rabbi and asked him to intervene. The rabbi, Angelo Sacerdoti, was esteemed by all. He was said to be a noble figure of a man and a Biblical scholar of the highest order. He was an ardent Zionist and also a proudly self-proclaimed Fascist, enjoying the full confidence of Mussolini. The dark-eyed rabbi listened silently to the man who pleaded for the dead Jews and the treasured symbols of their faith, which marked the sacred place. Then, when the case had been heard, the rabbi reached for a large and weighty book and carefully turned the yellowing pages.

The book was "very old," the man would always remember. "Translating from the Hebrew, he read me the following passage:

> When your king or other ruler demands that your cemetery be turned into a garden, you must do all in your power to prove to the ruler that it should not be done. But if he still insists, you must bow your head and listen to him, albeit against your will and that of your people. You must obey him. . . . You have no choice; you have no power to oppose that which your king wills or desires."[1]

The road was built. It was lined with garden. The rabbi died the following year. Mussolini and fascism fell in July, 1943. But yesterday, the 10th of September, troops of Hitler's Wehrmacht, blasting through Porta San Paolo, marched down that road. The Nazis had occupied Rome.

It had been an extraordinary week. Until Wednesday, September 8, Italy had been fighting on the side of the Germans. Though the Fascist government had been overthrown earlier that summer, the new regime, led by King Vittorio Emanuele III and Army Marshal Pietro Badoglio, had not quit the war. Under the pretense of remaining loyal to Hitler, Rome had initiated secret negotiations with the Allies, seeking an armistice. On September 3 the "armistice," which was in fact unconditional surrender, was signed. On the 8th it was announced, the Rome-Berlin Axis broken. The Allies invaded Italy at Salerno, hoping to drive the Germans into precipitous retreat; and the Italian forces turned against their former comrades-in-arms. The peace that had been declared really meant war.

But the Führer had not for one moment been fooled. He had used the forty-five-day period between the fall of Mussolini and Badoglio's surrender wisely. Twelve new Wehrmacht divisions were moved down the Italian peninsula, tripling his strength and outstripping Allied and Italian forces combined. Moments after the armistice was proclaimed, the Germans began to encircle Rome, with a will to wreak vengeance on the traitorous ally. The King and Badoglio, filled with terror, ran. While Rome slept, they fled the capital in the quietest hours of the night, leaving no one at the seat of command. The Germans began to push hard against the Allied invasion and all but forced it back into the sea.

On Thursday and Friday, the 9th and the 10th, scattered units of the Italian army and civilians in their shirt-sleeves tried to resist the German entry into Rome. But by nightfall of the second day, while the bodies of courageous men were being wheeled away on the flatbeds of fruitsellers' handcarts, the Nazis had reached the center of Rome. The city had already fallen at 4:00 P.M.[2]

The Romans that Saturday—the first full day of the occupation—moved circumspectly. Regardless of who one might be, there were new rules to be learned, old ways to be cast off—a new shuffle, a new deal. Everyone listened, be it to a returning soldier, a knot of people on a street corner, or a rumor whispered around like a scrap of paper caught in a city wind. Each man labored to build his own bridge, however rickety, across the peril of ignorance.

At 1:00 P.M. EIAR—Radio Rome—went on the air, with Giovan Battista Arista reading the news. At the broadcasting studios in Via delle Botteghe Oscure two German soldiers stood guard.

"Yesterday," the newscaster began, "a truce was agreed upon by the commanders of the German and Italian troops in the Rome area. . . . It is forbidden to carry arms. . . . Anyone killing a German soldier will be shot. Otherwise the truce remains in force."[3]

Confusion ran everywhere like an excited dog. In the afternoon newspapers, the Germans were proclaiming Rome an "open city," neutralized not occupied. Rome had not fallen, they said, it had merely agreed to an "armistice," under which German forces would remain at the periphery.[4] But along the Corso Umberto in the center of the city, armed Germans in full view of the Romans were sacking and looting stores and banks. The neighboring streets teemed with hostile troops of the Afrika Korps, strutting SS men, Luftwaffe officers, and bare-legged paratroopers. Wehrmacht soldiers were taking up posts at all key installations, and military traffic jammed the main arteries from every point on the compass. What kind of open city was this?

In the evening the situation became clear. Harshly printed posters had suddenly been pasted to the walls of the city. They were signed by Nazi Field Marshal Albert Kesselring, "Commander-in-Chief of the south."

Rome is "under my command," said the field marshal, declaring it a "war territory" subject to martial law. "Those organizing strikes or sabotage, as well as snipers, will be shot immediately. . . . Private correspondence is suspended. All telephone conversations should be as brief as possible. They will be strictly monitored."

The proclamation, printed in German and Italian, continued: "Italian civil authorities and organizations are responsible to me for the maintenance of public order. They will prevent all acts of sabotage and of passive resistance to German measures. They will cooperate fully with the German organizations."[6]

Order, restraint, and cooperation: This was the new law, handed down from Kesselring's hillside headquarters just outside the city. Many people in Rome, particularly those responsible men at the higher levels of the city's civil authorities and organizations, felt it had to be obeyed.

That night, the Führer spoke.

His voice, as a result of an exceptionally good recording made twenty-four hours earlier, was rich and forceful. The treachery of the Italians, he was heard to say over Radio Rome, would not pass unpunished. The measures to be adopted against them would be "very hard."[7]

The time of the new law had begun.

II

NOWHERE IN ROME was the new law more closely studied than in the city's small community of Jews. Though some Jewish women, hearing of the German lootings, had already hidden their best Sabbath candlesticks, the general reaction was one of near relief.[1] Calm had returned to the city and there was nothing in Hitler's or Kesselring's messages that might be interpreted as discriminatory against Jews. Doubts lingered, of course. No Jew in Europe could feel entirely safe, not even in Rome.

In the ghetto and the neighboring area, where the majority of Rome's 12,000 Jews resided, a man might say—to use the Hebrew-Romanesque words of the people—*"Pesah non è; mazzod nun ce só*—Passover it's not; matzohs there are none."* But in the

* Hebrew words phoneticized in Italian are usually spelled differently from the English rendition. Where I have used the Italian spelling, they are printed in italics.

present situation, the majority of the Jews of Rome, and especially those in the ghetto, were not alarmed.[2] There had been German officers and troops in the city since the beginning of the war. They had always been courteous and well behaved. They were good customers, too. Nothing, it appeared, had changed. *"Adonai, Adonai,"* the saying went, *"che pozza restá gelata dove stà*—God willing it stay this way."

The Jews of Rome, it seemed, could find their way in any turn of events. Indeed there were many non-Jews in the city who now looked to the ghetto as the best barometer of impending danger.[3] Life in the Diaspora, it was generally believed, had imparted a quality of national survival, and no community of Diaspora Jews had survived longer or was more durable than that of the Roman Jews. In 1943 they had already lived in Rome for 2,082 years. The only known living descendants of the people of ancient Rome, they had endured the crumbling of the Empire, the sword of the Visogoths, and the fiery stakes of the Counter Reformation Church.

As free citizens of the Roman Republic, they had mourned the assassination of Julius Caesar and had borne witness to the Senate's designation of the tyrant Herod as King of Judea. As a part of the people conquered by the Emporer Titus, they too had suffered the fall of Jerusalem, the destruction of the Second Temple, and the capture of its spoils. At the Portico of Octavia in Rome, they had observed Titus's inaugural of the ceremonious march of triumph over Israel. One among them, the renegade Jew, Flavius Josephus, described it in all its fulsome glory for the eighty generations who have followed him. He wrote, in part:

> At the break of dawn Vespasian and Titus issued forth, crowned with laurel and clad in the traditional purple robes, and proceeded to the Octavian walks. . . . A tribunal had been erected in front of the porticos with chairs of ivory placed for them upon it; to these they mounted and took their seats. Instantly acclamations rose from the troops . . . and then, having donned their triumphal robes and sacrificed to the gods whose statues stood beside the gate, they sent the pageant on its way driving off through the theaters in order to give the crowds an easier view.[4]

Here, by Octavia's Portico, scarcely a tenth of a Roman mile from the bend in the Tiber that accepts the hunch of the river island, the Jews had come to live. Sometimes freemen, sometimes slaves, they had seen Hadrian build his villa, Aurelian build his walls, and Constantine the Roman Church of Jesus Christ. They had lamented the anti-Jewish legislation of the medieval Lateran Councils, the confiscation of the Talmud, and the papal edicts requiring them to wear a yellow badge. They had rejoiced at the privileges extended to them by the republican government of Cola di Rienzo and by Pope Boniface IX, only to despair at the evil works of their successors. On the sea of time they had changed course as others would have it done, but they had never yielded the vessel of their faith.

In 1555 Pope Paul IV built a wall around them, establishing the ghetto. Those who did not already live in the new enclosure were forced to move there.

Dominated by the Theater of Marcellus, the ghetto extended west along the right bank of the river, from the old Bridge of the Four Heads for about 200 yards. To the north it ran almost that same distance, again terminating at the *pescheria,* or the fish market. It included the Portico of Octavia, which by then had already been reduced to ruins, as had the entire district. Just outside the western gate of the ghetto was a not unpleasant piazza with a fountain and a little church. It was named Piazza Giudea, or Jew Square. Within the walls, which were closed every dusk and reopened at dawn, were hellish alleys where the light of even the noonday sun could not fully penetrate and which were perennially covered with a layer of malaria-ridden filth from the bowels of the unquayed Tiber.

This imprisonment, with only minor lapses, lasted for the next 315 years.[5]

In 1870, with the unification of Italy and the secularization of Rome as the capital of the reborn nation, the walls of the ghetto were torn down. The emancipation of the Jews was proclaimed. The ghetto area was cleaned. The worst streets disappeared when embankments were built to contain the Tiber. But the memories of oppression were more tenacious. Many

Jews, wanting to breathe freer air, but limited in means, moved just across the Tiber. In the labyrinthine *vicoli* of poverty-stricken Trastevere, a Jewish settlement centuries before the institution of the ghetto, they lived as symbols of the new freedom, which was something far less than the freedom itself. In reality this movement had the effect of only changing the shape of the Jewish quarter, not its condition. The ghetto had given birth to a satellite community, the two, equally as poor and similar in appearance, straddling the Tiber island turn in the river.

The prosperous Jews, a class of which had always existed even in the worst of times, did escape, however. Many of them took up residences in the newer, more elegant parts of town, which were rising around the city center. Those who managed to break the bonds of the old existence, by wealth or by other means, found little resistance in integrating Italian society. They were joined by their counterparts from ghettos all over Italy who wished to be taken up into the lap of the nation. Accepted by their countrymen, they wore the cloak of bourgeois, nationalist equality with a full cut of pride, responsibility, and fraternity which could be gainsaid by no one. Many Jews rose swiftly to high places—like Giuseppe Toeplitz, the banker; the Modigliani family, whose son became the great painter Amedeo Modigliani; the Olivetti industrialists; and highest of all, Luigi Luzzati, the thirteenth Prime Minister of modern Italy.

But when all the shuffling slowed and the achievements of Italian Jews began to pass without special attention, the Roman ghetto was still there, and except for a new look, hardly changed. In absolute terms the poverty of the ghetto Jews had actually increased. In the more than seventy years from the emancipation to the German occupation the population of the ghetto and its mirror image on the other side of the river nearly doubled, reaching a figure of about 7,000.* In the ghetto proper the number of Jews, despite all the outflow, held

* This was about 60 percent of all Jews of Rome of 1943. The Jewish population of Italy at the time was about 45,000, or .10 percent of the country's 45,000,000 citizens.

steadily around 4,000, the same amount that had been maintained for hundreds of years. In the proclamation of their freedom, the ghetto Jews had found only the wherewithal to multiply.

By 1943 the original ghetto area looked nothing like the walled-in enclosure of old, though there were Jews still alive in Rome who could remember the last days of bondage. The "ex" ghetto, as it now was properly but never to be called, resembled any of the other old, poor sections of Rome, its only identifying feature being the great synagogue that had been built by the Tiber in 1904. The blackened pillars and arches of Octavia's portico still stood, but gone was the wretched *Fiumara*, the muddy street along the river. Gone were the tired Jewish women who used to sit among piles of rags in the late Via delle Azzimelle, or Street of Matzohs, stitching and darning that which by now had also disappeared. Gone was the Via Rua, street of the ghetto rich, and gone was the centuries-old fish market and the shameful Piazza Giudea.[7]

What had been left behind, however, was by any measure a city slum. The 400-to-500-year-old apartment buildings had never throughout the centuries undergone anything more than minor repair, and they looked the worse for it: wizened and worn, hunched and huddled irregularly, as if they had somehow moved from an original orderly row. They had no heat, of course, and often the toilet was only a hole in a pipe that plunged directly into the sewer. Even the grey palaces of the Roman first families Mattei, Costaguti, and others, which had been architectural masterpieces in the area long before the establishment of the ghetto, had been slummified by the Jewish poor and their exploiters. The innards of the *palazzi* had been cut up into one- and two-room dwellings, into which were squeezed an incredible number of people—as many as nine or ten in a single room.[8]

From the streets, however, all of this could not be seen. The ghetto seemed like a pleasant enough place. With its busyness and earthy ways, it had all that elusive "charm" of a Chinatown or a Harlem. Before the war it had been a tourist attraction, especially for American Jews, but oddly, also for Germans. They would come, first of all, to see the synagogue—the *tempio maggiore*—an experiment in eclectic architecture which did not quite succeed. Then they would walk up the slight incline of the Via del Tempio to wander in the little ghetto streets among the natives. The guide books of the day were full of spicy tales, in which there was some truth, about the early ghetto Jews having been "great astrologers" and "brewers of love potions." The tourists would make note of all the things the people of the ghetto would never see: the dangling wash that stretched from one side of the street to the other; the steep stone staircases that reached up almost like a ladder into the houses in the tiny Via della Reginella; the hanks of wool that hung outside the mattress shop in Via del Portico d'Ottavia, and the way the children and the cats played so unselfconsciously among the ruins of the portico and the Theater of Marcellus.

The people of the ghetto were hard to know. They had little trust in the *gojim*—or the *goits*—and were not very well understood by their fellow Jews outside. They dressed the same as other poor Italians and their names, although very decidedly Jewish, sounded Italian and could be distinguished only by those who knew the difference, which had to be learned empirically. Among the non-Jewish Italians it was often said that the Jews had the names of places in Italy. But this was a prejudice, only partially true and a very poor rule of thumb. Two thousand years of inbreeding had kept the number of names in the ghetto to about a score, which had to be shared by all, often with confusing results. Many times all the multiples of a single name—as much as ten persons with the same given and surnames—lived on the same street, or even in the same house. This situation gave rise to the wide use of nicknames, which were affixed when written to the full name, such as "Lazzaro Anticoli, *detto* [called] *'il pugliatore'* [the prize-fighter]" or "Marco Di Veroli, called 'the millionaire.'"

But names, other than to be entered into the well-kept files of the Jewish community, were rarely written. Nor was much else put down on paper. The ghetto Jews, as might be expected, were a poorly educated group. Like most underprivileged people they entrusted the responsibilities inherent in the written word to others who appeared to be wiser about such things. In the ghetto, the wisest men of all were unquestionably the Chief Rabbi, the President of the community, and his Councillors, titles that were always capitalized at the offices of the Community.

Life in the ghetto was the hard life, the daily struggle to earn one's bread. Centuries back the Jews had been barred from any economic activity other than peddling and dealing in second-hand merchandise. Now, long since freed of such restrictions, they nevertheless continued in the same occupations, at least in the ghetto where 70 percent of heads of families were either itinerant peddlers or small storekeepers.[9]

There was the used dress shop of Giuditta Di Porto and the *banco fisso* of other Di Portos who sold their wares from a "fixed stall"—the next best thing to a store—in the huge outdoor market in the Campo de' Fiori; there was Angelo Anticoli's jewelry shop, the peddling father and sons Amati, and the stands along Via Arenula where Jews sold souvenirs—"memories of Rome," as they called them—to the city's only tourists these days, the visiting troops of Hitler's Wehrmacht.

The life permissible from meager earnings eked out this way and the heavy weights of always difficult times were unburdened to some extent by the spiritual and earthly institutions of Rome's well-organized *cheilà*—the Jewish community. Imparting the values by which Jews lived, these institutions functioned to alleviate suffering, give meaning to ghetto life, and stabilize the community.

First and foremost there was the great temple on the right bank of the river, with its rabbis, vestments, and rituals for the care of the Jewish soul. Then there was the Tiber island hospital to care for the Jewish sick and the collateral services for the Jewish pregnant, the Jewish newborn, the Jewish destitute, the Jewish aged, and the Jewish dead. There were social workers for Jewish refugees, libraries for Jewish scholars, schools for Jewish children, and religious instructors to tug at the ears of puberty-aged Jewish boys and turn their restless minds to the study of the *Haftorah* in preparation for bar-mitzvah.

Above all else stood the council of Jewish leaders; a president and board of fifteen councillors, democratically elected but somehow always from among Rome's most "prominent Jews," save for the ever-present one representative from the ghetto.[10] By the example of their own success, it was generally thought that the prominent Jews knew best how to help their less fortunate brothers achieve a better, fuller life. They were given the trying duties of leadership, which they discharged by contributing of their superior intellectual, technical, and often financial resources. In practice this meant assuring the perpetuity of the apparatus which administered what they and their predecessors had formulated as the needs of the faithful.

But the leadership and their deathless organized community, for all their benevolence, dedication, and the useful services rendered, could not effect any fundamental change in the ghetto existence. Indeed the organization had arisen to help secure the prevailing social order.[11] There were, as will be seen, many untended needs of the faithful that were contrary to the needs of the leaders. One of these, tragically, was change.

Such conflicts, however, through the fault of no one individual, lay in zones covered by eternal darkness. The average ghetto Jew sensed them, but lacking an identity with anything outside that which was valued by the community, he was incapable of articulating any "non-Jewish" feelings. Differences, if they ever arose into conscious thought, were swaddled in the ideas of Judaism, which was the common denominator of all the social classes of the group.

This fraternity was clearly and regularly demonstrated anew every Friday at sundown, when rich and poor alike turned to the synagogue. The gates and the doors of the *tempio maggiore* would open wide, and from somewhere inside an ancient cabbalistic chant could be heard in the ghetto, beckoning the faithful to the Ark. "*Lehà dodì, lichrà calà*—Come, oh friend, and greet the Sabbath." And they would come and stand before the columns fluted with gold and the six menorahs that hung high upon the wall, to kiss the silver crowned Torah and pray to the *Signore* that they might be blessed with a brighter, more prosperous future.

Now that the Germans had occupied Rome, there seemed to be more reason than ever to pray.

III

IN HIS CHAMBERS on the second floor of the main synagogue in Rome, His Excellency, *Commendatore* Ugo Foà appeared to those who saw him then somber and preoccupied. The lines of his face expressed the heavy responsibility of his office, president of the Jewish Community of Rome.*

In the room beyond his door, this first Monday morning of the occupation, the chief rabbi of the city was waiting to see him.

* In Italy the president and the community had well-defined and extensive powers with regard to native Jews. A law enacted in 1930 had regulated the administration of the Jewish "cult," as one which was "not contrary to public order." The local community wholly controled the religious life and institutions of all its Jews. Membership in the community, according to the law, was compulsory for every Jew. In turn the community was compelled to adhere to a larger organism known as a "union" of communities. No Jew—legally described as the offspring of a Jewish woman—could leave the community unless he converted to another religion or formally declared himself a non-Jew. In either case he relinquished his rights to all community services and assistance. The purpose of this law, which was in no way discriminatory in relation to other non-Catholic religions, was to unify and subordinate under a central authority an Italian minority group that had been disorganized for 100 years. Promulgated in a Fascist state, the law cultifying the children of Jewish mothers in Italy, was hailed as the *magnum opus* of the late Chief Rabbi Sacerdoti.[1]

The president did not know exactly why the rabbi had made the request, but there was an urgency running through the air as clear as the crack of a whip. It would not be a happy meeting, and he would surely be forgiven if the rabbi were kept outside a little longer, while Foà postponed, if only for moments, whatever the encounter might bring.

The situation that had newly overtaken the city, Foà well knew, had created grave problems for the community. They had to be treated cautiously and there was little margin for error. To be sure, he had already received satisfactory reports from the highest levels of Italian authority in Rome. They had said that the Germans would respect the Holy City and were not interested in its small population of Jews.[2] Yet anything could go wrong, and there were persistent, unsettling rumors; voices even among his closest associates spoke of an incredible inferno to the north: camps of concentration, centers of extermination, chambers of gas.[3]

Downstairs, just below his windows, a small group of Jews had collected around the temple. They too had heard rumors —far more vague than those the president knew of—loose talk of Nazi persecutions, "things" that could never happen in Italy. Still, it was known, some Jews were going into hiding or running away from Rome. As they spoke quietly among themselves, they looked calm and easily broke into smiles, laughter, and even horseplay. Nonetheless they had been drawn there, like expectant fathers almost sure that everything would turn out fine, but waiting to be told.[4]

There would be no one to tell Foà, however. He would soon be called upon to make decisions that would affect the lives of thousands of his fellow Jews. Fortunately, his colleagues believed, he had already enjoyed a long career of service to nation, state, and religion.

For hundreds of years the Foà name had been prominent among the Jews of Italy. In the 1700s Mosè Beniamo Foà, of Reggio Emilia, had been a great book merchant and bibliophile. The following century father and son, Pio and Carlo Foà, had won international recognition as renowned physicians.[5] But

Ugo Foà was a leader, one to whom responsibility flowed like the natural course of a river. He felt comfortable in the role. He was stern at times, hard and impatient with less dedicated souls, but cut from that sturdy timber of men who possess an unbendable will to do what they believe good and right for their fellow human beings. Foà, almost all who knew him agree, was "an exceptionally sincere and generous man."[6]

He was born in Florence fifty-six years before the Nazis entered Rome. He grew up in Leghorn, a coastal town of Tuscany, where Italian Judaism had flourished in the sixteenth and seventeenth centuries as a privileged sanctuary for Jews who were persecuted in other parts of the politically divided peninsula. With the outbreak of World War I, he joined the infantry, receiving a commission as a captain. On October 21, 1915, he led a company of troops against a heavily defended enemy outpost. Twice wounded in the assault, he nevertheless remained in command, at the side of his men, earning him at war's end the *Medaglia d'Argento* for military valor.[7]

He returned home when peace was made. He studied law, married, fathered three children, and in 1932, as so many of his countrymen were doing in those years, he joined the Fascist party. He moved upward. In 1936 the capital called; the Ministry of Justice had appointed him a magistrate. His wife died that year, and the motherless family went to Rome, where he took up his new post and the full weight of raising and caring for his two young sons and a preschool-age daughter.

He moved into a nine-room apartment in Via Cicerone, in the Prati district. It was not the very best neighborhood, but he had wanted to be near his court in the Palace of Justice. Every morning the tall, white-haired, distinguished-looking magistrate would walk to his chambers in the Baroque *palazzo* in Piazza Cavour. There he would pass the day administering Fascist justice. Evenings were dedicated to the children, guiding their activities, helping with their lessons, sometimes with firmness, always with kindness. Theirs was a family, one son would recall years later, that never felt the lack of a mother.[8]

His high position in Fascist society; his presidency of the war veterans organization, Nastro Azzuro; his real and honorary titles; his first hand associations with some of the most powerful men in Italy; the deference and respect of his contemporaries; of such was the iron and steel of his convictions: a belief in the inviolability of law as the foundation of civilization; a love of fatherland and all honor to its institutions.

In 1938, following Hitler's state visit to Rome, Foà's orderly world began to crumble, but not his faith that it might one day be reconstituted. The Duce, aping the Nuremberg laws, adopted racial legislation against the Jews of Italy. Foà, like all his Jewish colleagues, was forced out of public life, slowly and gently, Italian style, with a pension. Made conscious of his Jewishness, he turned to the Roman community and asked what he could do to help his suffering coreligionists.

The prominent Jews made him president. They would never regret it.[9] No one was more dedicated to the cause of alleviating the hardships imposed by the racial laws than Foà. No one worked harder than he toward that end. His almost daily contacts with "more civilized" Fascist authorities and even some Germans in Rome, among whom his prestige had always remained high, had until now won many concessions, many winks at tough restrictions against the Jews.[10]

In these first days of the occupation, however, some of Foà's fellow Jewish leaders had expressed misgivings that the old relationships with the authorities, so carefully tended over the years, would hold together. Members of the community council and other prominent Jews were advising the president to go into hiding. But he refused categorically. He rejected their counsel as premature and chose to remain in the apartment in Via Cicerone with his children.[11] More than ever, he repeatedly told his colleagues, his presence at the head of the community was needed. It was not a matter of vanity, but of duty. There was much to be done for others—work that only Foà, by virtue of his standing, could do—before he could think of his own security.

Now, in his office overlooking the Roman ghetto, this work began. He rang a little bell that lay on his desk and it made a tinkling sound, which could be heard in the room outside. This brought a secretary to the door, and he let it be known that he was ready to meet with the chief rabbi of Rome.

The sixty-two-year-old religious leader of the community was a less confident man than Foà. His name was Israel Zolli. A mystical soul, he feared the wrath of the gentile invaders with an intensity that had been driven like a spike through the centuries. Some days before, when the Germans were penetrating the city, Zolli had prophesied a bloodbath in Rome. "Who knows," he had remarked to a synagogue employee, "how many Jews will pay with their life?"[12] The following day, at the height of the battle for Rome, he had begun to search for a hiding place for himself and his small family, finding temporary refuge in a vacant apartment near the Vatican. The calm that had followed the surrender of the city to Kesselring's army was, the rabbi believed, only a deceptive interlude. Now he had come to voice his fears to Foà, warning the Jews in his path to the temple to "disperse and go as far away as you can."[13]

Ushered into Foà's office, the chief rabbi noted that the president seemed sober and concerned. He regarded the rabbi attentively, his face wearing an inscrutable silence. After a few words of greeting, Zolli indicated the reason for his visit.

"Listen, Mr. President," he began pointedly, "give orders that the temple and all the oratories be closed. Send all the employees home and close the offices. . . . Draw one million lire, or even two, from the bank and give all the employees three months' advance pay."

The rabbi urged that Jewish funerals be conducted by the civil authorities and that despite the approach of the autumn season of high holidays, Jews must not assemble in large groups, and the religious ceremonies must not be held.

"The prayers can be said at home," he declared. "Let everyone pray where he is; after all, God is everywhere."

Foà remained taciturn.

Besides the Roman Jews, the rabbi continued, there were Jewish refugees in the city from all over Europe. "The Germans can surround the temple and the oratories with their cannons and guns exactly at the hour when those places are jammed with people."

The purpose of these measures, said Zolli, was to demonstrate the seriousness of the current situation to the "thousands of people who are going about the streets of the ghetto ignorant of the danger."

He advised the president to set up a committee to administer a sizable allocation of the community's funds, which would be used to subsidize the dispersal of the poorest Jews from their homes and the city. "You will see," he said, "the first ten families will be a good example to the others." Zolli was convinced that the only way to save the Jews was by organizing an underground exodus that would entail dismantling community life and fanning out the heavily concentrated Jewish population either in the homes of non-Jewish families, Catholic monastaries and convents, or in villages across the countryside.[14]

When Zolli had finished outlining his plan, Foà continued to sit quietly for awhile. He then rang his little bell, which produced the executive secretary of the community, Fortunato Piperno. As the rabbi later remembered it, the president inquired whether a certain female staff member had shown up for work yet. He was told by the secretary that the employee was fearful of being on the premises of the synagogue. Foà instructed the secretary to dismiss her, and Piperno went out.

At last Foà turned to the rabbi. "We are alone again," he said. "You should be giving courage instead of spreading discouragement. I have received assurances." As to Zolli's proposals, Foà replied that by his order the *tempio maggiore* and all other places of worship would stay open.[15]

There was no room for further discussion, Foà let it be known. Under the terms of Article 17 of the law of 1930 on the Jewish cult, the chief rabbi could not speak on nonreligious questions. The president and the council prevailed.[16]

IV

THE CHIEF RABBI of Rome took leave of Foà to return to his hiding place. Coming out of the office his eyes were drawn to two strangers. He heard one of them say as he passed them, "That's the man." The words had been spoken in German. The rabbi continued walking, hurrying to the crooked ghetto streets that wound behind the synagogue. He was certain he was being followed, but the pursuit broke off when he changed direction.

Israel Anton Zolli, normally self-restrained and forbidding, was a man in a panic. In his fears for the Jews of Rome he included himself, his wife, and his daughter. At the moment the occupation began, he had been told by someone he considered reliable that one hour after entering Prague the Nazis had killed the chief rabbi of that city. He had wandered through the streets that evening seeking shelter in the homes of two non-Jewish "friends," only to be twice turned away with lame excuses. He had returned to his apartment in the ghetto, he later said, trembling and "dripping in sweat." He had stretched out on his bed and prayed. "Will there be a sudden stroke of a bell?" he had thought. "A knock on the door . . . I lay motionless with eyes wide open and listened."[1]

The whole of his life experience told the aging man that peril lay ahead. Unlike most of the leaders of the community and almost all of the people of his flock he was a newcomer to Rome, and not a native Italian. He was born in Brody, on the threshold of the teeming pale of east European Jewry, in 1881, the year of the great pogroms.[2] The family name was Zoller. His father was a silk merchant, his mother from a long line of rabbis. As a boy he grew up in the debris left by the torrent of fleeing Russian Jews, tens of thousands of whom were stranded in Brody after crossing the Austro-Hungarian frontier. Under the impact of his early contact with the persecution of Jews, young Zolli drew back from the temporal world at an early age, turning inward to the spirit and the book.

He became a rabbi, studying at the University of Florence and the rabbinical college of that city, at the time a center of Jewish learning. Ordained in 1908, he also earned a doctorate in philology from the university. He went to Trieste, where he had been offered a post with the Jewish community and an opportunity to engage in Biblical scholarship and teaching.

Following World War I, Trieste, until then Austrian territory, became part of Italy. Zoller became Zolli, and before long chief rabbi of the new Italian city. He loved Italy. He had studied its literature under Mazzoni and had learned to speak the language impeccably with a richness drawn from the past. His wife was an Austrian, but when she died, he married an Italian, and he became a naturalized citizen of the country.

He was not a popular man among his colleagues and the flock, neither in Trieste nor in Rome.[3] Known for his stolidness and the cool countenance of his expressions, he was nevertheless given to sudden flashes of emotion. Sometimes such outbursts frightened other men and seemed to undermine his stability, which was deeply rooted in Mosaic law. Some said he was odd, others said aloof. His face was bony and unpleasant; he wore a pointed beard, his eyes were intense and myopic, and his gestures decidedly un-Italian, "typical of a Polish Jew," one of his fellow rabbis in Italy would recall.[4] Zolli himself would one day complain, "I know how to love better than how to make myself loved."[5]

With the rise of Nazism, the sleeping terror only a Jew of the pale can know began to stir. While still unopposed to Mussolini's Fascists, he began as early as 1933 to preach in the *tempio maggiore* of Trieste against Nazi anti-Semitism. He had received testimony and documents of Hitler's persecutions from Jewish refugees arriving in Trieste. Naïvely, he passed this information to Roman Rabbi Sacerdoti, seeking to employ the latter's influence with the Duce to bring pressure on Berlin. Zolli spoke out against the Nuremberg laws, which cost him his Italian citizenship and called the attention of the Germans to his name.[6]

By 1938, when Italy too turned against its Jews, Zolli had become an anti-Fascist, though not openly now that the circle of danger was closing. Nevertheless he found ways to make his views known to his fellow Jews.*[7]

In those late years of the 1930s a religious fire raged in Zolli's mind, which was slowly consuming the troubled outside world. He had had at that time a number of "experiences," during which he had seen a vision of Jesus Christ, to whom he felt strangely drawn. He did not know if the figure of Christ was "objectively real or only subjective," and he spoke of this to no one.[9] The conflagration soon dimmed, however, and receded from his conscious thoughts, at least temporarily.

Now, time, the death of Sacerdoti, and the emigration of his successor, had brought Zolli to occupied Rome. He had put aside his supernatural life and had turned again to his people. As chief rabbi of Rome he had learned from sources he considered trustworthy that the occupiers would treat the Jews of the Eternal City with no more consideration than those of the other great cities of Europe that had fallen under Hitler's rule. His chief informant was, he later said, "a high Catholic ecclesiastic." This man, who had direct contact with the German embassy, had told Zolli that the Roman Jews "might expect persecution."[10]

Once convinced of an impending physical threat to the

* One of them, a Triestian who was impressed by Zolli's antifascism, sought a final encounter with the rabbi before fleeing to America. He asked Zolli what fate he believed imminent for European Jewry. "Suffering and destruction," was the rabbi's only reply, the departing man later said. "His pale features were transfigured. I shall never forget their aspect of resignation." "Rabbi," the Triestian Jew persisted, "if you see what is before you, why do you not seek to escape it?" Zolli answered: "Most of my brethren and sisters are also unable to escape."[8] Such was the magnetic quality of his society.

Jews of Rome, he could hardly arrive at more than one conclusion. By his own admission "unable to escape" the attractive force that bound Europe together, even as it was literally exploding apart, he had to link his fate with that of the poorest members of his flock—the majority of the city's Jewish population. Only in the salvation of their place in the community could his own be saved; only in temporarily scattering them could his own flight be rationalized.

In the end, the differences between Zolli and Foà were narrow. Both men were, as will be seen, as equally dedicated to a common cause as they were mindful of their privileged and prestigious position in the community. The conflict between the two Jewish leaders was governed by the inner logic of their divergent views of the danger presented by the occupation and the manner in which it should be handled. They would consistently and invariably behave accordingly.

As for Zolli, his unsuccessful mission to the president had not yet exhausted his possibilities for further action. There were other influential Jews in Rome.

V

THE JEWS OF ROME were very much in the minds of the Germans. They were a "problem" of particular interest to Nazi Ambassador to the Holy See Baron Ernst von Weizsäcker—more so, at this early moment in the occupation, than to any other German in the city.

Von Weizsäcker until a few months ago had held the second highest position in the Foreign Office, only a step below

Reich Foreign Minister von Ribbentrop. Now that the war was no longer going well, Weizsäcker had grown inwardly opposed to Hitler. He had asked to be transferred to Rome. He nourished a secret hope that he could influence the course of the war by means of a Vatican-mediated peace between the Germans and the Western Allies.[1] On July 5th, in ceremonies held at the Vatican, he had presented his credentials to Pope Pius XII. The new ambassador, received in private audience, had then been told by His Holiness that at present he could see "no lead on which to base any kind of practical work for peace."[2]

If the time were not yet ripe for peace, Weizsäcker believed, he could at least do some practical work for the Jews. Few men in Rome were as well informed as he about the genocide taking place in the north. While still in Berlin, as early as 1941, he had received the daily reports of the Einsatzgruppen describing the mass murders of Polish and Russian Jews. He had read and initialed number sixteen of the thirty copies of the minutes taken at the secret Wannsee Conference preparing the "Final Solution" to the Jewish question.[3] He knew of the constant deportations, of the Polish town of Auschwitz, and the fate of the Jews who had already been sent there. As for the Italian Jews, Weizsäcker in 1942 had seen and transmitted to Ribbentrop the very first proposal to induce the Mussolini government "to bring about a final solution to the Jewish question also on their part."[4]

The duties of high office had severely compromised Weizsäcker, weak and fence-straddling man that he was. Nevertheless he had carefully sown the span of years with prudent protests, secret resistance, and kindnesses that might one day be harvested under the name of Christian charity. Always a gentleman from the old school, the baron was well regarded in Rome and highly esteemed—even, as will be seen, among some Jews.

Now that his countrymen had occupied the city, Weizsäcker was moved to act. He conferred with his closest aide, Embassy Secretary Albrecht von Kessel, who he knew could be trusted with the most delicate of affairs. One of the rare nonmembers of the Nazi party, Kessel was a man whose opposition to the Hitler regime, in the circle and style of the hesitant *Herren* resisters, would never be questioned. Only a few days earlier, at a quiet dinner among the German diplomats in Rome, "Teddy"—as he was called by his colleagues—had launched into a tirade against the Führer and his Nazis. "Teddy, Teddy," German Ambassador Rudolf Rahn had admonished in a friendly way, "the day is not far off when we'll have to intervene to get you out of a concentration camp. When will you ever learn to hold your tongue?"[5]

The meeting between Weizsäcker and Kessel, held in the elegant old villa Napoléon in Via Piave which served as Hitler's embassy to the Holy See, was conducted on a far more serious plane. It had been called, Kessel said later, "to discuss what we could do to help the Jews."[6] To men accustomed to recline on euphemisms this was a convenient manner of referring to a real problem that had suddenly arisen in Nazi-Vatican relations. Responsible for the Führer's diplomacy at the Curia, both Weizsäcker and Kessel had to be concerned with the reaction of the Pope, should an SS pogrom suddenly descend on the Holy City. There were humanitarian considerations too, at least in the case of Kessel, who was not above discreet friendships with persons he regarded as being merely one of the many races of the "Mediterranean people."[7]

Both men were in agreement that it was a foregone conclusion that the SS would move against the Jews of Rome.[8] Although no one in the city had as yet received any instructions on the Jewish question, "it was our conviction," according to Kessel, " . . . that the worst was to be expected." One method of dealing with this matter, they thought, would be to warn the Jews of the imminent danger and advise them "to go into hiding or flee." This, however, was an assignment too risky to be undertaken directly by themselves and "we could not work through the Italians because, we felt, they would certainly be indiscreet."

The meeting dragged on interminably. They were perplexed. "Suddenly," Kessel later recalled, "I thought of a friend of mine, a Swiss in Rome who might be trusted with this mission."

Kessel suggested that he seek out the man, Alfred Fahrener, the secretary general of the Institute for International Private Law, an agency of the League of Nations. Weizsäcker agreed.[9] There was no need to say anything further. Both men knew that speed was of the utmost importance.

Finding no difficulty in locating the Swiss, Kessel met with him that evening in the privacy of Fahrener's home. The German asked him if he knew "any of the leading members of the Jewish colony in Rome." He did.

"They must leave their homes as quickly as possible and seek shelter elsewhere," Kessel warned. It was a matter of urgency. He requested that Fahrener contact his Jewish friends and pass the message on, presumably with the assumption that they in turn would spread the warning further. Fahrener voiced no objections and said he would undertake this work at once.

"Greatly relieved," Kessel said later, "I returned home convinced that I had done my duty and had, with possibly a few individual exceptions, prevented a disaster."[10]

VI

THE VATICAN, AS Pope Pius XII had said privately months back, had acted since the war broke out "as far as was in its power, economically and morally" to help the Jews.[1] Now, with regard to the Roman Jews, the Holy See knew it would have to, and was already preparing to do more. A catastrophe for both Catholic and Jew seemed in the making.

The Nazi takeover of the Holy City, for one thing, seriously threatened to undermine the Pope's fundamental policy toward all the Jews of Europe. This, rigorously maintained until now, was the policy of silence. "There where the Pope would like to cry out loud and strong," Pius had confided to the Catholic bishops in Germany, "it is rather restraint and silence that are often imposed on him. Where he would like to act and to assist, it is patience and expectation that become imperative."[2]

The policy of silence had not been lightly assumed by the Supreme Pontiff, and it went beyond the Jewish question. For more than a year now, Pius knew the Jews were being systematically exterminated.[3] For an even longer period he had been kept informed that Catholics, too, particularly in Poland, were being oppressed by the Nazi invader. But the Pope did not protest because, as it would later be authoritatively stated, he thought "in more comprehensive terms."[4] There was, he had become convinced, a greater enemy to mankind than Nazism; it was called, at that time, Soviet atheist bolshevism. If he were to speak out against the former, he could not but criticize the latter in even stronger terms.[5] To protest Hitler's Germany would weaken what the Church often referred to as "the only possible bulwark against Bolshevism."[6] Moreover, to denounce Stalin's Russia would be a blow to the Western Powers with whom the Communists were allied. This was the substance of the policy of silence. While regrettably it imposed restrictions, it also, as seen by the Pope, opened many new possibilities for peace. It was through nominal neutrality that the Pope sought to maintain good relations with both the Western Allies and the Germans. He hoped in this way, should the Americans and the British come to understand that the true arch-enemy of the world was Russian communism, to act as a mediator in a general *rapprochement* in the West. As Ambassador Weizsäcker wrote at the time from his lookout post at the Holy See: "The Vatican's dream [is] that the Western Powers will realize in time where their real interest lies and will join the German effort to help save European culture from Bolshevism."[7]

But the policy of silence, at this date in the war, was beginning to show unmistakable signs of ruin. The Americans and the British, instead of softening their position on Nazi Germany, all but ignored Vatican diplomacy. They toughened their stand, declaring repeatedly that there could be no separate peace in the West, and the Germans would have to surrender unconditionally.

Further, the abandonment felt by persecuted Catholics and the mounting toll of the organized destruction of European Jewry had long ago rendered Pius's silence open to attack on moral grounds.

A Polish bishop wrote to the Pope early in 1943 imploring him to break his "inexplicable silence." The plea continued: "with the growth of persecution and daily spread of unheard-of crimes by the invader, the highest authority of the Christian world has kept silent for almost two years. . . . The facts prove that, even with the silence of the Holy Pontiff, the persecution is daily increasing. . . ."[8]

Now, in occupied Rome, the most crucial moments seemed at hand. Pius had not protested the distant slaughters, but should the Nazis lay the terror at the Pope's front door, could he still have nothing to say?

The Vatican quite naturally sought to prevent such a crisis and since the Jews of the city seemed a most likely Nazi target, it considerably increased its aid in their behalf.

Until now the Vatican's relief to persecuted Jews in Italy had consisted mostly of emigration assistance.[9] But as soon as the Pope received assurances, which came from Hitler himself, that the occupation forces would respect and safeguard the extraterritorial status of Vatican City and its multitude of enclaves in Rome, he personally ordered the clergy to open these sanctuaries to the Jews.[10] More than 150 monasteries, convents, and other religious institutions, including the Vatican itself, were to take in without discrimination any Jew who declared himself in need of refuge. The Germans, like everyone else in the city, were aware of this, and some of them, with Weizsäcker at the lead, now initiated efforts to guarantee the inviolability of these islands of safety.[11]

At this early stage of the occupation, however, few Jews felt the need to avail themselves of this generosity. The city was calm, the Germans were behaving correctly, and the Vatican was dispelling all rumors to the contrary.* The Pope, more than anyone else, seemed to have the situation in hand. Danger, by all appearances, was nowhere in sight, remote.

Thus the new, open-door policy of the Holy See was a poor prescription for the ailing policy of silence. In fact it created a new complication. Dependent on the good will of the Germans, the maintenance of the sanctuaries more than ever required the continuance of satisfactory relations between the Curia and the Wilhelmstrasse, which, in turn, depended on papal silence. But such a rapport, publicly attested to by the Vatican itself, helped make life in the occupied city appear normal, furthering the very illusion of security that was so much sought after and so comforting to the Jews of Rome, and of course so perilous. Indeed the open doors of the sanctuaries themselves enhanced the well-being of anyone who thought he might one day be impelled to pass through them.

For the Germans of the Weizsäcker stripe and the Vatican men of good will, sanctuary was a charitable work of which they approved. But, it did not take long to determine, the threat of Nazi action against the city's Jews had in no way been abated. The supreme test of the Pope's silence—considered so essential to the "larger" issues at stake—moved closer with each passing day. None of these men, German and Churchman alike, wanted that to happen. At all costs, the Jews of Rome had to be saved.

* This effort was undertaken by the Holy See by means of Vatican radio, its daily newpaper *Osservatore Romano,* and in the churches of the city. Pressed for by the German Foreign Office, it began almost immediately and culminated in October with a statement "to put an end to unfounded rumors . . . about the conduct of German troops with regard to Vatican City." The Germans, said the statement, had respected Vatican territory, as well as the activities of the Holy See, until now, and it had declared its intention to continue to do so.[12]

VII

THE EFFORTS BY both friend and foe to aid the Jews of Rome continued that first week of the occupation.

Two men who were in an especially advantageous position to help were Roman Jews Renzo Levi and Settimio Sorani, president and secretary, respectively, of the Jewish refugee service organization in Rome, DELASEM.* Levi and Sorani were exquisitely informed of the dangers faced by their fellow Jews. Levi, a wealthy industrialist serving DELASEM in an honorary post, had known of the concentration camps and the crematoriums "for a long time."[2] Sorani, as the chief functionary of the organization, had been aware since early in 1943 not only that Jews were being gassed but also of the most obscure details of the German persecution and destruction. "I knew then," he would say more than a score of years later, "as much as is known today. Everything."[3]

Their sources of this valuable knowledge were both disin-

* DELASEM (*Delegazione assistenza emigranti ebrei*—Committee for Aid to Jewish Emigrants) had been founded in 1940 by the leaders of Italian Jewry to assist the emigration of Jews who were being expelled systematically or were leaving voluntarily. Financed by the major Jewish organizations abroad, particularly in the United States, the agency had the support and approval of the Fascist government, which was happy to be relieved of the problem it had created, while at the same time enjoying a notable influx of foreign exchange (some $20,000 monthly from the U.S. Jewish agencies Joint Distribution Committee and the Hebrew Immigrant Aid Society alone). The Vatican was also active in the work of DELASEM, which by the time of the German occupation had broadened its functions to succor Jewish refugees who were fleeing to Italy from other countries under Nazi domination.[1]

terested and unimpeachable. Prior to the German takeover of Rome, Sorani had been in daily contact with the Vatican and the International Red Cross in the performance of his duties of assisting Jews who had succeeded in escaping from the terror in Nazi-occupied territories to the lesser evil of Fascist Italy. In this manner he had received reports from the most distant outposts of the Nazi *abattoir.**

As early as July 1940 Sorani had proposed to the leaders of Italian Judaism that measures be taken in the event of a German occupation. His suggestions at a time when Italy had just entered World War II as Hitler's closest ally had been considered preposterous[5]—though the Jews of Europe had already been publicly singled out by Führer and Duce alike as an enemy marked for destruction.

On the evening of the 8th of September both Levi and Sorani, who had equipped themselves with false documents offering new, non-Jewish identities, had acted individually on their superior knowledge. They and their families had gone into hiding. Both men had previously worked out their own separate plans for moving neatly and swiftly from the most dangerous place a Jew could live, his own home.

In this week of relative calm, they had emerged from their hiding places, spreading warnings once more among their fellow Jews.

Sorani spent much of the time at the Lungotevere Sanzio offices of DELASEM, diagonally facing the temple from across the Tiber. Going through the organization's files, he removed for concealment elsewhere everything that might be dangerous should it fall into German hands. The most compromising documents were burned, leaving enough old and innocuous material so as not to arouse suspicion in the event of a search.[6]

Jewish refugees, who were arriving daily from countries such as France, Yugoslavia, and even as far as Poland, were cautioned

* His informants were the high Vatican officials Monsignori Angelo Dell'Acqua, Cipico, and Dionisi, and the International Red Cross representative in Rome, Count De Salis. In addition, he had received reports of Nazi atrocities from the United States wartime diplomat in the Vatican, Harold H. Tittmann.[4]

by Sorani not to remain in Rome. There were about 650 refugees in the city that week, more than half of whom found their way to DELASEM.[7] Sorani advised them to proceed further south. Their safety could be assured, he told them, if they could cross the Allied lines—at that time not a very difficult feat. The majority, however, for one reason or another did not go. They were given money for food and quartered with false identity papers in the scattering of hotels and *pensioni* around Termini train station.[8]

More important than this work, perhaps, were Levi's and Sorani's appeals to President Foà and other leaders of the community urging them that the time had come for them and all the Jews of Rome to hide. By now, however, it was virtually useless to bring up this subject in the presence of Foà. The head of the Roman community had been kept constantly apprised of the information gathered by Sorani, and now, he let it be known, there was nothing new in what they had to say. As always he made it peremptorily clear that true or not "these things can't happen in Italy."[9]

There were at least three reasons why any "excesses," to use Foà's words, "the brethren in faith had fallen victim to in other lands invaded by German armies would not be repeated in Rome." According to the president's thinking, the Jews of Rome were protected because they were "relatively few in number." Furthermore the city in which they resided would be respected by the Germans, and finally the Jews of his community were making "every effort in order not to give any pretext for persecutions." Shortly after these arguments would prove themselves to have been wholly in error, Foà would say: "Not even Italy was immune."[10]

Faced with this attitude, which was shared in varying degrees by some other Roman Jewish officials, who were confident in Foà's and their own abilities to negotiate any future threat with the authorities, Levi and Sorani, the industrialist and the bureaucrat, concluded that there was little they could do.[11] They were unable to think of any plan of action acceptable to themselves to propose to the other leaders and members of the Jewish Council as an alternative to Foà's reputed contacts. All they could offer to such men, who were accustomed to the rewards that accompanied their station in life, was a suggestion that conjured ugly images of surrendering that in which they had invested all of their energy for the rootlessness of a common refugee, such as those tattered, pathetic souls who darkened the offices of DELASEM. This unjust and unequal exchange was to be made on the basis of inconceivable tales of horror taking place in a distant land—stories that no amount of evidence, sometimes even for Levi and Sorani themselves, could render entirely credible.

Like wounded messengers of doom, the two men were incapable of doing anything more than walk the streets of Rome sounding soft alarms to their friends and relatives, not one of whom in that September lull took their advice.[12]

VIII

One Jew in Rome whom Sorani had somehow neglected to warn was his young neighbor, twenty-nine-year-old Arminio Wachsberger. Wachsberger's flat, in Lungotevere Ripa, number 6, a comfortable building on the Trastevere side of the area around the temple, stood face to face with that of DELASEM's chief executive. Still, he did not know that Sorani had abandoned the place a few days ago—news that Wachsberger would have found troublesome at this moment in his life.[1]

Like many average Jews in the city, Wachsberger had given some thought to fleeing. Lately he had been hearing alarming information about Nazi behavior toward the Jews of other countries. It was not just the anti-Nazi propaganda broadcasts of the BBC—London's nightly voice of Colonel Stevens who told of Jews being slaughtered and gassed—which all the Jews of Rome had heard. Nobody believed those atrocity stories; or if anyone did, there would always be someone else to deride them. Wachsberger had had what he believed was harder news. To be sure, it was infinitely less authoritative than that which had driven Sorani into hiding. Nevertheless it was enough, given the other pieces of his existence, to make a man wonder about what to do.

At the place where he worked, Simoncini's photo-optical shop in Via Volturno, he had had an unusual opportunity to speak casually, even friendlily, with many German soldiers. Because of the shop's proximity to the military installation at nearby Macao barracks, they would often drop in to buy a roll of German film or leave a camera for repair. Wachsberger, born in Austrian Fiume a few years before it became part of Italy, spoke their language as his mother tongue. Whenever soldiers of the Reich entered Simoncini's, quite naturally it was Wachsberger who was called on to serve them. He was, name and all, always taken for a German or an Austrian, and never a Jew, since it seemed impossible that Italy, with its Nazi-style racial laws, would tolerate Jews in an Aryan setting.

Wachsberger would see the same faces returning again and again. For the most part they were worn by lonely young men who were happy to exchange a few words with him in the language of their homeland. Many had recently come from Russia and Poland, and they would tell their German-speaking civilian friend of the horrible things they had seen with their own eyes—all the grisly, benumbing details of how the Jews and other undesirables were being exterminated more efficiently than so many rats and roaches. On one occasion a German had come into the shop holding a souvenir he had bought from a stall in the Roman ghetto. Where had he gotten that? Wachsberger had asked, knowing all the while. "From the Italian Jews," he had said. "Happy souls, they're still having a good time here in

Italy, whereas in Germany and the other occupied countries by now they are all *kaputt*."

To Wachsberger it seemed so unreasonable, incredible. He preferred to think such reports were exaggerations of a few individual cases of reprisals against Russian partisans, among whom there may have been some Jews.

Though he withheld giving much credence to this news, the idea of flight, now that Rome was in German hands, did not seem to him to be foolish. In these first days of the occupation his wife's cousin, a well-known Italian-Jewish actor named Cesare Polacco, came to him and said that he and a group of his friends were going to try to cross the front lines into Allied-held territory. Would Wachsberger care to join them?

Running away was a difficult decision to make. It was not as if he were alone. There was his family to think of: his wife, Regina, and their frail little daughter, Clara, who was not yet five years old and was not a well child. Then there were his in-laws, Moise and Carlotta Polacco, an elderly couple who lived with him.

Furthermore, Rome in spite of the discriminations had not gone badly for him. He had come to this city some years before the war, newly drafted into the Italian Air Force. When he had completed his military service, he remained in Rome, where he had met Regina, a Trastevere girl who had been born in Venice. They married, lived near the ghetto, and partook in the life of the Jewish community. In November, 1938, their daughter was born. It was, of course, a joyous occasion—doubly so since it took some of the edge from the anti-Jewish regulations which were decreed by the King that very month. As any child would have been, Clara was a constant delight to her young parents, a sometimes annoyance, and always a cherished object of deep concern. When the little girl was hardly three years old, she was stricken with poliomyelitis, and even now she had not fully recovered.

It was not an easy life for Wachsberger, but shafts of bright light broke through, and there were places and things of warmth. Like the holiday eve of the *Giorno del Kippur*, when not an inch of space could be found in the synagogue, all the Jews of Rome having come to hear the chief rabbi intone the *Kol Nedarim*. Or like the Passover days: eating the corrugated *azzime* and reading from the *Hagadah* about the exodus from Egypt and the plagues God had visited on the enemies of Israel.

The son of a rabbi, Wachsberger carefully guarded the orthodox rites and traditions of Judaism, frequenting the temple more than most Roman Jews. At the same time he was an ambitious and energetic man. While most Jews of the ghetto-Trastevere district, as a result of the racial laws, were sorely unemployed, Wachsberger had two jobs and was diligently casting his hooks on the middle class.

There was the salesman's job at Simoncini's, which was, however, only part-time employment—daily until the hour of the siesta. His afternoons and early evenings were dedicated to a small enterprise he had started. Renting meager premises in the Flaminio district, he had opened a miniscule chemical factory for the manufacture of such commercial products as soap and wax. This, perforce, had all been done in the name of two agreeable Aryan friends, since Jews were not permitted to be owners of anything productive of capital unless it was valued at less than fifty dollars.[2] Wachsberger's laboratory was anything but a prosperous venture, and the work among the pungent chemical odors was extremely unpleasant. But there was enough activity to keep alive any dreams of success Wachsberger might have had, and it also provided a job for his sixty-eight-year-old father-in-law.[3]

From such roots a man does not easily take flight. Wachsberger told his actor cousin that after reflecting on his offer he had decided to remain behind. The Allies, Jews in the city were saying, were beginning to move, and before long—within days perhaps—they would drive the Germans from Rome. Besides, somewhere in Wachsberger's mind was the soporific thought that if matters really worsened, he and his family could always go into hiding in his chemical shop.

IX

IN THE MIDDLE of the week Chief Rabbi Zolli went to see the president of the Union of Italian Jewish Communities.[1] His plans to save the Jews seemed more imperative than ever, for Rome had just been stunned by news widely regarded as bad.

Monday's noon newspapers had announced that Mussolini, who was being held secretly by forces loyal to the King and Badoglio, had been rescued in a daredevil operation by commandos of the SS and flown to Germany. Now there was talk going around, on the basis of reports broadcast by Radio Munich, that the Duce would be reinstalled by the Nazis as chief of a new Fascist Italy. DNB, the German press agency, issued a statement from Mussolini, in which he ordered the Fascist party to reexhume itself and punish all traitors—a category of persons yet to be defined.[2]

In Rome and elsewhere party bosses and toughs, who had dropped out of sight immediately after the July 25 *coup d'etat*, were crawling out of their holes, bearing seven-week-old grudges that ached for revenge.

One of them, fascism's most venemous anti-Semite, Giovanni Preziosi, had already reached the Duce's side. He began at once to lobby for a harsher-than-ever anti-Jewish policy for the new regime and a post in its administration.[3] If anyone in Rome bothered to listen, even now they could hear Preziosi's Italian-language broadcasts over Munich radio. All of Italy's troubles, he continually blared, came from its Jews and the failure of the fallen regime to have recognized this. The first task of neo-fascism, he declared, was the "total elimination" of the Italian Jews.[4] Minister of State in the old Fascist government, Preziosi had earned the reputation of being a *Judenfresser*—a Jew eater. He was well thought of by Hitler and Goebbels, and now there was every reason to fear his return to a position of power.

If thoughts of these late developments weighed on Rabbi Zolli's mind, they only added to his sense of importance about his visit to the president of the Jewish union. In the hierarchy of Italian Jewry the head of the union stood at the summit. His name was Dante Almansi, properly referred to as His Excellency *il Cavaliere* Gr. Cr. Dr. Dante Almansi, formerly Prefect of the Realm. Should Zolli fail now, it would be useless to turn elsewhere.

To broaden the scope of his projected rescue operation, in keeping with the more comprehensive character of the union, Zolli thought now beyond the Jews of Rome to include all of Italy. The rabbi envisaged the deputation of a sort of Jewish Mercury, who would be dispatched "to visit the larger communities to notify them by word of mouth of the impending danger and to cause the same advice to reach minor centers . . ."[5]—the objective being the flight of all the Jews. It was a rather vague idea, and Zolli himself thought such plans might seem to others to be "like the product of childish fears."[6]

Impelled though he was to go on, however, he had little reason to think he would be more successful with Almansi than he had been with Foà. He had already spoken to the former on the telephone, and Zolli's suggestion that the Jews were imperiled had been politely scorned. Almansi had received "reassuring information." "Do not worry," the union president had said to Zolli, ". . . you can keep quite calm. And moreover, you must communicate absolute confidence to the people."[7]

Dante Almansi was by far the most influential Jew—and one of the most respected—in Fascist Italy. A bantam of a man, with a softness about his face that spoke for his kindly manner, he was, by profession, a police official.[8] Until the racial laws, he had served Mussolini's government for many years at the highest levels of the state police system, including the national offices of vice chief of police, and prefect of several provinces. Though unavoidably drenched with the contents of the Fascist cesspool, he had never borne any special affinity to the dictatorship, having entered the civil service prior to the rise of the Duce.

The rapids of the bureaucracy, which he had learned to ride with greater-than-average skill, had carried him far, with only one recorded instance where he had acted just a shade opportunistically. At the time of the Matteotti crime—the 1924 Fascist murder of Mussolini's chief political opponent, Socialist Giacomo Matteotti—Almansi had adhered to a request by a Fascist party official to delay by a few days the ordered expulsion of a foreign thug. The man had been picked by the Duce's henchmen to drive the car to be used in the Matteotti slaying. At the last moment the foreigner was replaced, and there is no evidence that Almansi knew in advance what was being plotted.[9] But as second in command of the state police, he had helped cover up the crime when a national outcry threatened the Duce's government. At that time he had also joined the party, reconfirming his commitment to the regime.[10]

For this show of faith he had been rewarded with a prefecture and the abiding trust of party Secretary Starace and the top man in the Interior Ministry, Buffarini-Guidi[11]—contacts that were to prove invaluable in his later efforts to help his fellow Jews.

In November, 1939, one year after the racial laws had stripped even *camerata* Almansi of his office, he was elected president of the union of Jewish communities. He had been pensioned out of the government without bitterness, and his influence, despite the official discriminations, had not diminished. The new president quickly proved himself, in the eyes of his fellow Jews, to be a valuable asset in softening the blows of Mussolini's anti-Semitism.[12]

According to one of his Jewish colleagues, however, Almansi had "one defect": he could not conceive of the danger to the Italian Jews inherent in the Fascist alliance with Hitler's Germany.[13] When Settimio Sorani, the DELASEM executive, had put this problem before the Jewish leaders in 1940, Almansi had replied with a benign, shrug-of-the-shoulder smile, "Well, let's hope to God . . ."[14]

Revered by all the Jewish leaders in the land, Almansi was said to be a generous, openhearted man. He was reputed to possess an "indomitable" spirit, which he employed with neither surcease nor guile in behalf of his suffering coreligionists.[15] But when the United States Fifth Army would liberate Rome, Almansi would be regarded less magnanimously. An American Jewish officer attached to the occupation forces would respond, perhaps unfairly, to the fine judgments of Almansi rendered by his colleagues by remarking, "tell them to stick their reports up their ass." The American would then quote from the official Allied police record on Almansi: "He is an intelligent and able individual . . . capable of any action to preserve his own safety and position."[16]

It was to this man that Rabbi Zolli had come with his half-baked idea of disbanding, if only temporarily, all of Italian Jewry.

Almansi, the rabbi later said, "listened to me graciously." When Zolli brought up the subject of the Nazi occupiers, Almansi replied, "I guarantee safety for you and for your wife also."[17]

Both Foà and he had had "categorical assurances from high personages in whom they had unshakable confidence," Zolli was further told.[18] They could not publicly reveal who had so assured them, but it was allowed to be known that their guarantors were highly placed in the Italian government. As proof of the Germans' good will they could point to the fact that since the arrival of Hitler's troops, almost a week ago, not a single Jew had been harmed.

Zolli thanked His Excellency for the promise of security, but he persisted in the notion that measures should be adopted to protect the Jewish population as a whole. "We must disperse the people," he said.

"I do not share your fears in the least," Almansi rejoined.

Zolli suggested that in any event there could be no harm in

merely discussing his plan and he proposed a meeting of community president Foà, Almansi, and himself.

"If you both wish to come," said the diminutive Jewish leader, "let me know, and I will await you with pleasure."[19]

On Friday the 17th Zolli returned to Foà in hope of arranging the meeting of the two presidents.[20]

Reaching the point of exasperation, Foà reminded the rabbi that if any precautionary measures were to be eventually adopted in Rome, such decisions, according to the law of 1930, were only to be taken by the duly elected local Jewish Council—to which both Zolli and Almansi did not belong.

Zolli, whose personal fear had reached the stage where he felt he could no longer risk walking the streets of Rome, urged as a last resort that the community's list of Roman Jews be destroyed.[21] There were actually two such lists. One was a roll of persons who contributed funds to the community. Since the law of 1930 had conferred on the community the right to exact such "contributions" in the form of a graduated income tax,[22] it was inclusive of almost all the city's Jews. There was, however, an even more extensive file in the second list. Recorded on thousands of neatly packaged index cards, this was a most up-to-date catalogue of names, addresses, apartment numbers, birthdates, and genealogy of virtually every living Jew in Rome.

Foà, in answer to Zolli's final plea, remained silent for a moment or two, and then, according to the rabbi, he replied: "If the Duce proclaims himself Head of State, we will have to remove the portrait of the King."[23]

On Saturday, the eighth day of the occupation, the Jewish leaders rested. In the great synagogue by the Tiber they gathered with the common people of the community. This, both circles would agree, was the embrace that brought them closest together.[24] The shoulders of every Jewish man were draped in the white cloth of the *taléd*, and their heads were covered with a skull cap fashioned like the Pope's and called a *"papallino,"* or "little pope." The oneness of the group was warmed in the temple's motherly caresses, as rich and poor alike filled the cupola with a single voice to the one God. It would have been hard to distinguish the leaders from the led, were the former not always seated nearest to the Holy Ark.

If anyone among the congregation feared the Nazi presence in Rome, he could find comfort in this day, like any other Sabbath of the less troubled past. *"Loro,"* or "they"—the name reserved for the leaders of the group—did not allow a shadow of concern to darken their faces. This required no special effort; everything, it seemed to them, was relatively under control. To be sure, one newspaper began again that day to use the Fascist date[25]—a Roman numeral affixed to the day, month, and year to indicate the year of the "Fascist Era"—but that was only a small figure in the masthead, hardly noticeable at all.

There was, however, one conspicuously unusual aspect to this Sabbath, although few spoke of it with more than casual interest. Chief Rabbi Zolli had not appeared that morning to officiate at the ceremonies and his place had been substituted by another rabbi, David Panzieri.[26]

Having spent his last hope to save his position, Zolli had yielded to his fear of losing his life. He and his wife and daughter had closed their ghetto apartment, finding shelter in the home of a Catholic family in the Prati district.[27] This had infuriated the community leaders—even those who themselves had hidden. They would forever accuse Zolli of abandoning his post and his people, at a time when they needed him most.[28] But now they said nothing, and for all that was known to the average Roman Jew, the chief rabbi's absence might only have been caused by his having come down with a cold.

X

BEFORE THIS FIRST week of the occupation ended, Albrecht von Kessel paid a visit to his Swiss friend, Alfred Fahrener. The German wanted to learn whether the mission he had entrusted to Fahrener had been executed. The League of Nations official replied that the warning had in fact been passed on to his Jewish acquaintances, but the feeling was that now that order had been restored in Rome, "there was nothing to worry about."*[1] Fahrener himself concurred with this view. There seemed to him to be no grounds for excessive concern. The Germans were behaving "extremely correctly," he said.[3]

Kessel was shocked, he later said. The Swiss and the Jews had failed to understand that it was order not chaos that the SS needed to carry out its work. "Once order was established," he said later but not then, "the deportation of the Jews became a certainty."[4] Instead of expressing these views at the time, Kessel lost his temper. The Jews of Rome must vanish, he shouted. "If they are killed, their blood will be on my head and on the heads of my friends—and we don't deserve that."[5]

* Attempts to find out precisely to whom Fahrener had spoken were unsuccessful. However, it was learned that almost certainly they were not in any way associated with the organized Jewish community of Rome. Further, Jews who were warned by Kessel himself were identified and on the basis of testimony given to me by one of them, it seems likely that Fahrener had met with some of the foreign Jews who lived in Rome, a number of whom were employed by the Vatican, and international and foreign scientific, educational, and religious organizations.[2]

Here their meeting ended. Convinced that the reaction of Fahrener's Jewish friends was the result of the "fatalistic attitude" of all Mediterranean peoples, among whom he included the "southern" Italians, the German diplomat felt that there was nothing more that could be done. Fatalism, he believed, was a "characteristic" of Jews, who were different from the "more active" people of the north. In Rome, the Jews "simply did not move, going about as if nothing had happened."[6] If these prejudices had been taken on to relieve the gnawing of his conscience, they would prove futile. Kessel would one day admit, "Everything I did . . . was too little. I feared being tortured by the Gestapo."[7]

In the meantime, however, he had contacted a friend at the German Archaeological Institute in Rome and let it be known that he regarded the present situation as being "difficult." This was a signal to be passed on to a German woman named Hermine Speier.[8] An archaeologist of Jewish origin, Dr. Speier was an employee of the Vatican. Though she had come to Rome in 1928, she had never had any contact with the Jewish community and was unknown there.

Some weeks before the 8th of September, Kessel, who had known Dr. Speier since 1930, inquired of a mutual friend at the institute, "Does Fräulein Speier know what to do should there be any difficulty?"[9] Apprised of this discreet warning, she had quietly made arrangements to hide in a nearby convent. Now the word had come. In her apartment on the sharply sloping Salita S. Onofrio in the Trastevere section of Rome, she began to pack a few things. Should anyone ask, her colleagues had been told to reply that she had gone to Naples.

In no way enmeshed in the dynamic of the community, Dr. Speier would find it relatively easy to escape the approaching fire by simply withdrawing from the fuel.

Across the Tiber at the Termini train station near the center of town another Jew who was unknown to the community was in the process of fleeing, though he was entering, not leaving Rome. His name was Giuseppe Levi Cavaglione. He had arrived in the city at 9:00 P.M. having come from Genoa, where he was being hunted by the Germans.[10]

Levi Cavaglione, not yet thirty years old, had already spent six years in concentration camps. His "crimes" had not been racial, but substantive acts of antifascism, for which he had been confined to the political camps set up by the Fascist regime. When Mussolini had fallen, he had returned to his home in Genoa, only to see the city fall to the Germans. On the 15th of September the local chief of the political office—the same man who had arrested him six years earlier—sent a message to Levi Cavaglione that the following morning he would have to take him into custody once again, on orders received from the German occupation authorities.

The Jewish anti-Fascist had immediately acted on the tip, taking refuge in a monastery, where he passed the next few days enjoying the seclusion. "That tranquil and comfortable life," he later said, "made me blush with shame at the thought of the groups of partisans that were forming in every part of Italy for the fight against the Germans."[11] He decided to go to Rome and make contact with the Underground, which in reality was still barely more than a wish and had only begun a few days earlier to organize itself under a National Liberation Committee (CLN).*

Now in the grey waiting room of Termini, Levi Cavaglione had arrived, a single suitcase gripped in his hand, and in his pocket, the addresses of three persons in Rome said to be in touch with the *macchia*. It was early evening as he began to walk through the unfamiliar streets of the occupied capital in search of the new comrades. But a few minutes before the cur-

* On September 9, as the first armed resistance was taking place at the Pyramid of Cestius, leaders of the six anti-Fascist political parties in Rome met in a villa in the northern part of the city and formed the CLN—*Comitato di Liberazione Nazionale*. The CLN immediately grouped into two factions: a tripartite right wing, led by De Gasperi's Christian Democrats; and a less-united left wing of Communists, Socialists, and a liberal-republican party. The following day, echoing Allied broadcasts and leaflets dropped on the city from American aircraft, the CLN issued a statement calling the people "to arms" and to resist as the only way to deal with the invading Nazis and the anticipated Fascist resurgence.[12]

few, he said later, "I found myself wandering aimlessly in a dark street of the great unknown city; the three addresses had been wrong."[13]

After 11:00 P.M. he would be in danger of immediate arrest. Nothing remained but to walk up to the first friendly face and ask for help. In the darkness he could make out the form of an elderly man walking toward him, a heavy-set figure who, it seemed to Levi Cavaglione, had a pleasant bearing.

"I am an Italian officer escaped from the Germans," he said abruptly, alluding to the fact that he had so served prior to his first arrest. "I don't know where to spend the night. Will you accept me in your house?"[14]

The old man was taken aback. He hesitated, then beckoned the stranger to follow him home. For Levi Cavaglione tomorrow would be time enough to pick up the trail of the partisans.

XI

IN THE SECOND week of the occupation the aid to the Jews took another form. Early in the week the head of the Gestapo in Rome, SS Major Herbert Kappler received an unusual telephone call from an officer of Reichsführer Himmler's staff.[1]

Kappler's prestige had soared in recent days, and he may well have been expecting to hear from the Reichsführer's office, even from Himmler himself. In August, on special orders from the RFSS—as the Reichsführer was often referred to—he had conducted the intelligence work necessary to locate the secret site of Mussolini's imprisonment. In a cloak and dagger operation he had twice outsmarted the Italians in finding the Duce, whose place of custody had twice been changed. He had then helped organize the dramatic expedition which had rescued Mussolini and returned him literally into the arms of the Führer.[2] Now the Gestapo major, who would celebrate his thirty-sixth birthday in a few days, could scarcely feign surprise if this telephone call from the Hochwald—code name for Himmler's headquarters in East Prussia—would bring words of praise, and perhaps an advance in his thus far brilliant career.

The call in fact informed Kappler that Himmler had promoted him to Obersturmbannführer (Lt. Col.) and had conveyed his best wishes. That was not all, said the voice at the other end of the line. The Reichsführer wanted to proceed with a roundup and deportation of the Jews of Rome. The action was to be prepared very soon. Further instructions would be sent shortly.[3]

The telephone call was followed by a "marconigram" radioed from Himmler's office. It read:

> The recent Italian events impose a final solution to the Jewish question in the territories recently occupied by the armed forces of the Reich. The RFSS therefore requests SS-Obersturmbannführer Kappler to actuate without delay all necessary preliminary measures in order to assure the precipitateness and secrecy of the operations to be carried out in the territory of the city of Rome. Immediate further orders will follow.[4]

Kappler, whatever his pleasure about having been promoted, was not happy about the idea of deporting the Jews of Rome. He felt this new order was "*eine neue grosse politische Dummheit*" —another gross political stupidity.[5]

He believed "a true Jewish question did not exist in Italy." The Italian Jews, he felt, "had not as in Germany grown rich off the backs of the people." Besides they were few in number, went Kappler's thinking, and linked as they were with the Italians to the Mediterranean, there was a strong affinity between the two, which did not exist between the Jews and the Germans.[6] In Rome, as far as he knew, they were poor, orderly, and passive—perhaps the least dangerous element of the population in spite of any connection they might have to the "international Jewish conspiracy." There were more important matters on the desk of the Gestapo chief than preparing the Final Solution—a term he had just seen used for the first time[7]—to the Jewish question in Rome.

The man who had been ordered to help solve this question was born in Stuttgart, the son of a chauffeur.[8] He entered the SS at an early age, having come from the ranks of the pre-Hitler police system. In 1939 he was sent to Rome as a police expert attached to the German embassy, his principal mission being to spy on the Italian police. There were difficult beginnings. "I had to be my own typist, my own driver, and even my own errand boy," Kappler later recalled.[9] With the war on, this seemed to him a squandering of his real worth. Five times he tried to be transferred to the front, going finally above his superiors in the SS directly to the military authorities. But he was reprimanded for this insubordination and he was forced to remain in Italy. Not that he did not like it there; indeed he came to "love this country." To use his own peculiar mode of speech, "I tried, by dint of study, to edify myself as to the historical basis of Italianity." Before long he invited his parents to come to Italy, "given that by now I considered this land as a second Fatherland."[10]

There was a wife, too, whom he despised and was trying to divorce, and a child, Wolfgang, adopted from those unfortunate bastards of the Lebensborn—children of Himmler's sexually degenerate scheme of finding and mating "perfect" German men with German women of equal perfection.

The Kapplers lived in a modest, rented villa at number 318 Via Salaria, at the north end of the city, almost in the country. He had a garden full of roses he loved and tended. His hobby was photography. His office, to which he often went dressed in civilian clothes, was on the other side of town in the sumptuous Villa Wolkonsky, the German embassy. But soon he would relocate. His work was rapidly expanding now that Rome was occupied.* New headquarters for the Gestapo, complete with its own twenty-cell prison, were being constructed in an apartment building in Via Tasso, which until now had served as the cultural office of the German embassy.[11]

Kappler, wooden in his movements, his steel-grey eyes frighteningly penetrating, was not a well-liked man, even among his colleagues. He had the reputation of being fiercely intelligent, a walking police archive, and in possession of an exquisite memory.[12] His dedication to his office was supreme, and in this sense he was without guile or pretense. He believed in the Third Reich and the righteousness of Hitler's *Kampf.* His duty, as he saw it, was to protect the security of his country, and in this work he had little time for anything else. Serious man that he was, he had consistently shown himself to be an incorruptible police official. He did not misuse his great power—as it was defined by German law—nor did he involve himself in minor affairs, which so many less competent Nazis used as straw men.

Loyal executor of superior orders, he nonetheless often sought to influence decisions before the orders were given. He had, for example, warned the Foreign Office of the danger of an Allied invasion of Italy and of the fall of Mussolini long before Berlin had been caught off guard when these events occurred, his reports obviously having gone unheeded.[13] He had also resisted the plan to rescue Mussolini as a waste of time, reporting that Italian fascism was dead. He had told this to Himmler personally, adding that any new government under the Duce could not stand without being propped up by German bayonets.[14]

Berlin did not know Rome as Kappler did, and for such reasons he considered the coming persecutions of the city's Jews a *Dummheit.* If Berlin were to persist in this, Kappler decided, he would oppose the Final Solution in Rome.[15]

* Officially Kappler was in section VI bureau B of the RSHA (Reichssicherheitshauptamt—Reich Security Main Office) of the SS. VI-B was the "German-Italian sphere" office of the foreign division of the SD (Sicherheitsdienst—Security Service). But in practice he did the work of RSHA section IV—the Gestapo.

XII

ON THE 23RD the situation in Italy changed somewhat, at least in appearance. The newly liberated Duce, reinflated by Hitler, proclaimed himself head of a new Fascist government called the *Repubblica Sociale Italiana* (RSI)—the Italian Social Republic. It was a puppet regime immediately nicknamed Pinocchio's Republic. The new government was too shaky to venture as far as Rome. It would be installed in the north of Italy, to where Mussolini flew now, from Munich, surrounded by Germans.[1]

This development was regarded by the Jewish leaders in Rome as favorable. The more power and authority that could be concentrated around the Duce, who, they persevered in believing, was really "soft" on Judaism, the less would be the threat to the Jews.[2] The Jewish leaders, especially Foà and Almansi, felt that they could negotiate almost any new twist in Italian anti-Jewishness with the government of a man who as late as October, 1941, had said:

> The Jewish patriot loses the characteristics of racial polemics. . . . I have Aryanized these men of great heart. . . . The ex-Prefect Almansi, who is in continuous contact with me, will become an Aryan—I pledge myself to that—as soon as he has resolved the grave problem he is studying for me [the emigration of the "politically untrustworthy" Jews].*

* Almansi's version of what he was doing for Mussolini differs slightly. His orders from the Duce called for the emigration of *all* Italian Jews, he says. The departure rate was to have been ten persons daily, which would have taken ten years to empty Italy of its Jews. "It was this calculation that tran-

It will be a question of a generation. Mixed marriages are slowly diffusing Jewish characteristics. A small percentage that might remain will do no harm in the veins of some future Italians.[4]

The absence of *Judenfresser* Giovanni Preziosi in the new government and the appointment of Guido Buffarini-Guidi as head of the Ministry of Interior—under which was the police system and the anti-Jewish Office of Demography and Race—were also signs the Jewish leaders could point to as auguring well for their coreligionists. The cunning and depraved intriguer Buffarini-Guidi, who was despised even by Mussolini and had entered the regime only because of his close relationship with Himmler, was said by the leaders to be one of the "moderates" on the Jewish question.[5] Buffarini-Guidi, as Undersecretary of Interior in the earlier Fascist government, had been the man responsible for administering the racial laws and the political persecutions. But he had shown himself to be a good-humored type with whom the Jewish leaders had little difficulty getting along.[6] Almansi, who especially enjoyed Buffarini's full trust and confidence, was exceedingly close and effective in his dealings with the Fascist, in whose service he had once been employed.[7] Buffarini was considered a hypocrite on the Jewish question, and he sold Aryanization certificates like a huckster. Nevertheless the Germans were satisfied with him, though in their eyes the obese, unctuous minister looked like a "Jewish cattle dealer."[8]

From the Mussolinis and the Buffarinis, the Jewish leaders were convinced, the flock had little to fear. That the Duce during this very week had proclaimed over Radio Munich that the neo-Fascist RSI would be national socialist in outlook

---

quilized me," Almansi relates, and after expressing his "pain and wonder" that such good citizens as the Jews could merit such treatment, he began at once to execute the orders. Enlisting the aid of all Italian Jewish communities, Almansi started with the expulsion of the Jewish youth, who were regarded by the regime as the most potentially anti-Fascist element of Italian Jewry and by the Jewish leaders as the biggest troublemakers. At no point did it ever appear likely to Almansi—or to anyone—that *all* Italian Jews would have to leave and in fact only 6,000 departed, of whom almost all were young people.[3]

and would "annihilate the parasitic plutocracies"[9]—common Fascist terminology for a group that included Jews—did not appear to enter into their calculations.

XIII

ON THE FOLLOWING day a message was dispatched from Himmler's office in Berlin. It arrived in the Villa Wolkonsky code room twenty-four hours later, Saturday the 25th. Drawn up on special paper bordered with a black stripe, the message bore the designation *Geheime Reichssache*—a secret affair of the Reich—which was a higher category of secrecy than the usual *Geheim* rubber stamped on such documents. It was marked "strictly confidential and personal," and was addressed to SS-Obersturmbannführer Kappler. It was, however, immediately opened, decoded, and brought into the office of the head of the occupation, General Rainer Stahel, Stadtkommandant of Rome.[1]

Until two days ago, Kappler had been under Stahel's command, placed there by Field Marshal Kesselring, but the Gestapo chief of Italy, General Wilhelm Harster, had come to Rome with orders moving Kappler into his organization. These orders had come from one of Kesselring's rivals in the division of supreme power in Italy, SS-Obergruppenführer Karl Wolff.[2] Thus, while there was no official reason for Stahel to be reading Kappler's mail, he was immediately caught on the flypaper of curiosity and intramural competition, familiar products of any bureaucracy, which in the end are used to strap it to the common cause.

The dispatch, Stahel quickly ascertained, called for a final solution to the Jewish question in Rome. All Jews, regardless of age, sex, and other considerations, were to be arrested and deported to the north "for liquidation."[3]

Somewhat ambiguous in that it did not set a date for the operation and did not actually order Kappler to move, the message continued:

> It is known that this nucleus of Jews has actively collaborated with the Badoglio movement and therefore its speedy removal will represent, among other things, a necessary security measure guaranteeing the indispensible tranquility of the immediate rear of the southern front. The success of this undertaking is to be assured by means of a surprise action and for this reason it is absolutely necessary to suspend the application of any anti-Jewish measures in the nature of individual acts in order not to arouse any suspicions among the population of an imminent *Judenaktion*.[4]

General Stahel, who had once been a door-to-door salesman of razor blades, was a sort who would be offended by this order, if only because he had not been previously consulted. A tough workhorse of an officer, he had risen in the ranks of the Luftwaffe, after having served as an air force captain in World War I. In Hitler's Wehrmacht he had acquitted himself superbly as a military man, earning the Iron Cross with oak leaf clusters. But as commandant of the occupied city, he was rapidly losing his prestige. Rome, as it had so often done to others, had possessed him. He saw himself as the guardian of the Eternal City and the center of Christendom.[5] To the astonishment of his fellow officers, Stahel had become a "political" man, driving around the city in an open green Mercedes with a motorcycle escort, much like a chief of state. He had entered into direct relations with the Vatican, which was pleased to expand its contacts with the authorities.*[6] But in dealings with the Holy See, mostly regarding local matters, he had irritated the neo-Fascists, the German diplomats, and Kesselring's chief of staff, to

* He developed particularly good relationships, according to Vatican sources, with German nationals Father Pankratius Pfeiffer, Pius XII's personal liaison between the Holy See and the occupation authorities, and Bishop Alois Hudal, rector of the German church of Rome.[7]

whom Stahel was increasingly neglecting to report, in violation of the field marshal's standing orders. This latter infraction of protocol had been especially foolhardy, since the chief of staff, Siegfried Westphal, was the youngest general in the German army and was fearful of being lightly regarded.[8]

Lately General Stahel had taken to sending naïve "political reports" with fatuous titles to Berlin—an action which was as inexplicable as it was insufferable to the chiefs of the other Nazi and Fascist authorities in Rome.[9] Stahel in fact would very shortly be replaced and swiftly sent back to the eastern front, which would cure him of his affair with Rome, only to be killed by a Russian bullet.

A little man, with rimless glasses and a triangular mustache, Stahel in the meantime was relishing his position as commander of the occupation forces, and at the moment he had intercepted the message to Kappler, he was apparently in a mood to use the instrument of his high office in a "political" way.

The general, whose headquarters had been set up in the spacious German embassy, went directly to the offices of the Reich's Konsul, the decoded message still clutched in his hands. By a curious twist in fate, the consul, Eitel Friedrich Möllhausen, had literally overnight become one of the most important men in occupied Rome. Late in the previous day the Nazi ambassador to the new Mussolini government, Rudolf Rahn, had been seriously injured in an automobile accident in northern Italy. It had now become clear that Rahn would be incapacitated for at least several weeks, and in any event most of his future activities would take place in the north, seat of the neo-Fascist regime. The consul in Rome, who was only thirty years old, was thus placed in charge of the embassy with the full powers of a chief of a diplomatic mission.[10]

Stahel showed Möllhausen Kappler's message. The general, Möllhausen later said, was very excited and said he would never have anything to do with this kind of *"Schweinerei."*[11]

"All right," Möllhausen replied, "then you shouldn't have any difficulty in aborting the plan."

Stahel flaked away a gesture of annoyance. "I came to you just because there's nothing I can do. The order was sent directly to Kappler, and unless he tells us, we'll have to pretend to know nothing about it. But I thought that you might be able to do something through the Foreign Office."[12]

Möllhausen, a suave, olive-skinned man of *Kultur*, pointed out to the general that if he, the Stadtkommandant, could do nothing, a second-ranking diplomat such as himself could certainly do no more. "Let me think about it overnight," he added, however. "I don't know what can be done, but let me think about it."[13]

With that, Stahel departed, and the order announcing the coming deportation of the Jews of Rome was hastily delivered to Kappler without trace of its interception.

Eitel Friedrich Möllhausen had been somewhat startled by this encounter with Stahel. The language of the dispatch from Berlin had cut deeply into his sensibilities. It was the first time he had ever seen the word "liquidation" used in reference to the persecution of the Jews.[14] He had long known that the European Jews were facing a "bad end," that many died in concentration camps, and that of those deported few might be expected to return. But it had always been a matter easily repressed, especially because he had managed to keep off the path being steamrollered by those who had the answers to the self-raised Jewish question. Now, however, with the unconditional term "liquidation" in an official document, the situation had become wholly "clarified," as he would later say, and from this day forward he would never be able to declare, should anyone in the future inquire, that he was uninformed as to the true fate of the Jews.[15]

The young diplomat, however, was still at some distance from being conscience-stricken. His entire life history had been rolled in noncommitment. The crust permitted a form of existential behavior that was often misinterpreted by his colleagues as politically *gauche*. He was a noncareer officer in the foreign service, and even now in Rome his post was contractual, an arrangement which came up for renewal from time to time.

He was born in Turkey, the son of a French woman and a

wealthy businessman of part-German extraction.[16] Although a citizen of the Reich, he had learned to speak Italian before German, having spent many of the early years of his life in Trieste. He was also fluent in Greek and French, and it was his knowledge of languages that gave direction to the drift of his youth and finally landed him in the German Foreign Office as a translator. Posted in the propaganda section, he was sent to Paris to work on the French-language *La Gerbe,* a German-financed weekly designed to win local intellectuals to the Nazi cause.

Möllhausen, who had consistently refused to join the Nazi party, seemed destined to a lackluster future. But in the course of his work he had fallen under the wing of Rudolf Rahn, who was rising fast in Ribbentrop's ministry. Before long he had become Rahn's closest aide, and after several tours of duty in the Middle East and North Africa, Möllhausen, despite himself, had been handed a "dream job" in occupied Rome.

Educated in France and having passed only brief periods in Germany, he had succeeded for the most part in eschewing the Nazi ethic and he had few illusions about a master race. Further, he was not infected with the intense anti-Semitism of the times and did not even talk the sour language of half-concealed prejudices common to the diplomatic corps. By his own admission, however, he had no special interest in aiding Jews, but on the other hand he was not opposed to being helpful to anyone in need.[17] He was a man with little pride in the red-white-and-black Nazi flag, and in appearance he looked more the swarthy Turk than the Nordic conqueror. He had a woman friend in Rome, an attractive Italian, who he had recently discovered was hiding a family of Jews in her home. To this shocking news he had reacted with customary urbanity, and for the remainder of the occupation he would bring extra ration books when he visited her in order that the fugitive family be well provided.[18]

Yet the system in which he took part had integrated him into its oily workings and had stamped him with a mediocrity he could not deny. At this grave moment in the war the problem that was uppermost in his mind was a pedestrian threat to his "freedom of action," which he saw as being "strongly compromised by the presence of Stahel and Kappler in the Villa Wolkonsky."[19]

He had come to believe—perhaps correctly so in some involuted way—that the autonomy of German diplomacy was in jeopardy because of the physical proximity of the representatives of the Wehrmacht and the Gestapo. As a result of hard bargaining and the intervention of Ambassador Rahn, he had already won concessions from Stahel and Kappler. They had agreed to contract their operations into the rooms of the *palazzo*, which were not absolutely indispensible to the functioning of the embassy. They had also recognized Möllhausen as master of the house.[20] Kappler was less the problem than Stahel. The Gestapo man would shortly withdraw to his new headquarters being prepared in Via Tasso. But the general, much to Möllhausen's displeasure, had rejected out of hand suggestions that he leave the embassy grounds and reorganize his command elsewhere in the city.[21]

It was this challenge, which Möllhausen would eventually win at the time of Stahel's removal, that was now coloring at least a part of the consul's thoughts, as he reflected upon what he might do to help the Jews of Rome.

XIV

EARLY THE NEXT morning—it was Sunday, the 26th—Möllhausen went to see Kappler. He had, in the short period he had known the Gestapo chief, developed a measure of respect for him. He thought Kappler to be a man of superior intelligence, and although he seemed a "typically obedient SS officer," Kappler, as far as Möllhausen saw, had demonstrated a certain wideness of views.[1] He never took part in matters of scarce significance, Möllhausen had observed, and it was only when he believed himself to be dealing with something that might menace the security of the Reich that "he knew no pity and became the blind instrument of the implacable Gestapo."[2] Doubtless the diplomat would have held his colleague in even higher regard, had he known that Kappler was aware—and had told no one—of Möllhausen's clandestine relationship with persons characterized as non-Aryans.[3]

Möllhausen spoke frankly to the Gestapo officer, coming right to the point. He asked if Kappler would cooperate in obstructing the order for the deportation of the Jews of Rome. Möllhausen said that when he had served in Tunisia under Rahn, the ambassador had intervened there in order to remove the Jews from the jurisdiction of the Gestapo. As a result of this, they had not been deported and had been used instead in a locally organized labor service for the benefit of the Wehrmacht. Now, said Möllhausen, he believed the ambassador would want to adopt these same measures for the treatment of the Roman Jews.[4]

A flash of anger and indignation crossed Kappler's uneven face. His eyes leered icily. "How did you know about these orders?" he demanded.[5] He was furious that the content of so secret a dispatch, which had been solely for his eyes, was apparently already common knowledge.

"What difference does it make?" Möllhausen replied, protecting his source. "The order exists and I would like to know what you're going to do about it."

"What can *I* do?" Kappler said. "I have nothing against these Jews. They're not the enemy—oh, yes, the enemy—" he interrupted himself, correcting a technical point, "but they don't bother anyone. They're here in Rome living peacefully and they won't make trouble. My problem is not the Jews, but the anti-Fascists. But the order has been sent and I don't see how it can be evaded."

"You can pretend you never received it," Möllhausen suggested weakly. But Kappler dismissed such a foolish notion summarily, fixing his penetrating gaze on the young diplomat with a frightening glint of suspicion. As Möllhausen later recalled it, Kappler's glare had not disturbed his composure, and the Gestapo man appeared then to want to "take a step in my direction."

The only way out of this situation, Kappler said, was to put the matter before Field Marshal Kesselring. If the commander-in-chief of the southern front were to oppose the deportations, Kappler went on, he would be willing to interpret Kesselring's word as countermanding his orders from Berlin, at least until new orders arrived.[6] Since Rome had been designated a war territory, it would be difficult for anyone but the Führer himself to overrule Kesselring.

"All right," said Möllhausen. "If you really mean it, let's go at once to Kesselring."[7]

They sent for a car and departed immediately to the field marshal's headquarters in the *Castelli Romani*, the cluster of low mountains just south of Rome. Within the hour the two Germans were in the Villa Avorio, to which Kesselring had moved after the September 8th Allied bombing of his elaborate command post in nearby Frascati. They were received without delay by the field marshal.[8]

Kesselring, who would one day be convicted as the perpetrator of war crimes against civilian populations, had nevertheless been in on the Tunisia affair, having responded favorably to Rahn's intervention. When the SS Einsatzkommando had arrested the Jewish leaders, Kesselring issued an order to mobilize Jewish workers for the construction of fortifications.*[9]

It was Kappler who spoke first to the field marshal. He related

* The Jewish leaders were released—on payment of a "fine" of 20,000,000 francs ($400,000)—in order that they might organize the able-bodied men of their community for the implementation of Kesselring's order. Platoons of Jewish workers were assigned to various detachments of the Wehrmacht, the SS totally excluded from the operation. The net effect of this incident, outrageous as it was, left the Jewish women, children, and elderly free, and the labor gangs were unmolested and finally liberated by the Allies.[10]

the situation objectively and impersonally, revealing the orders that had been received and the consequent necessity that they be followed.[11]

Möllhausen reminded Kesselring of Tunisia.[12] He argued further that the deportation would be "politically inopportune" and would only result in "damaging consequences" for the Reich. He purposely avoided any reference to humanitarian reasons. Such talk, he believed, was certain to bring negative results in meetings with high officials of the Nazi state.[13]

When they had completed their speeches, Kesselring looked at them silently for a long while. The commander-in-chief was always a quiet man, given to lengthy deliberation before making decisions. On this very day he was preoccupied with the Allied advance up the Italian peninsula, and first among his internal problems was a struggle with Field Marshal Rommel for complete control of all German forces in Italy.[14] Some days before, he had given an order to disengage his coastal defenses in order to move more troops to the Volturno River line, and now, with his flanks exposed, he feared a new Allied sea invasion.[15] For a man who had threatened to send 700 bombers to destroy Rome earlier in the month unless it surrendered, the well-being of the city's Jews could not have meant a great deal. There appeared to be only one consideration, and when the field marshal finally spoke, he expressed it succinctly.

"How many men will you need to carry out this operation?" he asked Kappler.

Kappler thought for a moment and replied that aside from his own personnel, an additional force of about one motorized battalion would be necessary.

"That settles it," said Kesselring. "Under these circumstances, I regret to say that I will not be able to give my approval. Information at my disposal indicates the possibility of an imminent invasion at Ostia, and I need all available forces for the defense of the city."[16] If it were important to do something with the Roman Jews, he would favor duplicating the Tunisian incident, using Jewish labor for defense construction work around Rome.[17]

That seemed to be the end of it. As the two visitors departed, the field marshal's face was as inscrutable as ever.[18]

On the return from Kesselring's headquarters, neither Möllhausen nor Kappler brought up the subject of their mission, choosing to speak of other, less weighty topics. But at the moment of parting, Kappler turned to the diplomat and said abstrusely, "I hope you are convinced that personally I have no desire to persecute for the sake of persecution. For my part the Jews can just as well remain where they are."[19]

Möllhausen was puzzled by this remark. Not quite certain what Kappler was trying to say, he replied benignly that he was pleased for Kappler's sake that Kesselring's decision meant that now the Gestapo chief would not have to undertake such a disagreeable task as deporting Jews. They then left one another, Möllhausen relegating the affair to the past.[20]

XV

KAPPLER KNEW SOMETHING the others did not.

In the past forty-eight hours or so he had found his own "solution" to the Jewish question in Rome, given that events had forced him to think about it. If the deportation demanded by Berlin was a political stupidity, the do-nothing policies of the Möllhausens were equally untenable. There *were* Jews in Rome; there was no escaping it, and, he had decided, they *were* an enemy, if only in an ideological way. But putting them in prison, sending them to a concentration camp, or even exploiting their muscle power, were not, in Kappler's view, intelligent methods of handling the problem.

He had already sent a number of messages to Berlin questioning the advisability of the deportation orders, but clearly they were having no effect.[1] Now he had decided on a new initiative; winning Kesselring's backing was a beginning.

The deportation, Kappler had concluded, would work completely at cross-purposes to the very reason for his presence in Rome. Security and espionage were his professions, not traffic and transportation; his work required him to be subtle, shrewd, ruthless, brutal, and even savage, but not savage alone.

Kappler, who accepted as unquestionable the Nazi shibboleth of an international Jewish conspiracy in which all Jews were somehow involved, had arrived at the conclusion that the removal of the Jews of Rome "precluded for us the possibility of obtaining useful information by exploiting the existing relations between Jewish circles in Rome and those of neutral or enemy states."[2] Furthermore, he had decided to tell his superiors in Berlin, the contacts between the Roman Jews and "Jewish financial groups abroad" comprised a distinct area to be penetrated for reasons of espionage.*[3] Finally he hoped that Berlin would comprehend that in "putting the Jews in prison or deporting them we would lose an excellent financial source for our own intelligence services."[5] Jews, it was his conviction, had but a single weapon: money. Kappler had decided that it was his duty not to deport them, but to disarm them.[6]

Prior to his meeting that morning with Consul Möllhausen, Kappler had contacted the Questura, Rome's police headquarters in Via della Gatta. He wanted to have a talk with the leaders of the Jewish community and requested the Italian police to act as a go-between in arranging the meeting. It would be convenient, Kappler had said, if the leaders could come to his office in the Villa Wolkonsky promptly at six o'clock that evening.

* There was some truth here, in connection with the large sums of money being sent to the DELASEM agency by American Jews. When the United States entered the war the money continued to reach the Roman Jews clandestinely, through Switzerland and the Vatican. Settimio Sorani was in continual contact with the American envoy to the Holy See, Tittmann, who acted as one of the couriers of these funds and exchanged information with the Jews of Rome.[4] Kappler, who was uncanny in his competence as a spy, could hardly have been unaware of this.

The Questura had immediately decided that this was an affair that lay within the provenance of the Office of Demography and Race, a bureau of the *Pubblica Sicurezza,* which was a larger organism encompassing the Questura and was itself built into the structure of the Ministry of Interior. Before the morning had passed, the chief of Demography and Race, Commissar Cappa went personally to see presidents Foà and Almansi.[7]

Cappa found Foà in the synagogue offices. He advised the president of Kappler's invitation. His manner was cordial and respectful of Foà, but the commissar could not tell him anything about the nature of the meeting. Almansi was similarly informed, and when the set hour arrived, the two Jewish leaders presented themselves at the gates of the Villa Wolkonsky and were ushered into the office of the Obersturmbannführer without delay.[8]

Foà was struck by a not unfavorable first impression of Kappler. Unfamiliar with the singular ranks of the SS, he mistakenly took him for a major. Kappler seemed to him to be about forty years old, and Foà took note of his blond hair, medium build, and the long thin scar that crossed his left cheek. "At the outset," Foà later recalled, "Kappler assumed a rather courteous demeanor. He regretted any inconvenience he might have caused; he asked about the number of Jews there were in Rome, and he dwelled for some minutes in general conversation, on the surface quite affably."[9]

Suddenly, it seemed to Foà, Kappler's tone changed, and the cast of his face became cutting and hard. He began again to speak, and as Foà remembered it, he said:

> You and your coreligionists are Italian nationals, but that is of little importance to me. We Germans consider you only as Jews, and as such our enemy. Rather, to be more precise, we regard you as a distinct group, but not wholly apart from the worst of the enemies against whom we are fighting. And we will treat you as such.[10]

Kappler himself would recall that, "I spoke of the unity of world Judaism, which constituted a unique hostile bloc against

Germany. I said that consequently the Jews of Italy and Rome also represented a part of that bloc. Their weapons were not firearms, but money and gold, and, as all enemies had to be stripped of their weapons, thus they too had to be relieved of their arms. . . ."[11]

Therefore, Kappler continued, according to Foà's account:

> it is not your lives or the lives of your children that we will take—if you fulfill our demands. It is your gold we want, in order to provide new arms for our country. Within thirty-six hours you will have to pay fifty kilograms of gold. If you pay, no harm will come to you. In any other event, 200 of your Jews will be taken and deported to Germany, where they will be sent to the Russian frontier, or otherwise rendered innocuous.*[12]

The first reaction of the two leaders to Kappler's extortion demand was that they might not have enough time to raise such an exorbitant sum of gold.[14] Both Foà and Almansi agreed that it was "perfectly useless" to oppose themselves to the demand, and they limited their response to making note of the time factor and similar difficulties, such as that of obtaining the precious metal.[15]

Kappler was willing to cooperate with the Jewish leaders, meet them at least part of the way. He was flexible on the thirty-six-hour limit, first setting it to expire at 11:00 A.M. on Tuesday, the 28th, then rounding it off at noon, which was actually more than forty hours from the present time. He also offered to provide some of his men and light trucks or automobiles to help the leaders get around the city to collect the gold—a gesture the presidents were too proud to accept.[16]

Almansi asked Kappler if the gold could be paid in its equivalent of Italian lire.

"If you want to give dollars or British pounds, fine," said the German. "But your money—I really wouldn't know what to do with it. I can print as much as I want of it."[17]

* Kappler later confirmed both Foà's and Almansi's accounts of the meeting, with the exception of his threat to deport 200 Jews. He said that he had warned that if the gold demand were not met, there would be a general roundup and deportation of the city's Jews.[13]

The leaders also wanted to know, in case they should be unable to meet the terms of the ransom, whether Kappler's threat would be carried out only against Jews inscribed in the Rome community. Or would he also take those who had formally disassociated themselves from the community, including Jews who had converted to Catholicism and the offsprings of mixed marriages? The answer to this question was important to the two presidents. It would help them guage the extent of the danger to their own Jews, who of course were their only concern.

"I don't make any distinction between a Jew and a Jew," Kappler replied. "Inscribed in the community or disassociated, baptized or mixed, they are all the enemy."[18]

Kappler had no knowledge of the subject he was speaking about. The Nazis had in fact formulated a complex set of distinctions often varying from territory to territory, which were strictly followed. The Italian Fascists had copied the system. But Kappler knew little, if anything, of this, never having had previous experience in persecuting Jews. He was, for the reasons he had worked out in the past few days, indulging in a perfect exercise in intimidation. He wanted his solution to the Jewish question in Rome to succeed. Perhaps he felt himself on unsure ground; he brought the meeting to a close. Inventing a frightening lie, he said, "Mind you, I have already carried out several operations of this type and it has always ended well. Only once did I fail, but that time a few hundred of your brothers paid with their lives."[19]

The two presidents left Kappler, convinced of the futility of offering any further arguments.[20] They were outraged, but wasted little time on emotion. There was a great deal of work ahead, and even now the clock was running down.

The first thing they did was contact the Italian authorities.[21] The old, comfortable method had always worked in the past, and their faith and ruts ran deep. Now more than ever it seemed absolutely necessary to use their influence to gain some form of relief through the representatives of the Mussolini government.

Commissar Cappa, of the race office, and *Commendatore* Rosselli, regent of the Questura, were placed *al corrente* of the meeting with Kappler. The two presidents informed them of the demand for gold, pointing out that if the Jews of Rome were to pay this ransom, the end result would be harmful to Italy.[22] Extortion by a foreign power on Italian soil would be a violation of the country's sovereignty. There was every reason for the Duce himself to be alerted and for him to intervene in behalf of the national honor.

Cappa and Rosselli, according to Foà, "were truly courteous and showed an understanding that merits special mention."[23] Cappa assumed the responsibility of immediately notifying all the officials in the Questura with the intention of learning what measures might be taken by the Italian authorities in order to thwart the German ultimatum. Several urgent telephone calls were made, but within a few hours it became plain to the Jewish leaders that despite the "good will" shown by the Fascists, no one was going to do anything.[24]

"Evidently," Foà later commented, "our Authorities could do nothing in the face of Teutonic insolence."[25]

The only recourse left to the two presidents, Foà thought, was to call a meeting of "the most esteemed and influential exponents of the community and hold counsel on what to do."[26] The Jews had to be informed, Almansi later wrote, "in order to invite them to offer those objects of gold which might be in their possession."[27]

In a way they were relieved.[28] If the ransom were paid, the Jews of Rome would escape the unspeakable horrors said to be afflicting the Jews of other parts of Europe, the thought of which was gnawing at the stability of the community. The trouble was that the possibility of raising fifty kilograms of gold seemed slight. As Foà and Almansi were aware, most of the richest Jews had quietly slipped out of Rome, and there was no way to communicate with them.[29] The bulk of the gold would have to come from the wretchedly poor ghetto-Trastevere Jews, whose only contacts with the metal were not much more than the wedding bands around their fingers, and in rare cases, the fillings of their teeth.

Now, the hour was late. Nothing could be done until morning, and there was no need to disturb the sleep of their fellow leaders. But before dawn Foà telephoned one of his aides, Rosina Sorani, a sister of the executive secretary of the DELASEM agency. He told her to begin calling all the members of the community council and other prominent Jews to an emergency meeting to be held in his office at 10:00 A.M.[30]

XVI

GOLD. FIFTY KILOGRAMS of gold. One hundred and ten pounds, 3.68 ounces—worth, on the 1943 international gold market, $56,-000—to save 200 Jews, $280 per Jew. Perhaps it would save the 12,000 Jews of Rome: $4.50 per Jew. A small price to pay for the life of a human being.

It was always gold. Where and when had they encumbered themselves with this infernal identification with gold? ("And the Lord spake unto Moses, saying, Speak unto the children of Israel, that they bring me an offering . . . and this is the offering which ye shall take of them: gold . . .") Was it the magnificent golden table of the Second Temple, with its astounding weight of many Hebrew talents? ("Thou shalt also make a table . . . and thou shalt overlay it with pure gold. . . .") Or was it the gleaming beauty of the slender-branched candelabrum, which Titus brought to Rome? ("And thou shalt make a candlestick of pure gold . . . of a talent of pure gold shall he make it. . . .")[1]

In the Middle Ages Peter the Venerable had said: "Let their lives be safeguarded; let their gold be taken away."[2]

In 1492 a Pope had summoned the Jewish leaders of Rome,

demanding 2,000 ducats, or nearly seven kilograms of gold. The Roman Jews had not wanted to accept their coreligionists who had been expelled from Spain and were arriving in Italy. The gold was the price of this privilege. It was paid, but the Pope betrayed them, and the bedraggled refugees were cast upon the bribers.[3]

Never had a people surrendered so much gold for so little in return. The gold of the Jews of Rome had helped finance the building of the Roman Empire, the medieval Crusades, and more than a millenium of persecutions against themselves.

Few Jews in Rome of 1943 could remember where it had all begun, if it were possible to locate a beginning. But almost everyone could recall an earlier time in the not-too-distant past when the gold of the Jews of Rome was offered in tribute to the ruler and the land.

The time was autumn, 1935. The armies of the Fascist realm had invaded Ethiopia, a dastardly act of aggression that was condemned, if not resisted, by almost all the nations of the world. Mussolini's forces were spreading terror across that country of impoverished black men, dom nuts, and senna. Their mission, audaciously proclaimed, was conquest and subjugation; step one in the Duce's repugnant and absurd campaign to resurrect the Roman Empire. It was a dirty war against a half-starved people. The Fascists fought with mustard gas, raining lethal poison on soldiers and civilians, cattle and plants; polluting the waterways and the pastures; killing, in a systematic way, all living things.[4] These acts, which would help teach other nations to do the same, would one day be characterized as "crimes against humanity," rendering the Italians, not the Germans, as the first people in history to have committed barbarisms so designated.[5]

It was a war in which the leaders of the Jews of Italy were exhorting their people from the very outset to participate "with fervor and generosity."[6] Indeed so great was the number of Jews who were fighting in Ethiopia for the Fascist empire, a synagogue was built in Asmara to administer to their religious needs.[7]

But that was little noted then. Italians of every creed fought side by side. There was no racism in 1935, no Jewish question in the kingdom of Italy. The leaders of the Jews could feel the throb of Fascist society and call it theirs. It was, after all, their own Giuseppe Toeplitz and his Banca Commerciale who had underwritten most of the bills for Mussolini's "March on Rome," which brought fascism to power in 1922.*[8] The poverty of their people, like that of the great masses of all Italians, who had one of the lowest standards of living in Europe, was something the Jewish and other leaders would deal with at a later date, perhaps after the current war. Fortunately for them, the Italians, as the Duce himself had once said, were a people who were not yet accustomed to eating several times a day.[10]

"Italy," the Jewish leadership, celebrating the tenth anniversary of "true fascism," had boasted, "[is] one of the very few countries where the Jew not only can live his life fully as a citizen, but he also can, if he wants to, live his life fully . . . as a Jew."[11]

No sooner had the Ethiopian aggression been launched, when the Jewish leaders sent out a "vibrant appeal" to all communities to make a voluntary donation to the Fascist war effort.[12] The type of contribution specified was gold, as well as other precious metals, the need for which had been disclosed by the regime. Each of the communities responded with gold offerings, but none was as notable as that of the Jewish Community of Rome.

The president of the community, Foà's predecessor, *Ing-*

* The Italian Jews could also count themselves among the other builders of fascism: the venerated *sansepolcristi*—the 150 founders of the Fascist movement; the so-called martyrs of the Fascist "revolution"; the Blackshirt *squadristi*—Mussolini's version of Germany's brownshirted Stormtroopers; participants in the "March on Rome"; and finally members of the Duce's first Cabinet, Fascist Grand Council, and Parliament.[9] The Jews of Italy, however, cannot be said to have been more or less avid followers of Mussolini than the general population. Though there were, at all levels of power, proportionately more Fascists from among the Jews than the non-Jews, this may be explained by their equally disproportionate representation among those who stood to gain most from fascism: the Italian ruling class and the social layers nearest to it. The one group most distant from this phenomenon was that of the ghetto-Trastevere Jews of Rome, who were close to the lowest strata of Fascist society and thus among its most exploited victims.

egnere Recanati, and acting Chief Rabbi Aldo Lattes, interim successor to the late Sacerdoti, went to the Palazzo Braschi, seat of the Rome branch of the party, to have their picture taken with the Fascist Segretario Federale.[13] With them they brought their gold, the gold of the synagogue. The gift, taken with no one's consent but that of the leaders of the community, was magnificent: the hand wrought menorah, the universal and solemn symbol of Judaism; the long and narrow *puntarolo,* a golden pointer with which to follow the ceremonial readings of the Torah; and most symbolically of all, the solid gold key to the Ark, resting place of the Torah, the two-posted scroll of the five books of Moses.[14]

These were melted down into yellow bricks to be hurled at the victims and enemies of fascism.

When the seven-month war was won, the leaders of Italian Jewry declared themselves proud and joyful of the victory and exalted "he who has led us to that goal."[15] They saw to it that the Duce received God's blessing in the synagogue, and more gold was handed up for the Fascist coffer.[16]

A new order had begun, they said. In their most popular newspaper, *Israel,* they wrote: "Italy in the act of proclaiming itself imperial, presents the world with an offer and a promise. An offer to the people of Europe of a fruitful peace; a promise of civilizing the conquered lands . . . which until now have been deprived of the benefits progress and Latin genius. . . ."[17]

Carving out a spiritual role for themselves, without mentioning the material benefits they would personally enjoy as members of the new imperialist class, the Jewish leaders cast their eyes upon the Falashas, a native colony of African Jews. They lamented the past sufferings of their black-skinned brethren and promised them that: "For the first time in history their faith in God, their devotion to the Laws of Israel, will be secured . . . and they will have assurances of this from their brothers in faith who have had the good fortune of being born in, and of living in the land of Italy."[18]

Then came the war in Spain. The Italian Jewish leaders took no heed of a prophet among their people, the profoundly anti-

Fascist Carlo Rosselli, who warned: "Attention! They are preparing a war in Europe. . . ."[19] To his fellow Italian Jews, he admonished from his place of exile in Paris, "Today in Spain, tomorrow in Italy,"[20] alluding with irony to the saw of the Diaspora, "This year we are here; next year in the land of Israel." But no one listened that year, and the next year Rosselli and his brother Nello were assassinated by the Fascists;[21] no one heard or saw a thing. Instead the Jewish leaders nodded approvingly as their younger coreligionists marched with their countrymen to fight, and some to die, at the side of Franco.[22]

But somewhere in those years when national pride could be felt at the very quick of the Italian Jewish soul, all the gold, the blood, and prayers yielded in good faith began to count for naught. Strengthened by the success of his African adventure, Mussolini started to drill into the British sphere of influence in the Middle East. He declared himself the protector of Islam and sought to win the favor of the Arabs by denouncing Great Britain's support of Zionism and its policy of creating a Jewish state in Palestine.[23] At the same time, the war in Spain led to closer cooperation with the new Fascist state to the north, Hitler's Germany, which was also fighting with Franco's forces. The Führer carefully wooed Mussolini ever closer to his side with Nazi support of Italian expansion in the Mediterranean and Africa and with a *Weltanschauung* that held great promise for the future of fascism.[24]

More than anything else, these two developments—the adoption of an anti-Zionist foreign policy and the creation of the Rome-Berlin Axis—unleashed the "Jewish question" in Italy, which had been growling restlessly for the past few years.

Muting to a certain extent the Nazi style anti-Semitism of the "International Jewish-Bolshevik Conspiracy," which was not yet well suited for home consumption, the Italian racists attacked their native Jews where it hurt most: at the heart of their patriotism. The idea of a Jewish homeland in Palestine, the anti-Semites began to roar, was nothing but a pawn of British imperialism. How then could Italian Zionists, of which there were many, claim to be good Italians if in aiding the establishing of Israel they were promoting British aims in the Mediterranean? Italian Jews were therefore in direct conflict with the best interests of the Fascist fatherland.[25] And those Jews in Italy who were not Zionists, it was suddenly being said, could not in any event be true Fascists for the sole reason of their Jewishness. The individuality and the separateness of the Jews, this argument went, made them suspect. The Jews do not feel patriotism the way other Italians do. If it were otherwise, why would they hold themselves apart? "It is a problem that must be abolished. Fascist Italy does not want it. To say more would be superfluous."[26]

The attacks mounted swiftly, and it soon became amply clear that the Duce himself, though he pretended to remain aloof, approved. The leaders of Italian Jewry, in the path of a rising wave of anti-Semitism, which threatened to completely wash them out of Italian life, decided to fight back. Accepting the ground rules laid down by the non-Jewish racists, they tried to show that their Zionism was nothing to fear and that the Jews were more-Fascist-than-thou.

They argued that support of Zionism was only a philanthropic pastime for Italian Jews, and it was the foreign Jews who participated in such subversive movements as antifascism.[27] It was thus unjust to accuse Italian Jews of coresponsibility. The Jews of Fascist Italy, they said, "felt an undiminishable pride in being Italian."[28]

But it was to no avail. The anti-Semitism of such incorrigibly fanatic party writers and editors as Preziosi, Telesio Interlandi, and Roberto Farinacci—some of whom were secretly receiving funds from the Nazis—was taken up by the "respectable" institutions of communications. "Scholarly" racist books, notably Professor Paolo Orano's *Gli ebrei in Italia*, and daily anti-Semitic articles in Italy's celebrated newspapers *Corriere della Sera* and *La Stampa* lent an irreversible quality to the cancerous affair.[29]

Though the Pope, Pius XI, was wary of racism, authoritative journals of the Catholic Church joined them. They deplored "materialistic" German racism, they said, but spiritually speaking, Judaism was a religion that by now was "profoundly corrupt."[30] Analyzing the Jewish question, the highly respected Jesuit organ *La Civiltà Cattolica* wrote at the time:

> . . . Judaism avails itself of the two most effective powers for world domination: one is material—gold . . . the other is an ideal—internationalism. As far as the gold is concerned, it already has most of it in hand. There remains only the monopolization of internationalism. . . . It is evident that this Jewish mentality is a permanent danger to the world.[31]

When Mussolini's own newspaper, the Milan daily *Il Popolo d'Italia*, in reviewing Professor Orano's book, declared that Italy had a "new problem," this was correctly interpreted as the Duce having given his *va bene*, and a massive second assault was launched.*[32]

In the meantime a split began to develop in the ranks of the Jewish leadership, particularly in the council of the Union of Italian Jewish Communities. There were those who said now that to prove to their countrymen the Italian Jews were truly Fascist, Zionism and any other kind of internationalism would have to be eschewed.[34] The Zionist group did not agree. Their point of view saw Zionism as an inseparable part of Judaism, and while many Italian Zionists were Fascists and loved the fatherland, they also loved the land of Israel and wanted to participate in building a Jewish state.[35]

Unable to resolve their differences, the anti-Zionists broke away from the union and regrouped in a "Committee of Italians of the Jewish Religion." They immediately met in Florence and issued a hysterical manifesto declaring themselves "categorical enemies of anything international, Jewish or non-Jewish, masonic, subversive, or revolutionary and above all anti-Fascist." Furthermore, they had "nothing in common with anyone who professes Zionist doctrine. . . ."[36]

The Rome secessionist group appended its own statement. "Fascists of the Jewish religion," they affirmed, ". . . can only

* Shortly before *Il Popolo d'Italia* took its favorable position on the anti-Semitic campaign, Mussolini, who had in the past denigrated Nazi race theories, told the newspaper's director, Giorgio Pini, "As you know, I am a racist."[33]

be anti-Zionists." They loved the Fascist fatherland, they said, and anyone who had any beliefs that "went beyond the borders of Italy" was harming the nation.[37]

But the Duce's regime paid scant attention to the secessionists and upheld the authority of the union as the true representatives of Italian Jewry. It would be far easier to persecute the "suspect" union than the super-Fascists, all of whom had an impeccable record of loyal service to the regime. Confused by the attitude of the government, the secessionist's committee soon crumbled and fell apart. For its part, the union adopted a wait-and-see strategy, and through inactivity took shelter in silence, hoping the storm would pass.

Matters only worsened, however, and following Hitler's triumphal state visit to Rome, in May, 1938, the Fascists drew up the racial legislation, patterned after the already infamous Nuremberg Laws.[38] When the Italian laws were promulgated, in November, 1938, one group of prominent Jews, the leaders of the Jewish community of Turin, reacted almost simultaneously, in hope of setting an example for all the communities. They bade the local Jewish Council "to guarantee, with the most applicable and immediate means, the absolute and conscious abnegation of the Jews of Turin in their activities and way of life in order that it correspond with the directives of the Regime and for the benefit of the Empire." Further, the Jewish leaders had only one objective: "to obey as faithful Blackshirts, without hesitation, and as their strict duty, the orders of the Duce. . . ."[39]

But the union, now incontestably oriented to the "moderate" fascism-with-Zionism school, remained circumspect trying to steer a course down the center. It had been watchful and guarded in the months during which the anti-Jewish decrees were being formulated. To be sure, when it became certain that the racial laws were imminent, the council of the union rushed forward to "reaffirm with all its heart the complete submission of the Italians of the Jewish religion to the Fascist fatherland, in this moment when superior exigencies require from them painful sacrifices. . . ."[40] But it had not gone as far as the more extreme Zionists who had said of the coming discriminations, "to endure them manfully will be a new sign of dignity, of faith . . . and of true love for Italy, which the Jewish citizens will continue to serve with abnegation. . . ."[41] Nor had it taken the road of the super-Fascists, a contingent of whom had physically assaulted their Zionist brethren and had finally openly asserted that all other Jews but themselves were the enemies of Italy and therefore their own enemies.[42]

It was the union the regime had counted on, and it was the union that would correctly interpret the Duce's will. In avoiding panic or any extreme, it had already slipped into its role like a cartridge clip in an automatic.

For all but a handful of Jews who were answering the call of antifascism, nothing was left but to accept second-class citizenship. It was here the union could serve. Despite the injustice, which doubtless would one day be righted, the Jewish leaders remained prideful of the flag and loyal to the Duce. Anything less would be treason. Besides they knew of nothing else they could do. The sandstorm that was their society had long ago abraded their souls and had cut the one path they would follow.

When, some months after the institution of the racial laws, the Spanish Republic was about to fall to the troops of the Fascist international, the union spoke up at last, revealing clearly where it now stood.

Spain was a shambles, its people beaten into the ground for which they had fought. Only gasping Madrid remained to be crushed. The union, taking time out from its new task of aiding those suffering under the discriminations, drew up and dispatched Protocol Number 217, dated Rome, February 1, 1939-XVII (the seventeenth year of the *Era Fascista*). Sent to all the councilors of the union, presidents of the communities, and chief rabbis, it read:

> When the national liberation troops entered Barcelona, reconquering Spain—martyred by the barbaric Bolsheviks—the heart and soul of the Jews of Italy, palpitating in unison with those of our fellow citizens of the Fascist Imperial Fatherland, rejoiced and gave thanks to Divine Providence for having granted the triumph of order and civilization

over disorder and destruction. And in the *Tempio Maggiore* of the Community of Rome the officiating Rabbi,* with the full consent of the faithful, who filled the synagogue, commemorated the great event with moving expressions of sentiment. Interpreting the general feeling, he turned his thoughts to He [sic] who guides the destiny of our great country, who is always the leader and arbiter of civilization and of peace, of peace with justice, which is also the ideal of Judaism. And he invoked God's blessing on the architects of the undertaking that conserves the ideal of civilizing Europe; on those who are animated by the will toward reconstruction and pacification of the world; and on those who died in combat, among whom number many of our heroic coreligionists.

It is known that in other communities similar noble ceremonies will be held and we invite all who have still not planned to do so to publicly express some commemorative remarks about this so very significant episode.[44]

The persecutions continued. But the loyal union began to find ways to work with the regime, each taking cautious steps toward one another. It was embarrassing and awkward at first. The functionaries of both the government and the union were hesitant when it came to putting their hands in the actual muck from which the discriminations had to be apportioned. They needed each other.

Nothing gave more impetus to this romance than the election toward the end of 1939 of Almansi as president of the union. He knew best how to deal with the gentile bureaucracy, and somehow, in the eyes of his colleagues, he managed to impart a strain of dignity to the ugly affair.[45] He tempered the union's unctuous displays of patriotism, and, it is said, he was firm in his negotiations with the regime. He showed the government how in many instances it would be immeasurably easier to use the agency of the Jewish leaders than to attempt to do the entire job by itself.[46] In some cases, he said, the discriminations could even be financially profitable to the regime. He pointed

* Rome was without a chief rabbi at the time. Late in 1938 the community's head rabbi, David Prato, a self-proclaimed Zionist-Fascist, who had had friendly personal dealings with Mussolini, was accused by Interlandi of "antifascism" and forced to resign. He fled to Palestine.[43]

this out at the time he sought Mussolini's authorization for the establishment of DELASEM, which brought large sums of dollar currency into the hard-pressed country.[47]

Though the extremists branded him a "false Fascist" and an agent of Zionism, the measure of his worth can be seen in the number of concessions he won from the government and the esteem in which he was held.

Educational facilities were organized for the Jewish children, who had been expelled from the schools by the racial laws. The government approved his assistance programs to aid the Jews it forced to emigrate and the Jewish refugees who escaped the Nazis by entering Italian territory. Conditions in Italian concentration camps for foreign Jews and anti-Fascist indigenous Jews were constantly being improved, and those who were pressed into forced labor gangs had only to serve briefly and even received some wages.[48]

Before long the regime and the union found themselves in a lopsided embrace, sharing the function of administering the politically "necessary" racial laws as painlessly as possible.

Apart from this organizational coitus, the anti-Jewish measures were slowly toppling of their own weight. This was Italy, not Germany. One difference was that a people who had never known anti-Semitism could not learn overnight to hate a defenseless group so small that one would have to knock at a thousand doors to find the home of a single Jew. It would take time. For now, however, most Italians felt sympathy for their Jews. The enforcement of the laws was lax. There were ugly incidents, but people generally extended themselves in the same way that a neighbor might lend a helping hand. The armed forces, which had no heart for discriminations—at least against white people—were protecting foreign Jews entering Italian occupation zones.[49] They had the support of the Italian Foreign Office, which was anxious about national sovereignty in the face of its ever more aggressive German ally.[50] Moreover, Italian Jews in German-controlled areas, as a result of Fascist diplomatic interventions, were immune to Nazi persecutions, at least until late in 1943.[51]

Even the king, whose name would appear for all time as the chief signatory of the anti-Jewish laws, said that he felt an "infinite pity for the Jews."[52] And Pope Pius XI declared, "antisemitism is inadmissible; spiritually we are all Semites."[53]

The methods of evading and of living with the persecutions became, through the ceaseless efforts of the Jewish leaders, ever more sophisticated and effective, polished to the fine art of the possible. They had, it seemed, found a way, and the Jews once again would survive.

But now events that appeared to have had nothing to do with themselves had reduced it all to this: the vulgar equation of Jewish blood for Jewish gold.

XVII

AT ABOUT 6:00 A.M. on Monday, the 27th, the telephone began to ring in an apartment in Via Panama, a scythe-shaped street in the elegant Parioli district. A maid answered. Hearing a prearranged code word, she understood that the call was for Signor Levi, the Jewish businessman and president of DELASEM, who had gone into hiding in the home of Aryan friends.

At the other end of the line was the voice of Rosina Sorani, President Foà's assistant, who inquired guardedly whether Signor Levi could drop by—it was not necessary to mention the place—at ten o'clock that morning for some rather urgent business.[1] Levi agreed and began at once to dress, although he was not very pleased about having to leave his place of hiding, which was about three miles northwest of the synagogue.

The streets of the occupied city—filled with neo-Fascist rowdies and imperious Nazis—were becoming increasingly fearsome for Jew and non-Jew alike, and it was always more difficult to get about. The number of buses and trams was continually being reduced, and the consequent crowding of the remaining vehicles was so great that people often entered and exited through the windows. This very morning an order would be issued by the Germans providing for the confiscation of all privately owned motor vehicles, an imposition which would make walking the only reliable means of transportation.[2]

Levi, and the other Jewish leaders who had been summoned to the meeting, including Almansi, arrived at the synagogue at the appointed hour. Only Foà was missing and did not appear until 10:30, at which time the meeting was immediately called to order.[3]

Foà summarized what had taken place the day before in the offices of Obersturmbannführer Kappler, emphasizing that the fifty kilograms of gold would have to be delivered by noon tomorrow, little more than twenty-four hours from now. Otherwise 200 Jews would be deported.

One or two of the leaders said that they did not believe that the Germans would keep their word; they would take the gold and take the Jews anyway. Others thought it simply impossible to raise the ransom within the time limit. Another group felt the Nazi demand might be a trick: a way of getting the Jews who would bring gold offerings to concentrate in and around the synagogue, at which time they would be taken.[4]

But the majority were of the opinion that the Germans, however despicable, were honorable men, and that the Jews should therefore comply.[5] On this decisive note, the meeting ended.

Levi, by virtue of the fact that he had been trained as, and bore the title of, a *ragioniere*, an accountant, was given the task of directing the operation.[6] A collection center was set up on the second floor of the synagogue in the *Sala del Consiglio*, or the board room. Chairs were placed behind a long table, and an employee of the temple was sent to fetch the Jewish goldsmith Angelo Anticoli, who lived a few blocks away in the old ghetto alley Via della Reginella. Anticoli rushed over bringing with him two other Jewish gold experts, and of course, a scale. The Questura sent a police officer to act as a guard and other members of the force to control the crowd that was expected to gather shortly.*

In the meantime word began to reach the people. It spread first in the ghetto and then beyond, but slowly and cautiously at the start, for some of the leaders still worried about a German double cross and did not want the Jews to flock to the temple.[8] The story that was going around was immediately distorted. The fifty kilograms were mixed with the thirty-six hours and came out with entirely new sets of numbers. Instead of 200 Jews in danger of being deported, it was now being said that the Germans would take 200, and in some instances 300, 500, and higher, "heads of families," which especially among the poor majority, sounded a great deal more frightening.[9]

Around 11:00 A.M. the gold collection campaign was ready to be launched. If it were for some other, more conventional cause it would have aroused all the excitement and pleasurable sensations felt under conditions of teamwork. *Ragioniere* Levi, Anticoli the jeweler, and the other two goldsmiths took their places behind the table. Anticoli, seated before the springless balance, had the job of weighing the offerings, which were first to be assayed by his fellow gold experts. Rosina Sorani, sitting off to one side, was given the assignment of tending the collected gold. Some of the female employees of the community were also in the room to write receipts for the donors.[10]

With the hastily assembled staff all at their places, and as the Jewish leaders looked on, the doors were opened; the collection could now begin. Everyone waited expectantly, but not much happened.

Partially because there had been some hesitancy in letting the news disseminate swiftly and also due to a normal amount of inertia, few people came forward in the first hours. Among those who did, many offered money, not articles of gold, which

* According to some observers there were Nazi spies among the police sent by the Questura, as well as among the crowd.[7]

were more difficult to part with given their sentimental and—especially in wartime—their practical value. The community leaders, observing this, communicated that they would not accept cash, after rejecting a suggestion to buy gold on the black market—then the only source—as too time-consuming.

By 1:00 P.M., after two sluggish hours, the situation appeared to the leaders to have entered into a serious crisis. The amount of gold received barely reached the five kilogram mark. At this rate, they were doomed to failure, for they would lose all of the nighttime hours to the curfew. Despair filled the room.

Suddenly, one of the leaders, Adriano Ascarelli, came forward with an idea. Perhaps the Vatican would help. He said he had a Catholic clergyman friend, the vice abbot of the monastery of the Sacred Heart, in Via XXIV Maggio, who could get a message to the Curia without delay. This was considered by all an excellent suggestion, and Levi agreed to go at once to see the man, taking Ascarelli with him to make the introductions.[11]

They arrived at the sloping street at two o'clock, entered the monastery, and after identifying themselves, they were led in to see the vice abbot, Padre Borsarelli. Levi explained the dire circumstances that had brought them there and concluded with a plea for help.

"Please contact the Vatican," he said, "and tell them we need to borrow gold." It was the only way they could meet the Nazi-imposed deadline. "It will be easy for us to repay you. It is just a question of time."[12]

Padre Borsarelli asked the two Jews to return at 4:00 P.M., at which time, he promised, he would have an official reply to their request.

When Levi and Ascarelli returned to the synagogue, they were greeted with an extraordinary sight. A great crowd had gathered at the street entrance to the community offices. They were mostly ghetto-Trastevere Jews, but there were many unfamiliar faces, too. All were waiting patiently for a long line of contributors to pass through the second floor collection center, in order that they too might make a donation for the ransom.

The movement of rumors through the city had suddenly and seemingly simultaneously caught hold of the people, and a river of gold began to flow. Not only Jews, many of whom felt their lives to be at stake, but a large number of non-Jews came forward with offerings.[13]

Levi rushed upstairs to his post. The operation was going well, he was told, but they were still at some distance from the goal. The Vatican's help, if it were forthcoming, would still be needed.

Some people were offering their gold for sale. Word was immediately passed along that the community would now accept cash contributions and that it would buy gold, from those who could not otherwise part with it, at the rate of 400 lire per gram. This was about three times the normal price. As the gold began to amass, however, the rate was dropped, then raised and dropped continually, according to the flow.[14] The woman vendor at the newsstand kiosk near the Ponte Garibaldi, one of the Tiber bridges that led to the ghetto, took on the job of reporting out the fluctuations of the community's temporary gold market.[15]

The gold donations continued too, coming from a wide range of kinds of people and social classes. The easiest to recognize were the non-Jews, who appeared uncertain as to whether gentile gold would be welcomed. That the *gojim* too had come, "and not few among them some priests," made a deep impression on the Jewish leadership.[16]

A Roman Jew who observed the timorous behavior of the non-Jews recorded the scene shortly afterward:

> Circumspectly, as if fearing a refusal, as if afraid of offering gold to the rich Jews, some "Aryans" presented themselves. They entered that place adjacent to the synagogue full of embarrassment, not knowing if they should take off their hat or keep their head covered, according to the well-known Jewish custom. Almost humbly, they asked if they too could—weil, if it would be all right to. . . . Unfortunately, they did not leave their names. . . .[17]

One of them, however, was a young Roman folksinger named Romolo Balzani, known as Romoletto. He gave a gold ring. It had been a gift from some Jewish friends, given to him when he had sung at the "Arenula," the ghetto movie theater. On the steps of the community offices, as others now were surrendering their gold, he sang in the Romanesque dialect:

Credi che chi cia' l'oro
sia un signore
L'oro pe'me nun conta
*conta er core**[18]

As had been expected, however, it was the ghetto-Trastevere Jews who were providing most of the gold. Theirs was piling far higher than anyone else's, in almost insignificant droplets. The majority of the receipts were being written for donations of less than one-eighth of an ounce.[19]

There was forty-year-old Signora Vivanti, who gave her wedding band, a gold chain, and another ring. "Whoever had anything, gave it," she would later say.[20] There was Cesare del Monte, who gave his wife's wedding ring, as did Vittorio Astrologo, a Jew from Trastevere.[21] Seventeen-year-old Michele Amati gave a family ring and the results of a collection he had taken up among his friends and relatives.[22] Angelo Di Porto brought his own ring, his father's, and his mother's wedding band and earrings. Before going to the synagogue, however, his mother had despaired that the offerings would be to no avail. "The gold will not be enough," she had said. "The Germans want blood."[23]

They came from more distant neighborhoods, too. At least one tram driver of the Circolare Nera line, which passed the Lungotevere side of the temple, was allowing passengers with gold contributions to debark at the entrance to the community offices, although there was no stop there.

A small delegation of Jews was sent out to their coreligionists who lived in the outlying parts of the city. The news of the ransom was brought to their doors, and requests for contributions were made and readily filled.

* *Gold may make the gentleman/ for thee/ but it's the heart that counts/ for me.*

One Roman Jew who lived far from the ghetto was Lello Perugia, in the populous San Lorenzo district. He was decidedly opposed to paying the ransom.[24] Perugia, who would soon be twenty-four years old, was a member of the clandestine Communist party. He had fought the German entry into Rome on those two days of resistance earlier in the month. A group of youths had attacked the Santa Croce barracks and seized its storage of arms. He had been somewhat hesitant at first, but when he had seen a child killed by the invaders, he had been moved to action. He had taken part in the battle at the Pyramid, and when Rome fell, he had continued the fight in the developing partisan movement. Nightly, Perugia and his small group were harassing German supply lines along Via Tiburtina, sniping and sabotaging to help block enemy shipments to the front.

When Perugia heard of the gold demand, he was outraged and wanted to strike back. "After the Jewish question," he argued with his mother, a Communist herself, "There'll be the Latin question." He said he knew what the Germans would do to the Jews: kill them as they were killing the Jews of other countries—a simple fact he believed was known to every Jew in Rome. There was only one answer to give the Germans, he said, and that was the Resistance. But his mother did not quite agree and the Communist Perugia family gave a gold donation, too.[25] Only a small amount was being asked for, and perhaps it would do some good.

A few blocks away another Jewish family of the periphery of the city was approached for a contribution. They were the Efratis: Umberto Abramo, his wife, Maria, and their eleven children.[26] They lived in a four-room apartment in Via Portonaccio. In July, when Rome for the first time in the war had been bombed by the Allies, they had fled, going north to Viterbo. Via Portonaccio was too near the railroad marshaling yards, the prime target of the air attack. A few weeks ago, however, they heard of the armistice concluded by the King and Badoglio. They thought the war was over and returned home, only to find Rome occupied. Umberto had fought in World War I, and he disliked and distrusted the Germans. He had heard others were fleeing the occupation, but the Efratis were poor, and it was simply too hard for the family to gather themselves and their belongings for a second time and run away again. He gave a ring and a gold chain instead.

In the street outside the temple the queue of Jews who were patiently waiting their turn to make a contribution grew longer. As time went by, they talked to one another with greater ease. Would the payment of gold, many asked, guarantee their safety? They had doubts, yet it was pleasing that the *signori* councilors were in direct contact with the Nazis; if any further trouble arose the leaders would be the first to know and would warn the others immediately. But the question remained unanswered and troublesome for many.

Elena Sonnino Finzi, for example, was one of them.[27] She was a teacher and was discussing the matter with some of her pupils whom she had unexpectedly met among the crowd around the synagogue. One of the students, a young girl, remarked that the time had come to go into hiding, and in fact she was planning to do so immediately. Signora Sonnino Finzi, the daughter of the chief rabbi of Genoa, was not wholly convinced, although she too had given thought to running. She decided to speak directly with President Foà.

"I presented myself," she later recalled, "and asked whether he thought it opportune that we should leave our homes." The president's reply was that he saw "no necessity" for such action and he added that he "really knew not what dangers could menace me."[28] Nevertheless, in a few days she would reject the president's advice and follow the course of her pupil.

No matter what, people were saying, the gold had to be paid. The 200 "heads of families" had to be saved. Further, there was a false rumor going around that unless the demand were fulfilled the Germans would burn down the synagogue.[29] The temple had to be spared. Whatever reservations they might have, said the Jews, it was better to pay.

For every doubt that arose, there seemed to be someone to put it out as if dousing a lick of flame. Rome was an "open city," went the reassuring words; Rome is the city of the Pope.

The Germans, warlike though they were, were honorable men. Besides, as everyone knew, the Allies would soon be here.

At four o'clock that afternoon, Renzo Levi returned to the monastery of the Sacred Heart for his scheduled meeting with Padre Borsarelli.[30] Levi was feeling a great deal less anxious than before. The community in the past two hours had collected some twenty-five kilograms of gold, bringing the total to thirty. They had also taken in a large sum of cash.[31] Whatever the Vatican's reply, it now appeared that one way or another they would reach the full amount.

When the priest and the Jew reconvened, Padre Borsarelli declared that he had in fact contacted the Holy See and had received an answer to the community's request.

"Yes," said Borsarelli, "we are ready to lend you any quantity of gold you may need. But it is obvious we want it back."[32]

Pope Pius XII himself had authorized the loan.[33] It could be repaid on installments, if the community so desired. There would be no time limit as to when the final payment would be due. Did the community want the gold in ingots or coins? Borsarelli inquired.[34]

Levi thanked him for this offer, but then added: "Now we are more confident that we will reach our goal. If I don't return here by 6:00 P.M., that will mean that we will not need the loan."[35]

Levi returned at once to the synagogue and reported the news. It was greeted with a feeling of relief, although the gold and cash donations were still arriving in strength. President Foà thought the Vatican had made a "noble gesture."[36]

The information was kept secret as yet, but somehow it got out, and the people clutched it and dressed it like a Christmas tree. The Pope was about to donate two-three-ten-fifteen kilograms of gold, it was suddenly being said. Someone had "seen" a car with Vatican City plates arrive at the temple with a message from the Holy Father. It was "a providential, most generous intervention. . . ."[37]

At the supper hour the Jewish leaders, the goldsmiths, the temple staff, and the guards remained at their posts. Their wives brought hot food and wine, and they ate as they continued to work. If there had been any fear that the news of the Vatican's offer would slow the flow of contributions, it was quickly put to rest. The three- and four-gram lockets, bracelets, watch chains, and wedding bands continued to come forward from the hands of the poor. The ghetto Jews seemed possessed of a compulsion to give, as if the surrendered objects were some kind of negative manna, in the absence of which its owners would survive. God willing, it might even bring misfortune to the Germans. *Che de senza se ne resta!*

By 8:00 P.M., the hour decreed by the occupiers as the *chiusura,* or closing time for the front doors of all the buildings of Rome, the pile of gold had reached the incredible weight of forty-five kilograms. In the time remaining before the curfew, Rosina Sorani, who had been putting aside the collected items in boxes, stacked them neatly. The cash was placed in the community's safe. The Italian guard remained on duty. Tomorrow morning, the leaders were almost certain, they would reach the required amount. The Vatican's gold was forgotten.

XVIII

EARLY THE NEXT morning Chief Rabbi Zolli was approached by a member of the Catholic family in whose house he was hiding and asked to undertake a risky mission to help the Jews.[1] Zolli, probably more than he was aware, was being sheltered by active conspirators against the occupiers. The head of the family, Amedeo Pierantoni, had been a Communist since 1921 and a resolute anti-Fascist well known to the regime and the turnkeys of the Duce's prisons. His son, Luigi Pierantoni, a physician who would later be captured and shot by the Germans in Rome, was a partisan in the non-Communist "Justice and Liberty" movement.[2]

The younger Pierantoni, hearing an incorrect report that the community was some distance from collecting the fifty kilograms of gold, had arranged for the rabbi to be spirited through the ring of German troops around Vatican City* under cover of a false identity. The object of this ill-considered adventure was to obtain that which had already been offered by the Vatican, and was no longer needed by the community: a loan of gold.[4]

Zolli, who was known to the highest officials of the Holy See, agreed at once to go. He was anxious to do something for his flock, especially because he had yesterday sent word to the community that his presence there during the gold crisis would not be helpful, since it pertained exclusively to "financial matters."[5] Instead, he had sent his watch chain. This response was presumably dictated by his overriding concern about the danger—particularly to himself—of a German raid on any open gathering of Jews. It would do nothing to dispel the unfair insinuations about the rabbi's courage that were now being sown in the community by some of the leaders.

Zolli, posing as a construction engineer, successfully entered the Vatican and met with officials of the treasury. From them he received what was in effect a reaffirmation of the earlier offer, of which Zolli had apparently remained unaware. The rabbi, ushered away by a Roman lawyer named Giorgio Fiorentino, who was cooperating in the scheme, then wrote a letter to President Foà reporting his encounter at the Holy See and suggested a rough draft of a receipt for the loan. He added that if the Germans would not keep their word and hostages were to be taken, he was prepared to offer himself as a volunteer.[6] Zolli's daughter Miriam and *Avvocato* Fiorentino delivered the letter

* The troops had been placed there by General Stahel as part of the agreement between the Vatican and the Reich, under which the territory of the Holy See would be protected.[3]

to the offices of the community, where she handed it to Foà. By all appearances Foà was not very impressed, and the meeting ended quickly, if not curtly.[7]

A bitter and lasting enmity was developing between the president and the chief rabbi. Foà was appalled by Zolli's independent behavior, which in fact was a challenge to presidential authority. The rabbi was only an employee. Feeling the gold situation under control, Foà had no need of Zolli's intervention. Indeed there was little time remaining before he would accuse the rabbi of "abandoning all religious services and care of souls,"[8] and by authority of Article 17, of Fascist law number 1731 governing the Jewish cult, order him dismissed and deprived of his salary.*[9]

Miriam Zolli, taking leave of Foà, was suddenly surrounded by the Jews outside the synagogue who were still coming forward with offerings of gold. They were anxious to know if she had any news. "I begged all," the rabbi's daughter later said, "in the name of my father to leave their homes, and above all not to congregate around the temple while the German spies were there."[11]

In the community offices Rabbi Zolli's redundant achievement was quickly forgotten, lost in the excitement stirred by the realization that the fifty kilogram goal was within sight. More than two hours remained before the noon deadline. A concerned eye was frequently turned to the clock, but among the leadership no one, in view of the continuing unbroken flow of donations, could have any further doubt about the outcome. On the other hand, the talk among the poorly informed majority at this late hour, if not pessimistic, was laden with anxiety. A Roman Jew who observed the approach of those final moments wrote at the time:

> The telephones were ringing, crisscrossing discussions, recriminations, and proposals . . . the Jews, spread out through the vast city of Rome, were running about, working agitatedly, sweating, searching,

* Nevertheless, it would be further stipulated, "in case of need, as for any other coreligionist, financial help [will] be granted him"[10]

calling on friends and acquaintances, and collecting from all who would aid them. . . .[12]

A little before 11:00 A.M. the fifty-thousandth gram of gold touched the pan of Angelo Anticoli's scale.[13] The collectors put aside further contributions amounting to 300 grams. They wanted to avoid any discrepancy that might arise should the German scales be either more or less accurate than their own. The entire sum was then locked in Foà's private chambers, and the police officer on duty was stationed outside.[14]

Further offerings were taken from people who wished to give and virtually no one, beyond the few who already knew, were told that the goal had been surpassed.[15] There was a reason for this.

President Foà now telephoned Obersturmbannführer Kappler's office with an appeal that the deadline be extended by several hours. The president feigned to have not yet reached the fifty kilogram mark. If he were conceded some more time, however, he felt the community would manage to raise the full amount, he said.[16] The purpose of this was to minimize the great success of the operation. Some leaders were concerned that should the Germans learn of the relative ease with which the Jews had met the terms, the price would be raised or the mulctings would continue.[17] It was a precaution that was deemed worthwhile to hazard, even at the expense of withholding the good news from their own people. It would help protect the community's remaining assets and permit it to continue to function.

Kappler agreed to a postponement until four o'clock that afternoon.

There was yet another precaution to be taken. Foà believed that the Germans might later deny ever having received the gold. That the episode was already a historical event affecting the lives of thousands of people did not appear as sufficient proof. His intention was, he said later, to provide the Italian Fascist authorities with an "official documentation of the incredible extortion that was taking place in Rome at the hands of foreigners and of the damages being suffered by the Roman

Jews, that is, being suffered by a considerable number of good Italian citizens."[18]

The evidence consisted of a brief message sent to the chief of police of Rome, in which Foà restated the terms of the German demand. Since "one hopes to be able to satisfy the request," he added, would the authorities provide a police escort for the transport of the gold to the German embassy?[19]

At about the same time a final intervention was initiated by the Jewish leadership to obtain at least a measure of relief from other Italian authorities. Earlier in the morning one of the prominent Jews of the community, Luciano Morpurgo, had come into Rome from his country home in Velletri, where he felt living was safer than in the occupied city. Arriving in Rome, he had learned of what was happening at the synagogue.[20] Morpurgo, a writer and publisher of considerable fame, had been an enthusiastic supporter of fascism and especially its leader. But he had become embittered since the racial laws. Once he had been among those prestigious journalists, writers, and artists upon whom the Fascists had lavished favors and secret funds to subsidize their work.[21] He had written and published glowing praise of Mussolini's greatness, words that made their way around the world. In this, few had surpassed Morpurgo, who had dedicated one of his books to the Duce, "the renewer and the creator . . . with devotion, admiration, and love. . . ."[22]

By now, however, he despised the thankless Fascists, although —wisely, he thought—he said nothing and maintained his contacts among them. Thus he had been able to make use of his connections in behalf of others. For example, he had won a special dispensation from the chief of the state police ("a man of heart"), as had some other Jews, authorizing him to keep in his employ an Aryan maid, who otherwise, for no other reason than the dictates of the racial laws, would have had to have been summarily discharged.[23]

Hearing the news of the gold demand, Morpurgo went to the temple and met with Foà to offer his assistance. It was decided between them that he could serve best by calling on some of his highly placed friends.[24] Morpurgo went first to the president of the Italian Red Cross, General Giuseppe Boriani. The Jewish publisher proposed that the Italians attempt to win a concession from the Germans by which the fifty kilograms of gold would be donated to the Red Cross to be used, for instance, in aiding the victims of Allied bombings in Italy. Italian Jews, Morpurgo pointed out, would be "happy and proud" to offer their gold in the same manner as their Italian countrymen had given their lives on the fields of battle.[25]

Boriani, in a friendly way, replied that he himself could do nothing but advised him to try his luck at the headquarters of the neo-Fascist party. Morpurgo agreed and went to see his personal friend Alessandro Pavolini, who had been recently named by Mussolini as head of the newly organized party. But Pavolini was not in just now, he was told; did he care to leave a message? Morpurgo concluded that the new party was too weak to be able to do anything with the Germans, and he returned to Foà to recount his failure.[26]

As the new deadline hour drew close, preparations were made for the delivery of the gold to the Gestapo. The remaining contributors were turned away with the announcement that the campaign was over. The goal had been met, it was said, and all doors were closed. The Jews of Rome relaxed again.

In reality nearly eighty kilograms had been collected.[27] This excess was secretly cached. It was stuffed behind thicknesses of paper in some of the community's file cabinets, never to be spoken of again until years later.[28] The 50.3 kilogram treasure that was to be turned over was packed in large cardboard boxes normally used by the community offices to store correspondence. Five kilograms of gold were placed into each of ten of these cartons forming tidy packages that would be convenient both to carry and to reweigh at the other end.[29]

The cash donations were counted, and the total recorded: 2,021,540 lire (about $20,000), the balance of a considerably larger sum, from which fifteen kilograms of gold had been purchased in the early hours of the operation from the uncharitable sellers, all of whom were said to be non-Jews.[30] This currency was placed in the community's safe.

Some of the staff went out for a leisurely lunch. Not until

now had they left their posts. There was a general relaxation of tension and a not unpleasant feeling among those who had taken part in the collection work that, all things considered, they had done a good job.[31]

XIX

SOMETIME BEFORE 4:00 P.M. that afternoon, the Fascist police escort arrived. It was led by a sergeant and a squad from the First Motorized Battalion *Piccolo Vincenzo*. By previous arrangement with President Foà, Race Office Chief Cappa showed up dressed in plain clothes. Foà had got Cappa to agree to go with them to the Germans "disguised" as one of the Jews, a maneuver, according to Foà, which would provide "incontrovertible proof of the payment."[1]

A delegation of Jews who would make the delivery was formed. Foà and Almansi would lead the group. Angelo Anticoli would go along as their gold expert. Two other members of the community were picked to help carry the weighty load, a task Chief Cappa also offered to perform in order to appear less conspicuous. Foà thought that very kind of him.[2]

Renzo Levi, because of his high standing in the community and the vital work he had done in the collection operation, was asked to join them. But Levi was being nagged by a grim premonition that the delegation was going to be arrested.

"Why take chances?" he replied. "You don't need me."[3]

At last the group was ready to depart. The ten boxes of gold were loaded into two taxis which had been commandeered by the police. The small convoy of automobiles and motorcycles roared its engines and departed for the Villa Wolkonsky, a short trip of less than two miles. As the delegation turned out of view, some Jews, who were watching from the sidewalk near the synagogue, shook their heads in sadness.

At the German embassy, the Jewish leaders suffered a new humiliation. They were told by Kappler's secretary that the Obersturmbannführer did not wish to see them. The payment had to be made at Via Tasso, 155, the new headquarters of the Gestapo in Rome. Kappler's refusal to receive the delegation was taken as an insult by the two presidents, as if he would not deign to "lower himself" to the petty formality of accepting the offering.[4]

The group withdrew and went to Via Tasso, which was only two blocks away. The Gestapo headquarters was in a squat, five-story modern building which stood out awkwardly in a street of narrower, more graceful houses built in the Umbertine style. It had two entrances, one of which led to the prison side of the building, and the other—to which Foà and the others had been directed—gave on to the offices and living quarters of Kappler's command. Entering this wing of the building, the Jews filed past a striking color portrait of Hitler in uniform, announced their presence, and stated what business they had with the Third Reich.

They were greeted by a thirty-five-year-old SS captain, who introduced himself as Hauptsturmführer Kurt Schutz. He had been expecting them, and he immediately presented his own gold experts, an assayer and a second man who would do the weighing. Captain Schutz, who impressed Foà as arrogant and brutal, made it quite clear, without actually saying so, that the Reich could not be defrauded by Jews.

As the boxes of gold were being hauled inside, Foà, who wore his dignity like brass knuckles, said to the German officer: "I hope to come to Germany to get this back."[5]

The delivery was placed near a scale that had a capacity of five kilograms. Schutz's goldsmith began to fish into the cartons, placing handfuls on the weighing pan, while an SS man tallied the totals for the German side and President Almansi performed the same operations for the Jews.

When the array of objects had been weighed, the Germans huddled together for a moment as the column of figures was added. Captain Schutz then addressed the two Jewish presidents and spoke threateningly.

The Jews, he declared, had delivered not fifty kilograms of gold, but 45.3.[6] The figures did not lie. There had been nine weighings of five kilograms each, plus another 300 grams. Nine times five is forty-five. Adding the fractional amount still left a balance due of 4.7 kilograms. What was the meaning of this? Were the Jews trying to cheat?

Foà and Almansi protested, defending their honor and that of the people they represented.[7] A long and heated argument ensued, the central issue being whether there were nine five-kilogram weighings or ten. Finally the two presidents asked that the gold be reweighed. But Schutz refused. He had caught the Jews in their chicanery and that was the long and short of the matter.

The wrangling continued, and the incredible, almost farsical scene took on all the airs of the marketplace in nearby Campo de' Fiori. If anyone of the Jewish group thought that they were confronting some kind of diabolical Nazi trick, this was at least partially relieved when at last Schutz agreed to put the gold to the test of the scale for a second time.[8]

While the lengthy weighing process was being undertaken again, Jews throughout the community were living moments of anguish. Several hours had passed by now, and darkness had fallen, but the delegation had not returned nor had it been heard from. It seemed impossible for the simple delivery of ten cardboard boxes to have taken so long.

Renzo Levi, who for the past two hours or so had been telephoning Almansi's home without reply, was convinced that his intuition had been correct and the delegation had been arrested.[9] By eight o'clock the families and friends of those who had gone to the Gestapo were terrified. As one close to them later said:

The ticking of the clock in the silence of their homes, gnawed anxiously, as the families, more and more each minute, were assailed by the scenes of conjecture. An unreasonable screech of the telephone: but it was not them, only their friends . . . with words that sought to encourage, but expressed only grief instead.[10]

After the second weighing, the Germans, consulting the new figures, were forced to concede that the true total was fifty kilograms and 300 grams. Foà now asked Captain Schutz for a receipt, which he felt duty bound to obtain to show his fellow Jews that the payment had actually been made, and also to prevent any further dispute with the occupation authorities.[11] Schutz refused peremptorily. He was later to be backed up by Kappler, who would say: "To the enemy who is being relieved of his arms, one does not give receipts."[12]

Sometime after 8:30 P.M. the delegation of Jews returned. They appeared haggard, near collapse, but at the same time, unburdened. Like a man "who comes back from having brought a dear one to the cemetery," someone was to remark.[13] The repugnant business of the past forty-eight hours was completed. The Jews, it seemed to them, were saved. There remained nothing to do now but go to sleep.

XX

GIUSEPPE LEVI CAVAGLIONE, the young Genoese Jew who had come to Rome to join the partisans, could not sleep. Since arriving in the city some days ago, he had made contact with the Resistance and had been sent to Tor Paluzzi, in the *Castelli Romani*.[1] He was finding his new life as a guerrilla difficult to adjust to, and this night all the thoughts he had pushed aside during the day arose and kept him awake. Again and again he reviewed the series of disjointed occurrences that had brought him here, to a shack in the midst of a small vineyard in the Roman countryside.

The morning after he had spent his first night in Rome, in the home of the elderly stranger who had sheltered him, he had walked almost aimlessly about the city trying to get in touch with the Underground. At last he had met an official of one of the anti-Fascist parties. Following lengthy interrogations he was asked if he wanted to take an assignment with a partisan band in the *Castelli*, where the guerrilla fight against the Germans was developing more rapidly than anywhere else in central Italy, including Rome itself.

He was ready to go at once, he had said. But before departing, would it be possible, he timidly inquired, to get some clothes and a pair of shoes suitable for life in the hills? The civilian outfit he had on was his Sunday best.

Everything he might need would be furnished by the partisans, he had been told. "You can't imagine how well organized they are!"[2]

He had been given false documents, which provided a new identity, and had been introduced to a beautiful young comrade who would guide him to the partisan encampment. Dressed as elegantly as he was, the modest, would-be guerrilla had made a poor impression on the woman, and when she had turned him over to the leader of the band, he had overheard her whisper to the man, "He won't be with you for more than a week. He's a pansy!"

The partisan leader's name was Mario Colacchi, a youth who had seemed to Levi Cavaglione to have become a hardened veteran already. Colacchi had stared at length at the new recruit, disapprovingly and without a trace of friendliness.

"Why did Rome send you to this particular spot?" he had asked, speaking at last.

"Maybe," Levi Cavaglione had replied evenly, "Rome wanted me to see for myself that the wines of the *Castelli* are better than those in Liguria, where I come from."

Colacchi had fallen silent, not at all amused. "Those idiots in Rome," he had barked, "always sending you nuisances just when you don't need any. Okay! We'll send you to Tor Paluzzo. But watch yourself."

Levi Cavaglione had then told Colacchi that he did not have any weapons and that he thought it would be best if they were to give him a revolver.

The partisan chief had unleashed a loud guffaw, a mocking laugh, as if he had not heard something so foolish in years.

"A revolver?" he had shot back. "If you really want one, you've got to take it from the Germans."[3]

Reliving those moments as he lay awake in the partisan bivouac in the Roman hills, Levi Cavaglione jotted them on a scrap of paper, concluding: "I thought that was really not the right time to insist or to ask for some suitable clothes and shoes. So, looking regretfully at my low shoes and nibbling on a hard piece of bread, I crossed the fields and the rocky paths following the guide who led me here, to Tor Paluzzo."[4]

XXI

ALL OF NON-JEWISH Rome had been following the gold ransom affair intently. They suffered the once-removed apprehensions of a spectator to a surgical operation, some form of which he himself may one day be forced to undergo. Now that word began to circulate that the episode had been concluded, they too were relieved, and their reaction was swift.

There was an abundance of compassion for the Jews, but somehow, in the minds of a people—Jew and non-Jew alike—who were counting on the presence of the Vatican as their best protection, the Pope received the greatest share of the kindnesses for the success of the gold campaign. It had been Pius XII, people were saying, who had proffered an awesome gift of gold as the last moments were running out, saving the Jews from certain death.[1] Hence a mighty legend was born that still today lives on, among the people of Rome and especially the Jews.[2]

Such comforting thoughts notwithstanding, some people in the city saw ominous shadows in the events of the past two days. An American woman, hiding in a Roman convent, wrote in her diary that night: "Now that they have paid their ransom, the Rabbi [*i.e.*, the responsible party] out to destroy his register of Jewish residents in Rome. Although the Germans said that on condition of this payment they would leave them alone, how can they be trusted?"[3]

Another foreign woman in Rome, M. de Wyss, a journalist from a neutral country, who also kept a diary, recorded: "I have seen these proceedings more than once and know well that this is the beginning of Jewish persecution. The more they pay the worse they will be treated. But all I can do is to warn some of them not to trust the Germans, who never keep their word."[4]

Consul Möllhausen, the chief German diplomat of the occupation, learned of what Kappler had done from Albrecht von Kessel, of the German mission to the Holy See.[5] Kessel had heard the news from Vatican sources, and he characterized it as "complete nonsense."[6] Möllhausen was perplexed, unable to understand why Kappler had acted in apparent contradiction to the understanding they had reached a few days earlier when they had gone to see Field Marshal Kesselring. What was going on?

"I preferred not to know, not to ask questions," the consul said later.*[7]

* Möllhausen would come to believe that Kappler, opposed to persecuting the Jews of Rome, had tried to duplicate the Tunisian formula: extortion without deportation.[8] Kappler's own explanation, considering the solution he had arrived at for the Jewish question in Rome, is simpler and gives no reason to doubt its validity. Imparting nothing noble to his behavior, he later testified that the demand for gold "was my last attempt at trying to avoid the roundup. . . ."[9]

XXII

OBERSTURMBANNFÜHRER KAPPLER lost no time dispatching the gold to Berlin. A visiting major from the German capital was returning there and agreed to accompany the treasure chest.[1] Kappler had decided to ship it directly to the head of the entire Reich security apparatus, Obergruppenführer Ernst Kaltenbrunner, chief of the RSHA, the highest post in Himmler's police empire, save for the Reichsführer himself.

He chose Kaltenbrunner, who had only recently assumed this command, because as Kappler later declared, "until that moment he had remained extraneous to all the discussions that had been going on about the advisability of executing a roundup in Rome and also because he was interested in the intelligence services."[2]

Following the line of reasoning he had earlier worked out, Kappler composed a covering letter to Kaltenbrunner to explain the purpose of the gold shipment to Berlin. In it he sought to draw the RSHA chief's attention to his theory that the deportation of the Jews of Rome would constitute a double loss. First, the possibility of obtaining intelligence from local Jewish links to the Allies and neutral states would not be realizable. Second, "the Roman Jews were in contact with Jewish financial groups abroad and one would be able to exploit these contacts for the intelligence services."[3]

He felt this latter point particularly strong. He had heard that the espionage operations of the SS were suffering a serious shortage of funds, and here lay an opportunity of tapping what was believed to be the bottomless fount of Jewish wealth.[4]

The letter, which would carry the first news of Kappler's audacious and unauthorized initiative to Berlin, was encoded and sent to Kaltenbrunner's office. The gold, crated in a single case and placed on a train going north, was also addressed to the head of the RSHA. For Kappler, there seemed nothing further to do but to await a reply.

If Kaltenbrunner were in any way taken with the Obersturmbannführer's thinking, there was a great deal he could do to allow Kappler's plan to exploit the Jews of Rome to prevail. Kaltenbrunner's powers were almost limitless, and those in charge of deporting Jews—notably Adolf Eichmann, whom Kaltenbrunner himself had recruited into the SS—were directly under his command. But, in truth, Kaltenbrunner was not particularly interested in the development of his espionage services, especially in so unorthodox a manner as was being suggested by Kappler—a name that meant little to him, if he knew it at all.

Kaltenbrunner, a physical giant of a man who was possessed of a somewhat paranoic personality, moved in a world entirely unknown to Herbert Kappler. The RSHA, for its chief, was not an organization designed to deal with the multitude of enemies of the Reich. In a way that Kappler would doubtless have deemed shocking and immoral, Kaltenbrunner used his command as an instrument against his personal enemies, among whom he had designated Göring, Goebbels, Ribbentrop, and, of course, his direct superior, Heinrich Himmler.

A killer, an alcoholic, a totally corrupt opportunist, and a very recognizable figure in the history of Western hierarchal structures, Kaltenbrunner was a man whose sole interest was the improvement of his own condition through the destruction of all that stood in his way.[5]

Had there been one shred of a chance for such a result in Kappler's proposal—which when held up beside the figure of Kaltenbrunner shrinks to insignificance and appears as a perfect model of naïveté—it might very well have succeeded. In the end, however, the case of fifty kilograms of Jewish gold would be found after the war in a corner of Kaltenbrunner's office, at rest for more than a year and a half. No one, it would be discovered, had ever bothered to open it.[6]

PART TWO

The Books of Rome

Poor people always know things later.

— GIACOMO DEBENEDETTI[1]

1943

SEPTEMBER

SUN.	MON.	TUES.	WED.	THURS.	FRI.	SAT.
			1	2	3	4
5	6	7	8	9	10	11
12	13	14	15	16	17	18
19	20	21	22	23	24	25
26	27	28	29	30		

OCTOBER

					1	2
3	4	5	6	7	8	9
10	11	12	13	14	15	16
17	18	19	20	21	22	23

I

On the morning following the delivery of the gold to the Nazis, President Foà awoke at the usual time and prepared to go to his office in the synagogue. The daily routine was interrupted, however, with a knocking at the front door to his apartment. Responding, Foà was suddenly confronted with a small party of SS men led by a martinet of an officer who answered to the name of Captain Mayer.[1]

The president was shocked that the Germans had learned his home address. It could not have come from the telephone book because the racial discriminations prohibited Jews from having a listing in the directory. He made a mental note to investigate this breach of security.

Any fears he might have had that the Germans had come to arrest him, however, were quickly quieted. SS-Hauptsturmführer Mayer, one of Kappler's men, was in charge of Office 1/C, the intelligence section of the Gestapo in Rome. He announced that his presence meant only that Foà would have to accompany him immediately to the temple, where he was about to conduct a search of the premises. This measure, Foà later recalled being told, was needed "to find and seize confidential correspondence and documents of whatever kind."[2] More specifically, the Gestapo captain said there was reason to believe that the Jews of Rome were in collusion with anti-Fascists and "badogliani"—followers of the King-Badoglio government, which was now cooperating with Allied forces in the south of Italy.[3] Captain

Mayer had apparently been ordered by Kappler to ferret out the proofs that would back up his notions about exploitable Roman Jewish links with the enemy.

Aside from his personal displeasure at having to receive the SS in his own home, Foà was very disturbed by this new harassment of the community. He considered it highly irregular. He had not been previously notified of such an action nor had the Gestapo men "exhibited any decree or ordinance from the superior German Authorities."[4] What made it even worse, he thought, was that it was directly contrary to a communique issued a few days earlier and signed by Field Marshal Kesselring requiring a warrant or some other document, without which operations of this type would not be legal.[5]

Foà felt helpless, however, and went off with the Germans. When the Gestapo car carrying Mayer and the Jewish president reached the Lungotevere Cenci, the entire square block of the synagogue had already been sealed off by an SS police detachment of Ordunungspolizei of men in boyish short pants and rolled sleeves. Two tanks had been moved up to the temple entrance, their long guns pointed at the bronze doors. About forty German officers, interpreters, and soldiers armed with submachine guns were inside, and the employees of the community offices had been warned not to move from their places.[6]

Outside, Jews from the ghetto who were watching the assault on the temple could scarcely believe their eyes. In less than twenty-four hours since the mulcting of their gold, the Germans had apparently broken their promise to leave the community alone. When Foà was seen arriving in the Gestapo car, however, this was taken as a good sign. Many thought it meant that the president had matters under control, that the Jews "had nothing to fear."[7]

The search of the premises continued throughout the morning. The investigators worked from top to bottom, including the basement of the synagogue. They worked boldly rather than thoroughly, smashing through locked doors and cabinets like firemen without a moment to lose. Whole file cabinets filled with correspondence unread for years were moved onto the streets to be carried away. The minutes to countless meetings of the Jewish Council, which had been bound into books were taken too, as were a large part of the community's archives and its financial ledgers.

When the Germans arrived at the safe in the president's office, Foà, who had the only key, was forced to open it. Inside, mostly in small denominations, lay the more than two million lire that had been collected in the past two days during the gold campaign. Captain Mayer indicated that the money was no concern of his. But in the course of the search, Mayer received superior orders by telephone from Gestapo headquarters with instructions to take these funds, too. "He did so," Foà said later, "with evident regret. . . ."[8]

The search continued, moving into the temple itself. They were looking for a hidden radio transmitter, receiver, or other such incriminating equipment.[9] The searchers smashed open the Ark, throwing the two Torahs to the ground—an act of profanity to Jews. They broke into the oratorio for the Spanish rites—a temple within the temple—and cracked open the alms boxes.

Foà asked Mayer if they would at least respect the temple's sacred vestments and the *argenterie,* or religious articles of gold and silver. Some of the most important pieces of these valuable objects had been recently withdrawn from a vault in the Banco di Napoli for the coming high holy day services. They had been placed with other such items in the "Treasury," a locked room in the synagogue. To Foà's request the captain promised that they would not be touched, and the room was not even opened.*

About one o'clock in the afternoon a large van, which the Germans had waiting in front of the temple, was loaded with all the books and papers that had been dragged outside. In full view of the ghetto Jews who stood by and watched, the truck

* This was the one Nazi promise Foà did not believe would be kept, presumably because Captain Mayer obviously lacked the authority to guarantee it. In the following days, the Jewish leaders took elaborate, and according to Foà, dangerous but necessary steps to place the temple valuables—the "community's patrimony"—into safekeeping (see pp. 124, 125, 149).

was filled to the top and from back to front with a paper cargo that weighed hundreds of pounds. The functions of the community, in the absence of its files, had been rendered "completely paralyzed," according to Foà; the raid had caused "incalculable damage" to the morale of the Jews of Rome.[10]

The Jewish leaders felt themselves confronted with a major problem now. This was, as one of them put it: "how to continue the principal activities of the Community [and how] not to interrupt the *Tefilloth* [the daily religious services] . . ."*[11]

But as far as the search itself was concerned, there was really nothing to be concerned about, according to Foà. The compromising material the Germans were looking for, he later said, was simply nonexistent. It had been pure folly on the part of the Nazis to have thought that Foà's administration, and those of his predecessors, would have had anything to do with the anti-Fascists. For their trouble, the Germans had got only a truckload of paper with "not one secret document, or, anyway, nothing in the nature of being prohibited."[13] Nor had they found the excess of thirty kilograms of gold collected in the past two days.

Such sanguinity notwithstanding, the van that pulled away from the curb outside the synagogue carried with it the community's most valuable prize—more so than its gold, its sacred vestments, and its fetishes of precious metals. The president, his aides, and a few observant eyewitnesses to the raid had looked on as the registry of contributors and the thousands of index cards with the names, addresses, and other vital data concerning virtually every Jew in Rome had fallen into Nazi hands.**[14]

* This problem would be solved very quickly. The Jewish Council and the community administration in the face of all difficulties would in fact find ways to function in one manner or another with unbroken continuity throughout the entire period of the occupation.[12]

** Foà later claimed that part of this material had been hidden from the Germans and had not been confiscated. Further, he maintained that the files of Jewish names and addresses the Nazis had taken—unhidden, he said, because of "more pressing daily exigencies"—were never used by them.[15] A controversy arose over these lists and is said to still be unsolved. For an account of this affair, including new material uncovered by the author, see pages 301–303.

As soon as the Germans had left, Foà launched into an attack on his assistant, Rosina Sorani. He had concluded that it could only have been her who had informed the SS of his address. Accusing her in a strong rebuke, he said she should never have given this information to them.

Signorina Sorani was deeply hurt. She denied the charge and said it was especially unjust because she had in fact fought with the SS men to prevent them from getting the address. It had not been her who had told them, she insisted. She accused the executive secretary of the community, Fortunato Piperno.[16]

Foà let the matter drop. But later in the day Signorina Sorani, who since the gold ransom demand had begun to keep a diary, recorded her side of what had happened when the Germans had appeared at the temple offices in the morning:

> Since the Signor Presidente had not yet arrived, they demanded that I turn over the keys to the safe and the desks. When I said I didn't have them, they threatened me, saying that if I didn't give them the President's telephone number or his home address, I would have to pay with my life. But with all their threats I didn't tell them either one. . . . Then the Germans, who could get nothing out of me, went to the other members of the staff and especially to *Commendatore* Piperno . . . who on the first demand and the first threat immediately gave in and told both the telephone number and the address of the Signor Presidente.[17]

It was, that late September day of 1943, the eve of *Rosh Hascianà*, the coming of the Jewish new year 5704. If that which was passing had been filled with gathering clouds, perhaps next year the light of peace would break through. As the saying went: *"L'scianà tovà tachtvò*—Happy New Year!"

II

In apartment number ten of a building facing the temple on the Trastevere bank of the river Regina Wachsberger was very upset. Like most Jewish housewives that day, she was overburdened with the multitude of preparations for the important holiday that would come on at sundown. But her work had suddenly been made to appear as folly.

She had gone out that morning, and walking through the streets of the ghetto, she had seen the raid on the temple. She had stood among the gathering of Jews and had watched the Germans carry away among the mass of documents the open boxes of index cards containing the registry of the Jews of Rome.[1]

Now, putting aside her holiday chores, she telephoned her husband, Arminio, at the photo-optical shop in Via Volturno. She related what she had observed to her husband. She was certain about the lists of Jews being taken, she said, because she had actually seen the *schede*, or file cards, go into the German van.[2] Expressing at least a measure of her anxiety, she said that she could not help but think that "the SS had in mind some new action against the Jews."[3]

When Wachsberger returned home later in the day, he agreed with his wife that there was reason to be alarmed.

Ominous events had been occurring at a pace too rapid for a man to be able to absorb the impact of one before being stricken by another. The cumulative effect was beginning to be felt, not only in the Wachsberger household but in others throughout the community. More and more, Jews were taking flight, as were many non-Jews in the city, particularly Roman men, who were being called up for service in Mussolini's neo-Fascist army, and more often, for German forced labor.[4] It was getting so that Stadtkommandant Stahel was heard to remark, "Half the population of Rome lives in the homes of the other half."[5]

On the other hand, the flight of the city's most endangered residents was little more than an illusion, of which the great majority of the people at this date knew virtually nothing. Never during the occupation would it amount to more than a statistical twitch, and infinitely larger numbers of people were entering the city seeking its "protection" than were escaping its dangers.[6] The truth was that both Jewish and Christian Rome were charmed by a concert of authoritative voices intoning the city's invulnerability.[7] Thus Rome sat still, confident the ordeal would soon pass them by like the nasty winds of the *tramontana.* One eyewitness wrote at the time: "You are considered a pessimist if you think the Allies will not be here until the middle of October."[8]

The two edges of this condition cut deeply into the Wachsberger home that *Rosh Ha-scianà* evening. Arminio was very disturbed by what his wife had seen while passing the synagogue earlier in the day. They discussed the matter quietly among themselves, so as not to disturb their daughter and Regina's elderly parents. Suddenly Wachsberger decided on what had to be done.

"Prepare a few things," he said. "The time has come to run, to go into hiding."[9]

Regina agreed. Her husband outlined a plan, which seemed to her to offer the desired safety. They would conceal themselves, Clara, and the Polacco couple on the premises of Wachsberger's chemical laboratory in the Flaminio district. It was a quiet zone, which lay outside the Roman walls between the Tiber and the western precipice of the Villa Borghese. Some prominent Fascists lived in the neighborhood, and Via Flaminia itself was constantly filled with the heavy trafficking of

German military movements to the south. But few Jews were there, and the unimportant Via Carrara, where Wachsberger's workshop was situated, seemed far enough away from any nearby danger, certainly a haven when compared to the ghetto. More important, the little factory was not in Wachsberger's name, and anyone in the area who knew him or his father-in-law was unaware of their religion.

No longer doubting the need for escape and convinced of the relative security of Via Carrara, the Wachsbergers now found themselves faced with other considerations. When should they go? Tonight? After the holidays? And what of the problems of living in the limited space of the chemical laboratory, which after all had none of the facilities of a home? Would there be room enough for five persons? Two of them, Regina's parents, were perhaps physically incapable of surviving the stringent regimen that would be imposed upon them. And what of Clara? She was, her mother knew, such a fragile child and still convalescing from her polio attack.

The thought of Clara getting sick again weighed heavily in the minds of her parents. There could be no doubt that the chemical laboratory would be an unpleasant, if not an impossible, place to hide. As Wachsberger and even his wife were well aware, pungent and intensely disagreeable fumes constantly saturated the air of the poorly ventilated place. Perhaps it might be entirely polluted, dangerous to breathe over an extended period. Then there were the noxious chemical products stored there—acids and poisonous compounds—and children were so inquisitive.

What of another place? A shack in the countryside; a cave in the mountains?

"Our child is sick," Regina reminded her husband. "To hide ourselves with the baby in some damp cave won't help her get better."[10]

Maybe, one of the Wachsbergers suggested, the Germans were *not* planning any further persecutions against the Jews of Rome; certainly not in a physical way. By all appearances, Arminio and Regina told one another, the Nazis seemed to be interested in Jewish gold. That could explain today's seizure of the documents. They were checking the community's finances, probably looking for ways to extort more money from the Jews. But why did they take the lists of all the Jews? To get the names and addresses of the largest contributors. It might be as simple as that.

Perhaps there was no reason at all to hide. The Wachsbergers knew that other Jews were hiding, but they really amounted to only a few. It was obvious that the majority considered themselves safest at home. This was Rome not Poland; this was the center of civilization not the Russian wilderness.

"We decided," Wachsberger said later, "to renounce our idea of fleeing, hoping that the lists of contributors were taken by the Germans solely for the purpose of finding names of rich Jews from whom to demand further payments of gold and money."[11]

If it were true, a man could thank God, this high holy day, he was poor or even lower middle class.

III

THE ONE MAN now most directly concerned with the fate of the Jews of Rome sat behind a busy desk in a four-story building almost 1,000 miles away. He was growing impatient, eager to resolve the problem.

His name was Adolf Eichmann. An Obersturmbannführer in Kaltenbrunner's RSHA, he was the chief of Section IV- (Gestapo) B- (Sects) 4 (Evacuations and Jews), with headquarters in the Kurfurstenstrasse in Berlin. Although his name appeared on only one of the bitter fruits that hung near the top of the RSHA organizational tree, Eichmann's IV-B-4 was by far the most developed and extensive department of all. Continental in scope, his operation, however, functioned along very limited lines. In the division of labor systematized by the motion of the Third Reich, Eichmann headed a department upon which had devolved but a single function: deportation. In his own words, "In every European country under our jurisdiction it was the job of the Jewish Adviser (the representative of my office) to work through local officials until he had attained our goal: a roundup of the Jews and their delivery to the transports."[1]

In almost every case these transports were German freight trains, and no matter from which station in Europe they departed, very often they went to one of six places in Nazi-occupied Poland—Chelmno, Maidanek, Sobibor, Belzec, Treblinka, and Auschwitz. In Eichmann's view his was the most impersonal sort of work. "Whether they were bank directors or mental cases," he had long ago decided, "the people who were loaded on these trains meant nothing to me. It was really none of my business."[2]

He felt no strong animosity toward them, although as a nation, he believed on the authority of the German state itself, Jews *were* an enemy. But had the enemy been Eskimos, Negroes, or even bus drivers, they too would be required to ride his trains. Indeed he admired the Zionists, especially their leaders. He had often negotiated the exigencies of the Final Solution with them. He found these Jewish leaders especially trustworthy and "immensely idealistic."*[3]

Though he labored at the fulcrum of the Final Solution, it would have continued without him, and not having any tend-

* In his memoirs Eichmann relates two such encounters. "Dr. [Paul] Ep[p]stein from Berlin once said to me," he wrote, "that Jewry was grateful for the chance I gave it to learn community life at the ghetto I founded at Theresienstadt, forty miles from Prague. He said it made an excellent school for the future in Israel." The second represented his well-known dealings with Dr. Rudolf Kastner, the Zionist official in Budapest, which resulted in the exchange already noted (p. XIV). " 'You can have the others,' he [Kastner] would say, 'but let me have this group here.' And because Kastner rendered us a great service by helping keep the deportation camps peaceful, I would let his groups escape."[4]

ency toward self-aggrandizement, he felt no responsibility for what happened once the passengers debarked from his trains. He had in the course of his work witnessed the slaughter of Jews, and he had found it offensive. But no one else seemed to care, at least not enough to act. By his own account he did not regard himself competent to have his "own thoughts in this matter."[5] It was not his affair; it was an affair of the Reich.

Uncompromisingly faithful to superior authority and selfless in his devotion to duty, Eichmann was a skilled and talented official. He was a family man, a good provider with a wife and young children, but he knew and desired no other life than that of his office and expending the energy required to build a bigger and more efficient organization. "Officialese is my only language," he once said.[6] The papers that crossed his desk were his only concern. Yet there was some truth in his one time remark, "I was a regular guy."[7] He had dreams and frustrations, and like others he was trying to move up in a cruelly competitive world.

At this very moment in the war he was anxious about his career and he desperately yearned for a full colonelcy, to be a Standartenführer.[8] He was growing self-conscious about his failure to obtain a higher rank. At the age of thirty-seven he had not had a promotion in two years now, and younger men were passing him by. Take Schellenberg, head of Section IV-E (Gestapo Counterintelligence)—a smaller department than Eichmann's. In the same two years Schellenberg had rocketed from a rank below Eichmann's to Brigadeführer (Brig. Gen.) and at only thirty years old. And then there was thirty-three-year-old Ohlendorf: three promotions since the war broke out, and now a Gruppenführer (Maj. Gen.).

The good fortune of others made his own stagnation all the more embarrassing, causing him, he later said, "grief and sorrow."[9] It was no fault of his. He had done everything to favor a promotion. He had even asked to be sent to the front. It was inevitable that others would soon think, if they had not already begun to, that Eichmann did not merit a higher rank. In the RSHA, if a man was not going forward, he was going backward.

Moreover, Eichmann was lately besieged with difficulties that were hampering the effectiveness of his operations. Many of the western European countries—most recently Denmark—were offering an increasing amount of resistance to scheduled deportations. Also, it was becoming always harder to obtain the necessary number of trains from the Ministry of Transport, and only a few days ago Eichmann had been temporarily blocked by the Foreign Office from shipping Jews in the occupied territories with citizenship of neutral and allied countries to the "East."[10] Such situations would one day cause Eichmann to lament, "Whatever I prepared and planned, everything went wrong . . . I was frustrated in everything, no matter what."[11]

The thorniest problem plaguing Eichmann at this particular time was the deportation of the Jews of Rome. For almost two years now he had been trying to relocate Italian Jews. It had been Eichmann himself in preparation for the Wannsee Conference on the Final Solution who had drawn up the list of the number of Jews to be deported from each country. He had gone on record establishing a goal for "Italy and Sardinia" of 58,000 to be included among the approximately eleven million European Jews to be handled.[12] But now, at this late date in the war, not a single Italian Jew had yet entrained.

Everything had gone wrong. While Italy remained Hitler's most important ally, efforts to deport Italian Jews, even those in German-controlled areas, were continually forestalled by the German Foreign Office, which was reluctant to interfere in Italian affairs.[13] When the Duce fell, it was clear that the Badoglio government, continuing the Italian policy of sheltering Jewish refugees from Nazism, would not cooperate. Even now, with the Germans for the first time in complete control of Rome and everything to the north, opposition to the deportations was mounting from diplomats, military men, and even the local Gestapo, all of whom were wholly incapable of comprehending Eichmann's unique set of difficulties.

Earlier in the month he had begun to press vigorously for the deportation of the Italian Jews, and especially the Jews of

Rome. The first thing done had been to obtain permission for, and to dispatch, a top secret *Schlussverfügung*, or final decision to SS officials in all occupied zones *except* Italy. This ordered the deportation "at once" of Italian Jews "still remaining in the Territories under German sovereignty."[14]

As for the Jews on the Italian peninsula, he had started with Rome. The office of Reichsführer Himmler himself was requested by Eichmann's IV-B-4 to take the unusual step of personally intervening in Rome.[15] Having foreseen the possibility of obstacles arising from local officials, Eichmann had sought to firmly establish his authority on matters of competence or precedence with regard to the Roman Jews. This maneuver had resulted in the telephone call to Kappler in Rome, in which he was told of his promotion and that Himmler wished to proceed with the roundup and deportation of the city's Jews. It had also brought on the written messages from Himmler's office ordering Kappler to assure the secrecy of the imminent *Judenaktion* and not to undertake any anti-Jewish measures, in order to quell suspicion among the Jewish population.

But Kappler, for reasons unknown to Eichmann, or at least unappreciated by him, had disobeyed these directives on all counts. Moreover, in his communications to Berlin, Kappler had reported that the operation desired by IV-B-4 would face difficulties that appeared to him to be insoluable.

These impediments, Kappler had telegraphed, were both of a technical and psychological nature. In the first place there were not enough SS police in Rome to bring off the roundup, and those who were available were totally inexperienced in such actions. Further, the non-Jewish population of Rome could be expected to be hostile in the event of a raid on the Jews, and the possibility of passive and even armed resistance on the part of the Romans was very high.[16]

This intelligence had been designed to dissuade Berlin, but when it had come into Eichmann's possession it had had the opposite effect. Eichmann decided now that Rome needed special attention. He called in his chief troubleshooter, the young "Jewish expert" SS-Hauptsturmführer Theodor Dannecker.

Dannecker would know what had to be done. He was the man who had organized and directed the *grand rafle*—the great roundup—of the Jews of Paris.[17]

The complicated situation in Rome was explained to Dannecker. He was provided with a document conferring the necessary authority, signed by the head of the Gestapo, Eichmann's direct superior, Gruppenführer Heinrich Müller, and instructed to present himself to Kappler. Kappler, though he did not yet know it, was to be placed at Dannecker's disposal, notwithstanding the latter's lower rank.[18]

In the meantime a group of fourteen officers and NCOs and thirty troops were detached from a Waffen SS Death's Head formation deployed at the eastern front. They were serving there in the Einsatzgruppen, Himmler's mobilized killing units.[19] These men were placed in Dannecker's command, and as the month of September dissolved in the dawn of October, they packed their bags on a southbound train moving toward the call of still summery Rome.

IV

LIKE VULTURES HEARING the drum of the dead and the doomed, other Germans, who were in no way involved in the Eichmann operation, began now to pick at the naked parts of the wounded community. The Nazi intellectuals came to the Eternal City to study the Jews of Rome.

On the first of the Jewish new year, the final day of that September, two such intellectuals quietly appeared at the offices of the Roman community. Due to the holiday they found no one in except Rosina Sorani, Foà's assistant. They wanted to meet with the president, they said, but there was no cause to disturb him. Tomorrow would be soon enough. In the meantime they wondered if they might have a look around. They were particularly interested, Signorina Sorani was able to discern, in the community's library facilities.[1]

The two Germans examined the second and third floors of the temple. They found their way to the two libraries maintained by the community, which were called the Biblioteca Comunale, and the Biblioteca del Collegio Rabbinico. Without remaining very long and barely opening a book, they left.

They were refined men of culture, superior education, and scholarly pursuits, incalculably distant from the provincial organization men of the SS. They and their many colleagues were associated with a unique academic adventure, which had been formulated in an institution called Einsatzstab Rosenberg. Founded in 1940 by Nazi party ideologist Alfred Rosenberg, the Einsatzstab was an integral part of the dream of the intellectuals to reinvigorate European thought and culture after winning the war. To accomplish this task Einsatzstab Rosenberg was combing occupied Europe, collecting books and objects of art of high value for the purposes of research and accumulation of knowledge. Eventually an ideological "Hohe Schule" to be known as the Central National Socialist University was to be established. It would be dedicated to the advanced study in academic fields that had hitherto received scant attention from bourgeois scholars.*

Somehow, however, Einsatzstab Rosenberg could not escape the temptations of unrelated cultural research, such as amassing the priceless private art collection of Reichsmarschall Göring; or undertaking such operations as "Action M," which had been

* Some institutes of this university were already functioning in 1943: among them, one in Hamburg for colonial research; another in Halle for religious research; in Kiel for German "living space"; in Stuttgart for biology and race; and in Frankfurt am Main for research into the Jewish question. This latter faculty employed Jewish scholars from the liquidated Polish ghetto at Vilna.[2]

directed against the Jews of France and the Low Countries. Here Einsatzstab Rosenberg carried away to Germany 59,500 tons of privately owned *"objets d'art,"* such as furniture, rugs, silverware, pots and pans, bottles, medicines, clothes, and kitchen and toilet sinks.[3] Of the Einsatzstab, Rosenberg himself would one day remark that it was "the biggest art operation in history."[4]

On the day following Einsatzstab's visit to the Rome community, the two German intellectuals returned and were received by President Foà.[5] That same day Foà experienced an unpleasant encounter with two officers of the SS, apparently from Kappler's command. They were seeking further information about the finances and holdings of the community's richest Jews. Though they threatened him personally with the prospect of "rigorous measures" unless he told them what they wanted to know, Foà refused to betray such confidences and the SS went away.[6] These men, however, were obviously of a different sort. They had introduced themselves as Orientalists. One of them, in the uniform of a captain, said he was a professor of Hebrew language studies from the Hohe Schule in Berlin. With scholarly interest, they asked if they could browse among the books of the community's libraries. The president agreed.[7]

The Biblioteca Comunale, unlike the less important library of the Rabbinical College, had a magnificent collection, one of the richest in Europe, not only for the study of Judaica, but also early Christianity. A heritage of 2,000 years of Jewish presence in Rome, the library contained vast treasures that had not yet even been catalogued, let alone researched. Among the known material were the only copies of books and manuscripts dating from before the birth of Christ, from the time of the Caesars, the emperors, and the early popes. There were engravings from the Middle Ages, books from the earliest printers, and papers and documents handed down through the ages.

The German visitors were very impressed. They spent long hours silently examining the library's holdings—"with suspicious attention," it seemed to Foà.[8]

Incapable of realizing that the Jews of Rome were being eaten alive, Foà was, however, getting suspicious. The longer the Germans stayed, the more distrustful of their intentions he became. When the Einsatzstab officers declared at the end of the day that in the interest of their studies it was necessary for them to remove the catalogues of both libraries, Foà was convinced of their bad faith.[9] After they left, he immediately telephoned President Almansi, since, as Foà was to point out, it was the union and not the community, under Title II, Article 36 of the law of 1930, which was responsible for the administration of the libraries.[10]

The two presidents agreed that the situation had not yet matured to warrant any action on their part, but obviously they would have to note any further developments with the utmost of care and with a readiness to intervene, if need be, to the full extent of their authority. To be on the safe side, Foà had some of the manuscripts thought to be among the most valuable placed in a safe in the temple Treasury.

He later said, speaking in the third person: ". . . the two Presidents [were] well aware of the irreparable loss the plunder of such precious material would have meant for Italian culture. . . ."[11]

The next morning the Einsatzstab Orientalists, with the aid of a locksmith, broke into Rabbi Zolli's abandoned apartment in the ghetto street Via S. Bartolomeo dei Vaccinari. Searching the place, they confiscated some Hebrew language books, as well as the rabbi's private papers.[12] But almost no one took note of this first assault on the property of an individual Jew. Most people in Rome that particular day were celebrating the happy news that had just arrived from the south.

There had been a four-day uprising in Naples, ignited by harsh measures imposed by the Nazi occupiers, which included an attempt to round up Neapolitan men for forced labor service. On the night of September 27, thousands of civilians secretly armed themselves, and the insurrection was launched. They forced the Germans to release the captured men, and continuing the rebellion, made them withdraw entirely from the city on October 1. By now the Allies had entered Naples, finding it already liberated.[13]

Though all the details were not yet known in Rome, even the German and Fascist news sources were reporting that there had been a civilian revolt—which they attributed to "Communist" civilians—and that Naples had fallen to the Allies.[14] The implications of this spectacular event were not lost on the principal authorities in Rome—the Germans, the Fascists, and the Vatican—all of whom, for differing reasons, were trying to prevent an insurrection in Rome.* The immediate effect of the Naples incident was a tightening of security in Rome.

The occupiers began to step up their police forces and anti-partisan activities, especially in the *Castelli Romani*.[16] The Pope, partly as a direct result of the Naples uprising, summoned the city's parish priests, calling on them to urge the faithful to maintain calm and self-control in any circumstances. They were also warned to eschew any acts of violence that might provoke the Germans.[17] In addition, Pius XII asked the occupiers to increase the number of police in the city.[18] These measures were needed to assure the rule of law and order in these hard times through which the Holy City was passing, it was said.[19]

The calm continued. A new watchword entered the Roman vocabulary: *attesismo*. It described the doctrine of waiting passively for peace. Opposed by the weak partisan movement, it was an idea cherished and fostered by the Authorities. For most Romans peace meant the arrival of the Allies, and Naples was that many steps closer to Rome. Some people in the city had it calculated. "Naples," the American woman in hiding noted, "is only three hundred kilometers from Rome, and an army can advance at the rate of ten kilometers a day if all goes well. Must we wait the whole winter? Surely not."[20]

* The reasons of the occupation forces were of course determined by the need to guarantee an iron hold on the city, which was psychologically and militarily essential to the Nazi-Fascist war effort. The Vatican's motives, aside from its campaign to mediate a German-British-American settlement, stemmed from an expressed fear that an anti-Fascist insurrection would result in the city falling to the left-wing Italian political parties, particularly the Communists.[15]

In the ghetto the news from Naples meant all this and more. The 670-member Neapolitan Jewish community was free. Two thousand Jews were already behind Allied lines.[21] The turn of Rome would be next.

A few days after the good news from Naples, one of the German intellectuals, with an escort of SS men, returned to the offices of the community. It was morning, and Foà had not yet arrived, but that was incidental. The Einsatzstab officer, a new face this time, wanted to examine the libraries.

This new man, a lieutenant whose name would never be known, said he was a paleographer and a specialist in Semitic philology. "He was a strange figure," the Roman Jewish writer Debenedetti, who lived the experience of those days, would later recall; ". . . to look at him, one would have said he was a German official like all the others." But, as an intellectual, there was a difference. Debenedetti continued:

> While his men began to rifle through the library of the Rabbinical College and that of the Community, the officer, with artful and meticulous hands like fine embroidery, touched softly, caressed, fondled the papyrus and the incunabula; turned the pages of manuscripts and rare editions and leafed through membranaceous codices and palimpsests. The varying attention of his touch, the differing artfulness of his gestures were at once proportionate to the volume's worth. Those works, for the most part, were written in obscure alphabets. But in opening their pages, the officer's eyes would fix on them, widening and brightening, in the same way as some readers who are particularly familiar with a subject know where to find the desired part, the revealing passage. In those elegant hands, as if under keen and bloodless torture, a kind of very subtle sadism, the ancient books had spoken.[22]

After a while the officer left the library and returned to the community offices on the second floor. Foà had still not arrived, and only Rosina Sorani was there.[23] As she looked on with chagrin, the German picked up the telephone receiver and called the firm of Otto and Rosoni, an international shipping company with its main office in Piazza di Spagna. He wanted to know, Signorina Sorani overheard, when they could be prepared to pick up the books.

When he hung up, she reported at the time, "he turned to me and said that he had carefully noted how many books there were and in what order they lay and he then declared the two libraries under sequestration. Within a few days they would come for the books and all of them had to remain in the same place he had left them. Otherwise, I would have to pay for them with my life."[24] In fact, he said she would be shot.

The German philologist departed. His heels could be heard clicking down the flight of marble stairs that led to the street.

It was still morning when Foà appeared and Signorina Sorani immediately related what had happened. Angered anew, the president instructed her to lock both libraries at once and under no circumstances to give the key to anyone, including himself. He then contacted President Almansi and they decided that there was not a moment to lose; something had to be done.[25]

They wrote a letter:

> This morning a German official called at the offices of the Jewish Community of Rome. . . . After visiting the library of the Community and that of the Rabbinical College . . . the official declared to an employee present at the time that all the books of the two above-mentioned libraries were to be sequestered and must not be removed, threatening bodily harm to the person of said employee in the event of noncompliance. . . .

The letter went on to describe the immense value of the libraries, the loss of which would constitute a misfortune for Italy. It concluded with this sentence:

> The undersigned in their quality as President of the Union, which administers the Rabbinical College, and as President of the Jewish Community of Rome, respectively, in view of the impossibility of being able to oppose themselves to the demands of the German Authorities, and also in order to discharge their responsibilities, feel it their duty to inform the Honorable Minister of that which has been indicated above for measures to be taken within his competence.[26]

This letter, signed by Foà and Almansi, was typed four times. It was assigned protocol numbers 264, 265, 266, and 267, and sent for the attention of the appropriate ministers at four different addresses, deemed by Foà to be the most directly interested in "the conservation of that national patrimony," and agreed upon by Almansi.[27] They were: the library division of the Ministry of Education, the Directorate General of Cults, the Directorate General of Public Security, and the Directorate General of Civil Administration, all of the latter three being under the command of the neo-Fascist Minister of Interior, war criminal Guido Buffarini-Guidi.

Perhaps now they would see some results. "Those anguished advisories," Foà later wrote, "would have sounded the alarm for whoever took to heart the patrimony of Italian culture."*[28]

V

EARLY IN THE first full week of October—the fourth of the occupation—Haupsturmführer Theodor Dannecker arrived in Rome. He quietly checked into a small hotel in residential Via Po and went directly to meet with Obersturmbannführer Kappler. It being their first encounter, Dannecker formally presented himself and stated his mission.

* Dispatching the letters was not the only thing Foà did. The few manuscripts hidden in the Treasury safe, which seemed to have escaped the attention of at least this latest German visitor to the libraries, were removed and copied. A safe place was found for the originals in the municipal library Biblioteca Vallicelliana. Apparently Foà was too modest to report this minor rescue operation, although he spoke of it years later. Its significance, however, should not be overlooked. Involving at least fifteen other Jewish officials and trusted friends of the community administration, it further demonstrates the good faith of the leaders, and like the incident concerning the concealment of the temple's vestments and holy articles—noted above and below (see pp. 107, 149)—shows their willingness to take risks for what they decided was in the interests of whole group.[29]

As Kappler remembered it:

A captain in the SS showed up at my office and introduced himself as Dannecker. And in his hand was a document empowering him to carry out a *Judenrazzia.* It was a definitive authorization, containing an order to the local police commands to furnish all aid requested by Dannecker himself for the action. This power of attorney . . . was signed by General of the SS Müller.[1]

In short, Dannecker indicated, he had been appointed *Judenreferent* for Italy, and he had come to deport the Jews of Rome—as many as was humanly possible.[2]

"I understood," Kappler said later, "my attempts to avoid the persecutions had failed."[3]

There was nothing further he could do, he felt, but lend a measure of his assistance to his colleague, but "only when I could not refuse."[4] Kappler was not going to be bullied.

Dannecker, although he often made attempts at being amiable, did not make a pleasant appearance. The thirty-year-old "Jewish expert" had a tic that continually kicked his head to one side with relentless violence. He was awkwardly tall and poorly coordinated in his body movements, physical traits which combined to give others the impression that he was under the influence of alcohol.

Presenting Kappler with this image, Dannecker began to sketch out what had to be done in order that he might successfully carry out his assignment in Rome. At the outset, he said, speaking from experience not only in France, but more recently in Bulgaria, there were two main problems to be solved.

The first was the preservation of the secrecy of his mission, and the second was his need for a list of the names and addresses of all the Jews of Rome.[5] Time had taught him that these were the keys to success.

In Paris he had had an excellent list of every Jew in the city. It had been cross-indexed four ways: alphabetically, by street address, occupation, and nationality. With this *embarass de choix* he had been able, for example, to pick up in one sweep all the Polish Jews living in the city, and on another occasion, all of the

Jewish intellectuals.[6] Had it been necessary, at a moment's notice he could have deported, say, all Paris-born, fortyish, unmarried Jewish tailors who lived on streets beginning with any of the vowels of the alphabet.

But secrecy had been a problem in Paris. On the eve of the *grand rafle*, in the summer of 1942, the French police, who took on the shameful tasks of arresting the Jews on Dannecker's list, had nevertheless warned the rich Jews of the coming raid. Thousands were thus able to escape the net.[7]

In any event, Rome was another place, another time, another case. If Kappler's intelligence reports were to be credited as accurate, the Romans were even less trustworthy than the Parisians. For this reason he had brought his own men with him, those reliable veterans of the Deaths Head Corps. They would form a nucleus of his raiders, to be supported by local SS police or Wehrmacht troops—but not Italians. The rich Jews would not be warned again.

Discussing his problems with Kappler, it quickly became clear to Dannecker that the help of at least some Italians would nevertheless be required in the preliminary stages.

Kappler later stated: "I told him that first of all I had no men who could be placed at his disposition. When he asked me for topographical information, which he needed in order to organize the method of operation, I said that none of the persons in my command knew the city well enough. . . ."[8]

Kappler, since the very inception of this affair two weeks back, was unquestionably losing face at an alarming rate. If loyalty prevented him from trying to sabotage the deportation, he certainly was not going to cater to the wishes of a mere captain, especially not at the very start. Years later, when someone would suggest that at this point he should have completely disassociated himself from Dannecker's activities, Kappler would remark with some bitterness, "I told Berlin that if they didn't listen to my reports . . . they would do better by removing me from Rome and sending me into combat."[9]

Now he demonstrated this antagonism in telling Dannecker that if he wanted help for his project, he would have to do as all the other Germans did in Rome: deal with the Italians. The channel through which one normally had to go, Kappler said, was the Questura and the person to see was the liaison officer between the Italian and German police, a man by the name of Commissar Raffaele Alianello.[10] Kappler related this information "in the certainty that through the Italian police the news would be leaked. . . ."[11]

But Dannecker was unperturbed. Section IV-B-4 was used to unfriendliness from the local officials toward visiting representatives from the main office. In Paris, Dannecker could recall, it had been General von Stülpnagel who had been troublesome.[12] In Bulgaria, Kappler's counterpart, SS-Obersturmbannführer Hoffmann, had not been very enthusiastic about the deportations.[13]

A resourceful man, Dannecker did not really need or expect much cooperation from the local people. The amount that was required could always be obtained. Neither did he invite inquisitiveness. There was more to the intricate business of deportations than the layman could ever know. In Paris, for example, it had—as practiced by Dannecker—embraced the operation of a chain of nightclubs.[14] Though little related to the Final Solution, it had a great deal to do with Dannecker's well-being, which in turn could be expected to have a positive influence on his dedication to the SS.

The captain, a lawyer by profession, often welcomed the challenge posed by the men in the field, who were almost always his intellectual inferiors. Overcoming such difficulties was part of the job. Indeed in Dannecker's work—that of troubleshooting—it was the major part and a not unattractive one, though one always pretended otherwise. Only recently he had hurdled an obstacle resulting from the reluctance of a local official to turn over stateless Jews. The challenge had been met with just the right amount of exasperation as a seasoning for his pride of accomplishment. "I told him," Dannecker reported on that incident, "that it was not to be supposed that Germany found it easy to welcome so many Jews, but we were determined to resolve this problem for Europe in spite of all the difficulties."[15]

As for Kappler's recalcitrance, Dannecker said that if it were necessary to use Italian officials he would do so. To assure secrecy, he would simply seize them at the proper moment and lock them inside some nearby German compound for the duration of the action.[16]

"I could not oppose that," Kappler later said.[17]

Nor could he see any point in withholding the registry of the Jews of Rome, which had come into his possession on the day of the confiscation of the Jewish community's archives and files.

Concluding this first meeting with Kappler, Dannecker went to work. His inconspicuous hotel room in Via Po became headquarters for the operation. The men of the Waffen SS, whom he had brought to Rome, were quartered in the Collegio Militare, a military school on the left bank of the Tiber, where they awaited Dannecker's further instructions. In the meantime they were told by him to devote all of their time to a geographical study of the city, as well as to orient themselves to its habits and customs.*[18]

Dannecker's visit to the Questura met with satisfactory results. Assistant Commissar Gennaro Cappa and nineteen other men were assigned to work with him. Not to be confused with the Cappa of the race and demography office, Gennaro Cappa headed a special squad that was being formed to assist the occupiers in rounding up Romans for forced labor service. Working with Dannecker would be useful experience for him.[19]

With Cappa and his men, Dannecker was almost ready to begin. He lacked only an interpreter. The man who was found for the job, was given the additional assignment of acting as Dannecker's personal spy on the Jews of Rome. This person has never been identified. All that is known about him is that he was of

* Knowledge of the local way of life could mean the difference between success and failure of an operation. In Paris, Dannecker had committed the blunder of scheduling the great roundup at a time when the city would be celebrating its most patriotic national holiday, Bastille Day. The coincidence, which might have provoked the already resistant population to counteraction, was noted by another of Eichmann's representatives in the French capital, and the roundup was postponed for two days. In Rome, as will be seen, this lesson would not be completely learned.

Hungarian origin, and he qualified for his double role as a result of his knowledge of Italian and German and the fact that he was a Jew.[20]

VI

On Monday of that week, Giuseppe Levi Cavaglione, the Jewish partisan in the *Castelli Romani,* went with the leader of his formation, Commandante Orlando Gabbarino, to examine the terrain around Tor Paluzzo, the area of operations to which the seven-man group had been assigned.[1]

Cautiously, the two men advanced along a light slope that extended from their camp, discovering only mangy little vineyards and olive orchards. They circled back and climbed a hill that rose in the opposite direction. From the summit they looked across the brick-colored countryside which descended lazily to meet the sky above the distant sea. A mountain stood behind them. It was covered with a mantle of green and studded with tiny villages. It all appeared so decisively peaceful. The sun shown brightly, and it was hot. In the first hours of the afternoon they stripped their sweaty clothes and lay naked under the cloudless sky.

Until now Levi Cavaglione had not even seen a German, much less fight one, and he was beginning to wonder how the partisan organization operated, if it operated at all. The squad at Tor Paluzzo had almost no weapons—only the commandante was armed—and Levi Cavalione was encumbered with the self-consciousness and physical discomfort that came from his only clothes, his elegant suit and his frivolous dressy shoes.

The living conditions were far worse than he had imagined they would be. Seven men in a small hut had to sleep in nests of powdery straw. Water was almost a mile away and had to be drawn from a muddy well. It was yellowish and cloudy; happily they did not have to drink it, for wine was bountiful and delicious, but the water did not even seem fit for cooking or even washing.

Moreover, Commandante Orlando—as he was called—was a grim young man, who bore the additional, imperious title of political commissar, and he was not very comradely. To Levi Cavaglione he had said with a coldness that had the ring of truth: "When the time comes to go into combat, I'll shoot anyone of you who looks like he's going to run away."[2] Grammatically it had been addressed to all the men, but to Levi Cavaglione it seemed to have been pointed to him alone.

The other men were *simpatico,* though, he decided. One of them, a Roman, was a Jew. His name was Marco Moscati, and he and Levi Cavaglione had immediately become friends. Moscati, a tall, athletic man with a shock of long blond hair and a ready grin, had sensed Levi Cavaglione's difficulties in adjusting to the life of a guerrilla. He had taught the Genoese how to make the straw sleeping place and had given him one of his blankets. He had shown the understanding of a true friend in subtle ways, which was helping Levi Cavaglione overcome what he described at the time as "the bewilderment I feel in an atmosphere so different from where I lived until now."[3] There were those in the group who wondered whether the Genoese Jew could be trusted, or at least counted upon. In the *macchia* a man had to be suspected of everything from incompetence to treason, until he proved his worth.

But the warmth of that October afternoon sun felt good. He smoked his last two fancy cigarettes from a package of *Macedonie Extra,* and when he threw the empty away, he knew there would be only the local uncut tobacco leaves for the foreseeable future. But it did not upset him. The old life was slowly slipping away.

On the return from the scouting mission, Levi Cavaglione discovered a deposit of German arms and ammunition. He and Orlando took cover and then carefully surveyed the zone. The munitions dump lay about a hundred yards outside an encampment of Wehrmacht troops. Heavy and light machine guns, rifles, and crates of ammunition were heaped in an open field. Being of Italian manufacture, the material probably had belonged to Badoglio's regular forces, the two partisans surmised, and had fallen to the Germans after the debacle of September 8. The area was patrolled by Germans, they saw, but there appeared to be several gaps. A silent assault on the cache might succeed and go unnoticed until well after the partisans would withdraw.

The commandante decided it was worth the risk, but only under cover of darkness. They returned to their camp, noting the distance and the landmarks along the way. The raid was set for the following night.

Two of the men were sent out: Levi Cavaglione and the Roman Jew who had befriended him, Marco Moscati.

A heavy rain was falling. The ground had turned to sloppy mud, and Levi Cavaglione slipped and fell again and again, cursing his low-cut, expensive shoes. When they reached the field where the weapons were piled, they lay in wait until the sentries passed, then crept along the ground. They loaded their arms with as much as they could carry, but as they were about to steal away again, a machine gun slipped from the pile with which they had tampered. It crashed to the ground, making a clattering and frightening noise. It seemed certain that the Germans had heard the crash and would soon have them surrounded. But the sound of the torrential rain was even louder, and it had washed out the danger. Following this the men retreated with the utmost of stealth.

The downpour, a phenomenon peculiar to that place and time of year, fell with a heaviness that could beat a man to his knees. *Gioccioni*—giant raindrops, any one of which could fill a quarter of a tumbler—pelted the men. It soaked their skin, made a mop of their hair, and a malodorous sponge of clothes that had absorbed the perspiration of heat and fear. The landscape by now had turned into a muddy pool. When they tried to climb the hill that lay between the German camp and their own, they fell at every step, the heavy bundle of steel tumbling from their arms. Each time they gathered up the precious haul and then advanced another step.

The Genoese, perhaps because of his shoes, found it even harder than the Roman. After a while he could no longer get to his feet. He placed the weapons across the crook of his arms, and digging his elbows and knees into the sod, he crawled to the top.

At last they arrived at the camp. They were covered with mud. It had filled the crevices of their flesh and had coated every hair on their head. Their bodies ached. Their arms and legs were swollen and oozing blood, where the skin had been lacerated from so many falls. Nevertheless they decided to go out and raid the weapons dump again. In the end, it might save their lives.

They retraced their steps, though the going had become even harder than it had previously been. But before long they returned with a second load, and they sat with the others and counted the sum of their efforts: three Breda machine guns, six ancient, but still serviceable muskets, two rifles, and a healthy supply of ammunition.

"Even the straw hut was as drenched as my clothes," Levi Cavaglione wrote in a diary he had begun to keep, "but I felt happy and proud of myself." He was sure he had won a measure of esteem from his comrades, even the commandante. "For the first time since I got here Orlando spoke to me at length and quite affably, too."[4]

Somewhere around this time, Levi Cavaglione decided to use his childhood nickname, "Pino," as a *nom de guerre.*

VII

DESPITE THE SECRECY of Dannecker's mission in Rome, word began to leak in high places, and seep downward.

Realizing that their separate, earlier attempts to thwart a pogrom in the Holy City had failed, the three Germans most anxious to foil the plans of the SS—Consul Möllhausen, Ambassador Weizsäcker, and Embassy Secretary Kessel—undertook a somewhat more coordinated, *in extremis* action. The aims of this countermaneuver, according to Kessel, were to save the German people from having to suffer "a loss of dignity"; prevent a situation in which the Pope might be forced to break his policy of silence and protest publicly; and to help the Jews.[1] According to Möllhausen, the objectives were to avoid a disturbance in diplomatic relations between Berlin and the Holy See and to help the Jews.[2]

Since the gold episode, Kessel, representing Weizsäcker's embassy at the Holy See, and Möllhausen, tending Ambassador Rahn's embassy in neo-Fascist Rome, had been in "constant communication."[3] Now that it was again apparent that the Jews were to be taken by the SS, the two men agreed that an intervention at the Wilhelmstrasse was necessary.[4] The Foreign Office had to be alerted of the impending threat to German foreign policy.

At some point, while this new opposition was ripening, the Stadtkommandant of Rome, General Stahel, was brought back on stage. Stahel, who was at the height of his own short-lived diplomatic career at the Vatican, agreed that before any action against the Jews could be taken in his zone of command—Rome—the Foreign Office would have to give its blessing.[5]

The question now was: Who would do the intervening? Who would step up to the front lines of a battle, which if not hopeless, ran contrary to the entire thrust of the Reich? Obviously the matter called for special treatment in order to attract Berlin's attention and elicit a favorable response.

Kessel and Weizsäcker felt that Möllhausen should intervene.[6] Their own direct relationship with the Holy See, they believed, weakened their position with respect to Berlin.[7] Möllhausen's voice, which theoretically would be speaking for the interests of the Reich in all of Italy, could be expected in this case to carry more weight than theirs in Ribbentrop's ministry.

Möllhausen, who was still at a loss to explain how his earlier plotting with Kappler had gone so completely wrong, apparently concurred with the view of the others that now, with regard to the Jews, he was the most influential man in Rome. In any event, he decided to act on his own initiative, that is, without first consulting Rahn or anyone else outside of Rome.[8] Literally and figuratively a young Turk, Möllhausen devised an intervention scheme, which would provoke an unprecedented diplomatic exchange and perhaps the most startling one in the history of the Third Reich.

Bearing in mind his talks with General Stahel, Kappler, and Field Marshal Kesselring, Möllhausen translated those scenes into the skeletal language of memoranda, in such a way that, when read at the other end of the diplomatic line, they would come alive again.

The first act was set to paper, encoded, and at about noon of October 6, telegraphed to the personal attention of von Ribbentrop. It was marked "very very urgent!" (*supercitissime!*)—a classification which did not exist, the highest being "very urgent" (*citissime*). Apart from the content of the message, such eagerness alone was guaranteed to raise an eyebrow in Berlin.

The telegram arrived at the Wilhelmstrasse precisely at 1:30

P.M. It was unscrambled, typed, with at least three carbon copies, properly stamped, and recorded. It was then circulated to the departments concerned. It read:

> Rome, 6 October 1943. Received: 6 October 1943, 1330 hours. No. 192 from 10/6. *Very very urgent!* For Herrn Reichsminister personally. Obersturmbannführer Kappler has received orders from Berlin to seize the eight thousand Jews resident in Rome and transport them to Northern Italy,* where they are to be liquidated [*wo sie liquidiert werden sollen*]. Commandant of Rome General Stahel informs me he will permit this action only on approval of the Herrn Reichsminister for Foreign Affairs. In my personal opinion it would be better business to employ the Jews for fortification work, as was done in Tunis, and, together with Kappler, I will propose this to Field Marshal Kesselring. Please advise. Möllhausen.**[9]

Thrown through the air like a Roman spear, the intervention went deep and was irreversible now. News of what Möllhausen had done could no more be contained than a full-term baby, at least from German diplomatic and military circles in the city.[10] The Vatican too was informed by Weizsäcker of Möllhausen's intervention; it was good news of course, but from that moment on the highest authorities of the Church, including Pope Pius XII, knew beyond any doubt that the Germans were planning to deport the Jews of Rome.[11]

About twenty hours later, Möllhausen sent in the second act, which was received in Berlin at 10:05 A.M. on the 7th:

> No. 201 from 10/7. *Very very urgent!* For Herrn Reichsminister personally. In connection with telegram of the 6th, no. 192. Field Marshal Kesselring has asked Obersturmbannführer Kappler to postpone planned

* The figure "8,000" and that the Jews were to be sent to "Northern Italy" were inconsequential errors apparently originating from assumptions or misunderstood oral communications.

** Why Möllhausen said he was about to propose that which had already taken place ten days earlier has never been learned. In a letter to the author dated January 16, 1968, Möllhausen himself cannot explain this discrepancy, although he suggested that his meeting with Kappler and then with Kesselring may not have occurred until the 6th. This, however, according to evidence independent of Möllhausen, and his own earlier testimony, all of which has been documented above, is virtually impossible. The most plausible explanation is that Möllhausen was simply transmitting on the 6th what he neglected to do on the 26th of the previous month, having thought then that the matter had been disposed of.

Judenaktion for the present time. If however it is necessary that something be done, he would prefer to utilize the able-bodied Roman Jews in fortification work near here. Möllhausen.[12]

With this, Möllhausen's part came to an end. It corresponded closely enough to the facts of the near past to stand any test of its veracity. He had passed on the story to the Wilhelmstrasse, he later said, "with the conviction that I was giving good news—above all because all responsibility had been assumed by Kesselring, and the Minister of Foreign Affairs would have nothing to fear . . ."[13] But the drama was far from over. The conclusions were yet to be written in Berlin.

Ribbentrop, informed of Möllhausen's cables from Rome, regarded them as anything but "good news." Indeed, he was furious, but for reasons that had almost nothing to do with either the content of the messages or the set of complexities they implied. What disturbed the Nazi Foreign Minister most was that for the first time someone in his worldwide organization, speaking in reference to the Jewish question, had used the word "liquidate" in an official document. Moreover, this Möllhausen had set the forbidden combination of letters of the alphabet to paper in a telegram addressed *personally* to Ribbentrop himself.[14]

The Foreign Minister demanded that Ambassador Rahn be summoned at once. A telephone call was put through to Rahn, who was at Mussolini's headquarters in northern Italy. Asked to explain this irregularity, the ambassador told Ribbentrop that he knew nothing of Möllhausen's intervention, but he would certainly look into the affair, which he agreed was most regrettable.

Rahn then called Möllhausen to account for his strange behavior. Had he actually used *liquidate*? "I confirmed," Möllhausen later stated, "to have expressly included in the telegram the word contained in the orders imparted to Kappler, precisely because it was this word that had upset me and compelled me to intervene decisively."[15] This explanation notwithstanding, Rahn told Möllhausen to report in person at his headquarters in the north. He wanted a full report on the machinations taking place in Rome.[16]

In the meantime, Himmler's command in the Nazi capital had learned of Möllhausen's cables and begun making inquiries at the Foreign Office. The SS, presumably Eichmann most of all, wanted to know the meaning of this interference in their domain. What was Ribbentrop up to? Himmler let it be known that he could only look upon such overstepping of authority with distrust.[17]

Ribbentrop was embarrassed.[18] He had not the slightest objection to the work of the SS in the area of the Jewish question. The Foreign Office, in which he had established the Inland II-A section (SS/Jews) for the purpose of cooperating in the Final Solution project, had always sought to be helpful, asking only that it be represented when Himmler's organization operated abroad. Least of all did he want to arouse the Reichsführer's enmity. The man had been decent to him, most recently in the Luther affair.* Now, as a result of his inexperienced man in Rome, it appeared as if the Wilhelmstrasse were trying to infringe upon the plans of the Kurfurstenstrasse.

To extricate himself from this disturbance, Ribbentrop gave instructions to assuage the hurt feelings of the SS. Then, speaking by telephone to a senior staff man in his own Büro RAM (Office of the Reich Foreign Minister), he ordered that Rahn and Möllhausen be notified "not to interfere in any way in this affair . . ." and that the latter should be so directed in unequivocal terms.[20]

The orders pulsed along the lines of interoffice communications, coming to a momentary halt on the desk of the chief of Inland II-A, von Thadden, who promptly dispatched a "very urgent!—priority!" telegram addressed to Consul Möllhausen *persönlich*:

> On the basis of the Führer's instructions, the 8,000 Jews resident in Rome are to be transported to Mauthausen as hostages.** The RAM

* In this case, one of Ribbentrop's senior officers, Martin Luther, who was scheming for his chief's post, secretly wrote to Himmler that the Foreign Minister was insane. Himmler without hesitation reported the incident to Ribbentrop, and Luther was sent off to a concentration camp, from which he never returned.[19]

** Mauthausen was a concentration camp in Austria. The notion of Jews requests you not to interfere in any way in this affair and that you leave it to the SS. Please inform Rahn.[21]

A copy of this message was sent to Büro RAM, which seemingly found it unsatisfactory, for Thadden on the same day sent out a second telegram to their troublesome man in Rome. This one was more explicit; it brought the matter to a close. It read:

The Herr Reichsminister for Foreign Affairs insists that you keep out of all questions concerning Jews. Such questions, in accordance with an agreement between the Foreign Office and the RSHA, are within the exclusive competence of the SS and any further interference in these questions could cause serious difficulties for the Minister of Foreign Affairs.[22]

Möllhausen, who until now believed he was properly carrying out the functions of his office, got the point. He passed it along to Weizsäcker's embassy, which in turn enlightened the Vatican.[23] If the Jews of Rome were to be saved, an even greater effort would have to be made. There were still Germans and Churchmen in Rome who would not—in view of the manifold repercussions the deportations would unleash—shrink from this task.

VIII

NONE OF THE mounting secrets being collected and traded like so many precious postage stamps by the various authorities in Rome was known in the ghetto, of course. Not yet. But other disconcerting pieces of news were accumulating, swelling the

---

being sent there as "hostages" seems to have come from Ribbentrop's conversation with Büro RAM. In any event, this information was inaccurate.

festering fears of even the most ignorant Jews. These were sores that had to be salved.

Radio London all week long had been broadcasting information coming from Stockholm of a roundup of the Jews of Denmark, launched by the Gestapo on the eve of the Jewish new year.[1] By a coincidence Field Marshal Kesselring at the same time had issued a new ordinance in Rome against listening to the "enemy radio" on penalty of fine or imprisonment.[2] Nevertheless the broadcasts were heard by Jews in Rome,[3] and there could be little doubt that this latest news was not Allied propaganda, but from the neutral voice of Sweden.

First reports indicated that the raid on the Danish Jews was being carried out irrespective of age, sex, or state of health. Jewish property had been confiscated. Many Jews were fleeing in rowboats and fishing smacks, attempting to cross the narrow straits separating Denmark and Sweden at the port of Helsingör and other points along the Sund. Among the 3,000 Jewish refugees who had thus far succeeded in reaching Sweden, it was stated in Stockholm, was Niels Bohr, the Nobel physicist.[4]

About 1,600 Danish Jews, the reports continued, including infants and elderly persons—among them Denmark's oldest citizen, a 101-year-old woman—were taken in the first wave of arrests. They were being transported by ship and rail to concentration camps in Poland, Stockholm said.[5]

Early in the week the Swedish Foreign Office issued the following statement, which was also repeatedly broadcast by the BBC Italian-language service beamed at Italy:

> For some days it had been known in Stockholm that measures were being prepared against the Danish Jews similar to those already taken in Norway and other occupied countries. On the instruction of the Swedish government, the Swedish Minister in Berlin informed the German government on October 1, that such measures would have serious repercussions in Sweden and also offered, on behalf of the Swedish government, to give sanctuary to all Danish Jews.[6]

Joining the protest, as far as was known at this time, were the people of Sweden, the Danes themselves, who had never in their entire history discriminated against Jews, and all Danish

Lutheran churches. A strong reaction was also reported in Finland. The Wilhelmstrasse on October 5, issued a communique declaring that it had "nothing to say."[7]

One Jew who heard these broadcasts in Rome, which, he noted, also included comments on Nazi persecutions in other parts of occupied Europe, later said that they were scarcely noticed. "In general," he stated, "one continued the everyday way of life, adapting it only to the conditions of a general nature being imposed on the Roman population as a whole." The leaders of Roman Jewry, he said, "had decided to simply await the development of events."

This commentator, Michael Tagliacozzo, an Italian historian of Roman Jewish background, observed that the Jewish leaders as well as the faithful continued to nurture the widespread opinion that the Germans were "men of honor." As for the news reaching Rome about atrocious Nazi behavior abroad, "one found consolation in considering that the measures, if true, were adopted only against the so-called '*Ostjuden*,' the Jews of Eastern Europe."[8] In Rome, even the Jewish Danes, French, Norwegians, Dutch, Belgians, Luxembourgers, and ironically, the German Jewish coiners of that suicidal, intraracist word, were *Ostjuden*.

But if consolation could be found, there were always more reasons to look for it and renew it. The sum of the events of the first four weeks of the occupation could be seen in the eyes of the general population, and felt like the hand of winter. One journalist in Rome wrote at the time:

> The people's dominating reaction is fear. . . . This impression is deepened by hundreds of rumors about the coming persecutions, about the SS having three thousand men in Rome already, and so forth. The population is half crazy: young men and their families look desperately for hiding places, get them, then look for better ones . . . convents and seminaries have become the most "sought after" hideouts. Another famous one is the Lunatic Asylum: scores of people have entered and have filled it to the bursting point. Rome never had so many madmen.[9]

More and more the people looked to their leaders. In the same way the Catholic Romans were being pacified by an anxious

Church, the Jewish faithful were stroked and coddled too. This was done not so much with the well-pronounced words of the prominent Jews, although whoever heard them could not fail to be impressed. Words were for the leaders themselves, who wished more than anyone else they were true. But it was their deeds that denied all danger, including the war itself. Their composure, their polished shoes and manicures, the stiff white collars Almansi liked to wear, the look of confidence in Foà's eye, were mighty, too.

Nevertheless, by now almost all the prominent and educated Jews of Rome had almost imperceptibly disappeared from their homes. To be sure, these men of standing continued to count on nothing happening. It was unthinkable that the society in which they had invested their body and soul could cease entirely to exist. Yet they saw no harm in vacating their known address, especially since many of them were aware that the lists of Jews were now possessed by the Germans.[10]

Leading this silent exodus was President Almansi. In the first week of October, without calling any attention to himself, he took refuge in an apartment in Via Tagliamento, a street in the quiet Salario district.[11]

Unfortunately, these changes in residence, which usually meant moving to an empty apartment, the home of a non-Jewish friend, a religious sanctuary, or leaving the city, required almost total secrecy to have any meaning at all. Thus the ghetto-Trastevere Jews, who were the most dependent on the leadership and lacked the financial means and the knowledge to make such an exit, were largely uninformed of this immensely important development taking place in the upper levels of the community.[12] Far from being a cue, this change meant nothing to the poorer Jewish majority. The upper level Jews did not live in the Jewish quarter. Hence their flight was undetectable to the others. Theirs in fact was the disappearance of the already invisible.

At this point—despite their 5,000-year-old spiritual bonds—the social differences between the upper and lower layers of the Jewish community entered into direct and irreconcilable conflict. While it was in the best interests of the prominent Jews to do as much as possible to hold together the old society, it was a matter of life and death to the poor majority to dismantle the community and disband it precipitously. In controlling the community institutions, however, the leaders guaranteed that their interests would prevail. The majority, burdened with a system—whatever its benevolent intentions—that engendered dependency and ignorance could not even become aware of its plight, much less act on it.

As a consequence, the world of the ghetto Jew had become a place where up was down. These have-nothing Jews had the least stake in the establishment so dear to the leaders. They therefore constituted the most mobile subgroup in the community, having the least to lose in fleeing. Yet it was they who now became most riveted to their places. Unable to perceive the flight of the elders, their view of things tended only to strengthen the sense of security. The more fears welled within them, the more foolish such thoughts appeared. From the windows of their crowded flats and in the streets and the shops of the ghetto, they were daily confronted with the changelessness of their socially equal neighbors, who in the same way confronted them. Everything was in place, as it had always been, and it seemed, would forever be. Kept from a view of the real world, they were seeing nothing else but themselves in a mirror, within a mirror, within a mirror.

Reinforcing this illusion was the tenacious, unshakable faith in the Authorities professed by President Foà. He was by now one of the few leaders who persisted in remaining in his own home, still rejecting the idea of hiding.[13] His daily business-as-usual appearances at the community offices was a tonic to all who watched him come and go—a tonic, but deadly poison. That much of the staff, who had come face to face with the SS, had quit by now and had fled in fear was hardly known to anyone, and in fact, was kept secret.[14] Up there, on the second floor of the temple, Foà and his remaining colleagues labored at that which had become the order of the day: spreading a religion of trust in the fundamental goodness of the Old Order.

Another portentious incident took place that week, but it slipped pass the Jews like an agile thief.

On the morning of October 7 the Germans surrounded the barracks and armories of the Rome Carabinieri and began rounding up these forces, which had remained loyal to the King. More than 1,500 of the local force of 6,500 men were captured throughout the city either in their quarters or in flight. They were taken off in trucks and forced to board a train of freight cars. They were deported to the north, eventually to Germany.[15]

All of Rome silently lamented the fate of the Carabinieri, but scarcely anyone, least of all the Jewish leaders, saw any connection between the roundup and deportation of the King's forces and themselves. Always, even for the Jews, it was one's neighbor or some other group for whom the peril seemed greatest. In this case the Jews, whom the racial laws had excluded from service in any of the armed forces, felt most distant of all.

Yet there was a connection. A dangerous precedent had been set, making any future deportation from Rome appear—in the absence of organized protest—one large measure easier than before.* This connection was tightened, if only by coincidence, when a woman was killed by an Italian Fascist during the roundup of the Carabinieri. She was shot while resisting a search of her home, where her son, falsely suspected of being a member of the force, was in hiding from labor service. Her name, Rosa Guarnieri Calò Carducci, indicated that somewhere in her family, there was, or had been, a Jew.[17]

On Saturday, the fifth Sabbath of the occupation, the situation took a naked plunge which no Jew in Rome could fail to note. It was the Day of Atonement, *il Giorno del Kippur,* the holiest in the Jewish year. While the Jews were at prayer, the Germans, by design or by chance, chose this sacred moment to sting the community again. In a sudden stroke several Jews in

* At the same time the incident helped to strengthen the armed Resistance in Rome in real terms beyond its obvious anti-Fascist propaganda value. Many of the surviving Carabinieri had escaped with their weapons and now entered the Underground. Trained and experienced in warfare and police work, they were an important asset there and distinguished themselves in the fight against the occupiers.[16]

the city were arrested, for unannounced reasons.[18] Word rushed through the ranks of the faithful, chilling them. It was thought that this might be the beginning of a new and more sinister persecution than the earlier outrages. Was it, some asked, the start of an all-out physical assault on the Jews of Rome?[19]

The leaders went among the flock to quell and heal the unrest. The Roman Jewish writer Debenedetti recorded that to deal with this new alarm "reassuring news was circulated immediately (and responsible elements of the Community, doubtless with good intentions, abetted its dissemination)." Those arrested, went the story that was spread, "were exceptional and special cases." Acting on the assumption that the detained Jews had been taken on suspicion of being in the Resistance, it was said that they were "all persons already known for anti-Fascist activities." The Germans had arrested them "as individuals and not because of their race."[20]

One had to say, the Jews were told by their prominent coreligionists, "the Germans continued to show themselves discreet, almost human." And it had also to be borne in mind that: "With their overwhelming power, with their absolute authority, they could have done much worse. . . . No, there was no particular reason to distrust them, to take these things so seriously."[21]

The next day President Almansi, who without showing it was becoming less sanguine than Foà, closed the Lungotevere Sanzio offices of the union. Until now it had functioned at full strength. But Almansi, and his fellow councilors, decided it would be wiser to operate "clandestinely" for now.[22] Unfortunately, the reasons given were quite logical, and no one could misconstrue them as signs of any impending danger. It was simply explained that because of the war situation, which prevented regular postal and telegraphic communication with the Jewish communities outside of Rome, the union had been rendered temporarily incapacitated. Further, Almansi wanted to avoid the fate to which Foà's offices had been subjected. With the help of his employees, the union president had begun to secretly remove the organization's archives and liquid assets.[23]

The major part of the union's funds, however, had already

been secured. They had been invested in the Axis war economy in the form of bonds.[24] These were on deposit at the Cassa di Risparmio, one of Italy's largest savings banks. The dividends on the union's holdings were to fall due November 17. Almansi now instructed the bank not to renew them, but to collect both interest and principal.[25]

Whatever might have been Almansi's loss of faith in the Fascist system, his cashing in of the union's debentures was not in any way a form of protest.* It was dictated of necessity. Most of the union's income—especially contributions from the communities, interest on inheritances, and rents from real estate—had been cut off in the same way as the postal and telegraph services. Part of the bond money was needed to pay the salaries of the union's employees, the maintenance costs of its headquarters in Rome, and local taxes. In spite of the temporary closure of the offices, these payments had to be kept up, according to Almansi, "in order to safeguard the patrimony of the organization."[27] The institution had to be protected and cared for, or else it might die. This eventuality forestalled, Almansi reorganized the union on a temporary emergency basis so that it could continue to function—within its sharply reduced range of possibilities—by other means.

By now the two Jewish officials responsible for DELASEM, Renzo Levi and Settimio Sorani, had also gone underground. They too had removed vital documents and closed the doors of the refugee agency, which was just down the street from the union. Sorani had first organized the refugees secretly quartered around the city, in order that they could continue to be provided with DELASEM's services. Now numbering more than 400, the foreign Jews in Sorani's care were divided into small groups. A leader was appointed from among each unit to maintain communications with the organization. The contact person was found in an extremely cooperative Capuchin monk named Padre Benedetto de Bourg d'Iré, who had been the secretary to the Archbishop of Genoa.[28] Both clergymen had long

* The money from these holdings was not withdrawn. It remained with the bank, converted into four separate savings accounts.[26]

been engaged in unsung activities to help the Jews, often at some risk to themselves.

Now that Almansi had joined Levi and Sorani in having gone into hiding, he apparently began to draw closer to them. They were constantly in touch with one another, Almansi later reported. "The three," said the union president, "in order to deal with matters relevant to carrying out their different mandates, would meet in the late hours of the evening at different places in the city, which had been designated from time to time."[29] Nevertheless, according to Sorani, Almansi continued to persist in his "one defect"—his belief in the tenet that the Jews of Rome were really invulnerable.[30]

This "defect," of course, was only one side of the wholly defective penny, the other being the notion that the lives and safety of the city's Jews were the responsibility of higher authorities, from Foà and Almansi to the Church and State. On one or the other face of this coin lay the hopes of all the Jewish leaders in Rome, who differed only on how best to make the dream come true. It bore the wish to emerge from these trials unscathed into the world of yesterday's peace. All the worry, the heartache, and the dangers to one's personal safety were for this.

IX

ON THE MORNING of the 13th the staff at the offices of the community looked out of the second floor windows on a most unusual sight. Downstairs, in the middle of Lungotevere Cenci stood two full-size railway freight cars from the German national railroad. They had been rolled up on the tracks of the Circolare Nera trolley line and now were resting at the front door of the temple.

Moments later an employee of the shipping company Otto and Rosoni entered the offices, and speaking to Rosina Sorani, announced that he had come for the books and everything else in the two libraries. He had instructions to remove them, he said.[1]

The four appeals Foà and Almansi had sent to bureaus and departments of the neo-Fascist government had had no effect, both presidents later lamented. "Not one of these Authorities," Foà would painfully conclude, "budged an inch or even acknowledged receipt of [the letters]. . . ."*[2]

Signorina Sorani, who had been told not to surrender the key to the libraries, feigned not to know what the shipper was talking about and called his company for an explanation, which she promptly received. A German officer, she was further informed, would soon arrive at the temple to supervise the shipment. But the day passed without the appearance of this man, and nothing happened.[4]

During the wait the eternal subject of the gold and silver religious articles arose again. It seemed certain that these too would soon be lost to the occupiers, now that the attempts to save the books had failed. Foà and his aides spent long hours thinking of where these items might be safely concealed on the premises until a permanent secret place could be found. Someone put forward the idea of hiding them in the tank of holy waters that supplied the temple's *mikvà*, or ritual baths. A trusted artisan was called in, and the project was studied to see

* The new government at this time was occupying itself with other problems regarding its Jews. Apart from the cooperation being given Captain Dannecker, Buffarini-Guidi's Ministry of Interior, in which the Jewish leaders had invested so much hope, was preparing new anti-Jewish decrees, far more severe than the 1938 legislation. In spite of this, however, the minister was under attack in Berlin as a "friend of the Jews" by Giovanni Preziosi, who had been kept out of the government. Advocating a "whole solution" to the Jewish question in Italy, Preziosi rapidly gained the support of Hitler and Goebbels, and Buffarini was placed under suspicion. Preziosi some months later would enter the neo-Fascist regime as chief of a newly created anti-Jewish bureau and be given the title "Inspector General of the Race."[3]

how the tank might be adapted as a fit receptacle for the sacred objects.[5]

At eight thirty the following morning, the Germans, their armed escorts, and a team of moving men finally arrived for the books. Work was begun at once, the *facchini* loading the railway cars, and the Germans directing. The Einsatzstab bibliophiles took great pains to prevent any harm befalling the precious material. The books were placed flat side down on the bed of the freight cars like pieces in a jigsaw puzzle. In this way layers were formed and between them sheets of corrugated paper cushioned the books for the long journey to Germany.[6] Nevertheless some of the *facchini*, who either sought to deprive the Germans of some of the booty or simply wanted to break up the heavy work with a diversion, were surreptitiously throwing books away. They hurled them from the second- and third-story windows at a group of workers who had gathered at the side of the temple that faced the Theater of Marcellus. Some of these priceless works were later seen among the ruins of the Roman theater, ripped to shreds.[7]

While the libraries were being emptied, the workman who was helping Foà conceal the temple's *argenterie* returned to complete the job. Unnoticed by the Germans, who were occupied with the books, he and his apprentice slipped into the *mikvà* and drained the tank of its holy waters. In the meantime Foà, the synagogue's porter, and two other aides gathered the items from the Treasury, while Rosina Sorani and the porter's wife stood guard. The real danger that the Germans might burst in at any moment pushed the conspirators hard. But the tense operation was completed swiftly and without incident.*[8]

* This preoccupation with the *argenterie* continued throughout the occupation. Pieces were eventually added to those in the ritual baths, buried in gardens, and hidden in homes all over Rome. In November, 1943, learning of an imminent decision by the Fascists to appropriate all Jewish wealth, Foà arranged for the removal of seven large cases of gold and silver articles and two trunkfuls of vestments and tapestries which had been deposited in the Banco di Napoli. This material was hidden in a warehouse. Not one of these religious objects was discovered by the Germans. "Thus," Foà was to write proudly, "with the help of God, they were saved, kept intact for the Sacred Cult. . . ."[9]

The staff then returned to join the others in the second floor offices who were looking on glumly and helplessly as the removal work continued.

Someone, watching the street below, made note of the markings and serial numbers stenciled on the freight cars, which indicated that they came from the rail yards of Munich.[10] Perhaps, it was thought, this information might lead to the recovery of the stolen goods.

Rosina Sorani was pressed into service by the Germans and required to assist in the supervision of the movers. The main library was emptied entirely, except for a few books that had been in Chief Rabbi Zolli's study. The contents of the Rabbinical College library was only partially taken, although the Germans said they were not quite sure when, but they would return for the balance. When the work was finished, sometime that afternoon, one of the Nazi officers thanked Signorina Sorani. He said she had been *brava.* She said later that day: "I replied that I would have been very willing to have been something less than *brava.*"[11]

The two freight cars were loaded to capacity. They were hooked to a third, motorized car and hauled away on the tram tracks, coursing the bank of the Tiber.

President Foà, having suffered this new mortification in utter impotence, was wholly dispirited, exasperated, outwitted, sour, disgusted, and if only temporarily, run aground. To him it seemed everyone in the community felt as he did.

It had become a "nightmare," he said a few weeks subsequently, adding:

> By now the continuous presence of German officers, their armed escorts, and their invariable accompaniment of demands and repetitious ultimatums, was spreading always more oppressively in the offices of the Community; and from those offices it overflowed into the midst of the entire Jewish population in Rome.
>
> All the Roman Israelites by now felt themselves abandoned, without any defense and at the mercy of an enemy deprived of both scruples and compassion. . . ."[12]

Yet, according to Foà, even now all hope was not lost. The Jews of Rome, he went on:

> in their innocent hearts, supported by the high sense of civility, which they derived from having been born and raised in this beautiful country, mother of the morality and law given by eternal Rome to the entire world, refused to believe that Hitler's gangsters would dare to repeat the incredible slaughter which had already victimized their brothers in Poland and Germany, in Holland and Belgium.[13]

Lest anyone think that Ugo Foà did not believe hardest of all, it was now allowed to be known that the raid on the community's books was no cause for alarm.[14] The sacking of the libraries had been witnessed by hundreds of Jews, and the old questions began at once to reappear, which in turn brought out the community's defenders, who engulfed every haunting fear omnivorously.

For this, the quilt of the now customary replies was dragged out again, and a new patch was found and sewn on: A crime against books, it was asserted, is not a crime against people.[15] To the ghetto Jews, many of whom had never been taught to read at all, this seemed to make sense.

During the day it became known that several hours earlier the King's government, from its provisional seat of command behind Allied lines, had declared war on Germany. The United States, Britain, and the Soviet Union had recognized Italy as a cobelligerent.

In Rome the news was greeted silently, without emotion.[16] Though reality edged out in greater relief, the declaration of war changed nothing. The King might speak for the south; the Duce, perhaps, had some say in the north, but the Germans were the rulers of Rome. Here, only an individual could declare war, his own. If he did, there would be an army in which to fight. The times were such that this one decision separated every man in Rome from his chance to be free.

X

SS-HAUPTSTURMFÜHRER THEODOR DANNECKER held another meeting with Kappler that week. He had been in Rome less than a fortnight, but he was able to boast, according to Kappler, "that he was in possession of all the information that he needed."[1]

It had not been easy. The problem of the lists, for example, had been a particularly difficult one to solve. Dannecker, unsatisfied with the community files alone, had had to find and search other sources.* From these he had compiled the most comprehensive directory of Jews in the city. A study of their addresses, made with the assistance of the Roman Fascists who had been assigned to him, revealed the distribution of Jewish residences in the city and thus the problems involved in the roundup.

It had immediately become clear that there were three general characteristics of geographical Jewry in Rome: the concentration-camp-like ghetto; the heavy density of Jews among the non-Jewish population of Trastevere; and the apparently random spread of Jews throughout the remainder of the city.

* They were the Office of Demography and Race; the local branches of the Fascist party; and city's birth records. None of these files was as accurate or as current as the community's. Dannecker compared them with the lists he had, and apparently they also yielded several additional names. Which one or more of these secondary sources were consulted by Dannecker is unknown, although, as will be seen, there is evidence indicating that the birth records office was among those searched. Another source was the police file on the Roman Jews. These, however, had been rendered at least partially worthless by some uncooperative officials who had disorganized and confounded their records to hinder the Germans.[2]

Closer examination of this latter feature showed that these Jews were not thinly or evenly distributed at all, but were clustered at the ends of imaginary spokes radiating in every direction from the ghetto-Trastevere hub. Most of these lines passed through one or another entrance of the Aurelian walls—especially Porta S. Paolo in the south, Porta S. Giovanni in the southeast, Porta Maggiore to the east, Porta Pia to the northeast, and Porta del Popolo in the north. Not very far beyond, or just inside, these limits of the center of the city, and also in the Trionfale and Prati districts adjacent the sloping north wall of the Vatican, lay the clusters of Jewish homes—unaware of the convenient pattern they formed.

With this knowledge, Dannecker had been able to divide a street map of the city, according to the exigencies of his plan. On his map the traditional municipal divisions of the twenty-two *rioni* and the eighteen *quartieri* were struck down and redrawn. Rome could now be viewed through the grid of twenty-six *Judenaktionsbezirken*, or Jewish "action precincts."[3]

Like the framers of election districts, he had attempted, as far as possible, to place an equal representation of a selected population within any given precinct. The purpose of this was to balance the work among the men who would actually do the rounding up, a factor, experience taught, which helped to stabilize the entire operation. Where the zoning of equal representation could not be effected—as in the ghetto and parts of Trastevere—the common denominator was to be achieved by increasing the number of men who would operate in the high density zone.

In any unpopular police action—as all deportations had to be regarded—a man under orders to commit acts he would normally condemn would usually perform reliably and efficiently as long as he thought he did not have the worst or the most burdensome job. Effectiveness was further improved proportionately with the reduction and simplification of the task each man had to perform. These were the axioms of Dannecker's trade, but they had been borrowed from the universal laws of the assembly line.

Dannecker, in his meeting with Kappler, had not come to report these details, however, although he could not resist vaunting some of his abilities at problem-solving.

It was about the little things, which no outsider ever thought of, he seemed proudest of all. One did not just go out and round up thousands of people; there was complex planning involved, and even the smallest detail was Dannecker's concern. He wanted Kappler to know this.

"He showed me a little box that contained many envelopes," Kappler recalled some time afterward.[4] While Kappler was wondering what was inside and what the young captain was getting at, Dannecker explained that every one of the twenty-six zones would be assigned a police squad, each of which would have "a well-defined function to perform in previously specified streets and houses."[5]

Dannecker then picked up the box and withdrew an envelope at random. He opened it and showed its contents to Kappler, "in order to demonstrate the perfection of his organization to me," thought the latter.[6]

The name and address of every Jewish home had been entered on an individual piece of paper. These papers had all been folded neatly and put into an equal number of envelopes, presumably for ease in handling. From this, typewritten lists were compiled according to the twenty-six zones. Selected members of each police group would carry the list of Jews in their zone, and the entire arresting squad would call at the door of every addressee.[7]

It was the shotgun method. There were ways, beyond secrecy and surprise, to increase the rate of capture, such as striking when people were most likely to be at home and in the most defenseless posture—during the hours of sleep. But no one could guess how many Jews would be caught when the Germans arrived, how many apartments had already been abandoned, or how many persons would escape during the action.*

* There is no record of Dannecker or anyone else estimating the number of Jews expected to be taken in the roundup. Considering the size of the community and the problems Dannecker had to deal with, however, his mission would be regarded as a success if he could fill one train. Fuel limits imposed by the war determined a train's capacity, the longest generally being twenty

Upon arrival at the door of the Jewish home, a message from the Third Reich would be handed to whoever answered. This had already been drafted and mimeographed on paper rectangles the size and shape of a postcard. It consisted of a set of six instructions ordering the recipient to prepare to depart at once "to be transferred."[8]

The police teams would then have the task of loading the Jews into trucks and delivering them to a central point. It would not be possible to go directly to the train station. For one thing, the pressures of the war precluded holding a train waiting until the roundup would be completed, and trying to synchronize the two coordinates was very difficult and unnecessary. Instead, the Jews would be held in wait for the train. Marshaling those taken in the roundup at some staging place was also necessary in order to comb the group of any human errors on the part of the arresting squads. Human errors were what made inhuman acts even more inhuman, and thus, men believed, had to be minimized. One had to make an effort, above all in Western countries, to be sure that everyone deported was in fact a Jew, as defined under German law. Aside from the "injustice" of deporting a non-Jew, such mistakes, particularly in so sensitive a city as Rome, could be harmful to foreign policy.[9]

Drawing on his Paris experience, where 6,900 Jews who had been caught in the roundup had been coralled in the Velodrome d'Hiver sports arena, Dannecker had looked for a similar enclosure in Rome. He decided on the Collegio Militare, the huge military school in Via Lungara, where his Waffen SS men had been quartered. The prisoners would be kept there until the train would be ready. Then, if all went well for Dannecker, the deportation of the Jews of Rome would take place. Their destination: Auschwitz. Purpose: *Sonderbehandlung*—special treatment.

---

cars, or about the length required to transport 1,000 passengers. In Paris, many months of negotiations had yielded less than 10 percent of the city's Jews. A full trainload of Roman Jews would duplicate that ratio in a single day's work.

Admittedly Dannecker would not be able to do as much as was possible in Rome. The Italians who had worked with him, notably Gennaro Cappa and his men, had been taken into custody, ordered held until completion of the action. But the presumed untrustworthiness of the Italian police was a problem that could never be fully overcome and thus imposed limits on the operation. Moreover, since Rome was an "open city," some token concessions might have to be made to the diplomats and military men who were saddled with having to defend the misnomer.[10] Then, the Vatican's rights would have to be respected. Since the inviolability of the territories and properties of the Holy See had been guaranteed by Hitler himself, the Jews known by Dannecker to be hiding in the religious sanctuaries could not be taken. Under this agreement, if a Jew on Dannecker's list could put a foot in Saint Peter's Square or run into the doorway of, say, the Church of Saint Mary Major, the Gestapo would have to retreat. In spite of these handicaps, or perhaps because of them, Dannecker was nonetheless proud of what he had accomplished in the planning stages. The results of the action would, he had every reason to believe, prove worthwhile.

Kappler, however, seems to have been somewhat skeptical. He was not sure the younger man had thought of every contingency. The generally antagonistic attitude of the Romans was a security problem not only the Gestapo in Rome but also the Wehrmacht commands of the occupation were treating with growing solicitude.[11] In the past few days an increase in the number of acts of sabotage had been noted. This was an indicator of the developing strength of the Resistance movement. No one could predict how the people of Rome would react to the *razzia*—a factor that did not appear to have been fully appreciated by Dannecker. Kappler was taken with the observation that Dannecker's squads, judging from the addresses in a few of the envelopes he had examined, would have to "move from one end of the city to the other."[12] To a security expert such as Kappler, it was clear that this was a flaw. If the deportation were going to be resisted in some way, the German squads, passing through hostile streets, could be easily outnumbered and overwhelmed. They would become ready targets for ambush or encirclement.

Here was where Kappler's assistance was needed, Dannecker felt. He had not yet secured the personnel for his roundup squads, and the forty-four Waffen SS men he had brought with him were hardly enough. Kappler had already said he could not spare any of his own men, and even if he were able to, their number was not sufficient. The additional manpower would have to come from the Wehrmacht.

This fact had forced Dannecker into a weakness. He now had to ask Kappler, an opponent of the deportation, to formally request troops from the commands of either Field Marshal Kesselring or General Stahel, both of whom had also been recorded as looking with a quantity of disfavor on Dannecker's business in Rome. If the Wehrmacht men would persist in their opposition, a thoroughgoing morass would rapidly develop, which only an order from the Führer himself could undo—and not necessarily in Dannecker's favor.

The young captain, having no better alternative, simply asked Kappler to use his good offices. Kappler, mindful of Dannecker's directives from Berlin, could find no reason to involve himself at this late date in a struggle against superior orders. Obviously his advice and his best thinking on the matter had been rejected. It was Dannecker and not he who would be responsible for deporting the Jews of Rome. That much was on the record. Routinely, a request for troops at the strength of a minimum of one motorized battalion—Kappler's original estimate—was put through. It went via the Gestapo command in Via Tasso to General Stahel's office across the street in the Villa Wolkonsky.[13]

At the other end it immediately created a problem at the lower levels of command. A check by the Stadtkommandant's headquarters of the details assigned to its police disclosed that a battalion-size force was not available. At least three companies of men would be needed to form a battalion. But only two—Company 3 of the 20th SS-Police Regiment and Company 11 of the 12th SS-Police Regiment*—could be spared. Lacking one-

* All police were part of the SS organization. But in Rome, being a "war territory," the entire complex of German armed force was under Kesselring's

third of the required minimum force, the deportation action would be in jeopardy. Even at battalion strength, Dannecker would not have enough personnel to form squads larger than six men and in many instances only two or three.

Someone in General Stahel's office, however, discovered that the 3rd Commando unit of the 2nd Parachute Pursuit Regiment was not at the moment engaged in any essential activity. It was suggested that this formation, inexperienced in police work, be moved in as a replacement for Company 5 of the 15th SS-Police Regiment, which was performing commonplace guard duty at the German wing of the Roman prison *Regina Coeli* and at the Rome radio station.[14]

General Stahel approved, and the request from the Via Tasso was fulfilled.[15] Clearly, as Stahel saw it, this was a matter many times removed from the *"Schweinerei"* he had vowed days before never to involve himself in or permit at all. If it ever became necessary to reexamine the facts, he could spread them out like a deck of cards and show how he had allowed himself to be represented by Möllhausen as unwilling to consent to the deportation without the approval of the Foreign Office. Ribbentrop's reply was now a matter of record. As for Kesselring's earlier opposition, the field marshal was never reported to have mentioned the Jews of Rome again. Somehow the problem had been solved for the Wehrmacht, and it was, or would be very soon, disengaged from this affair at no cost to the war effort.

In the Stadtkommandant's office the keeper of the general's war diary noted the temporary transfer of the police companies to the Gestapo. Then, with an aloofness that reflected the "noninvolvement" of the Wehrmacht, he added: "How the action will turn out is not yet foreseen. It is assumed that our many hostilely disposed Italians, as exemplified by the perpetrators of the recent . . . cases of sabotage, will hold back."[16]

In any event, Dannecker now had a well-equipped combined force of 365 SS police and Waffen SS, which included nine offi-

---

command, and in the city itself under Stahel. Administrative confusion and overlapping of authority were especially well-developed features of the Third Reich. They worked like levers in shifting the unsupportably heavy weights of responsibilty.

cers and thirty NCOs.[17] A very light battalion, it was still something less than adequate for the job he felt capable of doing in this city of so many limitations. Nevertheless he could not hope for a better set of circumstances, and the press of time was an element that could not be slighted.

He now set the date and hour for the *Judenaktion* in Rome: Saturday, October 16, at one hour before dawn.

XI

ON FRIDAY, OCTOBER 15, at a little before sundown the streets of the ghetto began to empty. It had been rainy and gloomy, a bad day for peddling from an open cart. Most people had finished work, what little there was, and some had gathered in small groups to chat for a few moments before going in for the night. The Sabbath was nearing.

The streets were darkening rapidly under the overcast sky, and they wore the heavy stillness that tightens down in a neighborhood without any traffic. The tack of footsteps against the wet cobbles was keen, and even the hush of the Tiber, which had risen in the autumn rains of the past few days, could be heard. The lights in the Ministry of Justice, just across Via Arenula, were being turned on, but they were immediately draped behind the blackout curtains. The Via del Tempio entrance to the synagogue was closed and dark—strangely so, for normally on Friday evenings a blushlike glow would light the cloisters and spill onto the streets like molten amber. This week, however, as a precaution the rites were being held in semisecrecy at the Jewish Home for the Invalid on Tiber Island.[1]

Inside the honeycomb apartments of the ghetto buildings, Jewish women were lighting the Sabbath candles, having prepared a supper from the skimpy rations they had been able to shop. The food situation was worsening daily. There was even a water shortage; milk was almost nonexistent; and one had to wait in line for hours to buy a box of salt. Tomorrow eggs would be distributed—one to a customer—and there was a rumor about that next Tuesday a ration of 2½ ounces of meat per person would become available, for one day only.[2]

Downstairs the stragglers spoke among themselves, although without having much to say. There were complaints and speculations about the war, the weather, the callups for labor service, and the possibilities of selling on the black market, which was becoming the only market, and for thousands of Romans, the only means of earning enough to stave off starvation. One good thing: Tomorrow the tobacco shops would have cigarettes for sale, the weekly allotment. But one had better queue up early. The lines would be unbearably long.

It was nervous, almost senseless talk, the kind that discharges tension. But there was nothing unusual about it, like any other Friday.[3] Before long they grew silent and they broke up like a struck triangle of billiard balls, disappearing into the dark, open doorways that gaped on the streets.

Just when nearly everyone in the ghetto was in his home, a loud cry could suddenly be heard from outside. It was an unintelligible shrieking pitched at the level of a woman's voice, and it rifled through the streets and alleyways. Heads began to appear in open windows and doorways, as everyone attempted to find out what the terrifying noise was about.

There was a distraught woman running up and down the street.[4] She was calling for attention in a voice choked with tears. She was dressed in black, and her clothes were rumpled, torn, and slovenly. They were drenched from the rain, as was her hair, which was packed wildly around her face. Her head was turned up, and her eyes darted along the sides of the buildings seeking contact. Whatever she was crying got trapped in the knot in her throat, and all that emerged was a fearsome sound and an excess of saliva that began to run from the corners of her mouth.

Almost everyone recognized her. They came out of their houses, and they crowded around the woman, trying to calm her and learn what was wrong. She was a poor woman, poorer than most of the Jews, who was known in the neighborhood simply as Celeste. She lived in Trastevere, but would often be seen in the ghetto visiting relatives there.

After a while she settled down somewhat, and though she still was sobbing violently, she could at last be understood. She had run all the way from Trastevere, the woman in rags explained in the choppy, truncated speech of the Roman poor. She had just come from the home of a *signora,* the wife of a *Carabiniere,* where Celeste worked half-days as a maid.

The woman of the house had told her that her husband had spoken with a German that day who had in his hands a list of 200 heads of Jewish households who were to be rounded up and deported together with their entire families.

No one believed Celeste. She was somewhat odd, as everyone knew, a chatterbox, given to hysteria. Who in the ghetto was unaware that everyone in her family was somewhat touched? Her son, a dull-witted, singularly dark-skinned young man, had the reputation of being the village idiot.

Celeste was plainly mixed up, or else overtaken by the fear that had clutched both banks of the river. Anyone could see that she had only just now learned of the threat the Germans had made to deport 200 Jews unless the community turned over its gold. She had, it seemed, merely heard an echo that had traveled around the city and had at last reached her, utterly confounded. But all that had happened more than two full weeks ago; the danger had long since passed. Celeste was confused, they were certain, and they tried to tell her so.

"Listen to me!" she continued to cry, rejecting their incredulity with strange authority. "Run for your lives, I tell you!"[5]

The Jews laughed at her. It was unkind, but she was implacable. Some people whispered she was mad.

"I swear it!" she shouted in desperation now. "It's true. I swear on my life, on my children!"[6]

The more she cried and ranted, the less serious she was regarded by her audience. Intensely frustrated, she squeezed fresh tears to her flaming eyes and embraced two children who were standing near her as if to shield them. Rainwater dripped from her ugly hair; it mixed with her tears and streamed along her hot cheeks. Then she spoke again in a hoarse, tremulous voice.

"You'll be sorry!" she warned. "If I were a *signora* you would believe me. But because I don't have a single lira, because I wear these rags—"[7] Saying that, she released the two children and grabbed furiously at her clothes to show them the rags she spoke of, and unintentionally she tore them even more, exposing her flesh.

The crowd of Jews looked away and began to disperse. It was unsafe to be on the streets at this hour.

Upstairs, in a ghetto apartment in Via del Tempio number four, thirty-three-year-old Lazzaro Anticoli was unaware of what had just taken place in the street below. He and his wife, Emma, were wholly preoccupied with one of their three children, who, they had been told by a physician some hours earlier, was going to die.[8]

Until that afternoon they had been living in hiding, at the home of a Catholic friend a few blocks south near the Palatine Bridge. They had fled the ghetto soon after the Germans entered Rome, fearful not so much of the unpredictable Nazis but of the Italian Fascists, who had been turned loose by the occupiers.

Emma, a woman of twenty-six, had given birth to twins that summer, a boy they named Mario and girl, Rosella. Despite the difficulties involved in moving, Lazzaro had felt that the ghetto was too dangerous a place for his young family, and when his friend offered to shelter them, he accepted. They had hurriedly packed whatever they could carry with them and Lazzaro, Emma, the twins, and an older child, their two-and-one-half-year-old daughter, Grazia, departed.

Life in hiding had been all but impossible. The Catholic family, like the Anticolis, was very poor. The Jewish guests, even the two three-month-olds, had had to sleep on the floor. Lazzaro, a skilled mechanic, was unemployed and had been daily forced to suffer the painful embarrassment of having to take food from his friend, however willingly offered, sharing meals that were not even adequate for the hospitable family. Each day he had gone looking for any kind of work, sometimes earning a few lire, but scarcely enough. Still he would never have left the security of the Catholic home, had his older daughter not fallen frightfully ill.

That morning of the 15th Emma had sent him to the pharmacy to buy *pastiglie*—lozenges—something that might help to relieve the child. Her throat was inflamed, and it was hard for her to breathe. Instead he had gone for the family doctor. His daughter was burning, comatose, and clearly in pain. The physician had examined her, called the parents to one side, and told them the girl might not survive the night. She had diphtheria, he had said. There was nothing further he could do.

Lazzaro had not wanted his first-born to die on the floor. They had packed again, and after dinner, the twins in Emma's arms, they had dragged their belongings through the drizzle and had brought the bundled sick girl home, to her bed in the ghetto. Tonight they prayed the doctor had been wrong.

In the mountains the band of partisans at Tor Paluzzo was getting ready to go out on a sabotage raid.[9] In the past few days the guerrillas in the *Castelli Romani* were beginning to show their strength, but they had also suffered some grave losses.

They had launched their first actions against the Germans, attacking Wehrmacht food depositories. In this way they had been able to disrupt German supply operations, seizing quantities of grain and other foodstuffs, including live cattle. Providing for their own needs, they had also distributed this goods to co-operative peasants in the zone. The Germans had struck back on Tuesday of that week, locating and swooping down on several partisan encampments. They had captured almost 200 men, and prior to shipping them north, marched them through the villages, hands clasped behind their heads, before the eyes of the townspeople—parents, wives, and children of many of the partisans.[10]

The Tor Paluzzo band had escaped unharmed, however. Now it was necessary to show the Germans that the movement could bounce right back from a defeat. Since the two Jewish partisans "Pino" Levi Cavaglione and Marco Moscati had raided the munitions dump, their group had had no contact with the enemy. Pino, who was the only one who remembered his military training well enough to demonstrate how to dismantle and reassemble a Breda machine gun and the other Italian weapons, had been giving instructions to his comrades, but they had done little else.[11] Tonight he and the others would undertake a minor operation, cutting German telephone lines in the area. It was not much more than a harassment, but it was good for morale and the fight had to go forward.

As they set out under the black lid of the nighttime sky of the countryside, Pino's morale was already high. The men had taken to him now, and Marco had become his special friend. Furthermore, he had learned that the women in one of the *Castelli* towns were making uniforms for the partisans: blue woolens and a Basque beret, to which, it was said, would be sown a red star.

"I need any kind of clothes now and a good pair of mountain shoes," he said. "I'm dirty and in rags and my city shoes by now are broken through."[12]

Sometime before the hour of curfew that Friday night, the doorbell rang at the home of the Arminio Wachsbergers in the Jewish district. An answer brought an unexpected visit from Regina's brother, Elio Polacco, his wife, and their two-year-old son, Vittorio.[13]

Though the Polaccos lived but a few blocks north in Via della Luce, it was a welcome surprise, not only to the Wachsbergers, but also to the other members of the household, Regina's and Elio's parents. It being the Sabbath eve, and coincidentally the second day of *Succod,* the Feast of the Tabernacles holiday, imparted an air of festivity to the reunion.

But when it came to discussing the reason for the call, the illusion of joy was dampened by the unhappy reality of the times. Elio and his wife had planned to make a weekend trip to the Roman countryside, visiting the nearby farms in the hope of being able to buy some extra food. There simply was not enough to eat in Rome. Elio asked his sister and brother-in-law if it would not be too burdensome to leave their child at the Wachsberger home for the one or two nights they would be away. And since they were leaving quite early the next morning, probably before dawn, could the boy spend this night too with them?

There were no objections of course. Arminio and Regina found the child a fine playmate for their daughter, Clara, even if he was three years younger than she; and naturally the elder Polaccos, the grandparents of both children, were delighted.

In the ghetto a little before midnight a few shots rang out, cracking the integrity of the night like an egg. People who were awakened by the volley of gunfire and others who had not yet fallen asleep thought nothing of it. Almost every night sporadic shooting could be heard coming from one or another part of the city. There were looters, gangs, and drunken soldiers in occupied Rome, a fact of war one had to live with.

But the shooting suddenly became intense. As the firing increased, it also drew closer to the heart of the ghetto, until no one could sleep, for it sounded as if the whole neighborhood were under siege.[14] A rain of bullets struck the sides of buildings, then splintered and ricocheted, whistling eerily down the streets. People sat up in their beds and paced nervously around their apartments, but few approached the windows. It seemed too dangerous to even look. The light from bursts of gunfire flashed stark shadows on the walls inside the Jewish homes, and the trill of the fusilades made little objects in the room dance the tune of the fireworks.

Those who braved a glimpse outside saw a pack of helmeted soldiers running wildly in dizzy circles. Gun held high, they fired aimlessly into the fine rain that was falling from a heavily clouded night sky. From minute to minute the frenzy reached new heights. The soldiers shrieked madly, unleashing unnatural sounds like the shrill of a locomotive. Some of them threw hand grenades at the foot of the buildings, as if the old stones had been fighting off the intrusion.

Inside the buildings the people grew increasingly terrified. Babies began to wail. One woman who had given birth that evening, suddenly bundled up the newborn child and ran hysterically through the dank, unlighted halls, finally collapsing in the apartment of a neighbor. Women from other apartments on the floor succored her, while whole families in their nightclothes moved about in the darkness, seeking out their friends. They were looking for comfort in one another, and, fruitlessly for someone wiser than themselves, who might offer a reasonable explanation for the fiery convulsion that was banging at their doors.

They listened for the sound of shops being broken into—the splash of plate glass or the growl of a rolling storefront shutter. If the ghetto were being looted, there would at least be a reason for the attack. But there was only the endless shooting and the screaming of the frenzied soldiers.

An hour passed, two hours, three, but the seizure had not abated. The firing would erupt in spurts, volcanically. It would grow quiet for a while, and just when people would dare to think the soldiers were going away, it would start from the beginning again. In the absence of any *ex cathedra* explanation from the daytime machinery of the organized community, the ghetto Jews put forth their own ideas as to the meaning of this latest assault. Most everyone concluded that the Germans wished to continually intimidate and scorn the Jews of Rome. Beyond that, all the theories broke up into incoherent parts, and no one, as Giacomo Debenedetti observed, any longer recalled the warning of a few hours earlier cried through the ghetto by the woman in rags named Celeste.[15]

About 4:00 A.M. the shooting spree subsided, and the soldiers wandered away.* According to Debenedetti's account of the incident:

> It was cold, and the dampness of the rainy night penetrated the walls. Everyone stood about in their nightshirts and slippers, a few with shawls or overcoats draped around their shoulders. Perhaps the abandoned beds still held a little warmth. Tired, with that sense of letdown and hollowness that follows intense emotions, with aching bones and chattering teeth, everyone returned to his own home, to his own bed.[17]

Soon it would be daylight. And looking back, it would be as if the nightmare had never really happened.

While the Jews of Rome found sleep at last, elsewhere in the city a man was stealing through the last hours of the night. In one hand he carried a can of red paint; in the other a brush at least four inches wide. He was a courageous man, whose name would never be known. He risked being shot at any moment. To be outside during the hours of curfew could mean sudden death from the guns of the *lumpen* Nazi-Fascists who policed the occupied streets. But to this man, there were some things more important to him than his life. There was tyranny in the land, and it had to be fought.

With bucket and brush he walked along an empty street, taking care to crush the sound of his footsteps softly in his shoes. His hands were cold and wet. The light rain fell into the open paint can, but not enough of it to make a difference, to alter the consistency of the deep red color. As he moved from

* The origin and purpose of the wild shooting in the first hours of October 16 would always remain a mystery. Debenedetti and others have suggested that the Germans had wanted to force as many Jews as possible to remain in their homes prior to the roundup.[16] This seems highly unlikely. The curfew was the best guarantee of keeping people indoors, and the shootings could have had the opposite effect of sounding an alarm throughout Rome. Considering Dannecker's strivings for secrecy and his security problems, the most probable explanation is that the disorder was a coincidence—a spontaneous outbreak on the part of a group of soldiers who suddenly stumbled upon the Jewish quarter and decided to demonstrate against the enemy.

shadow to shadow, his eyes darted, picking at the city's walls for a place to hit and run. At last he found what he had sought. When it seemed safest, he rushed to the wall and began to paint. He worked fast. It did not matter that he splashed the words and that the letters dripped and ran. As long as they could be read, tyranny would suffer, and the cause of man would gain. In the time it took to lay down some twenty strokes of paint, he was finished, and he fled. His work began at once to slowly harden on the wall.

In the irrational world in which this man lived, where human beings had learned to nudge themselves, hand in hand, here gently, there rudely, into a machine they had built to exterminate themselves, he had struck a blow for freedom. He had done so with an ugly weapon, but in many ways, it was the only one he had. The painter had written:

VIVA STALIN![18]

PART THREE

The Jews of Rome

Then came the ill-fated 16th of October and things went from bad to worse. Nevertheless, it can honestly be said that although carried out on a reduced scale, the activities of the Community never ceased. . . . the daily rites went on, we buried our dead in our own cemetery, thanks to the grave-digger Settimio Spagnoletto (he too tragically taken away), marriages were performed, and we effected several circumcisions. . . .

—FROM A REPORT OF A LEADER OF THE JEWISH COMMUNITY OF ROME.[1]

1943

SEPTEMBER

SUN.	MON.	TUES.	WED.	THURS.	FRI.	SAT.
			1	2	3	4
5	6	7	8	9	10	11
12	13	14	15	16	17	18
19	20	21	22	23	24	25
26	27	28	29	30		

OCTOBER

					1	2
3	4	5	6	7	8	9
10	11	12	13	14	15	16
17	18	19	20	21	22	23

I

For the rest of the world it would be an ordinary Saturday.

In Moscow, middle-ranking diplomats from the United States, Britain, and the Soviet Union would put the final touches on preparations for the Foreign Ministers' Conference on Allied cooperation, which was to open in a few days.

In Washington, the Yugoslav ambassador would protest the "unfair picture of Yugoslav fighting which was being presented in the American press."[1]

Undersecretary of State Stettinius would write a memorandum to President Roosevelt on "the present status of the question of Rome as an open city."[2]

The number of Germans killed in the war would be reported: 4,000,000.

On the eastern front, the Red Army would kill 900 more.

Army would play Columbia.

In Albany Governor Dewey would order a stay of execution for Louis Lepke, who was to have been electrocuted today.

Greek guerrillas would engage Nazi troops at the town of Karditsa.

In Nashville an American Airlines passenger airplane would crash, killing ten persons.

Investors in the stock markets of both Allied and Axis countries would mark a week of steady gains.

On Broadway Milton Berle would perform in "Ziegfeld Follies," Mary Martin in "One Touch of Venus," and Paul Robeson in "Othello." "Oklahoma" would be sold out, standing room only.

In Italy the Allies would cross the Volturno River, some ninety miles from Rome.

The Sunday *New York Times* would be delivered to newsstands, its magazine section carrying a cover photograph of Field Marshal Montgomery and General Mark Clark with the caption, "On the Road to Rome."

Chicago would hold ceremonies formally opening its first subway line.

In London the Royal Air Force would lay further plans in its October series of very heavy air strikes on such German industrial centers as Frankfurt, Bremen, and Hanover.

Sumner Welles would discuss "Today's War, Tomorrow's World" in a radio broadcast over the Red Network.

Bookstores in the United States would enjoy heavy sales of *Thirty Seconds Over Tokyo* by Ted Lawson, and Betty Smith's *A Tree Grows in Brooklyn.*

In Brooklyn at the Loew's Boro Park movie theater children would pay twelve cents to see Bob Hope in "Let's Face It."

Across the East River, in the Temple B'nai Jeshrun on 88th Street near Broadway, Rabbi Israel Goldstein would address his congregation. He would say:

> Judaism is a democratic way of life stressing at the same time the worth of the individual soul as the image of God in man, and paramountcy of the best interests of the community as a whole.
>
> Judaism is thoroughly adapted to the modern world. Its social idealism and world vision are still ahead of the times.[3]

II

IN ROME IT was raining very hard, and the sky was black.

At about 4:30 A.M., an hour and a half or so before dawn, a Jewish peddler named Settimio Calò awoke. He dressed quietly in order not to disturb anyone in the crowded ghetto apartment. His wife, their nine children, and his young nephew who was visiting, lay fast asleep. Calò bundled himself in an old knit sweater and slipped out of the house. He walked down the part of Via del Portico d' Ottavia that runs north and south to the tobacconist's between the two bridges of Tiber Island. The shop had not yet opened, but a queue for the weekly cigarette ration, which was to be apportioned this morning, had already formed. Calò took his place in the line of smokers, most of whom were Jews from the ghetto-Trastevere streets on both banks of the river.

The downpour began to slacken. The queue of ghetto Jews grew longer. They waited patiently for the *tabaccaio* to arrive.[1]

In an apartment on the third floor of Via del Portico d'Ottavia, 9, Emma Di Segni opened her eyes and listened. The rain had been pounding and echoing in the roofless corridor just outside her door. But now it was quiet. She could hear only the sleeping sounds of her husband and their three grown children. The rain had stopped. She decided to take a bundle of wet laundry to the roof and hang it out to dry.[2]

From the roof, two floors above, the proprietor of a cafe in

Portico d'Ottavia could be seen coming from Monte Savello toward his shop. He was a non-Jew who lived in the Testaccio district. He had walked to the ghetto, noting nothing unusual along the way. Now he unlocked and lifted the rolling shutter to the cafe, and leaving it in a half-open, half-closed position, he began the daily chore of cleaning the pressure valves of his expresso coffee machine.

He had not been in the shop more than a few minutes when he began to hear the drumming sound of men moving in cadence. It grew louder, and he poked his head beneath the half-drawn shutter to learn what was happening. He saw two rows of German troops marching down the wet sidewalk. They wore helmets and carried rifles, and he guessed there were about a hundred of them. But the number was far less, closer to half that amount. In the middle of the empty street, two or three officers walked alongside the formation. They picked out men from the group and indicated points at the street corners as places to take positions.[3]

Within moments a small group of passersby began to gather and watch. The Germans paid no attention to them and continued to take their places. At the west end of Portico d'Ottavia, they set up a wooden roadblock, as well as at the other entrances to the ghetto proper: Via del Tempio, Via del Progresso, Piazza Costaguti, Piazza Mattei, and at the height of Via S. Angelo in Pescheria. Sentries were posted at each of these points, and others were ordered to walk in a circular route around the blocks of the area. Still others were placed at the east end of the Portico d'Ottavia, near the actual portico itself and the entrance to the ruins of the Theater of Marcellus. The black, canvas-covered trucks, which had brought the Germans here, blocked the north-south part of the L-shaped street. The ghetto was surrounded.[4]

It was just about then that someone known in the neighborhood as "Goggle-eyed Letizia"—a fat, misshapen little-girlish person in her early twenties looked out on the street and cried:

"Oh God, *i mamonni!*"—the Hebrew-Romanesque word for "the cops!"[5]

The signal was given and *Judenaktion* in Rome began. One of the Germans made note of the time: 5:30 A.M.[6]

III

JUST OUTSIDE THE ghetto proper, on the Trastevere side of the river, the doorbell rang at apartment number ten of the building in Lungotevere Ripa, 6. Arminio Wachsberger, who had been asleep, got out of bed. He looked at his watch. It was a little after five thirty. As he made his way to the front door, to answer the insistent ringing, he was certain he knew who it was. His brother-in-law, he thought, had come to call for his son, Vittorio. Elio and his wife must have changed their plans about going to the countryside; or perhaps they wanted to take the boy with them.

When he opened the door, he saw two German soldiers. They were armed, and Wachsberger's eye was caught on the double lightning bolt symbol of the SS sewn to their collars. He demanded to know what the intrusion meant. But they pushed passed him, without replying, and when they saw the telephone, they cut its wires.

By now his wife, the elderly Polacco couple, and little Clara and Vittorio had arisen. They stood about in a half-sleep, dazed and bewildered. Wachsberger, in his perfect German, tried again to speak to the men. In response they handed him a rectangular piece of paper with something printed on it in German and Italian. Wachsberger read it to himself:

(1) You and your family and all other Jews belonging to your household are to be transferred.
(2) You are to bring with you:
 (a) food for at least eight days;
 (b) ration books;
 (c) identity card;
 (d) drinking glasses.
(3) You may also bring:
 (a) small suitcase with personal effects, clothing, blankets, etc.;
 (b) money and jewelry.
(4) Close and lock the apartment/house. Take the key with you.
(5) Invalids, even the severest cases, may not for any reason, remain behind. There are infirmaries at the camp.
(6) Twenty minutes after presentation of this card, the family must be ready to depart.[1]

Wachsberger thought first of two-year-old Vittorio. "Listen," he said, "this child isn't mine; he's only spending the night here." He tried to explain the circumstances that had brought the boy to his home.

"Alles mussen kommen," one of the Germans replied.[2]

"All Roman Jews had to be transferred to a labor camp," Wachsberger later said they told him, adding:

> Its location was however unknown to them. They reassured us, saying that the old people would have to do only very light work, while the women would cook for everyone, mind the children, wash the laundry, etc. They advised us to bring money and anything else of value because we would need it for buying things at the camp store, such as certain foods and comforts, which would not normally be distributed. Naturally we followed their advice and I also took with me my very expensive Zeiss Contax camera.[3]

As they packed, Wachsberger continually asked whether he might, or whether he ought to bring one or another article he thought would be useful. To this the Germans invariably replied, "Bring it, bring it."

Within the twenty-minute time limit, the Wachsbergers and the Polaccos were dressed and ready. Arminio looked exceptionally well; he had put on a brand-new pair of suede shoes, which he was now wearing for the first time. Coming out of the apartment, he locked the door as instructed, and the group went downstairs. Their non-Jewish neighbors looked on incredulously. On the street a canvas-covered truck, with two more Germans in the cab, waited for them. The man sitting beside the driver was a noncommissioned officer, who seemed to be the head of the squad. He carried a submachine gun, and he leveled it at Wachsberger. He gave him the job of interpreter, to tell whoever else was to ride in that truck that any attempt to escape or assist such an act would be punished by immediate execution.

"As you know," he added, "the Germans don't fool around."

The Jews of Lungotevere Ripa, 6, boarded the truck. They were joined by the two Germans who had arrested them. The vehicle started up, moving slowly to the next address on the list.[4]

In a ghetto apartment in Via S. Ambrogio a woman with a broken leg heard someone calling her from the street below. Her limb in a heavy plaster cast, she hobbled to the window and looked.

"Auntie, Auntie," her young niece who lived around the corner was crying, "come on down! The Germans are taking everyone away!"

Two armed soldiers stood beside the girl. They were guarding the street and scarcely looked at her. The aunt, known to everyone in the ghetto as Laurina, thought as many people did that morning that the Nazis were taking only able-bodied men for the labor service call-up that had been so well publicized in recent days. Believing herself naturally immune, she dressed slowly, took her shopping bag and ration books with her and limped down the stone stairs to see what was going on outside.

On the street, she approached the two German sentries, one of them a man of about twenty-five and the other somewhat older. She offered each of them a cigarette, which they readily accepted.

"They taking all Jews," the older soldier said in poor Italian. He made a sweeping gesture with his hand, as if he were erasing a blackboard.

"But I have broken leg," said Laurina thinking it would be easier for them to understand her if she too spoke incorrectly. "Have to go away with family. To hospital."

"Ja, ja," said the German, indicating he would permit her to escape.

For some it was as simple as that.

Laurina alerted her husband and children, and they started packing, while she waited on the street.[5]

The arresting squads were working in other parts of the ghetto. Just around the corner from Laurina's a German soldier entered Via della Reginella, 2. It was a decrepit old palazzo, smaller than most, in the oldest street of the ghetto. Its dark halls held the smells and the memories of at least 400 years of life and death. Worn into its stone walls, obliterated by time but preserved by history, were the joys, laments, and desires of an imprisoned people.

The Germans had decided that it required only a single soldier to pick it clean of its Jews. He was a young man, almost still a boy. As he had been told to do, he began to work from the bottom of the building to the top, on the correct assumption that the front door was the only exit.

On the third floor the family of Mosè Spizzichino had already awakened when they heard a commotion from below. The Spizzichinos had given thought to the possibility of a German raid and sensed at once what the sounds might mean.

They had been warned to flee. Days back, friends who said they were going to join the partisans in the hills had told them it was unwise to remain in the ghetto. But Mosè's wife, Grazia, had shaken off such advice, replying hopefully, "We paid the gold; now they will leave us alone." She had even heard this said by the *signori* of the community themselves.[6]

Nevertheless two members of the household, the husbands of Mosè's married daughters, had gone into hiding some days earlier to evade the labor draft. Still living at home were Mosè, his wife, their other daughters, Settimia and Giuditta, the two married women, Ada and Gentile, and their children, a girl aged two and a boy eighteen months. Ada, however, about an hour or so ago had gone with her daughter in her arms to queue up for cigarettes, and she too, momentarily, was not at home.

It was twenty-two-year-old Settimia who ran from her bed to the window to examine the noise from outside. The disturbance was coming from within the building, however, and all she could see was the Jewish girl who lived in the apartment directly below. She was trying to get away from the house, but her mother was calling from the second-story window beneath Settimia's.

"Stella," the mother cried. "Don't go. Come back!"

"I'm going, *Mamma,*" said the dark-eyed girl of eighteen. "I'm scared. I've got to go." With that she turned around and ran.*[7]

Settimia Spizzichino, drawing back from the window, correctly assumed that the Germans had already entered the building. She alerted her family. They locked the door to the apartment and began to barricade themselves in the last room of the railroad flat. They hoped it would be thought that no one was home. But as they were closing themselves in, Settimia's younger sister, Giuditta, was suddenly stricken with panic. Still in her nightclothes, she broke out of the apartment, running downstairs toward the street. But when she saw the young soldier, her fear stopped her. For a moment she stood perfectly still. Then she reversed her direction and ran back to her mother. The German continued to climb the stairs.

Already under arrest was Angelo Anticoli, the ghetto jeweler who had had the weighing job during the gold collection. He lived on a lower floor. He was busy now carrying out the instructions according to the printed card he had been handed. With him were his wife and two young children.[8]

* "Stella," or "Star," was a nickname she had earned for her exceptional beauty. Her real name was Celeste Di Porto, She would escape the city this day and then return to Rome again, where she would be given a new name and live one of the most dismal chapters of the Nazi occupation. All of Rome would know her as *"Pantera Nera*—Black Panther," a ruthless spy who betrayed the surviving Jews of Rome, selling them one by one to the Fascist police at fifty dollars each (see footnote p. 296).

Now the Spizzichinos were arrested. Settimia on a sudden impulse protested that her married sister Gentile and her little boy were not members of the family. They were not even Jewish she said; Gentile worked for them as a maid. The rest of the family joined in and agreed. The young German appeared not to know what to do. He looked at the woman and her child, as if he were trying to find something Jewish about them. Finally he said to Gentile in words she understood only by their weight and texture, "Okay, beat it!"

The remainder of the family prepared to depart. Settimia was the calmest of all. A dark-haired young woman with an attractive figure, she was normally a person whose emotions could not be contained. But now she moved about with a sureness that had come on like a sudden change of season. Her feelings at the moment—fear, terror, even anger and hatred—fell away, if only temporarily. It was almost as if she knew what lay ahead: a singular destiny, uncommon to all the Jews of Rome. Settimia Spizzichino was to be the only woman to return from the great roundup now tearing the city asunder.

As much as was possible in the allotted twenty minutes, she helped put the apartment in order and get the family's belongings together. Then she withdrew from the apartment and joined the others in the building who were waiting to be taken away.[9]

In the street her sister Ada now returned from the cigarette queue, her baby still in her arms. She had seen the Germans in the ghetto and was afraid to approach her home. She wondered what to do and drifted aimlessly. Somehow she found herself marching with the captured Jews. She and the baby went too.[10]

IV

LAURINA, THE WOMAN with the broken leg, stood at the corner of the street, where it opens on the wide Via del Portico d'Ottavia. She waited for her family, who were still in the apartment, and she watched the Jews who were already under arrest. A long, single file of captives was being marched down the ghetto's main street to wait at the gates near the ruins of the Theater of Marcellus.[1]

A German soldier stood at the head of the column and another prodded the rear. The group consisted mostly of women, children, and older people. Many of the younger men—those between eighteen and thirty-five—were escaping at the first knock on the door, thinking the Germans had come only for them. They fled across rooftops or hid in cellars waiting for the onslaught to pass. The line of prisoners was formed by a motley crowd, disoriented people, their clothes in disarray and their arms laden with useless objects they thought they would need.

It was like a nightmarish parade. Some people were crying, others groaning, and still others asking questions of the Germans, who replied only by jabbing the air with the point of their guns. Among those Laurina later reported seeing was an eighty-year-old woman she knew as "Aunt Chele." Senile and half-mad, she was skipping along like a schoolgirl, greeting everyone with a great big smile. Another old woman, who had been paralyzed by a stroke, was being carried along seated on a kitchen chair. She was held aloft, like a king or a pope, by two strong men, they too under arrest.

A young woman carrying an infant suddenly broke from the ranks and rushed up to a German. She opened her blouse, brought out one of her breasts and squeezed the nipple to show the soldier that her milk had stopped flowing. It was the only way she knew how to communicate that her child was hungry and that she should be allowed to buy something for the baby to eat or drink. But the soldier, Laurina saw, raised the barrel of his machine gun and forced her back into the line.

The parade continued. Someone rushed up to a German, grabbed his hand, and began to kiss it, asking for mercy. With his free hand, the German slapped the face of the pleader, putting an end to the feelings aroused in both of them. Many children passed by. Their heads were almost always turned up toward their parents, it seemed to Laurina, as if what was happening could only be seen by reflection in their mothers' or fathers' eyes.[2]

The old reassured the young, the religious comforted the heathens, and the ignorant gave solace to the wise.

Another line of Jews was formed from those taken from the Via della Reginella and other north-south running streets. They were marched to trucks parked in Via del Tempio, the street of the main entrance to the temple. The Spizzichinos were in this group. They crossed Via del Portico d'Ottavia, and when they neared the next street, Via Catalana, Mosè Spizzichino whispered to his wife that he was going to attempt to escape as soon as they reached the corner. Their married son lived in that block. Mosè said he was going to try to get to him and warn him. He began to drift to the edge of the line, which was guarded by the one soldier who had arrested them.

"No, no," his wife urged in a low voice. "Don't leave us."

Mosè shook her off with a snap of his wrist. "Be quiet!" he said, and then, unseen, he unhooked himself from the captives and fled, running toward the home of his son.[3]

The Germans had hardly enough trucks for the large number of ghetto Jews they were raking in like so many fallen autumn leaves. They would have to make several trips to the Collegio Militare, the appointed gathering place for all who would be swept away. As soon as there were enough people to fill the trucks, the Jews who were already caught were ordered to mount them.

The paralyzed woman was lifted, chair and all, onto one of the vehicles and the other Jews followed her, the last one aboard lending a hand to the next one. Before long the first caravan of black German trucks departed, taking the Lungotevere Cenci to the north.[4]

In one of the trucks, Settimia Spizzichino sat between her sisters and her mother, cuddling close to the latter. Her calm had stayed with her all this time, and she looked out abstractly as they rolled on against the flow of the Tiber. But at the Ponte Mazzini, where the truck turned left to cross the bridge that faces Regina Coeli prison, Settimia suddenly began to cry, thinking the jail was their destination.

"I don't want to go to Regina Coeli," she wept, burying her head in her mother's breast. "I don't want to go to jail. I didn't do anything wrong."

"Don't cry," her mother said repeatedly, running her fingers through her daughter's hair. "It won't be bad at all. We'll be okay in jail. We'll eat well. *Ci stiamo bene.*"[5]

Settimia's mother, who had only recently been released from Regina Coeli after serving part of a six-month sentence for dealing on the black market, was almost relieved. But the truck passed the old prison and continued on to the Collegio Militare, which was in the same long street about a quarter of a mile further north. Now it was the younger woman who was happy. Her composure returned.[6]

In the meantime the Germans continued to pound at the ghetto doors. Emma Di Segni, who had been hanging out the wash on the roof of the building at Via del Portico d'Ottavia, 9, had seen nothing of what had already happened on the street just below. But now she began to hear a doorbell ringing and someone knocking hard. The sound was coming from beneath her, and she left her bundle of laundry and returned to the apartment. She was immediately placed under arrest, as was the rest of her family.[7]

On the floor below, her brother and sister-in-law, Abramo and Celeste Sabatello were captured, along with their six children.* One member of the family escaped via the roof.[8]

The Germans continued to empty the buildings in Via del Portico d'Ottavia while other squads worked in the side streets. A new file of Jews was formed. They too were marched to the gates at the ruins of the Roman theater to wait there.

The talk among them, while inspired by fear, was quiet and reserved, and most people felt everything would end well. Abramo Sabatello, for example, spoke scornfully of the Germans, almost with defiance. His wife and six children around him, he assured everyone who could hear his voice that there was really nothing to worry about.

"Where are they going to take us?" he asked rhetorically. When someone suggested they were to be sent to a concentration camp, he brushed such a thought aside. "They're taking us to work," he said. "Okay. We'll work. Then they'll let us go."[9]

It started to rain again, and the group grew sluggish and sulked. A crowd of non-Jewish Romans had collected behind the roadblocks. Francesco Odoardi, who had been out walking with his brother before going to work that morning came upon the scene by chance. The Odoardis had been stopped by an SS guard as they tried to pass through the ghetto. Now, in the rain, they stood by and watched.

They could see the captured Jews at the portico gates. There were about eighty of them, Francesco later said. They were idle. "It was as if they were waiting at the windows of I don't know what kind of welfare office or refugee agency." He went on:

* One of them, Leone, sixteen, would be among the fourteen male survivors of the deportation. Three of those who returned lived in this building. Another three lived in a building across the street, Via del Tempio, 4. See Appendix II for a list and further details of the survivors.

The men, some in jackets, some in overcoats, were sitting on the ancient rocks, or on suitcases, boxes, or sacks. They were looking down at the ground below, absently, without turning their heads. Perhaps they were saying a last goodbye to those familiar stones.

The women, however, were still the housewife, even in the open air, on the pavement, and under the rain. With slow and somber gestures, in some ways hopeless but always with love, some of them were tidying the little clothes and coats of their children. . . . One of the women, with a baby at her breast, covered the child with a shawl. Another put a kerchief on the head of her daughter, who was crying. She wiped the girl's tears and the drops of rain on her face, but always in silence. She had no words to comfort her. She could not even tell the child that Papà would know what to do; for he was there beside her, motionless, his blood turned cold with helplessness.[10]

If the Jews did nothing to help themselves, neither did the non-Jews of Rome rally to their aid. To be sure, there were acts of solidarity and comradeship, but the civilian resistance feared by Nazis would nowhere develop throughout the day. Jew and non-Jew alike were alone and divided; the Jew was already dying, the latter but a few steps behind him.

"At the door to one of the buildings in Via del Tempio," said one of the onlookers—a Roman on his way to his job in the nearby Ministry of Justice—

women and children were being pushed outside into the street with some rather rough treatment. The children were crying. Everywhere you could hear pleas for help and cries of distress. . . . It all seemed like a scene out of hell. . . . I was terrified, but I kept watching the scene, perhaps with an unconscious hope of somehow being able to help the victims. Suddenly a German NCO came up to me and told me to get away, accompanying his words with a persuasive push. There was nothing I could do but leave the place.[11]

The Germans now broke up the crowd of bystanders. They told them to keep moving.[12]

Among this group of Jews who had been taken from Via del Tempio were the Lazzaro Anticolis. They too marched to the gates by the portico. The twins were in the arms of their mother.

Lazzaro held his diphtheric daughter pressing her to the warmth of his body; to him she seemed closer than ever to death.[13]

The van in which Arminio Wachsberger rode was making the rounds of Trastevere. By now it had arrived in Via della Luce and had been joined by another truck coming from elsewhere in the district. The Germans had already arrested one family at the lower end of the street and were at the buildings of the next Jews on their list, one of whom was Wachsberger's brother-in-law, Elio Polacco.

Polacco and his wife were not at home, having already departed for the *campagna*. The other tenants, most of whom had awakened by now, saw the Germans in the street and were thrown into confusion as to what they should do. The Germans went first to an address across the street, and in the meantime people in Polacco's building gathered in the halls. Everyone thought it was a labor roundup. Some of the able-bodied men fled by way of the roof. Assunta Fratini, a Catholic woman who lived there, was asked by the others to go outside and see what was taking place. In almost every instance it was thought that women, as well as children and the elderly, had nothing to fear. Signora Fratini agreed and went down.

"I saw two large German trucks parked in a little opening in front of our house," she later said.

> Inside there already were some people. I went a little closer and then was petrified. There were not only men, but old people, women and children, frightened and crying. I looked around and suddenly, in the midst of all the confusion, I saw little Vittorio, a baby scarcely two years old, a lost expression in his eyes, holding the hand of his aunt.[14]

Looking out of the truck, Arminio Wachsberger recognized the woman as a neighbor of his brother-in-law. He made a tossing motion with his hands, as if to say that he would throw the child to her at the first opportunity. There was a German guarding the prisoners, but when he turned his head to light a cigarette, Wachsberger acted. He threw his nephew like a basketball, and the boy landed in the arms of Signora Fratini, who quickly disappeared into the hallway of the building.

When the soldier blew out the match, he looked puzzled for

a moment and then turned to Wachsberger and asked him if he thought someone was missing from the truck. Wachsberger replied that it seemed to him everyone was present, and the soldier returned to his cigarette.[15]

V

ROSINA SORANI, WHO lived not far from, but outside the Jewish quarter, stepped out of her house at an early hour, and as she did every day of the week, started to walk to the temple. She had not gone more than a few steps when a girl she scarcely knew ran up to her and warned her not to leave her house because the Germans were taking the Jews.

"I did not want to believe such a thing," she later said, "and I continued walking. But when I arrived near the flower shop at Ponte Garibaldi, I was told by a Jew that I should not go to the office because there was a danger of being arrested. Still not persuaded, I went on my way, but that same Jew who was at the florist's called me back and enjoined me not to go any further; he said there were black canvas-covered trucks passing by taking the Jews away. Just then, I saw one. It was loaded with men, women, and children."

For a few moments she did not know what to do.

"Finally, I decided to telephone the Signor Presidente. I told him that I had urgent need of speaking with him about a very serious matter. He replied that he understood and that he would come immediately to the office."[1]

Signorina Sorani said that was "absolutely impossible" and that she would go at once to his house.[2]

She arrived there some time before 8:00 A.M. and proceeded to relate what she had heard and seen. The Germans were rounding up the Jews of Rome, she said. She urged him to leave his house without delay.[3]

But Foà would not hear of such a thing. The "Germanic invaders" were demolishing his community like an old tenement, and it was almost as if he himself were the object being destroyed. He dressed immediately and rushed out of the house. The Jewish president went directly to the Italian authorities.[4] He had to alert them to this "premeditated crime," as he called it.[5] He wanted to employ to the full extent whatever might be left of the quarter-century of prestige and influence that had attached itself to his name in order that the Fascists stop the roundup at once.

It did not take very long for him to return home, however. The authorities were not going to do anything, he learned. From this and other signs Foà would soon declare that the Ministry of the Interior, the Office of the Public Security, and the Fascist organizations were "under the control of the German Authorities."[6]

Signorina Sorani continued to counsel Foà to abandon his apartment and flee with his young children. In this regard, she telephoned her brother, DELASEM executive Settimio Sorani, at his hiding place in Via Firenze.[7] He knew of literally hundreds of relatively safe rooms and apartments throughout the city.

"There's some confusion near the Ponte Garibaldi," she said mysteriously when the telephone connection was made.[8]

He understood. He told her to go to the Albergo Milano, a hotel in the center of town that was among the many which were cooperating with Sorani in sheltering Jews. She was to remain there, he said, until more suitable arrangements could be made.[9]

As for Foà, he was at last convinced that hiding was now "more than justified."[10] He chose nevertheless to remain at home. No amount of argument could alter his decision, at least for now.

The president seemed tired, broken. He had failed.

It had all come apart. All the tape and bandages; all the glue, the rubber bands, the patches, and the stitches; all the plaster and the gum, all the salve, the ointment, and the balm had not held the dream together.

It had been, Foà with admirable honesty would concede, "a vain illusion!"[11]

Yet there had to be an explanation. There had to be a reason why the plans of the community's most prominent Jews had run aground, why the Jews of Rome were suffering this fate. The president searched for an answer, drawing this pitiful, flatulent conclusion:

> With their Italian spirit, they could not have foreseen the events. Rather what was needed was the Teutonic mentality, which is accompanied by an intellectual acuity of the first order and a cold, unique culture arising from a mysterious fount of unchanged ancestral barbarity.
>
> Then the inevitability of terror would have seemed natural and logical even at only the sound of the name Hitler, who had already violated their coreligionists in Germany and Poland with unspeakable horrors.
>
> And perhaps then the *razzia* of 16 October would have claimed less victims.[12]

The leaders, the wealthy, the educated and otherwise prominent Jews were being taken, too. For reasons that would never become clear, some of them, such as Foà and the Jewish publisher Morpurgo, had been exempted—apparently without their knowledge, however. By error or plan, the Germans did not come to their homes that day.* Others, such as President Almansi, Renzo Levi, and Chief Rabbi Zolli, were secure in the homes of Catholic Romans, and still others had long ago left town. Nevertheless, prominent Jews would make up almost 5 percent of the captives.

* Morpurgo was at his country house in Velletri. He later said that some days prior to the 16th "someone," whom he could not recall, warned him of the impending roundup. "Other Jews" had been so notified too, he said, some of whom "did not believe."[13]

In Via Piemonte, just off the Via Veneto, *Grande Ufficiale* Lionello Alatri, a member of the Jewish Council, was arrested with his wife and her ninety-year-old father. Alatri was the owner of one of Rome's largest department stores. A member of an old merchant family who for centuries had played a major role in the administration of the Roman Jewish community, he had been repeatedly advised to hide. But he had refused. Even now, whatever might have been his private thoughts, he professed not the slightest doubt that everything would be all right.

Alina Cavalieri, benefactress of the Jewish hospital, philanthropist, and according to Foà, "a woman of high lineage and exquisite good will,"[14] was arrested in her apartment in Via Marghera near the University City district. By coincidence, Settimio Sorani, who had left his hiding place to warn the refugees in his care not to move from the safety of their hotel rooms, was passing through Signorina Cavalieri's street at the moment of her arrest. He watched the sixty-one-year-old woman climb aboard the police truck, which was otherwise empty. "She was serene," he later recalled.[15]

Signorina Cavalieri had been among those who had agreed with Rabbi Zolli that he ought to hide. "If they arrest you," she had said to him in September, "it is more probable that they will think of us too."[16] As for herself, she had felt secure enough. She had spent the previous night going over plans for a hospital she was going to build at her own expense. It was to be for the benefit of refugees from Allied bombings.[17]

A few blocks north, Retired Admiral Augusto Capon and his elderly servant were taken by the Germans too. Admiral Capon was the father-in-law of Enrico Fermi, the Nobel physicist who at this time was in Chicago, secretly engaged in the development of the world's first atomic bomb. Admiral Capon, seventy-one years old, was paralyzed from the waist down. He went quietly, leaving his house on crutches. He took with him a personal letter he had once received from Mussolini. He thought it would be useful.[18]

In Via Po, the same street where Captain Dannecker lived, the Germans called now at the home of *Ingegnere* Arrigo Tedeschi. Tedeschi, fifty-six, lived with his wife and their son.

Another son, Gianfranco, who would one day become a leading Jungian psychiatrist and a successor to Ugo Foà as president of the Jewish Community of Rome, had been sent to Switzerland to study.

This morning the Germans pounded heavily at the door to the Tedeschi home. "Open up!" they shouted. *"Deutsches Polizei!"*

It was a convenient warning. The Tedeschis began to flee rushing through the large apartment toward the service exit. Their non-Jewish servant would answer the front door, affording additional precious seconds in which to get away. Suddenly, however, Tedeschi told his wife and son to go ahead, and he would be along in a moment or two. When his family was out of view, Tedeschi inexplicably turned around and went quietly to answer the relentless knocking at the door, arriving there before the maid.

The Germans flung themselves inside. They cut the telephone wires and handed Tedeschi the bill of instructions. When the time was up, they took both him and the maid away, the latter being released in a nearby piazza where the Jews of this action-precinct were being gathered. Tedeschi boarded the black truck.[19]

VI

IN EVERY HOME the Germans entered, if there was a telephone, one way or another they disconnected it—a gesture of almost no significance. On the other hand they maintained excellent telephone service throughout the city that day, and wherever the SS struck, there was always an escapee or some other eyewitness who called his friends and relatives in zones where the Germans had not yet arrived. In this way the news of the raid spread rapidly throughout the city, and while the poorest Jews, who did not have telephones, were still in wait for word-of-mouth communication, hundreds of other Jews were running now. They found shelter in the homes of non-Jewish neighbors; they hurried to the mountains and the countryside, the city's convents and monasteries, and even hid among the ancient ruins on Palatine hill.

In one such case the telephone rang and a tremulous voice at the other end of the line reported: "Giovanni is here!" It was a prearranged signal at once understood.

"I hung up," the Jewish recipient of the call was to say, "and rushed to alert my mother and my kid brother who was still asleep."

> Then I grabbed a suitcase containing cash and valuables, which had been readied sometime before, and I ran with my wife to take her to the home of nearby friends. I left the valise with a friend at a store on the corner of our street and I went back to my building to pick up another suitcase, which was filled with clothes. Just as I got to the front door, I saw two helmeted SS men with machine guns looking at my house number. . . . My mother and my brother were still inside. Alarmed, I stopped a passerby, he too one of our neighbors, and asked him to warn them of the imminent peril. He calmed me, saying that he had already done so, and he told me to get away at once.

He returned to the apartment of his non-Jewish friends. From the window he and his wife could see the truck that had come for them. "Alongside of it were women and children, crying hopelessly. Other SS were entering the building facing ours. We knew that the Jews who lived there fortunately had abandoned their apartment long ago. The truck picked up its mournful course and in the street everything returned to normal."[1]

Lello Perugia, the Jewish Communist in the Roman Resistance, who lived on the periphery of the city, received a telephone call from someone he did not even know.

"This is Peppe," the caller said, "run!"

The sound of his voice was urgent, and it did not take too

many more words to convince Lello. The Perugias fled; they took to the mountains.[2]

They did not know that even as they ran, a German truck had been coming to get them. It had already made one of the two stops assigned to the SS men of this squad. They had called at the home of the twelve-member Efrati family who lived near the rail yards a few blocks away. They had taken all but one, a son who had spent the night in the home of non-Jewish friends. The Efratis owned a telephone, an old-fashioned model with a horn-shaped receiver. But that morning no one called. Now eleven Efratis rode in the black truck. An SS man watched them; two others were in the cab. They drove to the Perugias, but when they arrived, no one was in, and they went on toward Via Lungara, to the Collegio Militare. The Efratis believed the Germans were moving them because they lived dangerously close to the marshaling yards, a military objective of Allied bombings. Though they would rather have stayed in their own home, perhaps, they thought, it would be all for the good.[3]

Statistically, for every Jew who was taken, eleven others escaped. But for forty-four-year-old Settimio Calò, who had queued up for the cigarette ration earlier in the morning, the figures were exactly reversed. When he had returned to his ghetto apartment, his wife and nine children were gone; another daughter, newly married, who lived around the corner in Via della Reginella, had also disappeared.

"I thought I had gone mad," Calò later declared.

> No one was there. Someone told me they had been taken away. I began to run, I don't know where to. I found my way to Via Lungara. They were all there, everyone who had been taken. I threw myself against the doors. I wanted to go too. An Italian guard stopped me, pulled me by the arm, saying, 'Are you crazy, get out of here! Don't you know they'll grab you too, if they see you?' I didn't know anything. I kept pushing and shoving, but he threw me out. I walked a little, sat on the ground, and began to cry.[4]

Directly across the river, in Via Banco di S. Spirito, 3, the Germans were ringing the doorbell of the second floor apartment of the Reverend Emanuele Sbaffi, director of the Weslyan Methodist Church of Italy. The Protestant clergyman had been in his office on the fourth story and had seen the Germans from the window there. The truck was parked near Rome's only Methodist church, adjacent the building in which Sbaffi lived and worked. He had started to go downstairs, when he saw the two Fiorentino women, who belonged to one of the Jewish families who lived in the palazzo. Their elderly father had already been arrested, but the Germans had not seen them, and Sbaffi had hurried them into his home.

Now, as his wife was tending the two disconsolate women in a small room off the entrance foyer, the reverend answered the door.

"I found myself standing in front of two soldiers of the SS," he said subsequently. "Accompanied by the *portiere,* they showed me a typewritten page which contained the names of the Jewish residents of the building."

They had been trying to enter the apartment next to Sbaffi's, the Germans explained, but no one would answer the door. It was the home of the Ottolenghi family, Jews marked for deportation. Did the reverend know where they were?

"I replied that I thought they had all departed," Sbaffi's statement continued, "and that was why no one responded. Then the two soldiers began striking the door violently with the butt of their rifles. . . . But the door was resistant and would not give. They asked me if I had an axe. I said I had none. . . . I was afraid they would want to search my apartment. A couple of feet away from them was the entrance to my living room, and in there the Fiorentino women."

On the other side of the door the Germans were trying to fell, mother and daughter Gina and Giulia Ottolenghi listened to the thunderous blows against the wood. They could see the door wincing at every strike. The bolts were giving, and the hinges were slowly being driven from the posts they had clung to for so many years. It would not be long, it seemed to them, before the Germans would smash through.

They decided to jump from the window. The drop to the pavement below was about twenty feet, a frightening, almost impossible plunge. But there was a small terrace jutting from the apartment beneath theirs. It divided the distance to the ground by two. They leaped. Then again. Signora Ottolenghi's foot struck the pavement hard. It fractured, and her legs buckled under the weight of her body. Giulia lost her balance completely. She landed on her back, injuring her spine. But they went on, getting to their hands and knees and crawling to the shop of a marble worker in the nearby Via del Panico who took them inside.

The Germans, however, were unable to break down the door. They went away. Reverend Sbaffi's wife went to look for the Ottolenghis. She found them and did what she could to comfort them.[5]

By now the woman called Laurina had escaped the ghetto. Hobbling along with her family and their belongings, she had got as far as Largo Argentina, about 300 yards from her home, when she realized one of her relatives was missing.

Someone who was with her said that the missing person had started to go out of the house, but he had seen the two Germans standing at the doorway and had been afraid to pass them. They were the same friendly soldiers who had permitted Laurina to get away in the first place. She decided to return to escort the frightened man to safety.

Retracing her steps, she arrived at the doorway, finding the soldiers still there. They were surprised to see her, but said nothing. The look in their eyes, it seemed to her, indicated that she was still under their protection. She walked into the hallway and called upstairs.

"*Resciùd,* Enrico!" she cried, using the Hebrew-Romanesque word for escape.

Just then, however, the arresting squad arrived. They saw Laurina shouting, forced her back upstairs, and began taking everyone on their list. Laurina took hold of the situation. With persistent bluster, she tried to convince the Germans she was not Jewish and really had no time to argue with them, since she was on her way to the hospital to have her leg treated. She knocked on her plaster cast for emphasis. The Germans said she could go. At that moment four children came rushing down the stairs, a soldier chasing them.

"Help us!" they screamed. "Laurina, Laurina, save us!"

She caught the children in her arms and pushed them behind her, using her body to shield them. She insisted they all belonged to her and the Germans had better not harm them. They told her to leave, children and all.

When they reached the street, the children ran away. Laurina took two or three labored steps, stopped for an instant, and fainted, collapsing on the cobblestones. She was taken to a cafe near the Ponte Garibaldi, and when, some minutes later, she recovered, she left the ghetto and picked up the trail of her flight.[6]

While Jews everywhere continued to scatter like the splinters that splay from a bomb, German trucks from all over Rome moved inward to the Collegio Militare near the center of town.

Not all of them were covered. People were seen riding through the streets of Rome, drenched in the rain that kept stopping and starting throughout the early morning. They stood, crouched, leaned, sat, and squatted, their hair matted, their faces dripping water and often tears. Some still wore pajamas, others only a coat with little or no clothes underneath. The young covered the old. The old shielded the children. But the rain, when it fell, reached everywhere. It soaked whatever they wore, from the kerchiefs and scarves around their heads and shoulders to the socks inside their shoes.

Non-Jewish Romans who saw them pass, paled with feelings of shock, incredulity, and disdain and hatred for the Germans. A handful of others, the evidence shows, were secretly delighted, experiencing a perverse pleasure. But the overwhelming majority looked on in bitter silence or shook their fists with rage.

One eyewitness, a Roman newspaperman, two years later wrote what he had seen. He had stood alongside one of the trucks, he said, as the Germans were making arrests in a nearby building. The van was packed with people, including many children, he wrote, adding:

The eyes of the children were dilated and unseeing. It seemed as if they were asking for an explanation for such terror and suffering. . . . A poor woman standing beside me took a rosary from her pocket and began to pray and to cry, murmuring rhythmically with a spasmodic tremor in her lips: *"Povera carne innocente."* The truck departed, making a creaking noise. When it turned the corner, a working man, after declaring that he had been a fervent Fascist, started cursing Mussolini and his cowardice for having "teamed up" with Hitler in the persecution of "the people who had done nothing wrong."[7]

In the Campo Marzio district, near the Parliament building, two or three German trucks with an exceptionally large number of children in the vans were temporarily parked in Via Fontanella di Borghese. The Marquise Fulvia Ripa di Meana, a member of the Roman aristocracy, was passing through the street and saw the prisoner-children. She later described the scene:

I saw in their terror-stricken eyes, in their faces grown pale as if with pain, and in their little quivering hands that clung to the sides of the truck, the maddening fear that had overtaken them by what they had seen and heard, and the atrocious anguish in their little hearts in anticipation of that which yet awaited them. Those little children could not even cry anymore. Fear had rendered them mute and had inflamed their eyes with tears that did not flow. Only in the back of the truck, thrown on a wooden plank, some infants, who were hungry and chilled, were shrieking pitifully.[8]

Many of the German drivers of the trucks were unfamiliar with the city's streets, and in a number of instances they lost their way. They were to be seen entering dead end streets, going every which way, stopping to ask directions, turning, backing up, and getting on the wrong track again.

Trucks wandered off as far as some country roads that led out of the city. But the confusion was greatest around the Vatican, which was only a fraction of a mile from the Collegio Militare. Some of the lost drivers were using Vatican City as a landmark, searching for it to recover their bearing. But others, it seems, who were seeing Rome for the first time, had deliberately wanted to pass the Vatican for what might be their only chance to see the great Basilica of Saint Peter.[9] At one point there were several trucks parked adjacent to, or slowly circling the extraterritorial zone. While the Germans who were making this tour craned their necks at the imposing views, peering through the white embrace of Bernini's colonnades for a glimpse of the awesome dome, captive Jews from within the vans were shouting the name of the Holy Father in order that he might save them.[10] It is doubtful, however, that Pope Pius XII, several hundred feet away, heard them.*

But inside the Vatican, at an early hour of the morning, the Pope was informed that the Germans had struck. The expected *razzia* was taking place. The policy of silence was on the line. "Pressure from all sides," to use Ambassador Weizsäcker's words, was building up, calling for a "demonstrative censure of the deportation of the Jews of Rome."[11]

VII

SOMETIME DURING THE morning the Fascist newspapers began calling the German embassy at the Villa Wolkonsky. They had heard rumors of a roundup of the city's Jews, and they requested confirmation or clarification.[1] Consul Möllhausen was

* The closest possible approach to the well-known windows of the Pope's office—without entering Vatican territory, which the Germans were strictly forbidden to violate—is a point just north of the piazza today known as Pius XII Square, some 250 yards away. The Collegio Militare was about 900 yards from the Pope's windows, but less than 900 feet from the southern edge of Vatican City. Of the Jews who were arrested, the one who appears to have lived nearest the Vatican was sixty-nine-year-old Augusto Piperno, Via Giulio Cesare, 223, a distance of about 600 feet from the north wall of the city-state.

not in Rome.[2] He had gone to the north to meet with Rahn and explain his unauthorized telegrams to Foreign Minister Ribbentrop. The embassy in Rome declared it knew nothing about a roundup and began to make inquiries of its own.[3]

Between nine and ten o'clock in the morning Albrecht von Kessel appeared at Möllhausen's embassy in behalf of the Nazi mission to the Holy See. The highest ranking diplomat in the Villa Wolkonsky that morning was Gerhard R. Gumpert, legation secretary in charge of the economic section, who in the absence of the consul was acting in his stead. Kessel went to Gumpert, who apart from being his colleague was also his close friend.[4]

Kessel, somewhat agitated, explained what was going on in the streets outside. He adduced the reasons why something had to be done to stop the roundup, or at least alleviate the profound effects it was expected to have on German foreign policy.

Speaking in his heavily nasal tone, which his friends in lighter moments would take endless delight in caricaturing and imitating, Kessel was forced to go into some detail about the diplomatic problems involved, for Gumpert until now had scarcely heard of the Jews of Rome. The thirty-three-year-old legation secretary's assignment in Rome was to procure Italian foodstuffs and other indigenous products for the Reich, a job he had been ill-prepared for, since he had entered the foreign service as a lawyer in the legal department. He knew that the local Jews were experiencing difficulties, having heard from Möllhausen of the gold episode and the events that were associated with it. But this information had been of little practical interest to him, since he believed it would never enter into the matters with which he was concerned.[5]

Gumpert, though it had been his lifelong dream to be a diplomat, had since entering the service six years earlier developed a duodenal ulcer that was threatening his young life. His illusions too had long ago been ulcerated, and he had arrived at the conclusion that a good diplomat was nothing more than a man—preferably with a "woman's intuition"—"who understands nothing, does anything, and looks good while doing it."[6]

Von Kessel, who Gumpert considered the "classic" diplomat, concluded his exposition with the suggestion that for reasons of competence it was up to the Villa Wolkonsky, and not Weizsäcker's embassy, to act, at least in the first instance.

"Look, Kessel," Gumpert replied when at last his colleague had finished speaking. "What can *I* do? If you came to me for some barrels of potatoes or sacks of grain, then I could help you. But what do *I* know about these things?"

"Well, well," Kessel stammered, "something has to be done."

This talk went on for a while until an idea finally emerged, apparently from Gumpert himself, to bring the Vatican into the picture. If the Holy See were to somehow intervene—within the limits of the policy of silence, the salvation of which being the fundamental aim of this activity—Gumpert would be willing to take the matter up with Berlin.[7]

Protocol required that any such intervention be made at Weizsäcker's mission. But since the Vatican had had dealings with Stadtkommandant Stahel, it was thought wiser to utilize this relationship. It would inject still another high authority into the body of this countermaneuver, thereby strengthening it, and in reducing the individual responsibility of the Germans involved, it would enhance the immunity of all.

Kessel agreed to this approach.

"All right," said Gumpert. "I'll dictate a letter. But you'll have to get someone in the Vatican to sign it. Let them put it on stationery with the letterhead of the Holy See and take it to Stahel. Just be sure to tell me when whoever it is who's going to bring it will be there so that I can get the letter from Stahel and send it on to Berlin."[8]

The plan was for Gumpert to be in Stahel's office, which was not too many doors from his own, at the same time the Vatican's protest would arrive. In this way, Gumpert could immediately take it out of the hands of the general, who doubtless would be happy to be relieved of any additional burdens on his work and on his soul. It was of course not Stahel they were trying to impress. The Stadtkommandant, who had provided three companies of troops for the arrest of the city's Jews, was not now going to renege. Too many men had worked out their roles in this affair; too many bureaus had been set in motion. While it is not likely that the German diplomats who were preparing this intervention knew that Stahel himself had authorized and had made the roundup possible, no one could believe that the Stadtkommandant could stop the arrests any more than he could turn back the clock. The intervention was being rolled out like a red carpet not for Stahel, but for the benefit of Ribbentrop, Himmler, and the Führer himself. If any of them chose to move, there always had to be a path, something soft upon which to tread.

Kessel took up his end, and the Vatican was now brought into the plan, in the person of Father Pankratius Pfeiffer, Pius XII's personal liaison with the Germans in Rome. The Pope himself, according to Vatican sources, concurred, giving Pfeiffer "carte blanche," to speak in his name to the full extent of the established policies of the Holy See.[9]

The letter was to be handed personally by Padre Pancrazio—as Pfeiffer was called by all who knew him—to General Stahel. These two men had developed a very close friendship. According to one Catholic authority on Vatican affairs, Pfeiffer's "extreme good will, which at first had been exercised in behalf of the soldiers of the Wehrmacht, attracted the attention of General Stahel, military commandant of Rome and a practicing Catholic, who discovered that the padre, like himself, was a Bavarian. They became friends . . . [until] Berlin recalled its too-human chief. . . ."[10]

Pfeiffer, however, was unknown in Berlin, and he was not thought of as the signer of the letter. It had to be a man with a name of consequence, a person respected by the Nazis, if only for his title and his position in the scheme of Vatican-German relations.

The prelate finally agreed upon by all, since they could obtain no one of higher name and rank, was Bishop Alois Hudal, Rector of the German Catholic church in Rome, Santa Maria dell'Anima. Like Pfeiffer, he too was a citizen of the Third Reich. Hudal was also a friend of Stahel, as well as von

Weizsäcker. According to the bishop himself, he and the ambassador were collaborating on another project—which was to enjoy little success—issuing "letters granting immunity" from SS persecutions to Jews they considered meritorious of such treatment.[11]

Now the bishop was prepared to do whatever was thought appropriate in this emerging affair. Hudal seemed a logical choice for the assignment, but in fact he represented a compromise. Kessel had suggested that the Vatican "lodge an official protest."[12] But the Vatican, in agreeing to intervene, had qualified its action, in the name of "prudence" no doubt, as being "without any official mandate."[13] Thus the letter would not go on the stationery of the Holy See, but on Bishop Hudal's.

When it became known who the signer would be, Gumpert called in his secretary, Anneliese Krüger, a German national born in Rome. "Krüger!" he barked melodramatically, "roll a sheet of paper in your typewriter!" Then, like scriptwriters with a pressing deadline, Gumpert and Kessel dictated Bishop Hudal's historic letter of protest to the head of the occupation forces in Rome.[14] When finished and polished it read:

> I must speak to you of a matter of great urgency. An authoritative Vatican dignitary, who is close to the Holy Father, has just told me that this morning a series of arrests of Jews of Italian nationality has been initiated. In the interests of the good relations that have existed until now between the Vatican and the High Command of the German Armed Forces—above all thanks to the political wisdom and magnanimity of Your Excellency, which will one day go down in the history of Rome—I earnestly request that you order the immediate suspension of these arrests both in Rome and its environs. Otherwise I fear that the Pope will take a position in public as being against this action [*ich fürchte dass der Papst sonst öffentlich dagegen Stellung nehmen wird*], one which would undoubtedly be used by the anti-German propagandists as a weapon against us Germans.[15]

Kessel left with the typed draft, which was then prepared for Hudal's signature. Some minor, nonsubstantive cuts were made, but the text, as cited above, appeared in the final copy. The hour for Padre Pancrazio's appearance at Stahel's office was arranged. Kessel then called Gumpert and informed him that Pfeiffer would arrive precisely at 5:00 P.M. Gumpert said he himself would be there at 4:45.[16]

VIII

AT 11:00 A.M. the rain stopped, the clouds opened up as if to yawn, and the sun shone through. Arrests were still being made, but the rate of capture was rapidly falling off, and the streets were becoming more and more barren and silent.[1]

In the ghetto the latest group of captives waited at the gates of the Roman ruins for the shuttling trucks to come for them. The sunlight cast stark truncated shadows from the broken pillars on the sunken patch of unpaved ground that lay between the ancient theater and the portico. The bright light shone on the streets of the ghetto, making a sudden spectacle of the debris that had collected since dawn. The pavement was strewn with litter: broken dishes, fallen and discarded objects, clothing, scraps of paper, and even furniture, plaster and wood, which had somehow come from the now nearly vacant Jewish homes.

Inside some apartments children were hiding under beds or behind rows of clothes in the box-type wardrobes of the time. Their mothers and fathers, at the moment the Germans arrived had sent them or placed them there. And now that the parents had been taken away, there was no one to tell them to come out. In one abandoned house a baby girl lay on a bed, each of her captured parents having thought that the child had been led to safety by the other spouse.[2]

A few minutes past eleven o'clock the sky tightened down again, and the sun disappeared for the rest of the day.

At noon, as was the usual practice in wartime Rome, the first newspapers of the day came out. Though the entire city at this hour was aware of the roundup taking place within its walls, the press was silent.

"School begins again on November 8," wrote one Fascist paper.

"Whoever has permission to drive his own car," another item informed, "may not go faster than forty kilometers an hour."[3]

Il Messaggero, the city's leading newspaper, commented editorially on the war: ". . . the blame of the war is on the Jews . . . and all those, though they may be of Aryan blood, who have taken as their own the brutal, mammonistic Jewish mentality." It continued: "Today, as always, fascism considers the children of Israel as one of its mortal enemies and the Jewish threat as one of the most sinister of all those which concern our nation in these decisive hours."[4]

Il Giornale d'Italia, an important voice of neofascism, wrote of the worldwide prestige of Pope Pius XII. The presence in this city of the Bishop of Rome, the Vatican, and all its churches, said the newspaper, created a certain dualism of great significance. In the city, it went on:

> there are two ways of life, which intermingle, combine, and join together. They are: religious life and civilian life, that is, the life of a citizen of the most august city on earth and the universal life of the Catholic Church, which knows no boundaries. It is from the unity of these two ways of life that springs forth even today, in the midst of war, the inviolability of Rome.[5]

The Vatican's own newspaper, *l'Osservatore Romano*, the only non-Fascist, legally distributed newspaper in Rome, also had nothing to say about the *razzia*. This was not surprising, for it maintained a policy of being slow to react to temporal events.

There was one item in the Fascist press, however, which was

associated with the roundup. It could be understood by only a few, but in the history of the Nazi assault on the Jews of Rome it would become, in an indirect way, the first printed word of the chronicle of death. It read: "Italian officers scheduled to leave today at 9:00 A.M. for the north, will not depart from Tiburtina Station. The departure will take place tomorrow morning from Termini."[6]

The reason for the postponement and the change of terminal, which was not given, was that German and Italian railroad personnel had had to preempt the military departure for a train of higher priority. It too would soon leave Rome for the north, quietly and unannounced, and to avoid being publicly seen, other outgoing and incoming passenger trains to and from Tiburtina Station had been temporarily shunted to Termini. Now being assembled from freight cars in the Tiburtina marshaling yards, this special train was intended to carry the Jews of Rome to Auschwitz.[7]

IX

THE CENTURIES-OLD Collegio Militare was a massive, fortress-like structure, which lay between the river and the foot of Janiculum hill in a sparsely resided zone. It was actually four buildings in one. Each section stood at right angles to the other forming an almost perfect square. In the center was a large courtyard tiled with a mosaic of geometric shapes. This added an illusion of sinew and even wisdom to the powerful palazzo. A life-sized statue of Julius Caesar stood in a marbled hallway between the entrance and the courtyard. The figure had an outstretched, muscular arm and a masterful expression of fatherly severity. Above the entrance way, inscribed in tall, deep-set letters which would never fade, was the legend, "*Romana Virtus Romae Discitur*—Roman Virtue is Learned in Rome."

It had always been a forbidding building, and though it was situated in the heart of the city, few people in Rome had ever given it mind. Today its huge, irregular stone blocks were feeling the rumbling of a chaos the old military school had never known before. The number of captured Jews who had arrived there by now amounted to well beyond one thousand. They were an incongruously mixed mass of utterly disoriented and confounded souls, who, apart from being clawed from within by an implacable beast of unknowns, were also being barked and snapped at in a language they could not understand.

Trucks still arrived. They drove through the arched entrance way, passed the statue of Caesar, and into the courtyard, where all of the Jews were being jammed. The Germans, led by Captain Dannecker, were trying to bring some order to the crowd, attempting to break it up into smaller, more manageable groups. But no one comprehended the commands of the captors, who, interpreting this as disobedience, were expressing their discomfiture in the form of violence.[1]

Those who were being mistreated worst of all were some 250 non-Jews and less-than-full-Jews, who had been caught in the sweep, and were protesting their "innocence." The German guards, who had no notion of what they were saying, thought them the most unruly of all and beat them off with fists and gun butts.

In the midst of this, families who had been separated hours earlier pushed through the packed mass of humanity trying to reunite with one another. Children were getting lost in the crush, and they cried for their mothers. Relatives and friends who had not seen each other in months or even years greeted and embraced one another with tears, as well as joyful smiles. The press of Jew upon Jew, the tightness of it all, despite the fearsome circumstances in which it occurred, lent a quality of unity to the group, one in which there was pain-melting warmth and a feeling of security in numbers, which quelled one's fears. Whereas something dreadful could happen to a man alone, it was inconceivable that a group as large as this one was destined for anything less than an acceptable end. Hapless, however, were those who had believed their loved ones had escaped and now found them taken too. Settimia Spizzichino, for example, had been convinced, along with her mother and sister, that her married sister Ada had evaded the roundup because she had gone for cigarettes. But here in the courtyard they saw Ada and her daughter debark from a truck that arrived shortly after theirs.[2]

When Arminio Wachsberger climbed down from the truck that brought him and his family to the Collegio Militare, he was stunned by the utter babel. Like everyone else in the compound, he had never seen so many Roman Jews assembled in one place. He was surprised that even some of the prominent Jews of the city were there. He saw Alina Cavalieri, the grand dowager of the Red Cross, and as he later recalled it, "several physicians and professors." He recognized Admiral Capon, too. The old man was pushing forward on his crutches trying to show his letter from Mussolini.[3]

Wachsberger, almost at once, discerned the cause of the pandemonium, particularly the reason why no one was obeying the orders of the German soldiers.

"I therefore approached the officer who was commanding them [Dannecker], and speaking in German, I explained that the confusion was owed to the fact that no one understood his orders."[4]

"Okay," said Dannecker, "you're the interpreter."[5]

The SS captain, who had been standing on a desk dragged out from one of the classrooms, told Wachsberger to get up alongside him and the German and the Jew proceeded to bring order to the affair. "In this way," Wachsberger was to recall, "after a few minutes the atmosphere finally became a little calmer."[6]

When the group had been quieted and organized, the non-Jews and part-Jews began to shout at Wachsberger.

"Tell the commandant that we're not Jews!" one of them cried, with others immediately joining him.[7]

Wachsberger passed the request on to Dannecker, who instructed him to reply that all those who, according to German law, were not Jewish would be released following an examination of their identity papers, a procedure which would be undertaken later in the day.[8]

A little after 2:00 P.M. the last truck entered the courtyard; the roundup of the Jews of Rome was complete. The entire compound was sealed, the various entrances being reinforced with wooden boards nailed across the doorposts. The windows that gave on to the streets, many of which were already grated, were similarly blocked. Guards were stationed at strategic points. They were provided with submachine guns and orders to execute anyone caught attempting to escape.[9]

The men were separated from the women and children, and a count was made of the prisoners. The official figure reached was 1,259, of whom 363 were counted as men, and 896 in the women and children category.[10]

Now the Jews were redivided into groups ranging from seventy-five to one hundred, each of which were enclosed in the several classrooms of the military school which circumscribed the courtyard. Their capacity, however, was found wanting, and a large number of prisoners were gathered in one of the building's arcades. Some, who had put up resistance during the day or had otherwise been difficult to manage were also placed here and as a punishment were forced to stand close to, and facing a blank wall.[11]

A few prisoners were given the job of distributing the meager supply of food rations, of which there was not enough to go around even once. They were joined by several Italian NCOs who were being held in the Collegio Militare for refusing to obey an order to go north for service in Mussolini's phantom Fascist Republican Army. They went from one classroom to another trying to be helpful to the other prisoners. Many who had been taken from sick beds were in dire need of medicines, and others had been injured as a result of rough treatment during the roundup.[12]

Lazzaro Anticoli, the young mechanic whose daughter was ill with diphtheria, was among those chosen for the distribution team. He was able to move about freely from room to room, and he found that despite the discomforts, most people at this hour were more or less at ease.[13] They sat at the *banchi*, or schoolroom desks, doodled on blackboards, walked, leaned, and camped on the floor. The rations that were given out disappeared almost at once, but many had brought food with them in baskets and sacks, and suddenly it seemed everyone was eating.

Almost all of the Jews were convinced, on the basis of affirmations by the Germans, which were endlessly echoed by the prisoners, that the group was going to a labor camp. In room after room talk centered on what life might be like at the camp.[14] Depending on one's social status, it was envisaged as anything from being inferior to the worst imaginable situation to a condition in some ways an actual improvement on the customary ceaseless struggle to subsist. For an unemployed worker with a wife and several children, the prospect of an all-expenses-paid sojourn in Germany for himself and his family did not appear as a totally unpleasant prospect, no matter how hard he would have to work. Though there was no captive in the Collegio Militare who would not have preferred to have been released, no doubt many people were anticipating a more economically secure future than they had ever enjoyed in the past.

Anticoli himself was too busy to give much thought to what lay ahead. He was making the rounds of the classrooms and crisscrossing the circles and lines of the patio-like courtyard. At one point, despite the effort the Germans had made to close off the building, Anticoli turned a door handle and a moment later found himself standing on the street outside without a guard in view. He suddenly decided to go to a nearby tobacco shop which was known to him. Saturday being the only day to buy cigarettes, and considering his situation, he thought it wise to try to stock up on them. The tobacconist's was about 100 feet from the Collegio Militare in Piazza della Rovere, a busy square just off one of the Tiber bridges. Anticoli went inside and asked for some *Trestellas,* a popular brand of cigarettes. He was told, however, that there were no cigarettes remaining, but a note in the seller's voice communicated that the void could be negotiated. A deal was made. There being no *Trestellas,* Anticoli bought ten packs of *Africa* for 100 lire, which was about twice the normal price. He then departed, reentered the Collegio Militare, and closed himself inside.[15]

Later in the afternoon word began to circulate among the prisoners that all non-Jews and part-Jews were to come forward. They were to be released. Anyone caught lying about the extent of his Jewishness would be killed immediately, it was said. A big question rolled over the Jewish prisoners like a heavy thundercloud: Could a Jew bluff his way to freedom?

One's religion was not indicated on his identity documents. There was no manner in which the Germans could tell a Roman Jew, except if he were to give himself away by a look in his eye, or else, if he were man or boy, by whether or not he were circumcised. Was it worth the risk? Unless he were a Coen or a Levi, his name, no matter how Italian-Jewish it might be, protected him. Could the Germans know the difference between an Anticoli and an Antonini or a Segni and a Di Segni? Or could they?

In one of the rooms, the seventeen members of the Sabatello-Di Segni family, who had been taken from the second and third floors of Via del Portico d'Ottavia, 9, paid no attention to this new dilemma. They felt it in no way concerned them.[16] But in another room, on the courtyard level of the Collegio Militare, Settimia Spizzichino pleaded with her mother and sisters in order that they all try to get away. She had seen the non-Jews begin to gather, and among them she had recognized some who were entirely Jewish and were obviously about to attempt the deception. There were no males among the captured Spizzichinos, and their Jewishness could easily be concealed, it seemed. The idea was tempting, but fear won out and Settimia's importunations were rejected.[17]

In the meantime a group of nearly 300 "non-Jews" had collected. They consisted of Aryans—mostly servants or boarders of Jewish families who had been captured—spouses and offsprings of mixed marriages, and a small number of Jews who were hoping to "pass," or who had merely come to see if such a possibility existed.

Dannecker appeared now. Arminio Wachsberger, who had remained constantly at the captain's side as his *Dolmetscher*, or interpreter, stood by. The SS man told Wachsberger to instruct the group to form a single file in front of them.

"Whoever is not a Jew, line up here," said Wachsberger translating Dannecker's command. The SS man then ordered Wachsberger to remind them that, "If I find a Jew who dares to declare himself as not being one, the moment the lie is discovered he will be shot on the spot. And tell them that we Germans don't talk out of our hats."[18]

Wachsberger obeyed, and the examination of documents began. Dannecker looked at the papers and continually consulted with Wachsberger as to whether the name was of Jewish origin. As soon as he realized that Dannecker was totally ignorant of Italian Jewish names, Wachsberger began to signal with a nod of his head or a flash of his eyes to some Jews lingering at the fringes of the group to fall into line. He had recognized them, and knowing their surnames, he knew they would pass. One of them was a Venetian Jewish tailor named Diena, who lived in Rome, and another was a woman named Di Segni.[19] Dannecker himself, according to Nazi practice during the years 1941-1944, freed all Jewish spouses of non-Jews. In this way, 252 persons, among them several Jews, were marked for release.*

* Legend still persists in Rome that the Vatican obtained this "concession" from the Germans. One story goes that a cardinal appeared at the Collegio Militare, intervened with Dannecker in the name of the Pope, and won agreement that at the very least the above-mentioned categories of persons be discharged. The Holy See itself has never either confirmed or denied any role in this incident, although the Roman Jewish historian Tagliacozzo says that a Vatican intervention has been "discreetly admitted by persons very close to Roman ecclesiastic circles."[20] The legend, however, dissolves rapidly in the known facts. Survivors of the Collegio Militare experience agree that there was no visible intervention, crediting the initiative wholly to Dannecker.

On the other hand, one Catholic woman stayed behind. She had been arrested with a Jewish boy, an orphan who was afflicted with epilepsy, for whom the woman had been caring as a nurse. She chose not to desert the epileptic and did not stand in the line of non-Jews.[22]

With the release of the group of 252, which would not actually take place until dawn of the following morning, the number of captives was brought down to an official final total of 1,007.[23] This figure, however, was wrong. The German reputation for punctiliousness notwithstanding, the count was in error by at least fifty or sixty persons. Though the exact number would never be known there were at this moment more than 1,060 persons enclosed in the Collegio Militare who would be listed for departure on the Rome-Auschwitz train.[24]

X

SOME TEN OR fifteen minutes before five o'clock that afternoon Legation Secretary Gerhard Gumpert arrived at the headquarters of General Stahel. He was awaiting the delivery of the Vatican's letter to the Stadkommandant so that he might report the protest to Berlin. He took a seat in the anteroom to Stahel's office. There was another man waiting to see the general, a young lieutenant, and a moment later a captain entered the room apparently for the same purpose. The higher ranking man intro-

---

More important as will be seen, the release of the Aryans, the so-called *Mischlinge,* or part Jews, and the Jewish partners of mixed marriages represented not the slightest concession, it being carried out according to then existing German law and properly recorded and reported to Berlin.[21]

duced himself to the young officer as Toussaint, and the lieutenant said in quick reply that his name was Langenscheidt. This struck Gumpert as being very comical, and he began to chuckle, although the other men could find no humor in it at all. The two military officers were obviously unaware that when they clicked their surnames at one another, the combination formed the name of an internationally known Berlin publisher of dictionaries and the inventor of a popular phonetic transcription system, Toussaint-Langenscheidt.[1]

Still smiling, Gumpert noted the arrival of Father Pfeiffer, who was being led in to see Stahel. Pfeiffer, in the name of the Pope, appeared almost every day of the week at the general's office with a bill of particulars from the Vatican. But today was clearly special, even in the fact that he had come in the afternoon and not, as usual, in the morning. This was the day the friendly circle of Germans and churchmen had dreaded, their hour of trial.

Pius's representative did not remain very long with the Stadkommandant. Stahel presumably went through the motions of reading the letter and saying something he believed appropriate. He was in the foul position of an unexposed miscreant being asked to uphold the Ten Commandments. Nevertheless, he seems to have assured his fellow Bavarian that he would do all that was possible to help the Jews.[2]

The moment Pfeiffer left, Gumpert managed to appear at Stahel's side. The general, holding Bishop Hudal's letter in his hand, was visibly annoyed.

"Oh, Gumpert," said Stahel, seeing the diplomat, "I'm glad you're here." He showed Gumpert the letter, saying, "What is the meaning of this *Schweinerei*?"[3]—the final word apparently being the only one he knew to characterize any sort of inconvenience.

Gumpert assured the general that he need not concern himself any further. It was a matter that lay within the provenance of Nazi diplomacy. Stahel concurred.[4]

The next step was to inform the Wilhelmstrasse of Hudal's letter and its unprecedented threat of a public protest by the

Pope himself. This was to be done, according to plan, but also as required by form, by the Villa Wolkonsky first, and then by Weizsäcker's embassy at the Holy See. Gumpert almost immediately prepared a "very urgent" telegram. But it would not actually be sent until some five hours later, given the necessary steps before transmission could be effected, and it would not be received at the Foreign Office until 11:30 P.M. In the telegram he simply stated that Bishop Hudal "has just gone to Stadtkommandant General Stahel with a letter." He then reported the text without comment.[5]

Weizsäcker followed at a slower tempo, lest anyone think him rash—as Möllhausen was being lately regarded for example. The seasoned representative of the Nazi Foreign Office played on the oboe of diplomacy with a sense of timing which was understood as a factor of equivalent value as any other. It was not to be thought in Berlin that he was exercising a greater or lesser degree of his talents in this affair than in any other concern of the Reich of equal import. Indeed, he was not—insofar as he interpreted the best interests of the Fatherland, which it must be concluded and stated, had little to do with the lives of a large number of Jews.

After sampling opinion in the Vatican, the ambassador would have the following dispatch composed:

With regard to Bishop Hudal's letter (cf. the telegraphed report of October 16 from Rahn's office), I can confirm that this represents the Vatican's reaction to the deportation of the Jews of Rome. The Curia is especially upset considering that the action took place, in a manner of speaking, under the Pope's own windows. The reaction could be dampened somewhat if the Jews were to be employed in labor service here in Italy.

Hostile circles in Rome are using this event as a means of pressuring the Vatican to drop its reserve. It is being said that when analogous incidents took place in French cities, the bishops there took a clear stand. Thus the Pope, as the supreme leader of the Church and as Bishop of Rome, cannot but do the same. The Pope is also being compared with his predecessor, Pius XI, a man of a more spontaneous temperament.

Enemy propaganda abroad will certainly view this event in the same way, in order to disturb the friendly relations between the Curia and ourselves.[6]

Weizsäcker would not sign this until sometime much later in this day or the next, following which it would be sent off to the Wilhelmstrasse as a nightletter. As for now, with more than a thousand Jews of Rome in captivity, the Church and the diplomats could do nothing further but wait.

XI

All of Rome by now knew the Jews had been taken, and word of where they were being held was galloping too. As night fell, people began to gather outside the Collegio Militare. Jewish wives or husbands, who had been divided from their families in the sudden German thrust into their lives, brought fiberboard suitcases filled with outer clothing, pajamas, underwear, blankets, and toilet articles. They carried canvas bags with bread and wine, and messages hastily scrawled on odd bits and scraps of paper. They pretended to be Christian friends or servants of the prisoners, but no one, of course, could enter the guarded compound, and they placed these things at the portals as one might lay a wreath of roses at a grave. Relatives and friends also came, to see what could be seen. They too had news and sustenance, which they hoped could somehow be carried to the ones they loved. But the Germans chased the crowds away, and the things that had been brought never reached the prisoners.[1]

Inside the massive enclosure Dannecker called the Jews together once again. He had asked for someone among them who had secretarial skills to come forward, and a young woman had presented herself. Now she sat behind a little desk, a typewriter placed before her. The Jews, Dannecker had decided, had to be registered one by one.[2]

While the guards were summoning the captives to a central place, a table was placed beside the typist, and on it, two large, empty boxes. Dannecker and his *Dolmetscher*, Arminio Wachsberger, mounted the table as the group assembled. A murmur arose from the crowd, and expectations simmered in the air. Apart from the smallest children, everyone could sense they were about to learn something about their fate unknown to them before. They were easily quieted, for all of them wanted to hear whatever it was that was about to be said. A hush settled over them like a great shawl, as the captain told the Jew at his side what to say. To use Wachsbergers' words:

> Through me he told us that we were to be transported to Germany to a camp where each of us, according to his skills, would have a job to do. Since the old, the invalid, and women with children would naturally be unable to work and since the German government had no intention of maintaining them free of charge, all money, jewelry, and other objects of value that we had brought with us to the Collegio Militare had to be turned over to him in order to create a communal fund. . . .[3]

"The rich Jews will have to pay for the poor Jews," Dannecker had Wachsberger add. "Now in your right hand you are to place all jewelry, and in your left hand, your money. You will pass in front of me and deposit everything."[4]

Restating the now customary threat that anyone disobeying orders would be shot, Dannecker instructed the Jews to line up in single file, and as they went by, to put objects into the box on the right side of the table and cash on the left. At the same time the young woman who had volunteered as a typist was to record the name of each Jew.

The procession began. Rich and poor, old and young passed by the SS captain surrendering the things they had hurriedly grabbed that morning from the places of security in their homes. It was like a revival of the gold episode of two and one-half weeks ago. Once again the Jews were being asked to yield their gold to alleviate tomorrow's pain. At first no one withheld anything. Precious articles of real and sentimental value, as well as bank notes and coins were urged forward out of fear, but perhaps even more so by a belief in the communal future of the group, as sketched out by the youthful captain. But, according to Wachsberger, who was in an excellent position to observe the SS man, "whenever someone deposited a piece of jewelry of particular value, Dannecker put it in his pocket, and we soon caught on that it had all been only a trick to strip us of our goods."[5]

This information was passed quickly down the line. But most people felt helpless to resist, especially with regard to jewelry and other objects. Still, many others excused themselves temporarily and went to the toilet, where they tore their money into shreds and flushed it down the bowl.[6]

After the valuables had been collected, Dannecker decided to feed the people from the communal larder. The Jews, who at the moment of arrest had been ordered to bring their house keys with them, were now told to turn them over with their address and apartment number written on an accompanying scrap of paper. He then instructed some of his men to visit these homes and remove whatever food they might find there, returning it to the Collegio Militare to be apportioned among the group. He gave them several handfuls of keys and sent them on their way, assigning Wachsberger as their guide.

Dannecker cautioned him not to take advantage of his position. "Look, *Dolmetscher,*" he said, "you'll be on the outside, but remember, your wife and child are on the inside."[7]

Wachsberger had suddenly become the richest, most powerful Jew among all the captives. During the fleecing of the Jews of their money and jewels, he had remained constantly at Dannecker's side, and since the captain had not asked him to surrender his own valuables, he had not volunteered them. He was thus still in possession of his gold Longines watch and two diamond rings.

Clearly in a position of privilege in the eyes of his fellow prisoners, Wachsberger was now of considerable interest to the others, as someone among them who had risen to a high station in life might be. Many who had on occasion seen him in the synagogue or in the streets of the ghetto and Trastevere but did not know his name were asking one another who he was. Since he always responded when Dannecker called him *"Dolmetscher,"* some Jews decided that that was his name, concluding of course that he was not a native Roman Jew. This "name," as a result of the indirect way in which it had been learned, immediately became distorted or contracted to "Nemitch" and tenaciously attached to the young man in the minds of some of the Jews.[8]

He now departed with the SS men in a German truck to call at a random group of Jewish apartments. Like almost every other Roman Jewish home that night, they lay in darkness, devoid of human life. Disheveled beds that would never be made gaped like open wounds. Clothes hung limply over the lips of half-open drawers. Everything, everywhere, was frozen and rigid with the confusion of sudden death.

Much to Wachsberger's horror and genuine surprise, the Germans who were carrying out this supply mission showed almost no interest in the food contained in the apartments being searched. Instead they were looting whatever remaining things of value they could find. Jews who had sought to outwit the Nazis in the morning by hiding such objects instead of bringing them with them, were now being pillaged at night.*[9] The tour of the Jewish homes produced nearly a truckful of additional plunder and scarcely anything edible at all. When the party returned, Dannecker was unsatisfied with the results of the effort. He had a thousand restless and unhappy people in his care, and in such situations, where food was available, it was preferable to feed them, on the sound theory that they would thus be more manageable than a hungrier group.

* It would not take long for some Italians to realize how easily these homes might be burgled. Many Jews, who had fled during and prior to the roundup, found their apartments stripped bare, even of furniture, when they returned after the Allied liberation of Rome. These thefts were attributed to local thieves and bombed-out refugees who were billeted in abandoned Jewish residences.

Adopting a somewhat permissive attitude, however, Dannecker sent them out again. This time he reached into the box of collected cash and gave them a measure of money. He told them to buy enough bread for the remainder of the stay at the Collegio Militare and the coming journey to the north. Somehow the figure of 200 kilograms was arrived at, that is, considering the number of people to be fed and the distance to be traveled, somewhat less than one ounce per person per day. A list of medicines requested by the prisoners had been drawn up, and this too was to be bought by Dannecker's men and Wachsberger.

The bread was purchased at a *vapoforno* in Corso Vittorio Emanuele. While waiting for it, Wachsberger was suddenly taken with the temptation of escape. "The SS guard," he later recounted, "stood outside the entrance to the bakery, in which I had entered alone. Having also gone into the back room, I was told by the baker that if I wanted to I could unlock the rear exit. I was just about to act on his suggestion when I remembered Dannecker's threat regarding my family and I returned. . . . The same identical scene was later repeated at a pharmacy in Via Arenula, where we went to get the medicines. A back door in the rear of the shop gave on to a narrow street unguarded by the SS . . . but I climbed on the truck again."[10]

XII

News of the raid on the Jews of Rome, despite official silence, continued to move outward in an ever-widening circle. At the same time a strong implosion of non-Jewish reaction was closing down on the city.

Somehow the information had by now crossed Allied lines and

was being broadcast by Radio Bari, the voice of the King's government. This was heard in London and relayed across the Atlantic by the American news wire service United Press. Because of the five- to eight-hour time difference between Britain and various parts of the United States, American newsmen had an opportunity to include the story in their Sunday editions, which were still being made up. Thus, while the report was almost entirely inaccurate, Americans would be the first to read about what was happening to the Jews of Rome.

The New York Times, preempting space reserved for news already scheduled to appear in a corner on the front page of its Sunday paper, printed the dispatch as follows:

POPE SAID TO HELP IN RANSOMING JEWS
by the United Press

London, October 16—The Bari Radio reported tonight that Pope Pius had joined the Jewish community of Rome in paying a ransom of fifty kilograms of gold which the Germans demanded for the release of 100 Jewish hostages.

The Pontiff, according to the broadcast, quoting a report from Rome, contributed a considerable amount.

The Germans, after receiving the gold, refused to release the hostages, however, and instead began a general round-up of Jews, during which the Italians helped hunted families to hide and escape.[1]

In Rome itself the story was not much clearer than in New York, but feelings ran infinitely deeper. This was the city's first view of persecution with its robes down, and though there had been racial laws for five years, no one ever thought what lay underneath looked like this. Rome was horrified. Many non-Jews found a sudden need or desire to express their disbelief in the concept of racial differences and in the idea that Jews were in some way inferior to Aryans, that is, themselves. But such somewhat pathetic efforts only confirmed the "differences."

The Roman Christian Democratic journalist Carlo Trabucco called it a "black day for the Jews." Writing clandestinely, he said:

It was a pitiful spectacle, and at the same time contemptible and inhuman. Our Latin soul rebels against that of the ferocious Nordic man.

The millenarian Christian education of the Italians cannot accept it. . . . Among Jews it is necessary to distinguish the profiteers and the self-serving from the altruists and the indifferent. I knew Jews whose generosity and honesty could have been held up as exemplary to a great many Aryans from the financial world who stain and invalidate their baptism with selfishness, thievery, and exploitation. . . .[2]

Another chronicler of the times wrote that day:

This has made a deep impression in the city. People here didn't hate the Jews and got on well with them; now, on seeing the German procedure, they are shocked and more terrified than ever, for it is generally expected that other persecutions will follow the Jewish ones.[3]

Still another:

"It is a nameless horror. People you know and esteem, brave, kind, upright people, just because they have Jewish blood, treated like this. Some of them are heroic. . . ."[4]

Yet, however terrible this day had been, such were the divisions among men, that one could give thanks his veins were free of Jewish blood, or at least were not entirely so encumbered.

The Roman Resistance reacted too, if only in voice and not in deed. During the night on a clandestine printing press in Via Basento, issue number eleven of the underground newspaper *l'Italia Libera* was being run. This was the publication of the Action party, the organization of the Justice and Liberty movement. Its director was Leone Ginzberg, a Jew from Turin, who would be captured later in the occupation and tortured to death by the Germans. In the morning the paper would be secretly distributed throughout the city, slipped into letter boxes by cooperative *portieri* or passed from one man to another between the pages of a Fascist newspaper. In it, Romans would read:

The Germans during the night and all day long went around Rome seizing Italians for their furnace in the north. The Germans would like us to believe that these people are in some way alien to us, that they are of another race. But we feel them as part of our flesh and blood. They have always lived, fought, and suffered with us. Not only able-bodied men, but old people, children, women, and babies were crowded into covered trucks and taken away to meet their fate. There is not a single heart that does not shudder at the thought of what that fate might be.

But the soldiers who carried out such an inhuman task, so coldly, so fearlessly, and without a shred of pity in their eyes also have loved ones, far away: mothers, wives, children, sisters. And even they sometimes warm with nostalgia when they hear the songs of their youth. Any party or national discipline that dehydrates and petrifies a man's heart to such an extent, that muffles every human feeling, that degrades man into an automaton, is a poison that must be cauterized with fire and iron.

We do not hate anymore; we are horrified. Not until Europe is freed of this nightmare, can there be any hope for peace. No one thinks of taking revenge against German women and children, but these Nazi soldiers, their lackies, spies, and cut-throat Fascists, must be silenced for all times, buried forever in this very land that they dared to profane with so much shame.[5]

The word *Jew,* which was so often used unconsciously by the sympathetic and genuinely offended non-Jews as a cleaver with which they tried to chop themselves loose from the mortal dangers of the times, was not once employed in this anonymous article.

Sometime in the last hours of this night the Gestapo, probably Dannecker himself, prepared a report on the roundup of the Jews of Rome. Following standard procedure, it was addressed from Kappler's command and was meant only for the eyes of the highest officials of the SS. It was written in brisk, telescopic language and read as follows:

Judenaktion according to plan worked out in this office exploiting all possibilities was today initiated and completed. Put into action were all available forces of the Security- and Order-Police. Participation of the Italian police considering their unreliability in this affair was not possible. It was thus possible to carry out a series of arrests made in rapid succession in 26 action-precincts. Blocking off entire streets was not practicable considering the character of the Open City and also the insufficient aggregate of only 365 German police. Nevertheless during the action, which lasted from 0530 hours to 1400 hours, 1,259 persons were arrested in Jewish residences and brought to a central collection point at a military school here. After the release of the *Mischlinge,* the foreigners, (incl. one citizen of Vatican City), the members of mixed marriages, (incl. the Jewish partners), the Aryan domestics and subtennants, there remained in custody 1,007 Jews. Deportation set for Monday, 10/18 at 0900 hours, with through-accompaniment of 30 Order-Police.[6]

The report then went on to sum up the events that took place during the roundup and offered general observations on the local temperament:

The behavior of the Italian people was outright passive resistance, which in many individual cases mounted to active assistance. *E.g.,* in one case the police came upon the home of a Fascist in Blackshirt and with identity papers, which without doubt had already been used one hour earlier in a Jewish home by someone claiming them as his own. As the German police were breaking into some homes, attempts to hide Jews in nearby apartments were observed and it is believed that in many cases they were successful. The anti-Semitic part of the population was nowhere to be seen during the action, only a great mass of people who in some individual cases even tried to cut off the police from the Jews. In no case was it necessary to use firearms.*[7]

This was sent by wireless some twelve hours later to RSHA headquarters in Berlin. Going through normal channels, it bore Kappler's signature, required on all messages radioed from Gestapo headquarters in Rome. It was also appended to a routine report by Kappler to Himmler's headquarters, in which the Obersturmbannführer summed up his assessment of the over-all effect of the roundup. All the wretched fear, the trauma, the loathing and disdain, the despicable violence, and the infinite human suffering, were compressed into four simple words: "Situation in general unchanged."[9]

In a crowded classroom of the Collegio Militare, twenty-three-year-old Marcella Di Tivoli Perugia lay on the floor in

* A report drawn up in Stahel's headquarters for the general's war diary recorded much of the same information, although more briefly and with greater inaccuracy. Noting that there were "no incidents whatsoever," it said only 900 Jews were under arrest and that the operation ended at noon. It maintained the Wehrmacht's false position of aloofness, concluding, "What consequences the *Aktion* will have, remain to be seen."[8]

the middle of that night. From time to time she was wracked by a pounding pain within her body. Her two children, a girl almost six and a boy about five, were near her. Marcella had been arrested with them in the ghetto. Her husband had escaped. She was nine months pregnant and now her labor pains were coming. They had begun some time earlier in the evening, and by now everyone around her knew, judging from the intensity of the pains and the duration between them, the child would soon be born.

The Germans, notified of the woman's condition, had permitted an Italian physician to be called, and he was allowed to enter the compound. When the doctor arrived and had examined the patient, he immediately declared that it would be a difficult birth and that the woman would have to be removed to a hospital. The Germans said no. Instead she was brought into the courtyard and isolated from the other prisoners. There, under a still cloudy, nighttime sky, the child was born. An enemy of the Reich, he, or she, was automatically under arrest.[10]

XIII

SUNDAY WAS ANOTHER grey day. The city was still, the ghetto the most quiet part of all. As Debenedetti described it, "not a soul was to be seen; the desolation of Jeremiah's Jerusalem reigned."[1] President Almansi was to write, "From that day forward the Jews of Rome went out of their homes."[2] But these views were not wholly correct; they portrayed what might have been expected but not what was.

There were some Jews, escapees from yesterday's roundup, who now began returning to their homes both in the ghetto and elsewhere. To be sure, they were a relative few, representing the most credulous of all. But so refracted had the native Jewish view of reality become, it was still possible to believe that the enemy's desires had at last been satisfied.

The overwhelming majority of the survivors, however, were hiding now, though they continued to move about the city even today. They sought to locate and gather at least some of the fragments of their shattered lives. Many risked a brief return to their homes in order to remove things they had hurriedly left behind. The Jewish publisher Luciano Morpurgo, for example, returned from the country to his apartment in Via Dora. He found it intact, unvisited by the Germans. He quickly packed a bag and brought it to another apartment, in the Prati district, which he had prepared as his city hiding place.*

All over Rome Jews literally crawled out of holes and came down from the hills, seeking one another out in order that they might learn something about loved ones who yesterday had been so rudely torn away.

In the *Castelli Romani*, the Tor Paluzzo squad of partisans heard the news of the roundup. Pino wrote a letter to his family in Genoa to warn them of what had taken place in Rome. He wondered whether it was already too late. Marco Moscati, the Roman Jewish partisan, decided to return to the city to try to find out what had happened to his family.[4]

In Rome, people began making inquiries at the Italian Red Cross, the local authorities, and the Vatican. But there was nothing new to be learned.

The president of the Red Cross, General Boriani, went to the office of Stadtkommandant Stahel. Unsuccessful there, he tried the Gestapo. He was told that "it was useless to get excited, useless to concern oneself, useless to inquire. . . ."[5]

The Vatican, it seems, was in touch with Stahel's office during

* Morpurgo had been among those who had witnessed the Germans remove the registry of the city's Jews from the offices of the community. By his own account this had convinced him of the need to hide.[3]

the day, in the person of Bishop Hudal. He learned in a telephone conversation with the general himself that "in consideration of the special character of Rome, the arrests are to be stopped at once."[6] Taking a measure of credit for this "generosity" for himself, Stahel parceled out the major share to Himmler for having "given the order."[7]

In truth, there was never any intention of continuing the roundup beyond the one day sudden strike—principally because it was simply impossible to extend any such raid after it had run its natural course. That the arrests had actually come to a complete standstill at 2:00 P.M. the previous day, and the *Aktion* was then officially concluded, does not appear to have been mentioned by Stahel, though the fact was entered in his war diary this very morning.*[8]

While efforts continued by the forlorn to learn something of the captives, some of the Jewish leaders held a secret meeting. Foà was not heard from that day, but Almansi, Renzo Levi, and Settimio Sorani contacted one another at their hiding places and arranged a rendezvous in a dairy shop in Via Regina Margherita, a broad boulevard within walking distance of all three men. They believed that there was a slight chance that influence could be brought to bear to obtain the release of at least some of the Jews who had been arrested.[10]

When they met in the *latteria,* they showed the markings of hunted men. Levi had begun to grow a mustache. Sorani, who had already once changed his name since the occupation, had decided to do so again and would soon secure a new set of false identity documents. Almansi was wholly purged of his notions about the "open city" and from this moment on seems to have continually deferred to those few leaders who had foreseen the onslaught.

* In any event individual arrests of Jews, the only kind now feasible, continued throughout the occupation. As for Himmler assuming any role in preventing them, that was clearly invented by Stahel since the Reichsführer had not yet received any information about the roundup. No order to stop the arrests was given, and indeed one to the contrary was later issued. It should be added that the Vatican does not claim any credit for this, although defenders of its wartime policies invariably do.[9]

They discussed the possibility of aiding the Jews inside the Collegio Militare. It was felt that the Vatican might be persuaded to intervene. Sorani said he could get a message directly to the Pope through a diplomat friend of his, a high official of the Yugoslavian legation at the Holy See.[11] It was decided that a memorandum be drawn up, which was to be handed personally to Pius XII.[12] In it a request would be made to the Pope, asking him to attempt to free the captured Jews. The leaders, however, felt such an intervention would probably fail and thus alternative suggestions were to be included in the memorandum. They would ask for the freedom of the old, the sick, and the women and children. The community would further offer to pay any sum of money within its power in exchange for their release. If the Germans were to refuse, then still another request would be made for the salvation of the children.[13]

Sorani assumed the task of drafting the document and seeing to it that it reached its intended destination.

In the Collegio Militare the prisoners passed the day in waiting. Few had slept the night before, and now out of sheer exhaustion they dozed, nodded, and buried their heads in their folded arms, bent like so many withering plants.

They knew that soon they would leave, but not precisely when. Everyone tried to keep his belongings compact and stay close to his family in order that he might not be separated from either in the event of a sudden departure. Many people spoke of Marcella. Lazzaro Anticoli, who continued to make his distribution rounds, looked for her. He wondered what had happened to her and whether she had had her baby. His own child had in the last hours lapsed deep into a coma. He was unable to find Marcella in any of the rooms, and he assumed, like everyone he told, that she had been taken to a hospital and was therefore free.[14] But the young mother and her newborn child were still in the Collegio, separated from the others but waiting just the same.

Some of the prisoners wrote letters. They hoped there would be some way to post or otherwise dispatch them. There were so many people on the outside who had to be informed of their arrest; so many things were left unfinished, and only the prisoners themselves knew what had to be done.

On the outside, as the hours of the day mounted, the city began to respire with a rhythm normal for the times. The image of Jews being pulled from their homes by helmeted German troops began to fade. It happened imperceptibly, first among the people most removed from the event, then ever inward—the way a puddle disappears when the sun comes out and the storm has gone away.

It was Sunday afternoon, a time—so pitifully brief in wartime Rome—for rest and pleasure. The grey, wet weather was breaking up, the restaurants and movie theaters were open, and the Sunday newspapers were being hawked. No one could escape the war of course. It was everywhere: from the Nazi-Fascist propaganda posters on the city's walls to the look in the eyes of the bombed out refugees camping in the streets. Nor, for that matter, could anyone fail to hear the cry for resistance. The anti-Fascist sloganeers had painted their calls to arms for all to see: across the wide sweep of the Spanish Steps, in all the neighborhoods and shopping centers, and on the embankments of the Tiber.[15] The Fascist press itself reported the intensifying activities of these "Communists" and "bandits." Today's newspapers, for example, complained about three-pointed nails being strewn in the path of German military movements to the south and threatened "very grave sanctions" against civilians who lived in areas where this occurred.[16]

Yet, in spite of the war and the need for every man to fight for freedom, it was Sunday. And no matter what happened to the war, to freedom, or to the Jews of Rome, tomorrow would be Monday, and a man had to be at work at a certain hour of the day or else, it seemed in Rome of 1943, he could not live.

XIV

ON MONDAY, BEFORE dawn, the Jews in the Collegio Militare were ordered to gather themselves and their things together. This was the hour of departure.

The same insufficient number of black trucks that had shuttled them here was waiting in the courtyard. Always pushing toward a central figure in individual groupings of families and friends, the prisoners began to climb aboard the trucks. As soon as the first loading was completed, the vehicles left promptly.

Settimia Spizzichino, who had been in a classroom close to the main exit, was in this first convoy. It was still dark when they set out, she later recalled. They crossed the Tiber to pick up the wide Corso Vittorio. "We went right by the ghetto," she said, "through the Largo Argentina. And one woman, who lived only two or three blocks away and who had wrapped a message to her family around her house key, squeezed it through an opening in the canvas."[17]

The letter was retrieved by a passerby and delivered. Though only a personal note but a few words long—a farewell to the woman's loved ones—it was the first word of any kind from the prisoners. At last they had been heard from, and clearly they were being moved from the Collegio Militare.

The convoy continued to roll onward crossing all of Rome in an easterly direction. The city was wholly deserted, for the curfew had not yet lifted. There were no street lights or any other kind of artificial lighting, only the headlamps of the trucks, arched downward like dogs sniffing out a trail. Still the prisoners could make out the unmistakable contours of Rome; every district, every street, almost every building, to a Roman, was markedly different from another. Every old palazzo and its via had its own certain texture, which could be perceived only subtly in the quantity and quality of memories and emotions that had become attached to it over the years. There were monuments and ruins that were loved, hated, ignored, purposely avoided, and even feared, as one might fear witches and ghosts. And even today, though the most treasured landmarks of Rome were covered with scaffolding to protect them from bombardment, these feelings arose.

They passed through Piazza Venezia and the palace from which the Duce had governed his dwarf empire for a greater number of years than the lifetimes of many of even the grown prisoners. They went by the Vittoriano, the great white monument to the united Italy which had emancipated its Jews some seven decades ago. They went on, plummeting forward, through the invisible stone valley between the Quirinal and Esquiline hills, through streets that would soon bear new names they would never know, on past Termini, Policlinico hospital, and Campo Verano cemetery, where the remains of their ancestors had been moved when Mussolini razed the Jewish burial grounds on the Aventine.

The convoy had turned onto the broad Via Tiburtina, the ancient Roman road that bisects the Italian peninsula, ending at Pescara and the Adriatic Sea. It too was paved with memories, the most recent perhaps the most painful; for only little more than a month ago it was along the Tiburtina that the King and Badoglio had run away from Rome in its most trying hour since the coming of the Vandals. The German trucks had not gone more than a mile or so on this road when they came to a near halt at the Tiburtina train station. They did not actually draw up to the passenger terminal, but went somewhat past it to the entrance of a loading zone, from which cargo and cattle were shipped. Taking the tiny Via dello Scalo Tiburtina, they approached a rusty gate. It was swung open for them by police stationed in a small, concrete guard house just beyond the entrance way. The convoy continued another fifty yards or so, climbing a slightly sloping ramp. Then it stopped. The engines of the trucks fell silent, and now only the hush of low voices could be heard. Dawn was breaking, it was warm, and it looked like it might be a sunny day.[2]

The prisoners were ordered to dismount the vans. On the uncovered platform they could see now that they were standing almost in the middle of the rail yards, with a scribble of cross-tracks around them. Regular passengers never boarded from here; their part of the station lay at a not-too-distant, but incommunicable, lateral platform. Between these two points, immediately adjacent to where the prisoners were, a long, reddish brown freight train rested on the tracks. The sliding doors of its cars were open wide, showing their black interior, which was broken only by pencil lines of light that shined through the slits and cracks of their posterior walls.

The train reached out along the track for a distance of about 450 feet, some twenty cars long. These cars were not only of German and Italian manufacture but also that of almost every other European country.[3] All of them were made of wood, seasoned and hardened by time, weather, and endless travels; wood that had the touch but not the warmth of a workman's hand, the faintest smell of the forest, which it could never lose, and the powerful odors of heavily leaded paint and the manure and urine of generations of farm animals which had been transported around the continent. They were in fact freight, or cattle cars.

The Jews were told to get aboard. There was something repugnant, humiliating about riding in a freight car, but a complement of armed SS men drove every instinct of rebellion back into the well from which it had arisen. They began to climb into the cars. A German stood between them and the open door. Someone had divided the number of cars by the number of Jews, and a figure of how many persons should occupy each car had been calculated. The German counted now as they passed him, and when the figure had been reached, somewhere between the fiftieth and sixtieth person, his hand came down like the blade of a guillotine and the loading of a new car was begun. That a mother might be separated from a child, an elderly person cut off from a comforting companion, or a family split in two was a factor that could not be expressed arithmetically. It was therefore disregarded.

As each car was filled, the door was rolled closed, throwing the prisoners into almost total darkness. A heavy plunger was passed through an iron ring sealing the car from the outside. Only some light and air could enter, passing through the slatted walls and a grated window which was smaller than the breadth of the youngest child and set higher than the tallest man—although ways would be found to look out, and faces would always be seen in the window's frame. Inside the car there was scarcely enough room for each individual to choose whether to stand, sit, or recline on the bare wooden planks beneath his shoes. To move from one part of the car to another required the same effort as passing through a row in a darkened, crowded theater. At this early hour, most people sought a tiny patch of space to set their baggage down, and they remained on their feet.

When the first three or four cars were loaded and locked, the Germans returned in their trucks to the Collegio Militare to collect another group of equal number. Though the transport had been scheduled to leave Tiburtina at 9:00 A.M., this back and forth transferring operation went on throughout the entire morning and into the first hours of the afternoon.

The earliest arriving passengers had to wait as much as eight hours before the departure. The inconveniences that accompanied this situation were met with forebearance, however. To many it seemed simply a matter of getting the journey in motion, and as the hours went by, they grew more and more eager to be on their way.

To pass the time, some continued the writing of letters and others ate and drank from the rapidly diminishing stock they had brought with them.

The captured eleven members of the Efrati family, who

ironically lived but two or three blocks from Tiburtina station, had already exhausted their meager supply of food. Sixteen-year-old Cesare, one of the Efrati boys, was peering through the little window of their car, hoping to recognize someone he knew. Cesare and his brothers had often wandered and played near the rail yards and were acquainted with many of the personnel. At last he saw one of them and called to him. The workman approached the car, and after an exchange of a few friendly words in which he lamented the Efratis' misfortune, Cesare asked for his help.

"Please get us some bread," he implored, "some food to take with us." He turned to his father, who gave him a sum of money far in excess of what could possibly be purchased—funds he had risked concealing during the collection at the Collegio Militare. Passing the money through the window, Cesare also asked for some cheese and wine, items that would not quickly deteriorate. The family needed as much as possible. The man promised to do the best he could. He took the money and went off, but the Efratis would never see him again.[4]

During the morning it became known in the city that the Jews were being shipped out from the Roma-Tiburtina station. Some of the relatives of the prisoners ventured there, hoping for a chance to at least wave a last goodbye to those who had been taken from them.[5] They naturally went to the passenger terminal, from where the sealed train could be seen only at a distance. But some managed to approach it from the same entrance the prisoners had used.

One among this latter few, was Lilliana Calò. Her boy, who had been at his uncle's house the morning of the roundup, had been arrested there, while at her home she and her other children had succeeded in escaping. Now she walked along the platform searching for her captured son. Finally she found him. His eyes stared out from the small, barred window of one of the freight cars. He looked at his mother with bitterness, as if she were somehow culpable. Then, using the *Lei,* or formal manner of speaking, the boy spoke to her, coldly and evenly.

"Goodbye and go home," he said. "Go home and take care

that your other children grow up." His face disappeared from the window, and the mother went away.[6]

Another mother who succeeded in reaching the platform was, coincidentally, also named Calò. She had managed to get to the train at a moment between the transfer of prisoners. The station guards had apparently used this lull to go off somewhere, for there was no one in view, and the train, although securely fastened from the outside, was unattended.[7]

Signora Calò's full name was Costanza Calò Sermoneta. Her husband and their five children had been arrested in their ghetto apartment Saturday morning, but Costanza had been visiting the countryside and only today had she learned of the roundup of the Jews of Rome. She had come home to the city, finding the ghetto, her street, and her apartment wholly barren of human life. She had run frantically, picking up pieces of news here and there and at last had found her way to Tiburtina.

Now, still running, she went from car to car calling her husband's name in a loud and piercing cry.

Jews inside the freight cars urged her to be still. "Get away," someone shouted, "or else they'll get you too."

Instead she pounded her fists against the train. *"Fascisti!"* she cried, *"Fascisti!* Open up! I want to go too. I want to go with my husband."

At last she reached the car in which her family was held. Her husband told her to run away quickly. But she would not listen, shouting only, "Open up! *Fascisti,* open up!"

By now the Germans had returned. They saw and heard the woman and tried to drive her away. But she pleaded with them to permit her to board the train, and after a while they relented. They unlocked the car and acceeded to her wish.[8]

XV

QUIRINO ZAZZA, A non-Jewish Roman who lived in the Monte Verde district, arrived at Tiburtina station that day just as he had been doing for the past twenty-two years. Zazza, a slight, little man with a voice as soft as fleece, was employed by the Italian state railroad. He had entered the service as an apprentice brakeman and by now had risen to the post of *capotreno,* a rank equivalent to a chief conductor.

Reporting to work sometime after noon, he noted nothing unusual at first. Since the Germans had taken Rome, there had been many changes in his routine. They had taken over the railroad, installing personnel of the Deutsche Reichsbahn in key positions, trainmen who had impressed Zazza with their expertise. But today seemed no different from any other day of recent weeks. He had not, as usual, been given any advance notice of what he was to do, and when he was placed in command of a crew who were to take a freight train out of Rome, he naturally gave not the slightest heed as to what the cargo might be. It was always more or less the same; these days mostly war materiel and foodstuff.

But about 1:30 P.M. he went on to the platform to check the train he had been assigned, and he saw the difference.

"The train was surrounded by armed German soldiers," he later said. "Their faces were inscrutable, and they were very young. Most of the cars had already been sealed, but one was open, and there were people boarding. They appeared terror-stricken. Some of them, who were already on the car were throwing out messages written on scraps of paper."[1] He was struck by the fact that they were civilians, of both sexes and every age.

He looked across the tracks and saw another group of civilians who were watching the embarkation and assumed that they were the friends and relatives of the passengers. If he had heard of Saturday's roundup, he could not associate that which he had not personally witnessed with the astonishing spectacle now before his eyes. It took him some time to conclude that the human cargo were persons "who seemed to belong to the Jewish race."[2]

Zazza deplored this "act of bestiality" in the strongest terms, and he would later say so openly to his fellow-Italian employees, with whom he would invariably find complete agreement.[3] He would also record the nature of this transport in his log. But now he felt himself to be almost as much a prisoner as the Jews, certainly equally as helpless. In the apparent absence of any rational alternative, he climbed aboard the train himself and prepared to set it on its way. He was grateful he had to take the train only as far as Florence.[4]

By now the last car had been filled. Once again the arithmetic of the Germans had failed them. They had at the end of the loading process been left with a balance of about thirty Jews. Thus the final car of prisoners was the roomiest of all, a fact those now locked inside it considered a stroke of good luck. They had an equal amount of space as the accompaniment of German troops who rode in the very rear of the train in a species of caboose.

At five minutes past two o'clock in the afternoon, someone gave the signal, and the train began to move. It lurched at first, then half as much again. Then it clanked, creaked, and sighed, and it began, very slowly, to roll quite smoothly down the track. The people who had gathered waved, Italian style, either slowly chopping the air with a slightly arched palm and short, nervous strokes, or pumping the fist, half-open, then closed. Some people cried.

The track was perfectly straight for almost as far as the eye could reach and the train could be seen picking up speed and moving inexorably to that illusory place where all tracks converge and disappear. At last the train was out of view, and people turned away wondering where it might be going. By the compass, it was headed due north.

When almost all of the persons who had watched the deportation train depart had gone, the station porters came out with their dustpans and brooms, the way their counterparts appear after a ball game. A mess had been left behind, and it had to be swept and cleaned. There were bread crumbs, discarded, raggedy clothing, empty bottles, and other signs with which large numbers of human beings always mark their presence. Among the litter were the messages Zazza had seen being thrown from the train and others that had been similarly launched before. While some prisoners still retained such communications, these belonged to the Jews who felt there would be no other means of sending them, at least until they reached their destination.

The station personnel gathered them up and separated them from the rubbish. Most of them, it seems, were undeliverable, although attempts were made.[5] The Jews of Rome no longer had known addresses. But at least one of the messages arrived at its intended place, principally because the sender was well known in Rome. He was Lionello Alatri, the department store owner and member of the Jewish Council. His letter, written on a single sheet of paper, was addressed to no one individual, presumably to avoid compromising anyone at the store should the note fall into enemy hands. Hoping that his name would be recognized and his wishes respected, he had simply scrawled along the margin of the letter, "For humanity's sake, whoever finds this please post it."

It was written in a galloping hand, with many deletions and inserts, clearly by someone with an infinite number of things to do in an infinitesimal amount of time. It read:

Monday morning, 10/18/43

We are leaving for Germany! I, my wife, my father-in-law, and Annita. Notify our traveling salesman Mieli. Give 600 lire to the portress of my building at the end of every month and 250 lire to Irma, whom you are also to reimburse for the gas and electric. Show this letter to Signora Ermelinda. I don't know whether the merchandise will remain requisitioned. If we will be able to sell it remember that the prices in the first block must be sold proportionately to the type of merchandise. If you can make currency exchanges at the Bank of Sicily, do so contacting Signor Riccardo.

We are leaving with feelings of courage, but of course the presence of my father-in-law in his poor condition, alarms me.

Be brave, as we ourselves are brave.

I embrace you all.

Lione[6]

Immediately under this, Alatri appended a long postscript:

Tell the baron that Ettore and Elda and her cousin Lella are with us. Tell sales representative Riccardelli that his wife and children are with us and are fine.

Tell Bucellato that Vito of Via Flavia is with us and fine. Notify the porter at Via Po, n. 42 that sister and sister-in-law with us and fine. Notify porter Via Po 162 Lello and Silvia with us and fine. Notify porter Via Vicenza 42 that the furrier is with us and fine. Notify porter Corso Italia 106 the Di Veroli family with us and fine, Raoul with us and fine. Notify the porter Via Sicilia 154 Clara with us and fine.[7]

At about this hour, from a northern extremity of the city, President Foà was secretly slipping out of Rome. He was on his way to Leghorn, the town of his childhood and less troubled times. He had concluded that now a man had to hide from the Germans, and though, after a while, he would return to his work in occupied Rome, he would never go back to his commodious home in Via Cicerone.[8]

XVI

THE DEPORTATION TRAIN climbed out of Rome. Within minutes it had crossed the clackety bridge over the Aniene tributary of the Tiber and was racing parallel with Via Salaria for the northern slopes.

Prisoners who had ridden ordinary passenger trains before were immediately struck by the voluminous roar inside a moving freight car and the sensation of being in intimate communication with the wheels and the tracks, and even the crossties and the gravel between them. Every joint in the road bed, almost every knick in the steel rails could be felt intensely, and the varying lengths of track drummed differing rhythms on the walls of one's internal organs. These were sound patterns that would shake loose long forgotten memory barnacles from the brains of the prisoners; songs, sometimes happy, sometimes sad, here thunderous, there not heard at all, that would play an endless capriccio during the entire journey.

The train had not got very far out of Rome when it was suddenly attacked by Allied aircraft.[1] It was in the vicinity of Littoria airfield, which sprawled beside the north-south tracks just outside the city. Low-flying fighter planes swooped down on the transport, strafing it, then, arching upward, circled and zeroed in to attack again.

The lightning burst of gunfire sent a charge of excitement through the passengers, and they bristled to their feet. In one of the cars, sixteen-year-old Leone Sabatello could see the formation framed neatly in the grated window. He saw a star on the wing of one of the planes and shouted to the others, "It's the Americans!"[2]

In Settimia Spizzichino's car, just forward of the center, people thought the attack was being made for the purpose of liberating them.[3]

In the rear of the train the SS accompaniment began returning the fire. The planes made another pass over the moving target, riddling the source of resistance. One of the Germans was wounded slightly in the hand. But the others kept firing, and the assault was repelled.[4] No one else had been injured, and both the Jews and the Germans settled down again. The prisoners were not going to be freed after all. Many of them realized now that in all probability they had been mistaken for a shipment of guns, ammunition, or German boots and uniforms.

Inside the freight cars, the temperature rose swiftly to oppressive heights, as the afternoon sun made an oven of the train. The rush of air outside could barely find a way to enter the cars, and the prisoners breathed that which had already been in their neighbors' lungs. They shared it like a peace pipe, and before long it was foul and sluggish, something almost to be chewed rather than inhaled. Anything potable was rapidly consumed, and a great, overpowering thirst for liquids began to burn in the parching throats of the prisoners. Some of the more fragile among them were already dying.

For the most part, however, people adapted with astonishing speed and flexibility to the new conditions of their lives. The makeup of the train's population made a contribution to this adjustment. It formed a community of Jews, much as it had always been in Rome.

Despite the German arbitrariness most families had succeeded in remaining together, and the members or the property of one such grouping or another delineated part of a larger, familial circle or series of circles in any given space. Further, friends and peers and their families linked the circles in a chain. In this manner the ghetto-Trastevere Jews had become concentrated in contiguous cars, those near the center of the train and toward the front. They were separated from the middle-class Jews, who had gathered together, too, as had the non-native Roman Jews, and the foreigners. The rich and professional class of Jews had a car all to themselves. It was next to the last and they had had the good fortune of boarding hours later than the poor Jews up front, but the car was in no way different from the others. This replication of one aspect of the community social structure had all happened automatically, quite naturally and virtually involuntarily. There were many exceptions, of course, but there always had been. Thus even these had been faithfully reconstructed like a wound that begins to heal and become that which it used to be.[5]

Arminio Wachsberger was one of the exceptions. He, his wife, and his little daughter were with some of the wealthy and prominent Jews who had overflowed the car before theirs. The Wachsbergers' was the final, only half-filled prisoner car, which they had boarded as an outcome of Arminio's services as an interpreter being needed until the very end of the loading process. They now found themselves in the company of Admiral Capon, the dowager Alina Cavalieri, and an elderly woman who bore the illustrious name of Rothschild. For food this group would have to share some pieces of bread, raw potatoes, and one jar of marmalade.[6]

But hunger had not yet become a serious problem. Wachsberger, who was somewhat awed at being in the presence of the famous admiral and the nationally known benefactress suddenly found himself engaged in a conversation with them.

"You know," Signorina Cavalieri said to Wachsberger, "we are all going to die. Except you, perhaps, because they have need of you as a translator." She explained that as a result of her work with the Red Cross, she had repeatedly heard of the extermination of the Jews who the Germans had carried off, and she had no doubt of its truth.[7]

Wachsberger, however, refused to believe her.

"You don't know the Germans," said Admiral Capon, agreeing with the woman. "I got to know them well during the First World War." He too was certain they would never return.[8]

But the others in the car sided with Wachsberger.[9] As an expression of confidence in his future, Wachsberger released a message he had drawn up during the previous night. He had written to an Aryan friend, a business associate, telling him of his "transfer to a German labor camp" and entrusting him with his apartment and everything in it. He had somehow come upon an envelope, and in it he had placed the letter, the key to his home, 100 lire (about $1), and a note to whoever might find it to see that it reach its addressee—the money being a reward. He squeezed the little package through a crack in the freight car's wall and sent it on its way.

It fell to the ground, skidded along the side of the tracks for awhile, and then came to rest. Long after the train had disappeared, someone would find it. It would be turned over to the SS. Wachsberger's friend would be visited by the Germans, and although he would escape unharmed, Wachsberger's apartment would be stripped of everything he owned.[10]

The deportation train went on, following the trail of the Tiber, crossing from bank to bank wherever the river tarried to reach out for an uneconomical turn. The path lay between mountains. They rose on either side of the train and were not exceptionally high, having, except for two or three, a stunted appearance certainly devoid of any majesty. What gave them a special quality, however, were the necklaces of goats they wore around them, and the little towns nestled near their peaks or on the laps of every cliff—stone, medieval dwellings, towers, and churches, bunched and twined together as if they all grew from a single trunk or stem.

One such town, among the largest of them all, was Orte, at the 82-kilometer mark, an hour out of Rome. Here, where east-west railroad tracks cross the trunk line to the north, the train made its first stop.[11]

It had been flagged by a red signal, to permit the crossing of other carriers. *Capotreno* Quirino Zazza dismounted the train to see if it had been damaged in any way by the air attack. He was not aware that the train itself had been the target, thinking that it had passed through a general bombardment. Prisoners began to call to him. They had to go to the toilet. The message was passed along to the Germans. They opened two or three of the cars and about fifty persons descended.[12]

Meanwhile a southbound passenger train stopped on a parallel track. The people on board saw the deportees and stared at them. One young woman, a Jew returning to Rome from Milan, saw the face of a girl looking out of the barred freight car window, and though she could not be sure, she thought the child was someone related to her. She called to her, but someone else came to the window and signaled her not to do so. No one would ever know why. The passenger train continued.[13]

Conductor Zazza and the Germans waited for the prisoners to board again. Suddenly two or three youths, who had been among those who debarked, made a dash for freedom, running across an open field. The Germans opened fire. They either aimed poorly or above the targets, but the sound of gunfire and the spray of bullets were enough to convince the fleeing boys of their folly, and unharmed, they surrendered, returning to their places in the train.[14]

At the town of Chiusi, another hour's ride to the north, a second stop was made. An elderly man on board had died. Zazza informed the station personnel. A stretcher and two men to carry it were found, and the body was removed. The train continued on its way. At Florence it stopped once more, briefly. Night had fallen; the time was about eight o'clock. The train remained sealed outside the terminal, and the crew was changed; two brakemen, an engineer, and a new *capotreno* went aboard, and before long the deportees were moving once again.[15]

At the station in Florence, Quirino Zazza wrote a brief report, a requirement for every completed tour of duty. He said that "numerous civilians" had been aboard the train. He noted the stops at Orte and Chiusi and the reasons why they had been made. He then caught the next train back to Rome, a very sad, unhappy man.[16]

XVII

THE TRANSPORT OF Roman Jews dragged through the night, crossing the Apennines now. At a time when it should have been going fastest, it was actually moving unbearably slow. High in the mountains the temperature in the freight cars plunged by as much as seventy degrees. Those who had least been able to bear the heat of the afternoon now suffered most intensely from the cold. They tried everything to find warmth. They covered themselves with the clothes drawn from the bags they had carried with them, and those who had coats, used them like blankets.

The medicines were gone by now, and the sick got sicker. Some people were taken newly ill, but nothing could be done for them. The supply of food was virtually no longer existent, and only mothers' milk still flowed. But their babies had to work harder for it than ever before, with rapidly diminishing strength. The universal thirst that had begun half a day ago had spread from a dryness on the tongue to a fire that reached down the alimentary canal and burned from the lips to the walls of the stomach.

But though they had neither drunk nor eaten for so many hours there was a tremendous and recurrent urge to eliminate whatever waste was in the body. No one had been off the train since Orte, and there only a relative few had gone to the toilet. Many people had at that first stop anticipated a more comfortable arrangement, a longer stop at a larger station, later.

They had waited until the limits of human endurance, but it had not materialized. By now almost every group had been forced to make a toilet of their car. Some tried at first to erect a tent-like structure out of clothing and linens, or otherwise screen a designated corner. But at every turn or jolt it would collapse and at last prove more trouble than its worth. Some used empty bottles and dishes; others made conical cups of newspaper, and when used, hurled it from the little window of the train. In one car a man with a pen knife, bored through the floorboards, carving out a hole. But the motion of the train rendered it most difficult to use and it was the worst facility of all.

Depending on one's toilet habits in the past, the experience was accompanied by widely varying degrees of shame and humiliation. The ghetto Jews, who were accustomed to poorly equipped and rarely serviced communal toilets, were of course equally as uncomfortable as the others, but their embarrassment passed relatively quickly. On the other hand, those who had the largest and the best bathrooms at home were profoundly mortified, suffering a pitiful, irreparable trauma to their dignity and self-esteem.

Everyone tried to sleep. They huddled close to conserve the remaining warmth of their bodies. The train creeped over the lower peaks, wound around the others, and passed through the tunnels bored through the highest or most treacherous mountains. The noise fell at the low speed, the cars rocked not unpleasantly, and the rails and the wheels sang softly. But the physical discomforts were too many and too strong. Even the utter exhaustion could not bring on the sleep that might relieve them. Except for a fortunate few, it came only in brief lapses of consciousness, and the night was spent in a bedlam of delirium, a half-world in which it was possible to return to the past, but only with the pain of the present. People groaned all night long. They cried, whimpered, and prayed to God. Old people called out for mothers who had died a half-century ago, and children, like the boy at Tiburtina who coldly sent his mother home, felt a hatred toward their parents for permitting such evils to assail their young minds and flesh. It grew colder.[1]

In the morning, Lazzaro Anticoli's diphtheric child awoke from her coma of several days. No less feverish than before, she was perhaps thirstier and in greater need of nourishment than anyone else, but her parents could offer her only some powdered milk in a few drops of water they had conserved. She took it eagerly, then after a few moments fell back into unconsciousness.[2]

Between 10:00 and 10:30 A.M. the train pulled into the gable-roofed station at Ferrara. Some of the men of the German escort, who had not many more comforts than the prisoners, descended to guard the train, driving away all onlookers. None of the prisoner cars, however, were opened. The Jews stared through the openings, hoping that the purpose of the stop was to at least bring some water aboard. The cars, stoked by the morning sun, had already heated up again, and yesterday's discomforts were not only repeating themselves but were far more severe. Two or three persons had died during the night and now under the high temperature began rapidly to bloat and decompose.

The stationmaster at Ferrara, Mario Tagliati, and some of the other personnel tried to approach the freight train. They had observed, to their great surprise, that it contained human beings. When the deported Roman Carabinieri had passed through about ten days earlier, the Germans had permitted Tagliati and other station officials to provide food and drink for the prisoners.[3] But now they were prevented from doing so and were kept some distance away. Tagliati, however, at a moment when he was unseen by the guards, succeeded in getting alongside one of the cars. Someone from inside called to him and identified himself as *Ingegnere* Tedeschi. Tedeschi, who had been born in Ferrara, was a brother of a man who had been an executive of the state railroad and was well known to Tagliati. The Jewish engineer related details of the capture of the Roman Jews, which Tagliati was later to record.

The stationmaster would also recall:

The car was crammed with men, women, and children, who had not been given anything to eat or drink since the train had been sealed shut. In *Ingegnere* Tedeschi's wagon there was the corpse of a woman. . . . Tedeschi signaled that he wanted to throw out a message, which he succeeded in doing only as the train began to move again and the six or eight German guards jumped aboard.[4]

The train drew away. The passengers lost all hope of receiving even the slightest refreshment. Tagliati picked up Tedeschi's message. He read: "Ferrara, Tuesday, 10/19. I earnestly request that *Ing.* Ermanno Tedeschi be notified that his deported brother passed through here in transit to Germany. I hope that it will be he who will inform my dear ones."[5]

"The news of the passage through Ferrara of the brother of Inspector Tedeschi," Tagliati's account concluded, "became known immediately among the station's personnel, all of whom were startled and profoundly moved."[6]

Just about one minute out of Ferrara the deportation train crossed the long bridge over the Po. The crossing made a tremendous racket in the wooden cars, and it shook the passengers hard. But a moment later they were on the other side of the great river, picking up the normal rhythm and advancing along the scrubby plateau of the province of Rovigo. Over the Veneto flatlands, on the Big-Dipper-shaped run between Ferrara and Padua, the train began to take on speed. Any change in motion, any stop or start was viewed by the passengers as something better than what had already been and an opening perhaps toward a measure of relief. But matters, in total defiance of their wishes, only worsened. People, driven to the very edges of humanity, could move in only one direction, and any movement was better than none at all.

They began to argue and pick and screech at each other cruelly and nervously like caged, tropical birds. Husbands and wives bickered violently, unjustly, each blaming the other for their predicament. The parcel of space one occupied on the floorboards of the train became a subject of endless contestation, as if they were the disputed boundaries between two great landholders. The conditions that in less enlightened times caused clannish feuds arose, and families of long-term friendships suddenly hated one another. Perhaps greatest of all conflicts concerned the corner chosen as the toilet area. Now that it had begun to issue a fetid odor to which the prisoners had somehow attached their worst and most painful feelings and images, no one could bear being near it. Those who had a position closest to it tried to move away, but in doing so impinged on the space of others, provoking disputes with endless repercussions, echoes, and a chain reaction of ill feeling which deepened the suffering of all.[7]

In almost every car it was this way, and the only comfort, quite understandably, was the vision of the labor camp that lay ahead. No matter how far it might be, they were coming closer, and at least these hardships would there be left behind.

XVIII

SOME MINUTES BEFORE Padua the train developed technical difficulties. The engineer could feel that it was not pulling normally, and when they reached the station he brought it to an unscheduled stop. The time was about noon.

The trouble was quickly located. One of the center cars was breaking down. It was beyond easy repair, and someone decided that it would be simpler to change it for a new one.[1]

While the train rested on one of the station's three main tracks, the prisoners inside began to cry out to the Germans to get them some water. Some of the Jews were literally dying of thirst. They could see a fountain across the tracks, not very far away. It was gushing endless bucketfuls of fresh water. But the

German guards paid no attention to the importunations of the Jews.

Signorina Lucia De Marchi, a nurse who worked for the Italian Red Cross in Padua, was at the station, and she saw the imprisoned passengers. She went out on the platform, and learning that they were Jews being deported to Germany, she asked if her organization would be permitted to aid them.[2] She was in a position to offer a quantity of food and medicines to be placed on board, she said. The Germans refused. But the nurse was persistent and a loud argument developed, which began to draw a number of spectators. This in turn attracted the attention of some members of the railway militia, a uniformed Fascist police organization, which protected the state railroad.

Several armed militiamen approached the Germans now to learn what the difficulty was. Against the sound of Jews calling from the sealed train for a few drops of anything that might quench their thirst, the Germans attempted to explain. But the Italian guards did not listen for very long. They simply inquired why the prisoners were not permitted to have a drink.

"They are Jews," said a German, believing he had put his finger on the essential point.

"Yes," one of the Fascists replied, "but they are thirsty."[3]

The SS guards apparently believed they had failed to make their Italian comrades understand what kind of prisoners were being held and repeatedly asserted the fact of their religion. But the Fascists expressed not the slightest interest in having an explanation from the Germans. They neither questioned the legitimacy or the purpose of the transport nor had they any intention of hindering it in any way. But the prisoners, whoever they might be, were thirsty.

The Germans said that in any event they were not going to open the train or permit anything to be placed aboard.

The militiamen, with patient words, tried to soften the German resolve, but the latter held firm and the exchange then became increasingly heated. Finally, one of the Fascists raised the submachine gun in his hand to a level position. He held the weapon between his bent arm and the side of his body, the barrel turned on the SS men, and his finger curled around the trigger. The other Italians followed his lead. Everyone grew still, including the onlooking prisoners.

The Fascist, staring hard at one of the Germans, then said: "If you don't open that train and let those people get some water, we're going to kill you."[4]

The Germans hesitated. The tension mounted. By now a large crowd of civilian passengers, station employees, and local people had gathered. They, the Jews, and the militiamen waited, watching the Germans in silence. The militiamen's threat burned like a fuse.

Suddenly, one of the Germans shouted an order. The cars were to be opened. He told his men that only a few Jews were to be permitted to descend from each car to get water for themselves and the others.[5]

The militiamen seemed satisfied. Their guns still drawn, they now requested that the Red Cross be allowed to aid the prisoners. The Germans agreed, and the Fascists then urged them to get on with these tasks, overseeing the operation and helping wherever necessary.[6]

The complement of German guards stretched out along the full length of the train. They isolated it from the spectators driving them back into the terminal. Nurse De Marchi was permitted to come forward. She was accompanied by three other Red Cross workers and they observed the unsealing of the train.[7] Bearing the rank of inspector, Signorina De Marchi had many years of service in disaster and emergency work, both in natural catastrophes and those caused by the war. But she was to consider this experience the worst of all. Later in the day she would make note of the incident, writing:

> At one o'clock they opened the wagons, which had been closed for twenty-eight hours! In every one of them had been amassed some fifty persons: children, women, old people, young men and adults. Never have we seen a more ghastly spectacle before our eyes! It is the city people, torn from their homes, without baggage, with no one attending them, starved and thirsty, condemned to the most offensive form of mixed company. We felt ourselves disarmed and inadequate

before all their needs, immobilized by a pity that shuddered with rebellion, by a kind of terror that overwhelmed everyone: the victims, the station personnel, the spectators, the people. . . .[8]

After the train was unlocked and opened, Jews were chosen from each car and shown to two water fountains in the terminal, which were guarded by the Germans to prevent any escape. Many other prisoners descended from the cars, if only to stretch their legs or take a breath of air.

The Red Cross workers distributed bread, fruit, marmalade, and powdered milk, all in very small quantities. They also brought some medicines aboard and gave first aid where needed. The bodies of the two or three elderly persons who had expired were removed. The prisoners themselves tried to clean and freshen up their cars as best they could.

This busyness continued briskly for the next 2½ hours or so. The main activity was concentrated around the water fountains, with prisoners making endless trips back and forth to supply their fellow Jews. This system, however, was not at all adequate, for the fountains could not pump nearly enough water to satisfy everyone's needs and provide some reserve for the journey ahead and some people who had already had a drink were by now already thirsty again.

At some distance beyond the tail end of the train, a few prisoners could discern, lay another running fountain, which was neither in use, nor guarded. It was situated at the very end of the station in the center of a piazza which led to the street entrance to the terminal. A small number of Jews were so tempted by this sight they slipped off the train and managed to steal around it without drawing any notice from the guards. They crossed the tracks, followed a four-foot high retaining wall, and hidden by the train, they reached the fountain without any difficulty. A few others saw how easily this had been accomplished and joined them. Most of them had brought empty bottles along and now stood at the running water, filling them and drinking insatiably.[9]

In the meantime the car that had broken down had been replaced. Its passengers had come down from the old car and had boarded the new one. The train was ready to depart. The Jews at the fountains in the terminal were escorted back by the Germans. The four Red Cross workers withdrew. Only those who had succeeded in reaching the fountain in the piazza were left undisturbed, because none of the Germans knew they were there.

They began now, at a quarter of an hour or so before 4:00 P.M., to reseal the train. The straggling Jews were urged aboard by the SS guards, and the sliding wooden panels of the cars were rolled shut and locked in place.

Ing. Tedeschi managed to get off another hastily scrawled message, in which he wrote in the third person that he "blesses his family and asks that they send news by whatever means to wherever he will be."[10]

Other notes were dropped from the train, but far fewer than in Rome, because almost all the paper the prisoners had brought with them had either been consumed or conserved for future use. Of the messages that were thrown, one of them was written on a rough square of toilet paper. This one said: "Notify *Prima* a store in Via Nazionale that wife and mother are together with the Mieli and the Di Cave families. Greet—"[11] The final word was unfinished.

When the Jews at the street fountain heard the sounds of the train being readied, they took their last drops of water and hurried back. Though they had actually escaped and stood in a Paduan piazza as free men, they seemed not to be conscious of the fact, or if they were, they did not want to abandon their families.

But when they tried to reenter the platform, the Germans refused to let them pass. To the guards they appeared as trespassers; they had come directly from the streets of the city and therefore could not possibly have been with the deportees. That they were carrying bottles of water seems to have led the guards to the conclusion that they were local citizens attempting to aid the Jews.[12]

The blocked men protested, but to no avail. The principal difficulty was the difference in languages; neither the guards nor the Jews understood one another.

"No one is permitted in there," said an SS man in his native tongue.

"But we're part of that group," one of the Jews insisted.

"Sorry," said the German uncomprehendingly, "*kein Eingang*—no entry!"[13]

Arminio Wachsberger, who was preparing to take his place in the last prisoner car, was standing close to where this encounter was taking place. He watched it with passive curiosity, wondering how it would end. He knew they were telling the truth. He had seen them earlier as they moved stealthily toward the fountain. But he was also aware that they were free and he said nothing, not wanting to be the cause of their recapture.

Suddenly, however, one of the Jews recognized Wachsberger and called to him. "Interpreter!" he shouted. "Tell this man who we are!"[14]

Wachsberger was pressed into service. But the Germans were still unconvinced. A long discussion ensued. The Jews challenged the SS men to bring their families from the train as witnesses to their identity. This was done. It proved to be the solution to the problem, and the group was allowed to pass. They went aboard, as did the Germans, and the train began to move.[15]

Leone Sabatello, at this moment, was standing on the tracks, behind the far side of the train, urinating. A few minutes earlier he and some other boys had got down from their car for this very purpose and had chosen this spot because it was out of view of the crowded terminal. The others had reboarded, but Leone had lingered a while, and now he suddenly found the train rolling slowly down the tracks, leaving him behind. It had only gone a few yards when he began to run alongside it, calling for it to stop. He did not want to be cut off from his mother, father, and five sisters. Someone on the train, a German or a member of the crew, heard his cry and obliged. The train ground to a stop again, his car was opened, and he too was reunited with his family.[16]

At last the train left Padua. It rolled clear of the channel formed by the long station house on one side and the low retaining wall on the other. It was a smooth exit and the only changes in sound were created by the motion of the air around the train as it passed through the several trestles where the tracks and sidings give on to the north.

Among the passengers there was a feeling of reinvigoration, both in mind and body. The sun was setting, the afternoon heat was falling away, and the temperature in the cars was almost ideal. The food, the drink, the cleaning out of waste and garbage, the entire Paduan experience, was a narcotic, a syringeful of heroin plunged directly in the veins, which would take some hours to wear away.

In the car that had been exchanged for the one that had broken down, good spirits were running especially high. It was free of the choking smells which still lingered in the other cars. Moreover, this new car was of a different type than all the others. It had a large, open, unbarred window.

Michele Amati, who would tomorrow mark his seventeenth birthday, was in this car. He had been arrested in Trastevere during the first hour of the roundup with his thirteen-year-old brother, Alberto, an older sister, and their grandmother. His parents, who had been among those who had been buying cigarettes, had escaped. But his uncle, Giuseppe Piperno, had been taken from his home in the ghetto, and they had been reunited at the Collegio Militare, remaining together until now.

Michele and his brother had been studying the window of the car for the past few minutes. It was about 18 inches square. The bottom ledge was chest high. The window was just big and low enough for a small, agile man to scale and slip through. Michele was about five-feet-two-inches tall, his brother a bit less. They were wiry boys, who had long ago left school and had tempered their muscles performing the mule-like labors of the itinerant peddler. Discussing the matter briefly, the boys decided to jump. They would set a pile of the prisoners' belongings by the window and when the train would slow, as it often did, they would mount it and easily leap to freedom.

Michele, speaking for himself and his brother, now talked it over with his uncle. In the absence of their father the boys looked to him for guidance. Michele showed him how they could get away and said, "We're going to try it."

His uncle, a man of forty-four, thought a while. He then gave the boys his own advice.

"Listen," he said, "you'd better stay. They have all the names. If you get away, they'll kill everyone in the car."

Michele and Alberto did not wish to bear the responsibility for such a massacre, if it were to occur. Nor did anyone else in that car. The call of the open window was promptly silenced, and no one would speak of it again.[17] It was a cruel defeat, but in the new car a man could find at least some consolation; his was the airiest of all.

In a car further up the line, another escape plan was unraveling. A young man, who seems to have been named Lazzaro Sonnino, had plotted his own liberation and was about to carry it out. At Padua, when the car was open, he had tampered with the lock, hoping to prevent it from functioning. Now, with the full weight of his body he tried to roll the door open. The lock failed. He pushed a little harder, and the people in the car suddenly found themselves gaping at the open country-side, as clean air rushed in and swirled around.

The young man said a last goodbye and jumped. He hit the ground hard, tumbling and skidding in the same direction as the train. A moment later he was out of view, giving no sign whether he had been injured, or perhaps even killed. All that he left behind was the precious gift of the open door.[18]

This was the car which the Efrati family had boarded. Young Cesare thought at once of escaping, too. But his was a family of eleven, ranging from his three-year-old brother to his middle-aged parents. Most of them could not risk the jump. Cesare himself did not want to leave the others behind. So it was with everyone else in that car. The gift would remain unused. After a while, when the drafts from the onrushing air brought only additional discomfort, the open door was rolled shut again.[19]

It was evening now, and all the nighttime evils began again to overtake the prisoners. The train moved north-northwest, heading slowly for the Alps, the Brenner Pass, and the southern borders of the Third Reich.

XIX

ROME, AT THIS moment, was some 400 miles away. But it had not yet entirely forgotten its deported Jews; it would never entirely forget. People were saying that efforts were underway to obtain some relief for the suffering Jews of Rome.

The woman journalist de Wyss wrote that she had learned by hearsay that "the Jews have implored help from the Pope and that Pius XII has asked the German Ambassador Weizsäcker to stop this ill treatment and violence."[1] The American woman in hiding heard the same rumors. "It is understood that the Pope has asked the German Ambassador to make an effort to help the Jews," she wrote. "It is difficult for von Weizsäcker, of course, as the SS are independent of him. However, he did have some measure of success, for we hear that the women and children will be released."[2]

In reality, with the dispatch of Gumpert's and Weizsäcker's telegrams of the 16th and 17th, the German diplomatic corps in Rome had gone as far as they believed prudent. Today, the 19th, copies of these reports warning of the possibility of a public protest by the Pope were lying on the desk of Foreign Minister Ribbentrop. Within hours of one another, they had previously arrived at the Wilhelmstrasse bureau Inland II. The chief of this section, Group Leader von Thadden, had not acted on them until today. The step finally taken was to move them from his desk to Ribbentrop's office, Büro RAM.

Von Thadden was then informed that consideration of the

Gumpert-Weizsäcker messages by the Herrn RAM himself was "not yet possible," but that he would do so when he "has time."[3] The group leader made a note of this response for the Inland II files, and he, like the diplomats in Rome, waited for the voice of the RAM.

In Rome, Albrecht von Kessel discussed the matter privately with Möllhausen. The consul had just returned to the Villa Wolkonsky from having been recalled to the north to explain his own trouble-making telegrams in connection with the Jews.

"On this occasion," Möllhausen said of his informal meeting with Kessel, "we spoke at great length of the German drama, that drama that placed many Germans before the terrible alternatives of going over to the enemy or continuing to serve their own country. . . ."[4]

Toward the end of this friend-to-friend, lugubrious discussion, following which both men would carry on in the latter alternative, the "loose-tongued" Kessel made a rather lengthy speech about the shortcomings of his superiors in Berlin. The Nazis were foolhardy men, he felt, who were doing more harm to the Reich than good. He was clearly angry that Berlin's diplomacy had forced the Pope's policy to this, its severest trial. Pius might yet restrain himself, but in Kessel's view, the Germans would gain only a pyrrhic victory.[5]

"Whatever happens," said Kessel, "those gentlemen can boast of having lost the last bit of sympathy Germany enjoyed in the Vatican. . . ." He went on:

> Those gentlemen think that it's enough to merely pay tribute to the Church. But they're wrong. And by now they will have to win the war totally and quickly if they want to avoid many other disappointments, because no one will ever be able to forgive them for the persecution of the Jews and for the fate of all those unhappy people who suffer and die in the concentration camps. . . .[6]

While Kessel was speaking, Möllhausen's private secretary entered the office and handed the consul a message that had just arrived for him. It was in a sealed envelope, upon which had been written, "Personal—to be handed directly to the addressee." Möllhausen recognized the handwriting as Ambassador Rahn's.

It was a brief note, dated the 19th, which summed up the aftermath of the consul's attempt to block the deportation of the Jews of Rome:

> Apropos of the events of October 16th: You have got Ribbentrop's senior men on your neck; you have aroused the distrust of the central headquarters of the SS in Berlin; you have placed Kesselring in an embarrassing position and have weakened your own, and thus my position, in order to gain little or nothing at all. You should have reported to me and I would have tried to arrange something with Wolff. You have created chaos and have ruined everything. Very bad![7]

In the Vatican, Pope Pius XII waited, too, for word from the Germans as to what they might do in response to the Church's appeals for the Jews of Rome. Until then it would certainly be imprudent for the Pontiff to decide whether to break his long silence. Meanwhile, however, in a city of some two million Christians, in the very heart of the Catholic world, there were at least some matters of greater concern to the Pope.

Thinking always in broader terms, that is, beyond the fate of a thousand Jews, he was fearful that severe measures, such as the roundup of last Saturday, would drive the people of the occupied city into the arms of the "Communists." This was the word generally applied to those of the Resistance who advocated the use of force against the Nazis and who hoped to drive them out of Rome before the arrival of the Allies. Such a turn of events could bring the left-wing anti-Fascists to power in the capital and with them all the uncertainties of radical change.

For the Vatican, not only was it necessary to request the occupiers to restrain themselves, but they were also asked to strengthen their police forces in the city to assure that order would be maintained. That the weight of oppression and the breadth of "disorder," or resistance, would increase with the growth of police domination was a social phenomenon that apparently had not yet become clear in Vatican City.

Having received assurances from Weizsäcker that he would speak to Stahel about the "insufficient" police force in Rome,[8] the Pope on the 19th discussed the situation with the American diplomat in the Vatican, Harold Tittmann.

Immediately following his audience with Pius XII, Tittmann reported to Washington. He telegraphed that the Pope "seemed preoccupied that, in the absence of sufficient police protection, irresponsible elements (he said it is known that little Communist bands are stationed in the environs of Rome at the present time) might commit violence in the city. . . ." Pius XII, according to Tittmann, hoped that this point would be "given consideration by the Allies and necessary measures taken by them in time." Tittmann continued:

> The Pope said that so far the Germans had respected the Vatican City and the Holy See's property in Rome and that the German General Officer Commanding in Rome (Stahel) seemed well-disposed towards the Vatican. He added, however, that he was feeling restrictions due to the "abnormal situation."[9]

By "abnormal situation" the Pope may have meant the deportation of the Jews of Rome.

In the *Castelli Romani* this same day, a member of one of those "little Communist bands," the Jewish partisan Pino received a letter from his parents in Genoa. They wrote that despite the German occupation of that city, they foresaw no danger and were remaining in their home.[10]

At about the same time Marco Moscato returned to the squad's encampment. He told Pino what he had seen and had learned in Rome. His own family had escaped the roundup, Marco said. He then recounted everything he had heard in the city, describing the pitiless manner in which the Jews had been taken away.

Pino was profoundly angered by what he called the "savage fury" of the Germans. With rage and a yearning for revenge, he noted in his diary what Marco had told him, concluding with the question that burned in the minds of many of the partisans in Rome and in the hills. "When," he asked, "will we be able to start killing some of these brutes?"[11]

XX

THE DEPORTATION TRAIN reached the mile-high Brenner Pass in the first, dark hours of Wednesday, October 20th. It stopped at the frontier. The Italian crew got off the train. Their places were assumed by German trainmen. The freight cars were opened.

All of the benefits of the Padua stop had proved themselves by now to have been nothing but the briefest remission, a fresh coat of paint on a weary, sagging foundation. It had chipped and flaked away with every twist and turn in the road, and the reality of the prisoners' condition showed like the picture of Dorian Gray. They were exhausted, spent. They lay on the floorboards in attitudes far more disturbed than people already dead.

German border guards in greatcoats and boots stomped alongside the train looking in every car. Vapor poured from their mouths like the breath of horses running in the snow. But when the prisoners exhaled not the slightest mist was formed. Their clothes were too thin for this altitude, and there was simply no warmth in their bodies. If they could have at least trembled and chattered they would have generated some heat, but their muscles were too tired to shiver. Some of them did manage to get to their feet and move about, perhaps self-compelled to demonstrate that they were still fit candidates for the labor camp. But most of the Jews remained motionless, as if they had been sculpted rather than born.

A meticulous count of the prisoners was made. A German

entered each car, enumerated the individuals inside, and called out the total to another man who made note of it.[1]

Arminio Wachsberger was shaken by this procedure. He could clearly hear the entire operation taking place from car to car, as the Germans came down the line toward his own. Wachsberger later said that the man, a sergeant, "was crying out to his colleague who remained on the ground, '*sechzig Stück*' or '*funfzig Stück,*' which in German means 'sixty pieces' or 'fifty pieces,' that is he was not counting 'persons' or 'prisoners' or 'deportees,' but rather 'pieces,' as if we were so many heads of cattle destined for the slaughter house. That scared me very much . . . but after a little while I didn't think about it anymore."[2]

When the Germans had totaled their figures, the train was closed anew and waved on in the direction of Innsbruck. It was in Austrian territory now, but on the newest maps of the day, such a distinction did not exist; the borders of the Reich dipped into the Tyrol and stretched beyond Vienna. In fact, the Jews of Rome were in Germany.

Crossing the Alps, the train picked up a most circuitous route through Bavaria, headed toward Nuremberg, which was actually in the opposite direction of its final destination. Far from covering the shortest distance between Rome and the "labor camp," the Germans, for reasons unknown but probably as a result of Allied bombardments of the railways, followed a 1,150-mile course that was longer than the normal rail distance by almost half as much again. This alone, at the rate the train was moving, would add another hard days' travel to the journey.

Late in this third day out of Rome, the train stopped near the town of Fürth, just outside of Nuremberg. Women of the German Red Cross came aboard. They wore crisp clean uniforms and armbands with the red symbol of the organization and distributed hot barley soup to the wretched, malodorous prisoners. Some of the Jews sought answers to questions that were plaguing the group. Wachsberger repeated their pleas, which were also his own, in German.

"Where are we going?" he asked.

The Red Cross women continued dishing out the soup. It was as if only deaf-mutes had been chosen for this work. They managed to smile and tried to be helpful where they could, but not a word passed beyond their lips.

"Where are they taking us?" Wachsberger again inquired. No reply.[3]

The train went on, turning eastward. It had already passed about half-a-dozen labor camps.

XXI

SOME 450 RAIL miles further east, in a mire just north of the fiftieth parallel, Germans at the complex of installations known as Auschwitz were making preparations for the arrival of the Jews of Rome.[1]

The camp administration had received a teletype dispatch from Eichmann's bureau in Berlin announcing the approach of the deportation train. The shipment, it related, was due in on Friday, the 22nd. The estimated time of arrival was given, as well as the number of passengers, and the name of the city where the transport originated. Since the passengers were Jews, they were to be dealt with according to the procedure for "*Sonderbehandlung*—special treatment."

It was a standard teletype, the form of which did not vary from the countless others received in advance of trains arriving from all over Europe. At the base camp, Auschwitz-I, there were no particular measures to be taken, other than a coordination of this arrival with those of two larger transports, one coming in somewhat earlier from the Netherlands, and the other, scheduled for about the same time as the Rome train, from Szopienic, Poland.[2] The officials concerned at various points throughout the Auschwitz zone were routinely informed, including those at the extermination center, about two miles from the base camp. Appropriate instructions moved along according to an intercamp system of communication worked out for "special treatment" cases.

All of these operations were precisely those that followed the announcement of any approaching transport. Nevertheless the forthcoming arrival of the Jews of Rome was news of considerable interest at Auschwitz. From Camp Commandant Höss on downward, excitement began to whirl as word of the event reached every corner of the camp. It suddenly became a topic of endless fascination among even the guards who attended the gas chambers and crematoriums, and also the Jewish Sonderkommandos, the special squad of prisoners who were forced to assist them. They had been told of the arrival because they were the ones—both prisoners and guards—who would see to the actual killing and burning of the Jews of Rome.[3]

Italians had never been in Auschwitz before, and the fact that those on the way were Jewish Italians—an immense oddity in eastern Europe—and moreover Jewish Italians from the great city of Rome filled everyone with both awe and curiosity. It was as if an internationally celebrated company of performers were coming to town, cosmopolitan men and women who would not only entertain and delight them, but also bring tidings from the distant city and the bright lights of civilization.

Rumors churned. Among the Sonderkommandos and those who worked in the extermination operations it was being said that the Roman transport consisted of "five thousand rich Italian Jews."[4] Images of what they might look like were conjured and eagerly discussed. They envisaged how elegantly dressed the Roman Jews would be. Although they would have already been relieved of their jewelry, they would certainly be bedecked in precious furs and handsome clothing cut in the latest, most fashionable styles.

The highest officials of the camp wanted to be personally

present when the train from Rome was opened at the Auschwitz platform. Even Commandant Höss himself, who always remained strictly aloof from the camp's activities and never appeared in the presence of prisoners, planned to be there to take a look at the Roman Jews. Dr. Josef Mengele, the chief physician of Auschwitz, was anxious to learn about the dramatic developments that had placed Rome so much at the center of international news reports in recent months. Mengele, whose name more than that of any other German in Auschwitz would gain lasting infamy, would also personally greet the Jews of Rome.[5]

XXII

In the meantime the train pushed on, moving with the slow, excruciating sureness of a terrestrial tortoise in search of the sea. Early on Thursday the transport passed through Hof, which gave on to the Sudetenland and Bohemia, territory that had formed part of the now nonexistent state of Czechoslovakia.

In the wooden wagons, the passengers continued to deteriorate. The restorative effects of the last respite wore away faster than the previous one, and there would be none ahead.

In Wachsberger's car, the Rothschild woman had died. At every pause he had been trying to signal the Germans to remove the corpse. But they ignored him.[1] In the car with the open window, in which the young Amati brothers were riding, two persons had died, one of them a young, pregnant woman.[2] In Settimia Spizzichino's car, too, someone had died. People here fought incessantly with one another. Settimia's sister's two-year-old daughter had become unmanageable, screaming, twisting nervously, a grinding annoyance to the irascible people around her.[3]

Settimia herself had fallen into a disturbed melancholy. She had not eaten anything during the entire trip. Since receiving the food at Padua, her mother had been trying to induce her to take some. She kept it apart for her and from time to time she would say, "Eat it, eat it, it's good for you." But Settimia would shake her head no and remain silently disconsolate. Her mother would then stroke her and try to show that she understood, "Don't worry," she said. "Where we're going there'll be doctors."[4]

In Lazzaro Anticoli's car, his sick child came out of her coma once again. Lazzaro held the twins and his wife offered her some powdered milk, which she drank avidly, wanting more. Lazzaro touched her brow. It was cool. They gave her some margarine, then a large portion of marmalade, and then, still trying to satisfy her almost wolfish demand for food, a big piece of cheese they had conserved. When the child had eaten, she stood. She began to walk around. Her mother and father were amazed. Suddenly she was running up and down the car, stretching a week's accumulation of kinks and stiffness out of her little legs. She was laughing, giggling, ebullient. She dazzled the people around her with her partially toothless grin. The grownups, perhaps hearing an echo of pure child's pleasure, managed to smile. They played with her, and in the same magical way her illness had lifted and floated away, their suffering eased for a while.

The child was well again, her parents keenly delighted. But Lazzaro, even now, could not help cursing the Roman doctor who had prognosticized his daughter's death and had thus caused their return from hiding to the peril of the ghetto.[5]

It now became known or surmised, at least in Wachsberger's car, that the train was going to Poland. Both Admiral Capon and Signorina Cavalieri told Wachsberger that, according to the BBC broadcasts they had heard in Rome, Poland was the site of the Nazi extermination program against the Jews.[6] The admiral found a piece of paper and began writing his will. Signorina Cavalieri did the same. Believing that Wachsberger might survive because of his knowledge of German, they entrusted their last testaments to him. The admiral asked Wachsberger to try to get in touch with his son-in-law after the war. He wanted Fermi to know how he had died.

Wachsberger, since crossing the Brenner, was growing ever more doubtful about the story of the labor camp. Nevertheless, he still believed the admiral and the dowager exaggeratedly pessimistic. But he took their wills anyway, folding them neatly and placing them in his pocket among other papers he had brought with him. His two fellow Jews were both very old and before long would probably die in any case. Few people aboard the deportation train had any illusions about life in the labor camp being anything less than rigorous.[7]

Apart from the exceptions, however, hope was the one condition that remained indestructible among the passengers. During the journey it had died an infinite number of deaths, only to be born each time anew. At first they hoped every hope that the outermost limits of reason would allow. Then they hoped boundlessly. There were those who still hoped that they would be released; that the Pope, in the city from which they had come, had by now interceded in their behalf, and upon their arrival they would be turned around and sent back home to Rome.[8]

The train went forward. All day Thursday, the 21st, all day Friday it crawled across the fertile countryside of the Reich Protectorate of Bohemia, and part of Moravia. At about dusk on Friday, the passengers arrived at Ostrau, the German name for Czechoslovakian Ostrava, which lay on the edge of Poland. They crossed the frontier. The sun was setting behind the tail of the train. The darkness in the east was bringing on the evening and with it the Jewish Sabbath. There were no more borders ahead. They were on an open plain, and only some trees and farmhouses could be seen. There was some distance to travel as yet, but on German maps used by the administrators of the concentration camp system they were already in the *Interessengebiet,* or sphere of influence, of Auschwitz.

One Jew on the train had returned to his native land. His name was Paul Kaplan, born in Lodz, fifty-seven years earlier. He had only recently escaped Nazi persecutions in Poland fleeing to the West and settling finally in Rome. Now he had come home to suffer the fate of 3,000,000 other Polish Jews.[9]

Just over the boundary, the train stopped at a village station. The cars were opened, and the prisoners were permitted to descend. There was a sign in German that indicated a latrine for "Russian prisoners of war" and the Jews were urged to use it.[10] While this was taking place, the prisoners cleaned out their cars somewhat, although the dead had to remain with them. Hours later they were locked inside again, and the train moved on once more.

It was night now and totally dark. The prisoners could not even see one another and could see nothing from their little windows. Only the rails spoke for the world outside.

On these particular tracks, when the train went slowest, again and again, it said, "Click-click, di-da, di-da, di-da, di-da; click-click, di-da, di-da, di-da, di-da." At higher speeds: "Bi-bum, diddledum; bi-bum, diddledum."

Such was what the world had to say to the Jews of Rome.

Around 11:00 P.M. the train stopped. Though the passengers were not informed, it was standing at the front door of Auschwitz-II, the extermination camp, Birkenau. The transport had arrived too late to enter the camp this day.[11] The reception personnel had gone off duty hours ago. The evening *Appell,* or head count, had been made. The inmates and their jailers had retired. Except for the distant sound of barking dogs, and the chug of an occasional passing train, Auschwitz was silent. The Jews of Rome would have to wait until the morning to enter.

The train remained sealed. A complement of guards came out to relieve the SS men who had made the difficult journey. The passengers, however, were unaware that they had reached their destination, although many guessed as much. From their windows they could see the bright lighting that flooded the camp each night, a spectacular squandering of electricity that could be observed at great distances. The sky itself was lighted with a reddish glow, and they could smell a faint, strangely sweetish odor, as if something unfamiliar were burning. Many of the passengers were asleep. Now the others tried to do the same.

Sometime near dawn, Wachsberger awoke. Reclining on the floor of the car, he could look through a crack in the wall. He could make out the contours of a building. High flying balloons were attached to it. They swayed at the end of long wires and served as a protection against strafing from enemy aircraft. His little daughter awoke, too. He lifted her to the window of the car in order to point out the balloons in the lightening morning sky. Outside, an SS man saw the child. He suddenly bent to the ground, picked up a large rock, and threw it directly into her face. The girl drew back, frightened but unharmed, as the missile crashed against the bars of the window and dropped.

"After such an act of barbarity against that tiny harmless human being," her father would later say, "I finally understood that we had arrived on the threshold of hell."[12]

XXIII

AUSCHWITZ BEGAN TO stir. Passengers inside the waiting train could hear a great deal of activity outside, and before long the cars were being opened.

"Alle aussteigen!" the guards began to demand repeatedly, and while the words were not understood, it was clear enough that they were orders to detrain.

Day had not yet fully broken, but the platform upon which the Roman Jews descended was brilliantly illuminated. Huge reflectors drove out every shadow. The bewildered prisoners squinted at the brightness and stumbled onto what appeared as a set where a film was being made.

There were Germans everywhere shouting and gesturing confusedly. Men in striped uniforms moved silently through the growing mass of people. They began to remove the luggage, the garbage, and the dead from the open cars. Sewn to their shabby uniforms were two triangular pieces of cloth that formed the hexagram Star of David. To this was attached a letter indicating their nationality and a number of up to six digits.

Some of the Roman Jews stared at their coreligionists from other lands. To the Italians it seemed they were incredibly thin, their eyes empty and unseeing. Wachsberger tried to speak with them in German, French, Yiddish, and even the Hungarian he had learned from his mother. But they neither replied not gave any sign of recognition. At last, one of them, a French Jew, mumbled quickly, "If they ask how old you are, tell them that you're under thirty." Wachsberger wondered what he meant.[1]

Apart from the sight of the inmates, however, the scene was not very frightening. Indeed in some ways it was reassuring, for it seemed that everything the Germans had earlier said was now proving to be true. They were at the labor camp, and the terrible journey had at last been completed. The Germans were firm, but also patient and understanding. The Jews were grateful that the uniformed prisoners had been there to help them unload the cars, and that they were given ample time to gather themselves together. A sense of genuine relief swept through the group. They smiled easily and waved to friends from whom they had been separated throughout the trip. Settimia Spizzichino's mother discovered only now that her sister had been riding on the train and there was an emotional reunion, which the Germans left discreetly undisturbed.[2] They had learned that these were the ways to gain the greatest cooperation and to avoid disorder and panic.

While the Jews of Rome were assembling beside the train, Camp Commandant Höss and Dr. Mengele arrived with several SS officers. One of them asked of the escort that had accompanied the group who could act as an interpreter. Wachsberger was brought forward. As had been done at the Collegio Militare exactly one week ago, he was instructed to get up on a table and transmit the German commands. When the group saw him, they understood that they were about to be addressed. They fell silent and listened attentively. Wachsberger was to recall that moment as follows:

> They ordered me to say in Italian that our transport had arrived at its predetermined destination. That is, a labor camp in which the able-bodied men and women would perform jobs similar to those they were accustomed to and the old people, the weak, pregnant women, and children would be transported to a nearby camp where they would rest and do very light work. They assured us that in the evenings, after work hours, families would be able to be with each other. In the meantime, we first had to take showers and be disinfected. The men and women who were to do the heavier work would have to go on foot to the shower barracks, which were located in the principal labor camp. The elderly and weak, the pregnant women, and the children, in order not to tire them too much, would be taken by truck to the shower and disinfection building in the rest camp.[3]

At this point, Dr. Mengele, a dapper, handsome, young SS lieutenant of thirty-three, waved Wachsberger to his side. Mengele had a gentle manner and a quiet poise that almost always lay in a delicate balance between the edge of smugness and the height of charm. He liked to whistle Wagnerian airs and did so incessantly.

He told Wachsberger to inform the others that as medical director of the camp he was now going to choose those who in his judgement were physically fit for work. He sat on the table. All of the Jews were to approach him, he said, and he would divide them into two groups, one of which was to mount the trucks and the other to remain standing on the railroad tracks, women apart from the men.[4]

Wachsberger explained this in Italian and the selection—as it was called—began. It moved along at a steady pace, with only infrequent difficulties. These arose where people who had expected to remain together had been divided. The inseparable Amati brothers, for example, were sent in opposite directions. Michele, seventeen, was permitted to remain with his uncle among the work group, while Alberto, thirteen, had to join his grandmother on the other side. Alberto tried twice to steal over to his brother, but was stopped both times by the German guards.[5]

When the process had been completed, about 600 persons had been picked for the truck ride and 450 for the hike on foot.[6] Both groups were made up as had been expected, with many exceptions, however. The work group consisted of youths and young men and women, but also some older men. The larger group contained some able-bodied men who were younger than some of those in the smaller group, but had made a poor appearance, particularly because a week's growth of beard made them look older than they were. But few protested these inconsistencies, especially since Mengele now gave them an opportunity to partially rectify the situation.

Addressing those who had been selected for work, Mengele had Wachsberger say, "You are now going to another camp about ten kilometers from here. Anyone who feels he is too tired to walk that distance is free to join those going by truck."[7]

Of the 450 in the work group, some 250 persons accepted the SS doctor's invitation.[8] They hurried over to the trucks and rejoined their families, leaving behind those who for one or another reason thought it wiser not to call attention to their fatigue—an intense exhaustion felt by all, weak and strong alike.

The trucks were now ready to depart. Wachsberger, thinking his work was done, started to go to his wife and child, who had been selected for the larger group and had boarded one of the vans.

"Where are *you* going?" Mengele asked him.

"To my family," he said.

"No, no, *Dolmetscher*, you stay here."[9]

Both Mengele and Höss told him he would be needed as an interpreter. They instructed him to go with the Jews waiting to walk to the work camp. "They consoled me," Wachsberger was to remember, "saying that I would be able to see my family that evening at the rest camp."[10]

He obeyed. The divided work group now numbered exactly 154 males and forty-seven females.[11]

By now the trucks had started their engines and were beginning to roll away, kicking up dust from the soft earth underfoot. The prisoners called to one another and waved goodbye. Settimia Spizzichino and her sister Giuditta, both selected for work, bade a temporary *"ciao"* to their mother, their sister Ada, and her daughter.[12]

Lazzaro Anticoli, who had been separated from his wife, the twins, and his daughter, tried to find them among the faces in the trucks. But he was unsuccessful, and in a few moments they were all out of sight.[13]

Men and women SS guards now took charge of the remaining Roman Jews. Two columns were formed, one of each sex. A command was barked and they set out, dreading the march of the preannounced ten kilometers.

The train still stood on the track. It had been emptied of all its contents. Piles of baggage and rubbish lay on the platform, as if the train had vomited from its open doors. It was daytime now, and most of the Germans who had been so busy before had gone away. A depressing stillness fell. Wind blew over the marshy lands. It made a whispering sound as it rushed through the wild grass and crossed the ear. As they walked, the voice of the wind became more pronounced.

They had not gone more than half of one kilometer when they were halted and told that they had already arrived. They were standing at the center of the long, winged entrance to Birkenau. They passed through an opening in the massive, brick barrier. The men were led to the newly constructed male quarantine barracks, the very first ones at the right, and the women went to a similar facility on the left.

Many of them could not understand why they had been told they would have to walk so much further than the brief distance they had actually covered. They wondered why the Germans had permitted their group to volunteer to join the others who went by truck. But such questions were easily shrugged away.[14]

XXIV

THE GROUP OF 850 Roman Jews who were transported by truck went to Birkenau, too. They entered through a muddy roadway, which crossed then paralleled a railroad siding that penetrated the camp and went directly to the doors of two brand new white buildings. These facilities, which had been completed only a few months earlier, were designated K-II and K-III. The latter was on the right side of the tracks and the former to the left of the road. They were described as bathhouses. The inmates called them bakeries. In fact, they were Birkenau's newest gas chambers and crematoriums.

It was a tremendous camp, still in the process of being built. The new arrivals from Rome could look across the railroad siding and see orderly rows of long, low, wooden barracks which reached out almost to the horizon. On the opposite side there were barracks of a different construction, but equally as monotonous. The land was perfectly flat. The sky was everywhere. The camp seemed to embrace the entire world. Barking dogs and screaming birds could always be heard, but never seen, and in the distance there was the perpetual protest of trains moving to and from the direction of Krakow. From time to time they sighed, squealed, issued terrifying wails and most often a heavy, roaring breathing.

An endless curtain of barbed fencing, which stretched in every direction, could be seen by the Roman Jews. It was kept standing in a tireless upright position by a disciplined army of concrete supports, set an unvarying distance of about five feet from one another. These supports were long and slender and stood about eight feet high. They had a graceful turn at the top and bore an uncanny resemblance to a large snake that had been charmed to a standing position and, leaning back ever so slightly, was poised at the very instant before it would strike. This image was immeasurably enhanced by the presence on every third or fourth support of a silvery metal tongue that curled venomously from the place where the serpent's mouth would be. A lamp hung from the tongue. The snakes looked everywhere, and thus no matter where in the camp one might be, the dreadful object was staring. Running down its chest like huge buttons were porcelain insulators, where the fencing was coupled with high tension wire carrying 6,000 volts of electricity through the entire barbed curtain.

This latter fact was as yet unknown to the Jews of Rome. Those aboard the trucks would of course never know it. Within minutes after they had left the selection site, they arrived at the gas chambers, or as they regarded them, the shower and disinfection rooms. They were instructed to dismount the trucks. Two groups of about equal size were formed. They assembled outside the white building.[1]

In the concrete and steel anteroom to the gas chamber, into which the Jews of Rome were about to enter, the Germans and the Sonderkommandos were waiting for them with varying degrees of eagerness. But the curiosity which had been aroused days earlier, was felt by all—more than ever, it seems.[2]

About an hour earlier, just after the morning *Appell,* they had been told that the Roman Jews had arrived during the night. They had been in a state of readiness for them for the past twenty-four hours. Yesterday, at this time, there had been a false alert. Expecting to receive somewhat less than half of the "five thousand rich Italian Jews," they had been sent only a small group of "Mussulmen," weakened and diseased inmates who had been selected from the various labor camps and industrial installations at Auschwitz. Now, however, they had been given official information, and there could be no doubt that this morning they would stand face to face with the Jews of Rome. They imagined that today's labors would therefore be very intense.[3]

Outside, the first group of Jews was ready to enter the "bathhouse." It was below the level of the ground and they had to descend a ramp. On the land above it was a well-kept lawn, from which sprouted concreted objects shaped like large mushrooms. A little farther on, set upon the bathhouse roof, was an enormous white chimney.

The Roman Jews came down the ramp. The Sonderkommandos, dressed in striped uniforms and wearing rubber boots, stood by and observed them. One of the members of the special squad was a Czechoslovakian Jew named David Karvat.* He regarded the Jews of Rome with the same expectations as everyone else. He later described the entire event. The following is from a transcription of what he said:

> . . . the trucks arrived from the selection center, which was at Auschwitz-I, but not as many as had been expected. Perhaps 500 or 600 persons, but not more, while according to calculations, they were expecting that two thousand of the five thousand arrivals would be marked for elimination. We were surprised that among them were many young men and women, who should have been with those who had been selected for labor. Another surprise was that they were not as rich as we had been told. The rich Dutch and French were better dressed. Then the Italians were wearing clothes that were too light and anything but suitable to the climate here.
>
> It was difficult to make them understand. This was due to the language differences and these Italians spoke only Italian. The SS tried to explain the usual story about the showers. No one comprehended

* Like his fellow Sonderkommandos, Karvat was forced to watch the slaughter that was about to occur. Sonderkommandos, after a few months service, were invariably liquidated themselves. But Karvat was a rare survivor. In January, 1946, while waiting on a beach for an unmarked sea craft that was to take him and other Jews illegally to Palestine, he met the Roman Jewish historian Michael Tagliacozzo, who was among the refugees. In a series of transcribed talks that followed this encounter, Karvat revealed the details of the last moments of the Jews of Rome. Tagliacozzo has never hitherto disclosed this testimony, although its existence had been known. He has, however, now made it available to the author.

and there was some confusion. Then an old, well-dressed man showed a row of medals and shouted something in German, which I did not comprehend. At this point the group began to become upset and agitated. Some children tried to change places and join other small groups of persons and many of them succeeded, keeping very close to them. Then, unexpectedly, there were some loud cries from a woman. At this point one of the SS men rushed up to her and struck her with a cudgel and grabbed away the child she had with her. The child was shoved into the entrance to the structure. Here other SS men did the same thing with other women. Then everyone began to enter and the work became simpler. Only then did I see a little girl lying on the ground in front of the entrance with her head injured.

I have spoken only of the first group. The second group was waiting not very far away, but they could neither see nor hear what was happening, since there was a wall and some structures separating them from us. And then there was the usual chaos that overtook the camp each morning, which drowned out any other noise.

After everyone had entered, things proceeded as in any other elimination. . . .[4]

A "bath director" now took charge of the group. They were told to remove everything they wore and place whatever remained in their pockets and purses on a huge table. They hung their clothes on hangers, under which was the legend in various languages, "If you want your effects when you go out, please make note of the number of your hanger."[5] Towels and soap were distributed. Quietly, they began to enter the barren chamber. They had suffered a lifetime of deceptions, and now only one final trick remained to be played.

When everyone had gone inside, the heavy metal door to the gas chamber was closed and sealed. They could still be viewed through a small, but thick plate glass window set into the door. They filled the enclosure to only about 25 percent of its capacity. It was a long, narrow room, entirely barren except for some metal pillars and the "shower" facilities that ran along the low ceiling. Many of the Jews looked up at the pipes. They waited for the water to emerge.[6]

On the lawn directly above them, German personnel bent over the concrete mushrooms and turned them counterclockwise.

They were taken off entirely exposing the hollows of the perforated metal columns that plunged directly into the chamber. About six containers, in the shape of pound-sized coffee cans but approximately twice the size, lay on the grass. They had been brought by a truck falsely bearing the emblem of the Red Cross.[7] There were red and white paper labels around the cans, which read, *"Giftgas! [Poison Gas!] Zyklon."* They had cost the German government about fifty cents for each can. A skull and crossbones on the label warned that the contents were lethal, and bold print urged that the material be handled only by trained personnel. The Germans wore gas masks. One of them punched holes in the tops of the cans, exposing crystals that resembled little bluish-white pebbles that might be found in a garden path.[8]

The Germans by now had received a signal that the Jews had been secured in the chamber. They waited a few minutes to permit the temperature inside to rise several degrees from the body heat of the entrapped human beings. Heat facilitated the release of the gas from its crystalized form.[9] When the proper temperature was believed to have been obtained, a camp sanitary orderly poured the little pebbles into the shafts. They tumbled and slid down a spiral track, which had been constructed to slow the descent.

As they replaced the mushroom lids, the gas began to escape into the chamber. It seeped slowly from the openings in the pillars. Within a few moments, the prisoners detected the gas. For the next several minutes, depending on their constitution and condition, their bodies and minds struggled and reeled against it. With the utmost of violence they tried to tear themselves free of the hydrogen-cyanide acid, which they were sucking into their lungs. The more they fought, the quicker the battle was lost.

Inhalation of the gaseous acid was destroying the body mechanism which permits the red blood corpuscles to renew the supply of oxygen required for absorbtion by the tissues. The symptoms accompanying this rapid degeneration were vomiting, involuntary defecation, hemorrhaging, anxiety, and finally total paralysis of the respiratory system. Then they died. Death was caused by internal asphyxiation.[10]

"At the end," David Karvat's statement went on, "we began to extract the corpses from the chamber."[11] Twenty-five minutes had gone by since the door had first been closed, a week since the Jews of Rome had been fast asleep in their own beds.

Electric pumps were turned on to exhaust the poisoned air. The chamber was opened, and the high-booted Sonderkommandos, who meanwhile had put on gas masks, entered. They dragged hoses with them to wash down the blood, excrement, and vomit that fouled the grotesque mound of bodies. With specially designed hooks and lariats, they separated the dead from each others' clutches and embraces. Then they began the search for gold in the teeth of the victims. Even in death these Jews, who had given their gold to both the oppressor and the protector, would yield yet another tribute to the earthly ruler. When this was done, their hair was removed. The bodies were then transported by elevator to the furnaces, which had been stoked to an appropriate temperature. Here, another team of Sonderkommandos took charge.[12]

Karvat, in the meantime, had returned to await the second group of Roman Jews. According to his testimony, they were "calm and unaware of their fate. This time a prisoner who knew some Italian explained everything very well, following the orders of the SS, and therefore everybody entered peacefully."[13]

After the second group had been killed and disposed of, the Germans and the Sonderkommandos discussed their disillusioning experience with the Jews of Rome. Karvat continued:

> The SS explained to us later that the young people had been eliminated at once because they had been immediately qualified as being prone to laziness and thus unfit for work. A few days later, however, another SS man told me that they had been immediately eliminated because they were Badoglian Jews who had aided the King, he too of Jewish descent, in overthowing Mussolini.[14]

All of the Sonderkommandos who witnessed the extermination of the Jews of Rome, with the exception of Karvat, who would be transferred to another job, were shortly to be gassed themselves.[15]

By the late afternoon of that Saturday, the Roman Jews who had been killed in the morning had, for the most part, been turned to smoke that wafted in the Polish sky. The residue of incombustible bone matter was passed through a mill that ground it to a fine, white ash. This and the ashes of their flesh were trucked to the nearby river Sola, a tributary of the Vistula, into which they were dumped.[16]

The winds blew the smoke to the east and the waters carried the ashes to the west.

During this same day, coincidentally, the German Foreign Office acted on Gumpert's and Weizsäcker's telegrams. Group Leader von Thadden of Inland II, on the instruction of Büro RAM, sent a memorandum to Obersturmbannführer Eichmann of RSHA, IV-B-4, in reference to the Roman Jews rounded up a week ago.

In it, he informed that Bishop Hudal had delivered a letter to General "Stahls."[17] He then quoted the text of the letter as received in Gumpert's dispatch of the 16th. Furthermore, he said, the German embassy at the Holy See had confirmed that Hudal's reaction represented that of the Vatican. He continued paraphrasing Weizsäcker's telegram, arriving at the following conclusion: "The embassy has further pointed out that the reaction of the Curia could be somewhat dampened if the Jews were to be installed in labor service here in Italy."[18]

Copies of this gentle attempt to reconcile the several interests of the Reich were sent to the political, party, and—perhaps as a nod to the transcendental quality of the matter—to the cultural sections of the Wilhelmstrasse.[19]

As for Eichmann, he would later declare that on receipt of his copy, "I sent this report through regular channels to the chief of Section IV, Gruppenführer Müller, asking him, as usual, to indicate to me what was to be done."[20]

A reply from Müller has never been found. Any word at all

from the still-missing chief of the Gestapo is rare, although he has been quoted as saying, "If we had had fifty Eichmanns, then we would have won the war."[21]

XXV

THE 201 ROMAN Jews who survived the selection entered the camp according to established procedure. They were stripped of the things they held and wore, showered, and disinfected. An identification number was tattooed on their forearms. The men received numbers ranging in the middle of the 158,000 series, the women at the beginning of the 66,000s.[1]

They were given raggedy, wrong-sized clothing in exchange for their own, a watery turnip soup, and assigned places in the quarantine barracks. In the evening they were doled a liquid of dubious origin called "tea," a measure of bread, and a piece of blood-sausage. A few of the Roman men hesitated. They discussed whether they should attempt to preserve the *kashruth*, the religious laws that prohibit the ingestion of animal blood and declare that only kosher meats may be eaten. But a higher Jewish law insists on survival at the expense of the rituals, and the men learned to eat the blood-sausage.[2]

Before this first day ended, they witnessed brutality and violent death;[3] they learned the basic rules of the camp, became acquainted with its complex social structure, its classes of prisoners and the division of labor and power relationships among them. They discovered that regardless of where in life they had stood before, they were now in the lowest stratum.[4] At one and the same time they suffered the throes of change, mourned for the old ways, and began to take their place in the new society, which many were to conclude was not, in its general features, a great deal different from their own.

Their first day at Auschwitz had been worse than anyone could have imagined, but so far, not much worse, and the Germans could not be accused of having deceived them. Yet they had not kept their promise to allow them to visit their families that evening. Inquiries in this regard had brought very unsatisfactory replies. Some were reassuring; some less so. Others went so far as to say that their loved ones had been summarily killed. This, none of the Rome group believed at all.[5]

The following morning at about 10:00 A.M., the 154 Roman males were gathered before Dr. Mengele. With Wachsberger again serving as interpreter, Mengele questioned them individually on the state of their health and their medical history. While being tattooed yesterday, they had been cautioned by a Polish Jew, a veteran inmate named Nathan Gerovitsch, to withhold any negative aspects of such information.[6] This warning had been given when some Roman Jews, who had had malaria—then an endemic disease of the Italian south—inquired whether Gerovitsch thought they would be given favorable treatment were they to disclose their disability.

Mengele, following his interrogation of the prisoners, was impressed by their good health records. He said that in view of their having come from so civilized a city as Rome, and consequently so sanitary, they would not have to remain in quarantine for the usual period of forty days[7]—a circumstance that only hastened the death of many of them.

They were then dismissed, but Mengele asked Wachsberger to remain behind. When alone, the SS doctor began to question him about nonmedical matters. According to Wachsberger, he wanted to know "the details of our arrest, about life in Rome, the fall of fascism, etc."[8] Wachsberger answered as well as he could, but the German's curiosity was singularly insatiable. He told Wachsberger that he did not have time to listen now, but he wanted to continue the conversation in the evening, after their separate work day was done.

Thus began a brief but most irregular series of nightly encounters between the SS man and the Roman Jew. After the final *Appell* and the evening mess, they would meet in the registration barrack, at that hour deserted. "He wanted me to recount in every detail what had happened in Italy on July 25, 1943 [the date of the King's *coup d'etat*], and about the sentiment of the population with respect to fascism and Nazism," Wachsberger was to say. "Just before I would leave, he would hand me a gift of some morsels of bread, a bit of margarine or blood-sausage."[9]

Wachsberger learned quickly how to exploit Mengele's inquisitiveness. He perceived that the doctor had seized upon this contact with the important events that had taken place in Rome in order to assess the contemporary world situation. Mengele apparently felt himself to be a victim of Nazi propaganda and was seeking the truth as the best means of escaping the consequences of a German defeat. Wachsberger, the ghetto Jew, was hardly well-informed, however. He knew less than what had been reported in the Fascist press and only a handful of the worthless rumors that ran around. Yet he successfully pretended otherwise, and the rendezvous continued.

One such evening, in the last days of that October, Wachsberger saw that Mengele was more locquacious than usual, almost cheerful. The doctor, he thought, had had too much to drink, and he hazarded a question of his own.[10]

"Herr Hauptsturmführer," Wachsberger said timorously, "tell me, where are my wife and child?"

Mengele was not at all disturbed by this presumption. Without hesitation, without a moment's search for the proper words, he said, "Look, *Dolmetscher*, this is a labor camp. We need people who can work. The others . . ." An artful gesture of his hands finished the broken sentence. It proclaimed that there simply were no "others."

Wachsberger did not understand. But he was encouraged by Mengele's easy manner. "I asked him," he later said, "how come, contrary to what had been promised on our arrival at the platform, we were not allowed to see our families that evening."

"Deine Familie existiert nicht mehr," the doctor said softly, informing Wachsberger that his family "no longer exists." Had he not seen the camp chimneys belching smoke all day long? Mengele asked with some surprise at the Italian's ignorance. Had not anyone told him of the crematoriums?[11]

Wachsberger replied that he had seen all of these things, but he thought that this being a very large labor camp and a very difficult one, there were many more or less natural deaths. "I said to him that I had been told that the bodies of these persons, who had died in the camp, were the ones that were cremated, but that our families, after disinfection, had been transferred to a rest camp."[12]

Mengele, almost all of the prisoners who knew him and survived his selections agree, was a man of infinite patience. He now led Wachsberger to the registration files in the barrack. He opened a drawer and removed Wachsberger's card, showing it to him. It contained his name, number, and other personal data. He then invited the Roman Jew to search the records for any similar card for his wife and his daughter. The cards could not be found. Wachsberger was still unconvinced. If they had been sent to a rest camp, he thought, their records would be there.[13]

"But if you only need people who can work," he asked as if he had caught Mengele in a lie, "why did you tell those in the labor group that they could join the others on the trucks?"

Mengele chuckled. "Don't you remember that I said the camp was about ten kilometers away and that anyone who did not feel like walking could go by truck?"

Yes, of course he remembered. That was just the point. If this were only a labor camp, why would the laborers be destroyed? They had been robust young men and women, capable of prodigious work. It only proved there had to be a rest camp after all, where once they had regained their strength they would be put to work. Mengele was drawing him into a cruel and colossal joke.

"Why *did* you tell them they would have to walk ten kilometers when the camp was only a few steps away?" Wachsberger asked. "They could have worked. They were only tired from having been in those freight cars for five days."

It was almost as if it had become a trial or an inquisition, with Mengele in the dock. The Jew and the Nazi regarded one another. The long, wooden barrack contained not only them, but tens of thousands of silent witnesses, little file cards—tombstones in a way—memorializing all the prisoners Auschwitz had ever known by name, the living, the dead, and they who were about to die. Wachsberger waited for a reply. Everything, the entire thrust of all the involuted logic of the camp depended on what it might be.

Mengele, for his part, was still amused. He knew the answer in all the perfect contours of its rationality, and he turned it and toyed with it like the corners of a great mustache.

"Dolmetscher," he said finally, locking the words into place, "anyone who can't walk ten kilometers after spending five days on a train is not capable of the work we have to do here."[14]

The doctor had acquitted himself. Everything at Auschwitz made sense. At last Wachsberger believed.[15]

For the others the process of learning to believe in the reality of the gas chambers was less definitive than Wachsberger's experience, and thus, if it may be said, perhaps more painful. In any event, within days, most of the Roman Jews—though not all—were convinced that there was no rest camp. Inmates who had been reluctant to tell the Italians the truth on the first day now felt free to reveal what everyone else knew.

Lazzaro Anticoli remembers being told by a Polish Jew, "You'll be all right here. Don't think of your people. They've been dead since the very beginning."[16]

Michele Amati, when told that his brother had been gassed, warned his informant not to say such things. It was said again, and he burst into tears.[17]

Settimia Spizzichino actually saw a selection of new arrivals entering the gas chambers. To dodge a work detail, she had wandered off with her sister Giuditta. They came upon the biggest of the gas chambers, K-II. They too had already been told of the gassings, but still doubted. Now, at a distance, they watched as men, women, and children descended the ramp that led to the chamber. This group had somehow become aware that they were going to their death. They were being driven in like wild horses. Some of them saw the two sisters. They called out as if the young women could somehow save them. The sisters were terrified and ran away. Now they too believed.[18]

In the first week at Auschwitz, one of the remaining Jews of Rome developed pneumonia and died during the night. In the morning, as was the camp practice, his body was brought out for the *Appell*. It was then loaded on a cart and taken away by a Sonderkommando. Some of the Roman Jews followed behind. When they were prevented from going further, one of them, Angelo Fatucci, recited *kaddish*, the prayer for the dead, as their comrade was wheeled out of view.[19]

"We were all very sad," another man in the group was later to say, "because he was the first to leave us."[20]

Now they were 200. Very soon, as will be seen, all but the fifteen survivors would be dead.

XXVI

IN ROME THE limp aftermath of the forced departure of the city's Jews continued to unfold, as the fate of the deportees remained as yet unknown.

In that last week of October, Settimio Sorani attempted to deliver to Pope Pius XII the Jewish community's memorandum of proposals for a papal intervention in behalf of the deported Jews of Rome. He had made an early morning appointment with the Yugoslavian diplomat to the Holy See, Cyril Kotnik, the intermediary who had agreed to place the message in Pius's hands. When he arrived at the diplomat's home in Via Salaria, he was arrested by agents of the Gestapo. They entered the Yugoslav's apartment, taking Sorani with them, and finding no one in, began a search of the premises. Sorani managed to dispose of the memorandum, following which he was taken to Kappler's prison in Via Tasso and enclosed in a cell.[1] The community's document would never reach the Pope.*

Pius XII, in any event, reaffirmed the policy of silence during the same week, but not without some Vatican comment noting his disapproval. This appeared in *l'Osservatore Romano* in its issue of Monday-Tuesday October 25-26. The Vatican newspaper wrote:

> Persistent and pitiful echoes of calamities, which as a result of the prolongation of the present conflict do not cease to accumulate, continue more than ever to reach the Holy Father.
>
> The August Pontiff, as is well known, after having in vain tried to prevent the outbreak of the war by striving to dissuade the Rulers of the nations from taking recourse in force of arms, which today are so fearsome, has not desisted for one moment in employing all the means in his power to alleviate the suffering, which, whatever form it may take, is the consequence of this cruel conflagration.
>
> With the augment of so much evil, the universal and paternal charity of the Pontiff has become, it could be said, ever more active; it knows neither boundaries nor nationality, neither religion nor race.
>
> This manifold and ceaseless activity on the part of Pius XII has intensified even more in recent times in regard for the increased suffering of so many unfortunate people.

* Sorani was interrogated and after ten days released, the Germans apparently considering his false identity papers authentic. By this time President Foà had returned to Rome. He began drafting a general report on the period between the initiation of the occupation and the October 16th roundup. Dated November 15, 1943, a copy was sent to the Vatican. It received no reply other than an acknowledgment of its arrival.[2] Early in December, according to Sorani, the Jewish leaders learned from Vatican sources that the October 16th group had been "liquidated."[3] Historian Tagliacozzo, in hiding in the Vatican's church Saint John in Lateran, heard the news at the same time. He was told by the Reverend Father P. Palazzini, who was in charge of aiding refugees who had taken shelter in the Pontifical Seminary of Rome.[4] Efforts to obtain the release of the deported Jews then ceased.

Such blessed activity, above all with the prayers of the faithful of the whole world, who unanimously and with ardent fervor never cease to look to Heaven, can achieve even greater results in the future and hasten the day on which the shining glow of peace will return to the earth; and men, laying down their arms, will put aside all their differences and bitterness, and, becoming brothers once more, will finally labor, in all good faith, for the common weal.[5]

When Weizsäcker read this, he had it immediately translated into German. This version, presumably because of the haste in which it was done, was somewhat inaccurate, but not substantively so. The ambassador then sent it off to Berlin, under cover of the following letter:

In connection with telegraphed report n. 147, of 17 October last:

The Pope, although under pressure from all sides, has not permitted himself to be pushed into a demonstrative censure of the deportation of the Jews of Rome. Although he must know that such an attitude will be used against him by our adversaries and will be exploited by Protestant circles in the Anglo-Saxon countries for the purpose of anti-Catholic propaganda, he has nonetheless done everything possible even in this delicate matter in order not to strain relations with the German government and the German authorities in Rome. As there apparently will be no further German action taken on the Jewish question here, it may be said that this matter, so unpleasant as it regards German-Vatican relations, has been liquidated.

In any event, there is one definite sign of this from the Vatican. *L'Osservatore Romano*, of October 25-26, gives prominence to a semi-official communique on the loving-kindness of the Pope, which is written in the typical roundabout and muddled style of this Vatican newspaper, declaring that the Pope bestows his fatherly care on all people without regard to nationality, religion and race. The manifold and growing activities of Pius XII have in recent times further increased because of the greater sufferings of so many unfortunate people.

No objections need be raised against this statement, insofar as its text, a translation of which is enclosed, will be understood by only a very few as alluding in any particular way to the Jewish question.[6]

When received in Berlin, someone in the Wilhelmstrasse underlined the key words: *Pope . . . not . . . pushed into demonstrative censure of the Jews of Rome . . . done everything possible even in this delicate matter . . . it may be said that this matter, so unpleasant as it regards German-Vatican relations, has been liquidated.*[7]

Now not only the Jews of Rome but also the problems they created in their times no longer existed.

In the same last week of October, Pino Levi Cavaglione, Marco Moscato, and another partisan in the *Castelli Romani* lay in ambush at a turn in a country road. It was night and it was cold. German soldiers, they had discovered, often used this road, and during the afternoon they had decided to attack the very first ones who might come along. Now they had been in wait for two hours. The countryside was still. Pino, who was leading the assault, lay in a ditch on the bank of the road, the other two men covering him from a point in the rear.

Suddenly the sound of an approaching motorcycle could be heard. Then came the nodding beam of its headlight. Pino raised the sights on his rifle to his eye. In the next moment the hunched, dark shape of a German soldier straddling the vehicle came around the turn at a high speed. A gleam of light illuminated the circle of his face. It was trapped in Pino's line of fire. For the barest instant, the partisan hesitated. His finger froze on the trigger.

He had never in his life shot at any living thing. And now, despite the hatred that had long been welling inside him, he suddenly felt none of it. All of his desire to strike back simply vanished. Then, at the other end of that moment, he obeyed not his own command but that which he believed to be the will of his two comrades, his squad, and the guerrilla war. He fired. The German was less than six feet away.

"The crack of the rifle pounded my ears," he wrote that very night. "My throat parched. The cold and the trembling, which until that moment had overtaken me, disappeared. An intense and pleasurable sensation of heat flowed in my veins."[8]

The motorcycle kept going, wavering. Pino thought he had missed and expected his comrades to open fire so that the German could not get away. But after a few yards the motorcycle turned around and went into a spin. The soldier was jettisoned from the seat, and he sailed through the air. There was a violent storm of noise, fire and light, as the fallen vehicle spun out like a top. The German landed in a nearby ditch.

Then everything was silent and dark again, as if the attack had never occurred. The partisans did not move. In the distance a dog began to yelp, then howl. Pino shook himself to collect his thoughts. He wanted to appear disinterested, as if he were long accustomed to this sort of activity.

"Come on," he said to the others, "let's have a look and see if there's anything good to take."[9]

Marco Moscato went with him. The two Jews approached the German. He was dead. His body was twisted, half in the ditch, half stretched out on the road. He had on a gun belt with a .38 caliber revolver. He was also wearing an excellent pair of waterproof boots. Pino took out his pen knife and began cutting feverishly through the laces. He removed the boots first then cut the holstered gun free of the belt.

"I felt no repulsion; nor did I have any respect for the corpse," he wrote. "I was curious to see his face."[10] They dragged the body from the ditch in order to get the soldier's wallet and thus they could see what he looked like. Pino continued:

> The pallidness of his face stood out in the surrounding darkness. There was a black mark on the right side of his nose, just below his eye. A small flashlight hung from the button of his jacket pocket. I took it and shined it on him. The black mark was the bullet hole and a clot of dark blood. We threw the body back into the pit and went away.[11]

The money in the soldier's wallet was turned over to the local Resistance committee. Marco got the German's wristwatch and his cigarette lighter. The other partisan who had been with him took the raincoat the dead man had been wearing. Pino got the .38 caliber revolver and the waterproof boots.[12]

At last he was well equipped to fight.

PART FOUR

Epilogue

3rd Witness: We call them heroes
but their death was pointless

— PETER WEISS,
The Investigation[1]

1943

SEPTEMBER

SUN.	MON.	TUES.	WED.	THURS.	FRI.	SAT.
			1	2	3	4
5	6	7	8	9	10	11
12	13	14	15	16	17	18
19	20	21	22	23	24	25
26	27	28	29	30		

OCTOBER

					1	2
3	4	5	6	7	8	9
10	11	12	13	14	15	16
17	18	19	20	21	22	23

I

At Auschwitz, following the shortened quarantine period, the remaining group of 153 Roman men was divided. Seventy-five were sent to work in the nearby coal mines of Jawiszowice. Forty-two were shipped to Warsaw to recover bricks from the rubble of the liquidated ghetto in that city. Thirty-six remained behind.

Of the seventy-five, all but eleven soon died, the average life span at the 1,200-feet-deep mines being about three months. Among the survivors of this group were Michele Amati, Lazzaro Anticoli, and the two remaining members of the Efrati family, brothers Cesare and Angelo.

Of the forty-two sent to Warsaw, only three men—among them Arminio Wachsberger—did not die.

Of the thirty-six who stayed at Auschwitz, everyone died.

Less is known about the forty-seven women. At least two of them were still alive after about six weeks at Birkenau. They had been hospitalized and shared the same bed. One night one of them died. The other, Settimia Spizzichino, never saw any of the Roman women again. She was transferred to Block 10 of the Auschwitz base camp, where she served as a human guinea pig for Dr. Mengele's infamous experiments.[1] One of the rare survivors of this experience, she was transferred to the Bergen-Belsen camp. When the camp was liberated by the Allies, she was found among a pile of corpses, where she had slept for the past two days ("I felt more comfortable with the dead than with the living," she was to say).[2] Of the forty-seven, only she, as has been said, lived to return to Rome.*

In Rome the persecution of Jews continued throughout the occupation, spreading through all of Italy A "second wave" of quite a different nature from that of the October 16 *razzia* developed.

On November 30, 1943, Mussolini's neo-Fascist government decreed that all Jews, without exception, were to be arrested and sent to Italian concentration camps. All of their property, including liquid assets and real estate, was to be confiscated immediately, "for the benefit of the indigent refugees from enemy air attacks."[3] The purpose of these provisions, which had been advocated by the Fascist "moderates," was to remove the Jewish question from German hands and reaffirm a measure of Italian sovereignty. In this way, hoping to satisfy the German demand for a solution to the Jewish problem in Italy, and at the same time deceive the Nazis and spare the nation's Jews from the gas chambers, the regime sought to expand the narrow limits of the possibilities for its own survival.**

For their part, the Germans were delighted with the Italian measures. Following the October 16th roundup, the RSHA had concluded that German forces in Italy were insufficient for the remaining task.[6] Now that the Italians were willing to concentrate their Jews, the RSHA—doubtless Eichmann's IV-B-4—proposed to the German Foreign Office that the Fascists be con-

* For a list and further details of the survivors, see Appendix II.

** Apart from the expropriation of Jewish wealth, which was dictated by the regime's poor financial condition (confiscation was to yield some $25,000,000), this policy of shielding Jews from the Germans was a continuation of earlier practice in the pre-Badoglio period. Some Fascists hoped to use their sheltered Jews as a bargaining point, they too looking toward that illusory day when a separate peace with the Western Allies might be negotiated. It was a policy founded on the overestimated influence in Washington of American Jews. Under the Italian plan the Jews were not to be physically harmed.[4] As an extension of this policy the Duce's Foreign Ministry intervened at Berlin in behalf of a few deported Italian Jews, including one woman taken in the October 16th roundup.[5] Such attempts were unsuccessful, but interestingly this neo-Fascist puppet regime was the only government in the world to express any official interest in the affair.

gratulated.[7] Once the Jews would be gathered, however, the RSHA wanted them for shipment to the "East." But the Wilhelmstrasse, with far more expertise than the Jewish experts of the RSHA, put forward a counterproposal. The diplomats agreed that Germany should express its approval of the Italian initiative. But if Eichmann wanted to transport Italy's Jews, said Inland II, it would be better not to rush matters. The Italian plan would be carried out with greater facility, it said, "if the concentration camps were to appear as the final solution, and not a preliminary measure for evacuation to the eastern territories."[8] The Jews were to be lured into a net and then carried away. The RSHA agreed.[9] This proposal was adopted as policy, and thus the German diplomats set the stage for a double cross of the Italian double cross prepared by the neo-Fascists.

In practice, however, the intrigues of both Nazis and Fascists proved that there had never been any need for plot and counterplot. Italians simply arrested Jews and turned them over to their German counterparts.[10] The Nazis, who so mistrusted the Fascist police, found eager collaborators among them, but in a way that many Germans regarded as corrupt.

For example, on December 3, scarcely seventy-two hours after the launching of the Italian solution, the German consul in Venice reported the following incident to Berlin, which had been related by the Cardinal Patriarch of that city:

> The Patriarch pointed out that the Jewish question, as it was now being handled in Venice, was causing him grave concern. Last night, many arrests of poor, old and sick Jews were made in their homes by extreme Fascists, while wealthy and carefully screened Jews continued to move about freely in Venice, if they had not already fled from the city. This injustice was disturbing him so much that the only solution he could see would be for the measures against the Jews to be carried out by German authorities, because then justice would at least be guaranteed for all.[11]

In Rome the Fascists even disregarded the sanctuary agreement between the Vatican and the Germans. In February, 1944, they raided the Basilica of Saint Paul, where they captured nine

Jews who had taken refuge there. In this case the Germans intervened, putting a stop to such violations.[12]

During the same month the Rome police, under a new Questore installed by the neo-Fascists, launched a drive to arrest the remaining Jews in the city. It was relatively successful, especially with regard to the ghetto Jews, many of whom had by now returned to their apartments.* Those arrested were, for the most part, sent to Italian concentration camps, and then to Auschwitz, from where few came back.

Indeed the Fascists in Rome compiled a more impressive record than the Gestapo. Whereas Dannecker's raid netted an official total of 1,007 Jews, the Italians, working under infinitely more difficult conditions, officially turned over 1,084 Roman Jews, as a result of individual arrests made after October 16.[14] To this must be added another seventy Jews who were taken from the city's prisons on March 24, 1944—along with 265 non-Jews—and executed by the Gestapo on the same day in the Ardeatine caves massacre, a Nazi reprisal to a partisan attack on SS troops in Rome.[15]

The Germans, of course, lent a hand in this second wave, but so did some civilians, including Jews themselves.** Though throughout Italy many more civilians—thousands, perhaps tens

* Settimio Sorani learned of this campaign in advance, and his sister Rosina went to the ghetto to alert the Jews. "But they did not believe this warning," she said, "and many were taken, because they did not want to abandon their homes. Some even went to the Commissar of Campitelli [the district police official] to find out if it were true, and he replied that if they did not get away immediately he would be forced to arrest them. But with all that they continued to remain in the ghetto."[13]

** Among the scant captured files of the Rome Gestapo the author has seen several anonymous letters sent by Aryan Romans denouncing Jews living in hiding.[16] Most notable among the Jewish betrayers were the "Black Panther" Celeste Di Porto and her cousin "Powder Face" Enrica Di Porto, who was implicated in the former's crimes. Working for the Italian Fascists, the Black Panther turned over a total of about fifty of her fellow Jews for 5,000 lire ($50) per Jew. Twenty-six of them died in the Ardeatine caves massacre—among whom the Roman Jewish prizefighter Bucefalo (his real name was Lazzaro Anticoli, the same as that of the Auschwitz survivor), who left the following note behind in his cell: "I am Lazzaro Anticoli, called "Bucefalo" the prizefighter. If I never see my family again, it's the fault of that sellout by Celeste Di Porto. Avenge me."[17] Anticoli was arrested in the presence of the of thousands—gave aid, took risks, and showed solidarity with their nation's Jews, the heroic tales of Italian resistance to the persecutions are disproportionate to the truth.[20] Even in Italy, it must be said, the Final Solution was, as everywhere, a cooperative endeavor, involving to one or another degree the activity or the passivity of almost the whole of the people, including the victims, as it involved almost the whole of the world.

Beyond Rome, the details varied, but the results were the same. Wherever Jews lived, they were hunted by the Fascists to be killed by the Germans. As early as November 15, 1943, Eichmann was able to report that "a settlement of the Jewish question in Italy . . . is beginning."[21] In Florence, Venice, Genoa, Milan, Trieste, and smaller centers Jews were arrested and taken to Italian concentration camps at Fossoli di Carpi, Verona, and Bolzano, and then transported to the "East"—most often to Auschwitz.[22]

The behavior of the organized Jewish communities was much like that of Rome, characterized by a bureaucratic, conformist nature woven in the fabric of Fascist society.[23] One dramatic exception took place in Venice. The president of that community, Giuseppe Jona, was visited by Germans, who demanded the list of some 2,000 Venetian Jews. Jona told them to return the following day. During the night he warned his fellow Jews, destroyed the list, and committed suicide.[24]

A relatively large number of Jews in Italy turned to the Resistance. In the months between November, 1943, and March, 1944, the guerrilla struggle in the *Castelli Romani* was very fierce.

Pino Levi Cavaglione during this period went on to become chief of his squad and then head of a formation of armed units.[25] When the Allies opened a second southern front with the invasion at Anzio in January, 1944, the Germans, pushed by

---

Black Panther on the same day of the massacre.[18] At the last moment his name was added to those marked for execution and another man's removed. On the original list "Lazzaro Anticoli," typed on a narrow strip of paper, overlays the name of the person whom he replaced, another Roman Jew, Angelo Di Porto, the Black Panther's brother.[19]

the need to expand their supply lines, intensified their anti-partisan activities in the *Castelli.* The guerrillas suffered severe losses, and were virtually disbanded under this pressure. Marco Moscato was captured and shot in the Ardeatine caves massacre among those betrayed by the "Black Panther."[26] Pino survived, as the focus of underground action shifted to the center of Rome.*[27]

In the capital, however, the Resistance never succeeded in developing into a truly significant force, as it did in the north of Italy. There, too, the Jewish partisans were numerous. Many distinguished themselves on the different fields of battle. They fought with the Communists, the Socialists, and the brigades of the Justice and Liberty movement. Five of them—four men and a woman—were posthumously awarded Italy's highest wartime decoration, the *Medaglia d'Oro* for Military Valor.[29]

In the end, however, when all the deeds both good and bad were done, the remaining Jews of Italy looked beyond their heroes and their traitors. They searched for their deported and counted up their dead. After many years they would arrive at very detailed figures, which, however, would be inaccurate—too low. The true numbers would never be known, but at least 7,870 Jews were captured on Italian soil and deported to the north and to the east. Of this group better than 92 per cent are either known to have died in the camps or are still missing.[30]

* Lello Perugia, the Roman Communist partisan who escaped the October 16 roundup, fought with his three brothers in the Abruzzi mountains of central Italy. The Perugias were captured in April, 1944, brought back to Rome, and shipped to Auschwitz. Lello and one brother survived.[28]

II

ON JUNE 4, 1944, while the war in northern Italy was yet to be fought, Rome fell to the Americans and the British. The Germans pulled out without firing a shot. On the following day the Allied occupation government installed itself in the city, and one of its first acts was the abrogation of the racial laws.[1]

That evening a ceremony was held in the *tempio maggiore,* attended by American and British Jewish officers and troops. The surviving Jews of Rome gave thanks to the Allies for liberating them from the Nazis and the Fascists. Presiding was Ugo Foà.[2] For the shattered community, it would be a difficult reprise, Jewish leaders in Rome believed, but at least a beginning had been made. As always, Foà, Almansi, and their colleagues were ready to serve in this new endeavor.

The Allies, however, had plans of their own for the Jews of Rome. On July 7 United States Fifth Army Colonel Charles Poletti, Allied Regional Commissioner for Rome, dissolved the Jewish councils of both the community and the union. They were regarded by the new occupation as Fascist-controlled organizations.[3] Poletti reinstated Chief Rabbi Zolli, who by then had been fired by the Jewish leaders, and he named Silvio Ottolenghi, an ex-member of the Rome Jewish council believed to be uncompromised by fascism, as "extraordinary commissioner" of the Roman Jews.*[4] The task given to Ottolenghi was

* Ottolenghi, in fact, was one of the chief signers of the Fascist extremist manifesto issued by the cessionist "Committee of Italians of the Jewish Religion" at the time of the initiation of the racial laws (see p. 74).[5]

to reorganize the community and hold free elections establishing a new council.[6] Poletti then turned the matter over to his adjutant, an American Jew, Captain Maurice F. Neufeld.

These plans too were entirely consumed in a fiery, internecine feud, which had been brewing for months, if not years, and now erupted within the community. Its incredible climax literally startled the entire world.

One day after his reinstatement, Rabbi Zolli gave a long interview to the Rome correspondent of *The New York Times*. He used the opportunity to strike back at ex-President Foà, and as he called it, "his little clique of Jews who believed as he did."[7]

The Times, writing editorially that "Foà had driven around Rome ostentatiously in the company of a Gestapo leader, as if to say that the Jews had nothing to fear," quoted extensively from Zolli's own account of his efforts to provide for the dispersion of the community and of Foà's opposition.

Foà, said Zolli, insisted that "he had had assurances from the Authorities. He offered hope . . ."

The Rabbi justified his own flight as follows:

> Foà accuses me of having deserted my community, but let me tell you what happened elsewhere in Italy. The rabbis of Modena and Florence stayed with their flocks and were deported. The rabbi of Genoa did the same, and one day the German Elite Guard came to his office. They beat him until he was covered with blood. Then they dragged him to a telephone and made him call the leaders of the community asking them to come to the temple immediately with all their families. They came in good faith, three generations of them. When all had entered the temple the Germans surrounded it, herded the people into trucks and deported all of them, including the rabbi.
>
> I am an old sick man. I could die for my community, but suppose they had taken me and beaten me and burned the soles of my feet? How do I know what I would have done?[8]

The rabbi said wryly that he did not blame Foà for being a Fascist because the ex-President had joined the party as a young man. He concluded his reply with the ominous words, "Foà will be taken care of by your Colonel Poletti . . ."[9]

News of Zolli's interview was also reported in the Italian

Jewish press.[10] But neither this nor their ouster stopped Foà and his associates from continuing to advance their accusations against the rabbi. To the charge of abandonment, Foà added others of greater pettiness and denied that the rabbi had ever spoken to him "to present a project of yours intended to ward off the danger menacing our coreligionists . . ."[11]

The rabbi countered with the charge that Foà had permitted the community's lists to fall into German hands, implying that the ex-president was thus partially responsible for the October 16th roundup.[12]

Here was the most sensitive issue of all, one which remains so today. In view of what had taken place on October 16, it was a bombshell that fragmented the Jews of Rome in a way from which it would never fully recover. Powerful attempts were made at obfuscating the affair, and it is said today to remain a mystery as to how the Germans obtained the names of the homes they raided.[13] But despite any gaps that may still exist, the facts of the matter, as has been seen, were quite clear.

That lists of Roman Jews were taken by the Germans on the day they searched the community's office was not disputed by anyone. But immediately after the roundup Foà began denying that these files had been used by them. Foà maintained that many Jews who were arrested were not on this list and that many who were on the list were not arrested. This, he said, proved that the files were not used.[14] The community today insists on this version, declaring that it was confirmed by "information gathered by Allied troops after the liberation of Rome."[15]

It is difficult to determine how this relieves the community of its responsibility, since even if the lists were not used, the Jewish leaders could not have known this in advance of the capture of the material and should have therefore destroyed them. But they were used, as might be expected since the Germans went to the trouble of obtaining them. Further, Allied information confirmed Zolli's not Foà's version.

According to American Captain Neufeld, the person in charge of the "Allied troops" gathering the information referred to by the community, Jews were found who testified that their names and addresses could have been known to the Germans *only* from the community's lists.[16] The Germans had called at their addresses that Saturday, and they had succeeded in escaping.

Whereas Foà's contentions, if true, proved only that more than one list was used, Neufeld's statement clearly demonstrates that the files of the community were employed in the German plan—as were other sources.*

Unhappily, however, it appears that in this case, Foà was not even reporting the whole truth of the matter, which he may not have known. He asserted, as does the community of today, that "only" the contributors' lists were confiscated, and that the complete index card file of Roman Jews was not found because it had already been "transported elsewhere."[18] This contributors' list, according to Foà's own description of them, was a roll of names on sheets of paper contained in "file folders" or "*cartelle*"[19]—which is precisely the same way in which it is described by Rosina Sorani, in the unexpurgated copy of her diary.[20] When the ex-president speaks of the complete file, however, he refers to it as being an extensive "index of file cards," or "*schedari*."[21]

Apart from the eyewitness testimony of Regina Wachsberger, made available by her husband, and that of others who saw thousands of *file cards* being taken by the Germans from the community's offices (see p. oo), there is now further evidence to refute Foà's statements.

On the day the Germans withdrew from Rome, a retired Italian police official, Giuseppe Dosi, subsequently one of the founders of Interpol, captured the surviving Gestapo documents at the Via Tasso.[22] The Allies placed him in charge of organizing this material, most of which was in various stages of deterioration, an attempt having been made by the Germans to

* Of the other sources noted earlier (p. 152) the birth records office seems to be the most implicated. Debenedetti, hiding in the home of a neighbor that October 16, later reported being told by his neighbor, a woman, that she had known the roundup would take place. A friend of hers employed at the birth records office had confided that the staff had for several days prior to the raid been "worked to death" drawing up "certain lists of Jews, which had to be made ready for the Germans."[17] In any event, the nature of these secondary sources was such that they could only have been used to supplement and crosscheck the community's files.

destroy everything. Dosi eventually delivered these documents to the American forces in Rome—but not all of them. In the basement of Kappler's former headquarters, he found "the archives and the card index (*lo schedario*) of the Jewish Community of Rome"—a fact to which he later publicly testified, but without revealing the precise nature of the card file.[23]

In a recent interview,[24] however, Dosi disclosed that on discovery of this material he approached ex-President Almansi, who had been his chief during the period they both served in the Fascist police. He informed Almansi of what he had found and inquired whether the community would care to recover this material, since he assumed the Allies had no need of it, and would not mind if it were quietly restored to its rightful owner.[25] Almansi accepted the offer, and in a note dated September 4, 1944, signed by "F. Piperno" (then executive secretary of the Roman Jewish Community), and addressed to the Via Tasso to the attention of the "Allied Command"—which was no one but Dosi himself—the request was made for these documents and duly fulfilled by Dosi, on his own authority.[26] Dosi retained Piperno's note and the disappearance of the card file went unnoticed.[27] According to Dosi, the documents he returned to the community consisted of thousands of index cards (*schede*), on which, he said, "were the names and addresses of the Jews of Rome,"[28] that is, the same one Foà and others claimed had been successfully concealed from the Germans.

All of this, of course, was unknown at the time of the public clash between Zolli and Foà, except by a very few. All through the remainder of 1944, the Zolli-Foà dispute deepened in bitterness and recrimination—so much so that Neufeld, after many months of trying to resolve the community's differences, figuratively threw up his hands in disgust, declaring, "It's a community rent by factionalism and petty personal jealousies, sick to the very heart."[29]

The determined ex-leaders, however, very soon began to get the upper hand. Foà himself went around acting as if he were still head of the community, and his circle continued to call him "Signor Presidente."[30] In terms of popularity, Zolli was clearly at a disadvantage. Everyone seemed to be aware of Foà's charges, and few knew or believed anything the chief rabbi had to say. The Allies continued to support Zolli, although they too made note that he was "extremely unpopular in the community."[31] They were aware that the ousted leaders were "taking refuge under the six-cornered star in their flight from fascism," and Captain Neufeld said that two leaders in particular, Foà and Almansi, "have Fascist precedents that fill me with shame everytime I think of it."[32]

Some sympathetic, prominent Jews came to Zolli's defense, too, feeling he was being unjustly criticized.[33] But it was the old rabbi himself, sick and visibly suffering from the mounting attacks against him, who solved all of these problems and relieved the community of the burdens they imposed.

On the Day of Atonement, 1944, while presiding over the Yom Kippur services at the main synagogue in Rome, Zolli was overtaken by another supernatural experience. He had not had one in five years, but now, in the temple crowded with Italian Jews and American and British Jewish soldiers, the chief rabbi of Rome looked beyond earthly events at a vision which stretched before him.

"I saw with my mind's eye," he was to say, "a meadow sweeping upward, with bright grass but no flowers. In this meadow I saw Jesus Christ clad in a white mantle, and beyond His head the blue sky. . . . Within my heart I found the words: 'You are here for the last time.' "[34]

The rabbi told no one of this occurrence, but before long he resigned his posts, and on February 13, 1945, following some weeks of instruction by "a quiet unknown priest," he was baptized in the Roman Catholic Church.[35] As his baptismal name he took Eugenio—the same as that of Pope Pius XII.

The surprise apostasy of the chief rabbi of Rome was a major news story throughout the Western world. People of all faiths were stunned. There was a sudden outpouring of articles, sermons, and even one book on the case. They were authored by journalists, religious leaders, and persons who had known the rabbi and who wanted to "explain" his behavior. Outraged Jews, delighted Catholics, and disinterested Protestants were unanimously agreed that the rabbi had converted in gratitude for Pius's efforts in behalf of the Jews of Rome.*[36]

Among Jews the "significance" of the deed was sought, its effect being grossly overestimated. The noted British Jewish historian Cecil Roth, for example, called it a "spiritual catastrophe." He foresaw "rapid and widespread disintegration, which is likely to prove disastrous."[38]

In Rome, the rabbi was called a traitor by the Jewish leadership. "Those of us who still consider Zolli a teacher," said the Rome weekly *Israel*, "will hold the seven-day *avelùth* rite, during which we will mourn him as a dead man; the others—and they are in the majority—will not even do that."[39]

Captain Neufeld wrote two days after the incident that "Zolli's conversion has surely cleared the air."[40] Allied officers working with the community called now for a renewed attempt at unity, making it clear however that there could be "no room for the old Fascist hangers-on."[41] Before long elections were held and a new Jewish council was formed. Foà and Almansi had been prevented from being candidates for any office, but they were slowly rehabilitated by the new leaders—especially following the departure of the Allies—and restored to honorary positions of prominence and esteem.[42] Thus, in this manner, even before the end of the war in Europe the Old Order began slowly to reassert itself in the organized Jewish community of Rome—"purged" of course of all its card-carrying Fascists.

As for Zolli, he was given a post in the Vatican library. He made a study of anti-Semitism[43] and shortly before his death, published his memoirs, with a foreword by then Archbishop A. G. Cicognani, present Cardinal Secretary of State of the Holy See.[44] In it, the ex-rabbi, who had come out of the pale of European Jewry concluded, "I confess that I feel like one dying

* This "explanation" is still generally regarded as valid. Zolli, however, has said that he has always denied it, although he "renders homage" to Pius XII.[37]

without having lived: for one fails to live a good life when one fails to live Christ fully. . . . Christ, whom humanity puts to death because it does not know how to live him."[45]

III

ONE BY ONE, in the summer and fall of 1945, the fifteen survivors, liberated by the Allies from a collective ordeal in a score of labor and concentration camps, came home. Most of them weighed about half as much as they did when they had been captured more than a year and one-half ago.[1] On reentering Italy, they were interviewed by officials of the Jewish community, each returnee making a brief statement about his experience.[2] At Mantua they were greeted by an "assistance committee" organized by the Roman Jewish leaders. They were asked a great many questions. The men were given a packet of razor blades and a bar of soap;[3] Settimia Spizzichino received only a bar of soap.[4] Someone had apparently decided that the survivors should look clean and neat upon their arrival at home. They were then handed a second-class train ticket to Rome.

They came back to empty homes. Cesare Di Segni, the oldest of the survivors, who was taken from the ghetto that morning with his entire family, lay on a bed in his now barren apartment for two weeks, crying.* Cesare Efrati, returning to his family home near the railroad yards, discovered it had been completely sacked. The burglars had even taken the only photograph of his mother.

* He was to have the good fortune of learning shortly afterward that his eighteen-year-old son Lello survived. Oddly, beyond the father and son relationship, there were among the fifteen who came back two pairs of brothers and six persons who were cousins of one another.

They found postwar life difficult in Rome. Some of them were looked upon as freaks, even by their own families. It was difficult to get a job, make a friend, or find a wife. Cesare Efrati met a Roman Jewish girl, and before long they were to marry, but when she learned he had been in a concentration camp she broke the engagement. Her father had told her, she said, "they are all mad." Settimia Spizzichino suffered the same experience more than once.

They learned not to speak of Auschwitz. Few people were interested. It was fine to recall the "martyrdom" of those who were swept away on October 16th. This was done in ceremonies organized by the community on every anniversary of the event. But the survivors were rarely mentioned except in a statistical way.[5] It was as if they were not supposed to have returned. It was so much more difficult to monumentalize the "martyrs" with the fifteen real, live persons from the anguished past stalking the ghetto and all of the Eternal City.

Almost all of the fifteen had suffered either physiological or psychological impairment, or both. Lazzaro Anticoli, the mechanic, had damaged his hands and could no longer firmly grasp a tool. Another survivor, named Sabatino Finzi, spent years being treated for internal disorders. Settimia Spizzichino continues to suffer severe headaches and is "very nervous."

Luciano Camerino, who was only fifteen years old when arrested and was among the returnees, was stricken with the saddest fate of all. In November, 1966, at the time of the great flood in Florence, he joined a group of Italian Jews who went there to help salvage the treasures in the synagogue. It had been gutted by the storm, flooded chest-high with the waters of the Arno. When the group arrived, it still retained a residual layer of at least a foot of mud. Camerino, then thirty-eight, walked into the synagogue, and when he saw the mud and destruction he suddenly exclaimed, "Oh my God, it's just like Auschwitz!" In the next moment he slumped to the floor. He was dead.*[6]

* Recent research in medical science has established that heart disease among former concentration camp inmates now in their fifties or younger is a result of their internment. One scientist who performed more than 10,000 autopsies on prisoners who died during his own three years in a camp discovered that heart damage had occurred *without exception* in all prisoners

Despite their ordeal, the fifteen get no special services from the community; like all Italian survivors of the camps, they receive no pension from the state and, according to the terms of the Italian peace treaty with the Allies, are not entitled to indemnification from the Germans.*

Through the years, however, they managed to reenter their society at the levels they had come from and two or three have even prospered. But the blue numbers still look out from beneath the skin of their forearms, and among some of them there are signs of stress in their eyes and tight, twitching lines in their faces. They do not talk easily with strangers and do not like to see their names in print. Nevertheless they want their story to be told, for though they try, perhaps harder than anyone else, to live in a manner they hope will be somehow more pleasurable than that which they have already lived, they cannot forget. History has climbed upon their backs, and it grows heavier with every passing day.

---

between the ages of sixteen and thirty-four. A growing body of evidence demonstrates the existence of a prison-camp syndrome, which lay more or less dormant for many years and is now increasingly manifest in camp survivors, who are suffering somatic and psychic ailments.[7]

* It should be noted, however, that West Germany later acceded to an Italian request that at least some reparations be made. A bilateral accord was signed by the two governments in 1961 and after a period of further negotiations and technical procedures, the matter was finally concluded late in 1968. A "global indemnity" of $10,000,000 was turned over to the Italian government, settling accounts forever. This sum is to be divided among some 17,700 persons recognized by the Italian treasury ministry as the legal claimants of the award. They consist of 3,899 survivors of the Nazi camps (including those of the October roundup) and nearly 14,000 relatives of deportees who died there. These beneficiaries are to receive a one-time payment averaging about $564 per person.

IV

In July, 1947, Obersturmbannführer Herbert Kappler, who had been captured by the British at the end of the war, was turned over to the Italians for trial as a war criminal. He was charged by a military tribunal in Rome as having a major responsibility in the Ardeatine caves massacre. On a second count he was accused of extorting fifty kilograms of gold from the Jews of Rome. The indictment said that he had violated a Fascist law of 1942 in having taken advantage of his position in Rome to make an "unfair profit with considerable patrimonial damages to the Jewish community of Rome."[1]

The trial took place in May, June, and July of 1948. It was held in the Collegio Militare, an ironic coincidence, which few people took note of. Almost entirely it concerned Kappler's role in the massacre, for which he was convicted and sentenced to life imprisonment. Two days of testimony were devoted to the gold episode. The principal witness for the prosecution was ex-President Ugo Foà, who had by now regained his position in the state judiciary system having been appointed deputy attorney general in the court of appeals.

Interestingly, the court concurred with Kappler's contention that he had opposed Berlin's plan for the immediate deportation of the Roman Jews.[2]

The accused, the military judges concluded, tried "to carry out his own plan, which he hoped would be approved by the authorities in Berlin. . . . he thought of taking the gold, which for him constituted a weapon in the hands of those whom he sought to lure with this apparent act of clemency into the sphere of the German espionage services, believing they were linked to enemy financial circles, and, in this way, procure information from them."[3] His motive, however, said the court, was to eventually abandon them anyway to the fate prepared for the Jews of Rome by Berlin, after having exploited their value as spies.[4]

Unable to convict Kappler—with regard to the second count—on what were believed to be his intentions, they found him guilty of having "acted without the authorization of the competent authority."[5] The court cited the Hague Convention of 1907, which it said, provided that behavior such as Kappler's would have been permissible in an occupation zone only if it had been ordered by "commanders of large units."[6] He was therefore sentenced to fifteen years in addition to the life sentence, which he continues today to serve in an Italian penitentiary in the coastal town of Gaeta.

While Kappler was being tried in Rome, former Ambassador to the Holy See von Weizsäcker was before an American court in Nuremberg. He and other high officials of the Wilhelmstrasse stood accused of a long list of crimes, particularly those committed under the heading of the Final Solution.[7]

Many defense witnesses, testifying in Weizsäcker's behalf, spoke of how he tried to help the Jews of Rome. Pope Pius XII sent a letter praising the Nazi ambassador.[8] Bishop Hudal signed an affidavit in which he called Weizsäcker "courageous."[9] A half-Jew living in Rome named Hubert Jedin revealed he had once been invited to dinner by Weizsäcker, who later aided him.[10] Von Kessel told the story of how they tried to warn the Jews of Rome through the Swiss official Fahrener.[11] But the ambassador had signed too many documents in Berlin, which became the instruments sanctioning the slaughter of thousands of Jews. He was convicted and sentenced to seven years in prison.[12]

An effort was launched to gain his release. The *Osservatore Romano* wrote that he had got Berlin to stop the October 16th roundup of the Jews of Rome.[13] The Jewish archeologist Hermine Speier, who had survived the occupation taking shelter in a Roman convent, wrote a letter to the United States Military Governor in Berlin saying that Weizsäcker had been her protector. He was a "real Gentleman," she said.[14] Before long Weizsäcker's sentence was reduced, then canceled. He was released in 1950, wrote an autobiography, and he died the following year. In his memoirs he never once mentioned the Jews of Rome, but he alluded to his "humanitarian" labors in saying, "to anyone who could not of himself understand what I was doing I really had nothing further to say."[15]

During the trial of Adolf Eichmann, held in Jerusalem in 1961, the "Italian chapter," as it came to be called, was a subject of some interest. Eichmann's defense attorney, seeking to demonstrate that the persecution of Jews was a general feature of Nazism and not the responsibility of one man, the accused, took sworn testimony from Kappler in his cell in Gaeta. The former Gestapo chief of Rome declared, probably truthfully, that he had never heard the name Eichmann until after the war, and Kappler took full responsibility for the extortion of the fifty kilograms of gold.[16] Nevertheless the ex-Obersturmbannführer's affidavit served the prosecution more than the defense. Kappler for the first time disclosed in great detail Dannecker's mission in Rome, the latter of course being one of Eichmann's closest deputies.

Eichmann could not deny that Dannecker was working for him in the Holy City. But he insisted that the order for the roundup and deportation came from his superiors. In this, as has been seen, he was technically correct. Eichmann was convicted of "the murder of six million men, women, and children," among them, presumably, the Jews of Rome. He was hanged.

These trials notwithstanding, the three men most directly responsible for the roundup, deportation, and extermination of the Roman Jews were never tried, and it appears, walk among us today as free men.

Heinrich Müller, who signed the order for the *razzia,* was never captured, and rumors that he is still alive persist.[17] Dannecker, who would now be in his mid-fifties, is missing, unheard from and unsought for a quarter of a century.[18] Mengele, who sent the Roman Jews to their death one by one, is definitely known to be alive. Now fifty-eight years old, he is a citizen of Paraguay. He has given up the practice of medicine and is a very wealthy business man, one of the "sons" of the giant West German corporation Karl Mengele & Sons, makers of agricultural equipment.[19]

V

WITH THE DEPARTURE of Chief Rabbi Zolli, Ugo Foà, the Allied occupation, and the problems of their times, the Jewish Community of Rome began to reconstruct itself to its own design. It recalled the ex-Fascist Rabbi Prato to fill Zolli's vacated post. It installed a new set of leaders and drew upon the wisdom and the counsel of the old. Although the 1930 Fascist law on the organization of cults remained in force (and still remains today), the Italian postwar republic passed new laws reintegrating its Jews. The Jewish communities took advantage of their new freedom by linking themselves to the world Zionist movement, which seemed now to at last be on the winning side. They received funds from Zionist organizations abroad and in turn offered considerable aid in preparing the way for the birth of the state of Israel. They assisted Jewish refugees coming down the Italian peninsula to Palestine, and when the time came, sent Italian Jewish boys to fight and die in the latest noble cause, as they had fought and died in Ethiopia and Spain.[1]

The Roman Jews even gave their gold. In 1948 the thirty kilograms of gold, which had been collected five years earlier in excess of the fifty kilograms turned over to the Germans, was removed from its hiding place and turned over to representatives of the new Jewish state for benefit of the building of Israel.[2] This was done by a simple decision of the Jewish Council, quietly and without ceremony,[3] presumably because no one knew of the existence of the thirty kilograms in the first place.

Three days after the United Nations voted for the establishment of Israel in Palestine, a group of Italian and foreign Jews demonstrated their solidarity with the new country by marching under the Arch of Titus in Rome. For nineteen centuries Jews had refused to pass through the arch, which commemorated the conquest of Judea by the Roman Empire. Now, however, wrote the Italian Jewish historian Attilio Milano, "history had made a complete cycle and the humiliation could be considered canceled."[4]

A cycle begun within the cycle, according to the Jewish community of Rome, was completed in 1961. Fifteen years earlier the community had announced that it had recovered in Germany a "good part" of the books and other materials confiscated by the Einsatzstab from its libraries.[5] But the value of the missing part and the restitution of the gold or its equivalent could not be retrieved until an agreement on indemnification had been reached between the governments of Italy and West Germany. Such an accord was signed in June of 1961, and on the *Rosh Ha-scianà* holiday, September 11, or the Jewish New Year's day, the Roman Jewish Council announced that the community had received a settlement from Bonn of $625,000. It issued a statement in which it said that this money could not atone for what the Germans had done to the Jews of Rome, a deed which "is and remains irreparable, unforgivable, and unforgettable. . . ."[6] The Jewish Council continued:

But it is undeniable, from a strictly logical point of view, that between the double bestial robbery of that autumn of 1943 and the bureaucratic gesture of the Federal [West German] Government there exists an intimate nexus of causality and that the two events, while being of such a different nature, constitute the extreme poles of an historical cycle which has now been completed. . . .

The Lord gives, the Lord takes; eternally blessed be His name.[7]

To mark this climactic event the community made public three documents purporting to describe "the initial moment of the cycle."[8] These were the complete texts of two reports written in 1943 and 1950 by ex-President Foà and a part of Rosina Sorani's 1943 diary, the latter having been carefully expurgated to rid it of all statements and ideas believed by the community to be unfavorable to itself and its institutions.[9]

Today, the community, the ghetto, and the Jews of Rome are still where they have always been. A lot has changed. The community has refurbished and reinforced its institutions, the ghetto, according to the new chief rabbi, has been "taken over by the *gojim*,"[10] and the city's Jews have increased somewhat in number and in means. Foà, Almansi, Zolli, and his successor are all dead. The issues have cooled. Memories have faded and confound all but the most vivid events. Tears have dried. The vacuum left by the deportation has long ago been filled. Through those emptied spaces others pass today.

Yet there is much that remains the same. Jewish children and the cats of Rome play in the ruins between the Theater of Marcellus and Octavia's portico. The hanks of straw and wool hang from the doorposts of the ghetto mattress store. Anticoli's jewelry shop is there at least in name, and the Di Portos still have their *banco fisso* in the Campo de' Fiori market place.

Michele Amati still peddles every day. Many of the names on the doorbells are the same as they were that morning the Germans came to call, and there are knicks in the wooden doors where rifle butts sounded that cruel reveille, waking the Jews of Rome from their last peaceful sleep.

The synagogue looks out across the Tiber and stares endlessly at the building in Trastevere where Wachsberger and his family used to live. The furnishings in the chief rabbi's office have been moved around, but the view of the ghetto from the windows is as it always was. There is a new tenant now, but Kappler's villa is there, as is the small hotel where Captain Dannecker once stayed. The Gestapo headquarters in Via Tasso has been turned into a museum, but most of its prison cells are intact. The Villa Wolkonsky, the Collegio Militare, and the Tiburtina station are all in perfect order. The now 15,000 Jews of Rome are in their beds each dawn. The community still keeps lists of the names and addresses of every one. Auschwitz still stands, and there is violence and hatred in the world.

All the elements are there, even the blind ignorance of what the future holds. For them. For others. For us.

A Conclusion

IF WHAT HAPPENED in Rome has here been faithfully reconstructed, the implications to be drawn from the events emerge in almost direct contradiction to the generally accepted myths of the Holocaust.

Perhaps the clearest statement of the legend as a whole comes from Norman Podhoretz, the editor of *Commentary*, a periodical published by the American Jewish Committee. Calling for an end to the discussion of the Final Solution, especially by Jews, he wrote in 1963 that there was nothing to be learned and nothing further to be said about this matter. The reason was, according to Podhoretz, "Murderers with the power to murder descended upon a defenseless people and murdered a large part of it. What else is there to say?"[1]

The Nazis were "insane" and they were "madmen," said Podhoretz.[2] The European Jews, according to an authoritative voice in Israel, "were a God-fearing people. . . . They had *Bitokhen*, an untranslatable Hebrew-Yiddish word, which means 'reliance upon God.' "[3] The blood they shed, Israeli Attorney General Gideon Hausner has declared, was "the blood of the righteous."[4]

Certain refinements of these observations were offered by the Jewish scholar Jacob Robinson in his massive attack on the Hannah Arendt book. Robinson's 150,000-word exegetical dismantling of Arendt's work may be considered the definitive reply of organized world Jewry.[5] He wrote that the general view of those who had studied the fate of the Jews during World War II was that Nazi Germany was directly responsible "and that it was indirectly aided by the almost universal passivity of the non-Jewish conquered populations, the neutrals, and the Allies, who by action and inaction did next to nothing to prevent it."[6] As for the role of the Jews themselves, any cooperation they might have given was "negligible."[7] Jewish councils were scarcely involved, and in any case, "the ultimate results were not demonstrably influenced by their activities."[8] The overriding purpose of Jewish activity in wartime Europe was "survival with dignity."[9] The solace of the victims was the belief that "a remnant would return" to continue "the 'golden chain' of Jewish life and thought."[10] The position of the Jewish leaders, Robinson concluded, was "unutterably tragic."[11]

Such are the comforting tales being told by the surviving Jews to their children, and by now, by the children to their own children. Once again, as the Prophets had foretold, the Gentiles came down from wild places to devour Our People. Once again Our People endured. May it never occur anew. So mighty is this myth, so widely is it believed among Jews and non-Jews throughout the world, it may be said that the entire popular support of the state of Israel, both domestically and internationally, rests today on these two pillars of Gentile guilt and Jewish innocence.

In truth something other than what has been purported to have happened took place in the Europe of the Holocaust. Indeed the real activity of men and nations prior to and during the war remains hardly changed today, and there is therefore not the slightest reason to exclude that a new catastrophe is in the making for the Jews or any existing social group, whether alone or in combination with others.

While the first part of Robinson's statement about the direct responsibility of the Germans and the indirect role of the non-Jewish world is undeniably true, the aim of Jewish activity was not "survival with dignity." Nor did the victims, as we have seen, take any solace in abstract beliefs about the immortal spiritual integrity of their religion. They went quietly to their death, as any people would have done under the same circumstances, and were then slaughtered like cockroaches, simply because they were tricked. Tricked by their non-Jewish and Jewish leaders from the day of their birth until the moment they smelled gas coming from the metal columns rather than felt the spray of water from the phony pipes. They were not the victims of a sudden, unpredictable storm of anti-Semitism, but the victims of a whole, multi-faith system of oppressors and oppressed carried out to its logical and ultimate extreme, where, as the German playwright Peter Weiss has said, "the oppressor could expand his authority to a degree never known before and the oppressed was forced to yield up the fertilizing dust of his bones."[12]

To understand what was going on in all of Europe, let us first take another look at Rome. If we roll back the events recounted in this book to the time of the Fascist aggression on Ethiopia, the Jewish leaders, as we have already seen, are to be found in retrospect in a most embarrassing situation. They are not fighting for a dignified survival or for the golden chain of Judaism. They are fighting alongside the Gentiles, arm in arm, in a dirty, imperialist war against black people. Embracing the *gojim,* they melted down their golden chain, armed their own people, and sent them off to help in the murder of a defenseless people. In short, they committed crimes against humanity. Then, as if to make certain that everyone might know where they intended to stand, they are to be seen the following year in Spain, fighting for Franco, a Mussolini deified in their own synagogues, and no one else but Adolf Hitler.

There can be only one reasonable interpretation of this behavior. The Jewish leaders in Italy, until a very precise moment, which will shortly be located and discussed, were Fascists, partaking in a Fascist society. It was an authoritarian, freedomless society, exploitative of its lowest and most populous classes. In a world system of Big Power nation-states, of colonial and economic empires, it had embarked on an imperialist course with the expressed intention of subjugating weaker peoples for the benefit of the Fascist Fatherland, beginning with the ruling classes. Its mode of expansion was the concentration of national wealth, militarization, wars of aggression, conquest, and the expropriation of foreign resources as the first step in reinitiating the cycle on a higher level. In other words, the same method used by the other Big Powers of its time, and more or less since the beginning of all time.

Suddenly, in 1938, the internal logic of Fascist society—one which Jews as much as anyone else helped to fashion—declares that its Jews can no longer participate and must be ostracized. The Fascist Jews do not then overnight become anti-Fascist, such a turnabout being as inconceivable as it is ahistorical, asociological, and apsychological. No group is radicalized before it has exhausted all halfway possibilities. The Jews, that is—more so than in any other society—the *leaders* (since under fascism the nonleaders have the least control of their own affairs) now do what any other like group would do: They mobilize their strengths in order to reintegrate themselves in the beloved society, beloved because until this moment it had been beneficial to themselves.

By whatever means, they seek to persuade their fellow Fascists of the error of their ways and look forward to the day of restoration, the day when they can once again be as imperialistic as their peers.

This conflict between them and their own kind goes from bad to worse, however. Fascism's shoes are filled by its far more powerful offspring, Nazism, which has decided not only to ostracize its Jews but to exterminate them. The Jewish leaders, having learned only the ways imparted by the institutions of the beloved society, continue the debate, and, as Ugo Foà has said—unknowingly echoing Jewish leaders throughout the European continent—make "every effort in order not to give any pretext for persecutions."

In the end, it becomes apparent that the debate is lost. Inevitably, the next step is a salvaging operation so that the Jewish leaders may participate in the *future* society, which of course is envisaged in precisely the same form and content as the Old Order in its sweetest moments. Naturally the leaders wish to take part in the future society at the level of leadership, in a position of prestige, power, and esteem, which they had long ago come to believe as either their birthright or something earned by labors more socially valuable than those performed by their inferiors.

They therefore place the highest value on the preservation of their institutions, which to the extent that they remain intact, are the infallible instruments that assure the perpetuity of the Old Order, that is, their rule. Thus do we see Foà risking his life for the salvation of the synagogue's gold and silver fetishes and all the rest of the community's "patrimony." Of such is made the Kastnerian philosophy of expending the many to save the "biologically valuable" few or the philosophy that Dr. Robinson pointed out as having guided "our people"—"He who preserves a single Jewish life is as one who preserves the whole world." And what is a "Jewish life" if not a human life invested with whole substance of the existing Jewish institutions? This philosophy, says Robinson who believes in the solace of the *Shear Yashuv,* or the return of the remnant, proved itself to be "valid,"[13] which of course is true: valid as defined by the Jewish leaders. As for everyone but the remnant and the institutions, however, they were gassed.

It can be seen then that the Jewish leaders were really no different from the non-Jewish leaders. In fact they were, having come from the same social matrix, one and the same kind. Any murderers or madmen to be found among the latter could be similarly found among the former. The only real difference between the two groups arose when the unjust system in which the two so happily took part developed in such a way as to demand the exclusion of one. The difference was that one was now in and the other out. The excluded group happened to be the Jews. In another time and circumstance it could have been the other way around, as for example, in Israel, where Jews—for whatever reasons may be given—have objectively excluded non-Jews from full participation in their society.

If the leaders in Fascist Italy could not be truly distinguished from one another by the label of their religion, then the same must follow for the nonleaders, or the vast majority of the Italian people. Jew and non-Jew alike, they had almost no stake at all in fascism and almost no common interest with their leaders, Jewish and non-Jewish. Yet such were the oppressive institutions of Fascist society that they were unable to become aware of the most important cause they shared with one another: the overthrow of their leaders and of fascism. Instead Jew and non-Jew were fragmented by those who controlled the social sources of what men thought, alienated from their true interests, from one another, and in the end, in many cases, turned against each other.

This is what happened in Italy. What of the rest of Europe? Were the Jewish leaders there of more noble stock? Were they markedly different from the non-Jewish leaders? Did something other than the Italian episode take place on the rest of the Continent? All of these questions, as might be expected, must be answered negatively. All the evidence shows that the same sordid theme in meaningless variations emerges everywhere one turns.

Take Germany. At the time Hitler came to power the 600,000 Jews of Germany were almost completely integrated into the political, economic, and social life of German society.[14] They were as devoted as any non-Jewish German to its flag, its aims, and its ideology. They as much as any German had committed themselves to its obligations and hoped to enjoy its rewards on an ever-increasing grade. This was the same society that in the early part of the twentieth century had launched its cry for a "place in the sun" and had set out on a course of expansionism, aggression, imperialism, and the subjugation of Europe to German hegemony.[15] This was the society that after World War I and prior to the initiation of full-scale anti-Jewish persecution, sought to reestablish itself as a Great Power, its prewar aims unchanged. It is Nazi society without fully developed Nazism, or with Nazism and all its paraphernalia, including its concentration camps and gas chambers, as yet disembodied among the people, both non-Jewish and Jewish.

Historians, after some hesitation, are now generally agreed that Hitler did not represent a new phenomenom in the history of German foreign policy, but that there was a continuity of aims that reached back into the nineteenth century. Indeed, according to A.J.P. Taylor, who was one of the first to arrive at this finding, "Hitler, far from transcending his respectable predecessors, was actually being more moderate than they when he sought only *Lebensraum* in the east and repudiated, in *Mein Kampf*, gains in the west."[16]

Hitler's contribution was the construction of the institutions believed necessary to achieve the powerful imperialist state, wished for with the greatest intensity among those Germans in the highest social layers, including, it must be repeated, Jewish Germans of equivalent class. The attitude of non-Jewish Germans on this social level is well documented; far less so is that of their Jewish peers, the following illustration of which has been offered by Hilberg.

In July, 1933, six months after Hitler had come to power, a delegation of American executives of the DuPont Corporation visited the I.G. Farben offices. I.G. Farben was an industrial empire of the first magnitude, which many Jews helped build and which was shortly to become the *raison d'être* for the entire Auschwitz complex of slave labor and systematic killing. The members of the DuPont mission, in talks with their I.G. Farben counterparts, held a meeting with Dr. Karl von Weinberg, deputy chairman of the *Verwaltungsrat* (management council), a kind of consultative Senate or House of Lords composed of I.G.'s elder statesmen. A DuPont official, who attended the meeting, reported shortly afterward to DuPont's director of foreign relations: Part of his statement read:

> Dr. von Weinberg . . . discussed the situation in Germany, and although he is a Jew, has given the [Nazi] movement his full stamp of approval. He stated further that all his money is invested in Germany and he does not have one pfennig outside the country. We spoke of the proposed increase in collaboration with I.G., to which he was in hearty agreement. In touching upon I.G.'s interest in the U.S.A., Dr. von Weinberg indicated that I.G. was very well pleased with the investment, and by suggestion gave us to understand that they had no intention of retiring from that market.[17]

Unfortunately for Weinberg, who ended up in a concentration camp, and for all the Jews who were hoping to reap the harvest of the new imperialism, one of the instruments Hitler found indispensible for the success of his plans was anti-Semitism. The moment this element appears, the same pattern of response that was to be adopted by the Jewish leaders in Italy a few years later arises in Germany in a much more pronounced degree.

In March, 1933, the prominent Jews of Germany, most of whom were serving on councils and boards of directors of the various Jewish communities throughout the country, were invited to Berlin by the chairman of that city's Jewish council to deal with Nazi racism. They formed a national organization, the Reich Representation of the Jews in Germany, with the aim of entering into an "open debate" with the Nazis, "a dignified controversy," the subject of which was to be "anti-Semitism and the Jewish future in Germany."[18] When this and the sequential efforts failed, the final phase, salvaging the Jewish institutions for the future society, in which the Old Order would be preserved, was begun.*

If we pass beyond the boundaries of the home countries of fascism and Nazism in search of other kinds of Jewish leaders, our efforts are entirely in vain. No group of leaders did not depend on the stability of the world system of Big Power imperialism as the means of maintaining their own position of leadership and the social order they cherished, if only as a prelude to something better. Even the leaders of the most oppressed Jews, the disenfranchised masses of eastern Europe, had a stake in the Old Order, since for them the oppressive system was less oppressive than for their flock. And when the Nazis came, they behaved precisely as their Italian and German Jewish counterparts.

* A document offering a striking example of what the Jewish leaders in the Austrian sector of the Third Reich were doing in this regard has survived. In October, 1941, a high official of the Jewish Community of Vienna, Rabbi Benjamin Murmelstein, reached an agreement with Eichmann's office exempting six categories of Jews who were not to be removed for "the resettlement action." Number one on the list read: "Members of the Jewish administrative machinery, with their parents, brothers, and sisters." Men, comforted by their families it seems, were needed to operate the "machinery," or else the beloved apparatus would grind to a halt.[19] Rabbi Murmelstein, who went on to become chairman of the Jewish Council of the Theresienstadt ghetto, is the man who taught Eichmann Hebrew. In an interview with the war crimes investigator Simon Wiesenthal (Vienna, June 10, 1967), Murmelstein's cooperation with the Nazis was described to me as outright criminal collaboration. The rabbi, incidentally, today lives in Rome, according to Wiesenthal, and is working in the Vatican library.

Listen to them speak, directly from the rare surviving minutes of their meetings:

> Honorable Assembly! . . . How can we remain close to the abyss without tumbling down into it?
>
> Firstly: carry out one hundred per cent loyally the requirements of the authorities. Secondly: personal control, which permits us to dispell misunderstandings.* Thirdly: our industry, which expands daily and demonstrates concretely the usefulness of the Jews to the authorities. . . .[20]

Another speaker, chairman of the Jewish Council, at another time:

> Our task consists in maintaining the present situation, and extending it until the end, which, some day, must come. But what are the concrete means in our power to do so? . . . there exists only one way only [sic]: achievements.
>
> The ghetto must become a body, the destruction of which will be a loss, because it is useful.[21]

Moving to the socially integrated Jews of western Europe, we find their leaders prominent members of nations whose *Weltanschauung* was the mirror image of Germany's. They were dedicated to a nationalism that had no wish to see the Reich as a Big Power, but only because they themselves wanted to be Big, or at least always bigger than they were—at the expense of Germany and other nations. In whatever land they lived, their governments had all endorsed the Treaty of Versailles, a punitive instrument that oppressed and exploited the Germans and helped create Hitler and the very Nazism by which Jews everywhere were to suffer. It was one system, and no one was out of it.

When the conflict developed, these western European Jewish leaders, virtually without exception, sought to negotiate the fate of their people in exchange for the preservation of their institutions.[22]

* Here the speaker was alluding to an incident described earlier in his talk. Some Jews had been identified by the Germans as being in possession of radio transmitters, presumably for the purpose of resistance. Such acts had to be controlled, since, he said, they wanted to shoot the Jewish leaders.

Finally there were the Zionist leaders. They consistently rejected European society in any country and continually sought to leave the continent to build a new society. But they too were no different from the others. One need only look at the society they eventually succeeded in establishing in Palestine to be convinced of this: a nationalist state with expansionist aims, not above armed aggression, and fully integrated into the contemporary Big Power system of international relations.

They viewed Nazi anti-Semitism as an opportunity to apply the Herzlian law: "A nation is a group of people . . . held together by a common enemy." They acted according to the Herzlian dialectic: that the anti-Semites "will be our most reliable friends, the anti-Semitic countries our allies."[23] Thus the Zionist response to Hitler, whose immense success in Germany was seen by the Zionists as "the decisive defeat of assimilation" was designed to advance Zionist aims.[24] These were the same aims as those of both the integrated and nonintegrated Jews with one additional feature: the exodus of the preserved institutions and the Old Order and their restoration in Palestine, in order that they might be enhanced, strengthened, and removed from the source of future threats. Then, Zionist ideology had always held, they would survive *forever*.

Kastner, the chairman of the Zionist council in Budapest, has revealed what he and other leaders were doing in behalf of their fellow Jews. It was the job of the leaders, he wrote, "to decide who would go first [to the gas chambers], who later. In sacrificing to Moloch, cruel criteria came into being, including age, merit, and achievements"[25] If one had the "wrong" age or had not compiled enough "achievements," he obviously could not pass this version of what Mengele was doing at the selection site in Auschwitz. Naturally many Jews did possess these qualities. They were members of the Zionist youth organization, and Kastner tells us, those "who had worked all their lives for the *zibur* [the community]" as well as the "most prominent Jews."[26]

An attempt has been made here to offer a new perspective of the Jews in the Europe of the Holocaust. Jewish social structure, like that of all peoples of the times, into which the Jews were meshed in one way or another, was one of classes; and the interests of one class, notwithstanding the ties of a common religion, did not always correspond with the interests of all. The response of the Jews of Europe to exclusion and finally liquidation from their societies was the response of the leading or ruling Jewish class. It could only have been this way, since it was the leaders who decided what the response would be, for themselves, and in good faith, for *their* people. While this response, as Dr. Robinson says, proved valid, it was valid only for them. The lower the descent on the social scale, the greater is its nonvalidity, for it is toward the bottom that the Jews with the least interest in the preservation of the Old Order were to be found, and it was toward the bottom that the greatest number of Jews resided. A valid response for them would have been total noncooperation with the oppressive system, total resistance to the oppressor. To the extent that these Jews actually did resist (almost always in defiance of their leaders), they were acting in their own interests and that of all of their fellow Jews, except the leaders.

It may thus be said that every Jewish leader gassed by the Nazis died fighting for his beliefs and his freedom, a hero or a martyr of his social class. As for the others—the more than 95 percent of all the millions—deprived as they were of genuine leadership and dazzled by the glint of the golden chain of organized class Jewry, they went to the same death, sadly, tragically, for the preservation of their prison, fighting for their slavery.

Dropping the fictions about the Jews requires a radical modification of our views of every group associated with the period. Fortunately such a reappraisal has recently been initiated in various quarters independently of one another, although the most sacred cows remain as yet unscathed.

A.J.P. Taylor's redistribution of war guilt among all of the Big Powers, and not just the Germans, has helped pave the way for major revisions of our thinking. Hilberg's and Arendt's work have opened our eyes to the cooperation of Jewish leaders in the attempt to destroy the Jews of Europe. Arthur Morse has uncovered the documents that demonstrate the cold-blooded apathy of the Allies and particularly the United States, which consciously refused to take any action that might have saved thousands of Jews from certain death.[27] Rolf Hochhuth and the historians who have backed him up with shocking evidence have dramatized the significance of the failure of Pope Pius XII to protest in behalf of the Jews.[28] Peter Weiss has given us new insights into the workings of the concentration camps; he has shown the intimate cooperative relationship between prisoner and guard and has revealed the Auschwitzes to have been island societies, which far from being alien to us, duplicated in the extreme all of the general features of our mother social system.[29]

Events too are helping to discredit the shibboleths. It was France, not Germany, who tortured and slaughtered the Algerians. It was Stalin, not Hitler, who sent millions of Russian political prisoners to their death. It was the Indonesian army, not the Stormtroopers, who killed two million Indonesian "Communists." It was Washington, not Berlin, who used nuclear weapons on civilians, and it is Washington, not Berlin, who continues to commit acts in Vietnam, which were defined, when other Powers were the perpetrators, as crimes against humanity.

It is necessary to carry this process of revision to its completion. It is imperative to have a clear view of the Holocaust of World War II, if only because the same Big Power social system which created Auschwitz thirty years ago is the very same one in which we live today. Nations still seek to expand their power and dominate other nations; there is discrimination, racism, and hatred among the peoples of the world, and violence and force of arms are still the engines on which the system runs. The new Auschwitz, which will be infinitely more efficient than the old, is in the air, and there is not the least guarantee that it will not slowly gather itself together again and suddenly take hold.

Clearly then, if the Jews as much as any people took part in the system which created Nazism, it is a meaningless and dangerous abstraction to merely punish Nazis and to single out merely their people for condemnation. Murderers must be brought to justice; people must be shown the evil they have done, but it was neither Nazism nor fascism that created the system of Big Power imperialism, but the other way around. We must abandon the easy chair of Jewish mythology and get off the sofa of anti-German scapegoatism and rush to look into the mirror of truth. We must see ourselves and all people in the frame of the social system, for here is where the world is made, our world and theirs.

To the truth in Dr. Robinson's, or organized world Jewry's statement about the responsibility for the murder of millions of Jews during World War II, an addition, or a revision, must now be made. We do so partly on the basis of the evidence offered in this book, and more so, on the findings that have been made known in recent years by others.

Robinson, as we have seen, wrote that:

> the murder of six million Jews was the direct responsibility of Nazi Germany which carried it out, and that it was indirectly aided by the almost universal passivity of the non-Jewish conquered populations, the neutrals, and the Allies, who by action or inaction did next to nothing to prevent it.

To this we add: . . . and with the almost universal cooperation of Jews and non-Jews alike in support of a social system in which genocide was possible and was carried out. The leaders of all of these peoples, German and non-German, Jewish and non-Jewish, bear a corresponding responsibility greater than anyone else.

With the role of the Jews themselves included, there now remains no innocent people, and thus the guilt can at last be put in its proper place.

It would be easy, as has been done too often, to lay it at the feet of one or another man or group; or to spread it thin among us all under the senseless notion of "collective guilt"; or worse, to attempt to shrug it away as "man's inhumanity to man." But, in the case of the Jews of Rome we have seen otherwise. Their destruction was the result of a system that functioned independently of how men felt or acted. No one in Rome, with the exception of Dannecker, wanted to deport the Jews, much less kill them. Yet this same insignificant man defied the will of a city of 2,000,000 inhabitants, including that of the victims, virtually without incident. Either Dannecker—not to mention the countless others like him and ready to step into his place—was possessed of some overwhelming occult powers, or it simply did not matter in the slightest what 2,000,000 people desired.

If the truth is in the latter statement, then clearly the will of the 2,000,000 was reduced by the system to the impotence of the breath of a fly—as long as they partook in that system, which was rendering them powerless. As long as there were Jewish leaders to negotiate with Gestapo officers; as long as Nazi diplomats wrote reports to Berlin; as long as churchmen preached calm and forebearance; as long as a policeman enforced the law, a postman delivered the mail, firemen put out fires, workmen ran the power plants, trainmen the trains; in short, as long as the system which deported Jews was held together, what men thought meant nothing, and Jews could be deported.

But, just as it would be wrong to charge Dannecker alone with the murder of the Jews of Rome, it would be equally erroneous, absurd, to so accuse the city's 2,000,000 people. What else could they have done but partake in the system? The answer is: nothing. There was only one system; and only the rare exception, only the extraordinary man who was willing to use his own life as a weapon against the system—for oppression rules only those who value their own life over freedom—could act as a free individual. As for the 2,000,000, dedicated as they were to their society—to be sure, each man only to what he believed was the "good" in the society—they could no more have stopped the deportation of the Jews of Rome than a bullet can refuse to be fired from a gun. To believe that men, under a system of oppression, have control of their own or the fate of others, is not only false but cruel and harmful. To believe that under such a system what ordinary men think is a source of power, is nothing but vanity. Moreover, to believe that men have in any meaningful way changed the oppressive social system of only yesterday does not correspond with the bloody facts of today.

One cannot shrink from the implications of this condition. Let us reject the hopeless concept of individual guilt—hopeless because it engages us in an eternal labor of rooting out evil *after* it is done. Let us reject the static, antihuman ideas of "collective guilt" and "man's inhumanity to man," which say that the evil men do arises from the nature of man. The source of evil lies elsewhere. Though its rivers flow in every land, it springs—we say it once more—from a single, polluted well: our social system.

The social system is guilty of producing people who commit war crimes, crimes against humanity, and genocide. It is guilty of producing accomplices to these crimes and accomplices to the accomplices, until, as one writer has put it, "an ordinary man going about his ordinary tasks, thinking of his family and his personal problems, can find himself in a position in which every act of acquiescence in the policies of his government makes him an accomplice of its crimes."[30] It has done so in the past, and it must be concluded, will do so in the future. If this social system could have produced even one innocent people there would still be hope for it, perhaps. But there were no innocent peoples, although, thank goodness, there were great numbers of individual exceptions, Jew and non-Jew. This social system, then, in its present form, is hopeless.

Yet, for us, it is the source of all hope. So inhuman is the social system, it creates, in protest of itself, all that is human and just. It creates the exceptions, those men and women of all races and religions who refuse to cooperate with evil, and who are prepared, as others were before them, to resist the tyranny and injustice of the social system with their blood and with their lives, and to fight for the liberation of humanity, for us. Herein lies the hope. It is the hope that the social system can be changed. If we are to survive as human beings, it must be radically changed.

As for what changes must be made, I leave that to the philosophers and the poets. As for how and by whom they will be made, I leave that to the exceptions.

APPENDIX I

Names and ages of the 1,041 known passengers on the Rome–Auschwitz transport who did not come back.[1]

Aio, Abramo, 58; Aio, Celeste, 35; Aio, Elisabetta, 33; Aio, Grazia, 26; Aio, Pacifico, 21; Alatri, Lionello, 65; Almagia, Delia, 68; Almagia, Emma, 75; Almagia, Enrico*; Almagia, Erminia, 80; Amati, Alberto, 13; Amati, Rosa, 20; Amati, Rosa, 74; Anav, Adalgisa, 51; Anav, Anita, 57; Anticoli, Ada, 18; Anticoli, Adelaide, 41; Anticoli, Adolfo, 48; Anticoli, Alberto, 35; Anticoli, Angelo, 6 months; Anticoli, Angelo, 36; Anticoli, Anna, 4; Anticoli, Attilio, 5; Anticoli, Celeste, 18; Anticoli Celeste, 43; Anticoli Emma Limentani, 27; Anticoli, Emma Zarfati, 45; Anticoli, Enrica, 5; Anticoli, Esterina*; Anticoli, Fiorella, 2; Anticoli, Fiorella, 7; Anticoli, Fiorella, 8; Anticoli, Fiorella, 12; Anticoli, Fortuna, 18; Anticoli, Gemma, 10; Anticoli, Gemma, 33; Anticoli, Geremia, 21; Anticoli, Giacomo, 36; Anticoli, Giuditta, 7; Anticoli, Grazia, 2; Anticoli, Lazzaro, 8; Anticoli, Lazzaro, 63; Anticoli, Lello, 2; Anticoli, Letizia, 11; Anticoli, Luciana, 5; Anticoli, Marco, 5; Anticoli, Marco, 65; Anticoli, Mario, 4 months; Anticoli, Marisa, 9; Anticoli, Pacifico, 9; Anticoli, Rina, 13; Anticoli, Rosa, 23; Anticoli, Rosa, 25; Anticoli, Rosella, 4 months; Anticoli, Rosina, 22; Anticoli, Vanda, 25; Artom, Riccardo, 76; Ascarelli, Adele, 45; Ascoli, Ernesta, 83; Ascoli, Lidia, 74; Ascoli, Vito, 48; Astrologo, Adriana, 39; Astrologo, Aldo, 35; Astrologo, Anita, 32; Astrologo, Attilio, 16; Astrologo, Diamante, 23; Astrologo, Ennio, 4; Astrologo, Ester*; Astrologo, Fortunata, 31; Astrologo, Giuditta, 21; Astrologo, Italia, 63; Astrologo, Lamberto, 52; Astrologo, Letizia,

* Age unknown.

21; Astrologo, Maurizio, 3; Astrologo, Milena, 19; Astrologo, Rina, 18; Astrologo, Rinaldo, 53; Astrologo, Rosa, 65; Astrologo, Sara, 18; Astrologo, Sara, 50; Baraffael, Fiorina di Capua, 74; Baroccio, Clara Efrati, 52; Baroccio, Virginia Piperno, 58; Battino, Giuseppe, 52; Belleli, Eloisa Anau, 66; Belleli, Roberto, 68; Bemporad, David, 62; Bemporad, Elvira di Cave, 51; Bises, Abramo, 80; Bondì, Ana, 3; Bondì, Benedetto, 12; Bondì, Elena, 1; Bondì, Fiorella, 11; Bondì, Giuseppe, 5; Bondì, Leone, 41; Buetow, Vally, 63; Calò, Alberto, 4; Calò, Alberto, 4; Calò, Alberto, 7; Calò, Alberto, 41; Calò, Angelo, 8; Calò, Armanda, 8; Calò, Bellina, 22; Calò, Benedetto, 17; Calò, Benvenuta, 68; Calò, Cesira, 17; Calò, Davide, 13; Calò, Elena, 11; Calò, Eleonora, 6; Calò, Ester, 20; Calò, Eugenio, 46; Calò, Fatima, 3; Calò, Fiorina, 41; Calò, Giuseppe, 8; Calò, Giuseppe, 63; Calò, Grazia, 40; Calò, Graziella, 3; Calò, Graziella, 13; Calò, Ines, 16; Calò, Letizia, Piperno, 32; Calò, Margherita, 40; Calò, Mario, 10; Calò, Nella, 6; Calò, Raimondo, 4; Calò, Renata, 11; Calò, Roberta, 6; Calò, Romolo, 19; Calò, Romolo, 36; Calò, Rosa, 18; Calò, Rossana, 2; Calò, Samuele, 6 months; Camerino, Elena, 39; Camerino, Italo, 50; Camerino, Wanda, 25; Campagnano, Donato, 3 months; Campagnano, Teresa, 61; Campagnano, Vito, 58; Capon, Augusto, 70; Castelbolognesi, Federico, 66; Cava, Perla, 69; Cavalieri, Alina, 61; Caviglia, Adamo, 63; Caviglia, Eleonora, 79; Caviglia, Emma, 33; Caviglia, Enrica di Cave, 27; Caviglia, Grazia, 14; Caviglia, Letizia, 6; Caviglia, Renato, 31; Caviglia, Rita di Segni, 28; Caviglia, Settimio, 12; Caviglia, Umberto, 10; Cesana, Carlotta, 67; Chimichi, Evelina Alatri, 61; Chimichi, Eugenio, 90; Citoni, Angelo, 70; Citoni, Arrigo, 5; Citoni, Carlo, 6; Citoni, Colomba, Piperno, 63; Citoni, Ettore, 54; Citoni, Giuseppina, 3; Citoni, Guido, 53; Citoni, Prospero, 76; Coen, Ravà Amelia, 76; Coen, Levi Edy, 62; Coen, Enrica, 55; Coen, Etore, 60; Coen, Fortunata, 55; Coen, Franca, 18; Coen, Piperno Giorgina, 55; Coen, Guido, 65; Coen, Mosè, 53; Coen, Passigli, Virginia, 65; Curiel, Carlos, 48; Curiel, Bruno, 11; Curiel, Giacomo, 44; Curiel, Giorgio, 17; Cuzzeri, Ennio, 11; Cuzzeri Coen, Olga, 56; Cuzzeri, Pia, 57; Darmon, Massimo, 35; DeAngeli, Enrichetta, 74; Dell'Aricia, Ada, 28; Dell'Aricia, Alba Bella, 9 months; Dell'Aricia, Aldo, 41; Dell'Ariccia, Emma, 34; Dell'Ariccia, Franco, 6; Dell'Ariccia, Giovanni, 64; Dell'Ariccia, Lello,

* Age unknown.

2; Dell'Ariccia, Manlio, 32; Dell'-Ariccia, Mirella, 31; Dell'Ariccia, Samuele, 31; Della Rocca, Alberto, 34; Della Rocca, Angello, 20; Della Rocca, Chiara, 14; Della Rocca Diveroli, Costanza, 56; Della Rocca, David*; Della Rocca, Elisabetta, 21; Della Rocca, Emma, 37; Della Rocca, Enrica, 6; Della Rocca, Silvio, 12; Della Rocca Campagnano, Virginia, 52; Della Rocca, Viviana, 24; Della Seta Astrologo, Adriana, 28; Della Seta, Alberto, 26; Della Seta, Franca, 21; Della Seta, Giancarlo, 16; Della Seta, Lionello, 52; Della Seta DiNola, Livia, 57; Della Seta, Samuele, 74; Della Seta Torre, Cesira, 39; Della Seta di Capua, Ester, 78; Della Seta, Giacomo*; Della Seta di Porto, Ofelia, 29; Della Seta di Veroli, Vanda, 29; Del Monte, Amedeo, 64; Del Monte, Anita, 35; Del Monte, Costanza, 15; Del Monte, Franca, 5; Del Monte, Fornari, Grazia, 66; Del Monte, Margherita, 56; Del Monte, Rina, 22; Del Monte dell'Ariccia, Velia, 30; Del Vecchio Funaro, Paolina, 47; Di Benedetti, Giorgio, 47; Di Capua, Amadio, 17; Di Capua, Angelo, 54; Di Capua Valabrega, Anita, 53; Di Capua, Clotilde, 66; Di Capua Di Cave, Clotilde, 81; Di Capua, Elisabetta, 36; Di Capua, Elvira, 56; Di Capua Di Segni, Enrica, 28; Di Capua, Ernnesta, 68; Di Capua, Gilda, 64; Di Capua, Pacifico, 70; Di Capua, Pia, 58; Di Capua, Rosa, 6; Di Capua Romanelli, Rosa, 70; Di Capua, Rita*; Di Capua Di Porto, Serafina, 55; Di Castro, Adolfo, 3; Di Castro, Angelo, 66; Di Castro, Angelo, 28; Di Castro, Attilio, 2; Di Castro, Attilio, 55; Di Castro, Cesare, 18; Di Castro, Cesare, 3; Di Castro, Crescenzio, 40; Di Castro, David, 6; Di Castro, Emma, 26; Di Castro, Ferdinanda, 20; Di Castro, Giulia*; Di Castro, Graziano, 1; Di Castro, Leonello*; Di Castro Di Segni, Letizia, 63; Di Castro, Lidia, 71; Di Castro, Maria, 45; Di Castro, Mario, 2; Di Castro, Mario, 12; Di Castro, Michele, 31; Di Castro, Michele*; Di Castro Funaro, Teresa, 35; Di Cave, Angelo, 77; Di Cave, Beha, 18; Di Cave, Cesare, 54; Di Cave Spizzichino, Elena, 37; Di Cave di Nepi, Elisa, 25; Di Cave Vittorio, Emanuele, 53; Di Cave, Eugenio, 80; Di Cave Mieli, Eva, 80; Di Cave, Fernando, 52; Di Cave, Franca, 2; Di Cave, Franco, 13; Di Cave, Guglielmo, 46; Di Cave, Luigia, 56; Di Cave, Rosina, 78; Di Cave, Sandro, 11; Di Cave Efrati, Settimia, 74; Di Consiglio, Ada, 6; Di Consiglio, Ester, 42; Di Consiglio, Marco, 4; Di Consiglio, Mirella, 10 months; Di Consiglio, Regina, 31; Dickstein Abramson, Berta, 65; Di Cori, Angelo, 44; Di Cori Camerino,

* Age unknown.

Giulia, 49; Di Cori, Sara, 7; Di Cori, Settimio Renato, 44; Di Gioacchino, Cesira, 19; Di Nepi, Angelo, 20; Di Nepi, Pergola Celeste, 44; Di Nepi, Elisabeta, 5; Di Nepi, Elvira, 6 months; Di Nepi, Emma, 3; Di Nepi, Giacomo, 73; Di Nepi, Laudadio, 61; Di Nepi, Rina, 29; Di Nepi, Samuele, 16; Di Nepi, Ugo, 4 months; Di Neris Diveroli, Esterina, 50; Di Nola, Alfredo, 65; Di Porto Anticoli, Ida, 29; Di Porto, Adelaide, 45; Di Porto, Alberta, 35; Di Porto, Alberto, 6; Di Porto, Albertina, 3; Di Porto, Angela, 27; Di Porto, Angelo, 6; Di Porto, Angelo, 6 months; Di Porto, Angelo, 7; Di Porto, Bellina, 31; Di Porto, Celeste, 10; Di Porto, Celeste, 34; Di Porto, Cesare, 4; Di Porto, Cesare, 35; Di Porto, Cesare, 10; Di Porto, Cesira, 35; Di Porto, Costanza, 62; Di Porto, Costanza, 6; Di Porto, Costanza, 52; Di Porto, Crescenzio, 18; Di Porto, Elena*; Di Porto, Elvira, 30; Di Porto, Elvira, 30; Di Porto, Ester*; Di Porto, Ester, 68; Di Porto, Esterina, 1; Di Porto, Fenizia, 26; Di Porto, Fortunata, 6 months; Di Porto, Fulvio, 25; Di Porto, Grazia*; Di Porto, Graziella, 7 months; Di Porto, Graziella, 1; Di Porto, Graziella, 7; Di Porto, Giuditta, 27; Di Porto, Italia, 4; Di Porto, Letizia, 36; Di Porto, Mario, 18; Di Porto, Mario*; Di Porto, Mario, 15; Di Porto, Mario, 33; Di Porto, Perla, 45; Di Porto, Renata, 15; Di Porto, Rosa, 24; Di Porto, Rosa, 19; Di Porto, Rosa, 12; Di Porto, Settimio, 40; Di Porto, Settimio, 5; Di Porto, Settimio, 59; Di Porto, Settimio, 41; Di Porto, Vitale, 39; Di Porto, Vitale, 62; Di Porto, Vito*; Di Porto, Wilma, 10; Di Segni, Adelaide, 7; Di Segni, Adolfo, 43; Di Segni, Alba*; Di Segni, Alberto, 31; Di Segni, Angelo, 13; Di Segni, Angelo, 38; Di Segni, Anita, 12; Di Segni, Armando, 9 months; Di Segni, Benedetto, 33; Di Segni, Benedetto, 3; Di Segni, Bruno, 11; Di Segni, Cesare, 44; Di Segni, Clara, 18; Di Segni, Clorinda, 59; Di Segni, Colomba, 38; Di Segni, Colomba*; Di Segni, David, 3; Di Segni, David, 34; Di Segni, Elia, 56; Di Segni, Emanuele, 10; Di Segni, Emma, 2; Di Segni, Emma, 14; Di Segni, Enrica, 19; Di Segni, Enrica, 32; Di Segni, Ester, 29; Di Segni, Franco, 2; Di Segni, Gianna, 2; Di Segni, Giulia, 72; Di Segni, Giuseppe, 7 months; Di Segni, Grazia, 5; Di Segni, Grazia, 20; Di Segni, Grazia, 55; Di Segni, Graziella, 7; Di Segni, Graziella, 29; Di Segni, Italia, 22; Di Segni, Lello, 18; Di Segni, Lello, 32; Di Segni, Leone, 42; Di Segni, Leone*; Di Segni, Lilliana, 17; Di Segni, Luciana, 3 months; Di Segni, Marco, 30; Di Segni, Marco, 8; Di Segni, Maria, 47; Di Segni,

* Age unknown.

Mario, 7; Di Segni, Pacifico, 7; Di Segni, Pacifico, 57; Di Segni, Pacifico, 18; Di Segni, Pacifico*; Di Segni, Renato, 13; Di Segni, Riccardo, 34; Di Segni, Rina, 11; Di Segni, Rina, 24; Di Segni, Roberto, 4; Di Segni, Rosa, 26; Di Segni, Rosa, 28; Di Segni, Rossana, 5; Di Segni, Rosa, 24; Di Segni, Salvatore, 13; Di Segni, Settimio, 6; Di Segni, Umberto, 4; Di Segni, Virginia, 13; Di Segni, Vittorio*; Di Tivoli, Adelaide, 34; Di Tivoli, Albertina, 15; Di Tivoli, Angelo, 27; Di Tivoli, Fatima, 1 month; Di Tivoli, Fatima, 36; Di Tivoli, Lazzaro, 24; Di Tivoli, Leone, 18; Di Tivoli, Marco, 51; Di Tivoli, Mirella, 14; Di Tivoli, Pacifico, 10; Di Tivoli, Rossona, 10; Di Tivoli del Monte, Rina, 25; Di Tivoli, Salomone, 68; Di Tivoli, Speranza, 14; Di Tivoli Compagnano, Virginia, 26; Di Veroli, Abramo, 62; Di Veroli, Adolfo, 8; Di Veroli, Alberto, 15; Di Veroli, Alessandro, 61; Di Veroli, Asriele, 62; Di Veroli, Celeste, 12; Di Veroli Zarfati, Celestina, 71; Di Veroli, Delia, 55; Di Veroli, Donato, 25; Di Veroli, Donato, 47; Di Veroli, Elisabeta, 32; Di Veroli, Emma, 2; Di Veroli, Enrica, 17; Di Veroli, Ester, 12; Di Veroli, Eugenio, 21; Di Veroli di Porto, Fortunata, 43; Di Veroli, Giacomina, 27; Di Veroli, Giuditta, 6; Di Veroli, Giuditta, 14; Di Veroli, Giuditta*; Di Veroli, Gualtiero, 2; Di Veroli, Italia, 10; Di Veroli, Leonardo, 5; Di Veroli, Lello, 6; Di Veroli, Lidia, 4; Di Veroli, Lina, 27; Di Veroli, Lilliana, 5; Di Veroli, Marco, 40; Di Veroli, Mario, 32; Di Veroli, Mario, 26; Di Veroli, Michele, 1; Di Veroli, Mosè, 81; Di Veroli, Pacifico, 5; Di Veroli, Prospero, 12; Di Veroli, Rina, 10; Di Veroli, Rina, 15; Di Veroli, Rosa, 17; Di Veroli, Sara Tedeschi, 47; Di Veroli, Settimia di Nepi, 64; Di Veroli, Settimio, 22; Di Veroli, Settimio, 13; Di Veroli, Silvia, 28; Di Veroli, Silvia, 34; Di Veroli, Virginia Fornari, 17; Di Veroli, Virginia Terracina, 66; Donati, Clelia*; Efrati, Adelaide, 3; Efrati, Alda Fiorentino, 57; Efrati, Dora, 5; Efrati, Egle Fiorentino, 50; Efrati, Enrica, 20; Efrati, Fortunata, 15; Efrati, Grazia, 13; Efrati, Marco, 4; Efrati, Marco, 3; Efrati, Marco, 63; Efrati, Mirella, 20; Efrati, Olga, 43; Efrati, Pacifica, 26; Efrati, Rina, 9; Efrati, Settimio, 64; Efrati, Speranza, 54; Efrati, Lazaro, 23; Efrati, Umberto, Abramo, 43; Efrati, Umberto, 32; Esdra, Rosina, 37; Fano, Lina, 66; Fatucci, Amedeo, 51; Fatucci, Angelo, 41; Fatucci, Arnaldo, 51; Fatucci, Attilio, 8; Fatucci, David, 78; Fatucci, Emma Pavoncello, 45; Fiano, Amedeo, 36; Fiano, Chiara Esdra, 64; Fiano,

* Age unknown.

Emilia Olga, 5 months; Fiano, Fortunata, 2; Finzi, Adriana, 23; Finzi, Amelia, 12; Finzi, Carlo, 67; Finzi, Giuseppe, 39; Finzi, Enrico, 21; Finzi, Luciana, 19; Fiorentini, Ernesta, 40; Fiorentini, Piera, 21; Fiorentini, Salvatore, 58; Fiorentino, Alda, 60; Fiorentino, Cesare, 54; Fiorentino, Ester, 79; Fiorentino, Fortunata, 17; Fiorentino, Lello, 14; Fiorentino, Leone, 19; Fiorentino, Salvatore, 41; Fornari, Alberto, 6; Fornari, Alberto Renato, 30; Fornari, Angelo, 73; Fornari, Angelo*; Fornari, Carlo, 5 months; Fornari, Ermelinda, 43; Fornari, Guglielmo, 39; Fornari, Perla, 61; Fornari, Rossana, 7 months; Fornari, Umberto, 11; Forti, Bruno, 48; Forti, Carmela, 70; Forti, Emma Piperno, 63; Frascati, Clelia Calò, 45; Frascati, Emma, 35; Frascati, Ester Anticoli, 30; Frascati, Fausta, 23; Frascati, Fiorella, 11; Frascati, Giorgio 4; Frascati, Ida, 14; Frascati, Irma, 6; Frascati, Lello, 16; Frascati, Marisa, 11; Frascati, Settimia Calò, 22; Frascati, Settimio, 42; Frascati, Silvana, 14; Frascati, Vittorio, 6; Funaro, Ada, 34; Funaro, Adele, 28; Funaro, Angelo, 10 months; Funaro, Cesare, 35; Funaro, Cesare, 4; Funaro, Chiara, 35; Funaro, Dario, 13; Funaro, Ettore, 32; Funaro, Ettore, 60; Funaro, Giuditta, 44; Funaro, Giuseppe, 10; Funaro, Graziella, 7; Funaro, Leo, 45; Funaro, Marco, 45; Funaro, Lina*; Funaro, Mibena, 71; Funaro, Pacifico, 43; Funaro, Rosa, 14; Funaro, Rosetta, 5; Funaro, Wanda, 2; Gai, Ettore, 45; Garzoli, Crescenzio 2; Garzoli, Debora, 4; Garzoli, Mario, 6; Gattegna, Gabriele Enrico, 64; Gattegna, Gino, 46; Gattegna, Perla, 69; Greco, Gisella, 69; Herzer, Ada Forti, 74; Kaplan, Paul, 58; Leoni, Gabriella, 11; Leoni, Gustavo, 51; Leoni, Lauretta, 14; Levi, Giorgio, 72; Levi, Giorgio, 17; Levi, Mario, 55; Levi, Oscar*; Limentani, Alberto, 33; Limentani, Cesare, 4; Limentani, Cesare, 7; Limentani, Cesare, 48; Limentani, Cesira Piperno, 64; Limentani, Chiara, 54; Limentani, Costanza, 44; Limentani, Costanza, Di Porto, 35; Limentani, David, 49; Limentani, Elsa Gentili, 22; Limentani, Israel, 63; Limentani, Letizia Perugia, 47; Limentani, Massimo, 23; Limentani, Rosa 2; Limentani, Rosa della Torre, 26; Limentani, Rosa, 26; Livoli, Allegra di Porto, 38; Livoli, Elvira, 32; Livoli, Rachele, 90; Livoli, Speranza, 55; Livoli, Vittoria Sonnino, 32; Loevinson, Herman, 80; Loevinson, Sigmond, 22; Luzzatto, Riccardo, 54; Menasci, Enrico, 83; Menasci, Enrico, 12; Menasci, Raffaello, 47; Menasci, Tina Piperno, 50; Mendes, Marcello, 28; Mendes,

* Age unknown.

Maurizio, 67; Mendes, Umberto, 20; Mieli, Alba, 46; Mieli, Alegra, 53; Mieli, Cesare, 24; Mieli, Claudio, 4; Mieli, Enrica, 19; Mieli, Ester, 52; Mieli, Ester, 6; Mieli, Giacomo, 46; Mieli, Lazzaro, 22; Mieli, Letizia Astrologo, 53; Mieli, Marco, 56; Mieli, Marina, 6; Mieli, Nella Pontecorvo, 32; Mieli, Pacifico, 32; Mieli, Rossana, 17; Mieli, Sergio, 18; Mieli, Ugo, 45; Mieli, Umberto, 17; Milano, Angelo, 73; Milano, Elda, 49; Misano, Fulvio, 52; Misano, Lina, 50; Montefiori, Nella, 38; Moresco, Alberto, 15; Moresco, Angelo, 17; Moresco, Anselmo, 4; Moresco, Cesare, 45; Moresco, Grazia Mieli, 47; Moresco, Grazia Piperno, 47; Mortera, Abramo Giulio, 73; Mortera, Giulia Levi*; Mortera, Jolo, 39; Moscati, Alba, 3 months; Moscati, Angelo, 12; Moscati, Cesare, 14; Moscati, Elio, 4; Moscati, Eva Dornaga, 53; Moscati, Giacobbo, 69; Moscati, Giacomo, 11; Moscati, Letizia, 8; Moscati, Maria Limentani, 29; Moscati, Tina Reale, 34; Moscati, Rosa, 9; Moscati, Rosa, 27; Moscati, Rosa, 51; Moscati, Sarina, 21; Moscati, Vanda, 25; Moscato, Bruno Anselmo, 3; Moscato, Celeste, 14; Moscato, Elio, 2; Moscato, Franco, 36; Moscato, Giuseppe, 36; Moscato, Lazzaro, 5; Moscato, Lazzaro, 65; Moscato, Pace, 33; Moscato, Virginia della Rocca, 33; Muggia, Aldo*; Muggia, Anna Belleli*; Muggia, Lia*; Nemes, Ferdinando, 22; Numes, Olga, Philipson, 75; Orvieto, Rodolfo, 25; Ottolenghi, Lidia, 42; Ottolenghi, Mary, 51; Ottolenghi, Teresa, 58; Pace, Giacobbe, 72; Pace, Gino, 58; Pace, Sergio, 17; Palagi, Franca, 24; Palagi, Gino, 59; Papo, Sara, 59; Passigli, Guido, 61; Pavoncello, Alfredo, 7; Pavoncello, Allegra, 54; Pavoncello, Allegra, 59; Pavoncello, Anselmo, 51; Pavoncello, Camilla, 18; Pavoncello, Cesare, 61; Pavoncello, Cesare, 10 months; Pavoncello, Clelia, 16; Pavoncello, Dora, 50; Pavoncello, Elio, 34; Pavoncello, Emilia, 33; Pavoncello, Emilia, 51; Pavoncello, Enrico, 31; Pavoncello, Ester di Veroli, 31; Pavoncello, Giacomo, 31; Pavoncello, Giacomo, 38; Pavoncello, Giuditta, 5; Pavoncello, Graziella, 3; Pavoncello, Lina, 4; Pavoncello, Rebecca, 64; Pavoncello, Sergio, 13; Pergola, Aldo, 44; Pergola, Bixio, 40; Pergola, Eleonora, 12; Perugia, Clelia, 35; Perugia, Debora*; Perugia, Gabriella, 30; Perugia, Italia, 53; Perugia, Letizia, 48; Perugia, Marcella di Veroli, 23; Perugia, Serafina, 86; Perugia, Vittoria, 41; Perugia, Vittoria, 51; Philipson, Beniamino, 73; Piattelli, Dora, 57; Piattelli, Elda Fiorentino, 42; Piattelli, Luigi Ezechiele, 76; Piattelli, Servadio,

* Age unknown.

* Age unknown.

Sciunnach, Ada Fortunata, 35; Sciunnach, Alberto, 63; Sciunnach, Giuditta, 15; Sciunnach, Letizia, 27; Schiunnach, Leone, 13; Sed, Ester Rina, 10; Sed, Gioia, 78; Sed, Giuseppe, 29; Segre, Elena, 33; Segre, Ida Luzzati*; Seppili, Allessandra, Perugia, 55; Seppili, Emma Piazza, 86; Serend, Clara 32; Sermoneta, Alvaro, 10; Sermoneta, Amelia, 35; Sermoneta, Anna, 33; Sermoneta, Bennedetto, 45; Sermoneta, Bennedetto, 13; Sermoneta, Celeste, 32; Sermoneta, Costanza, 11; Sermoneta, Costanza, 43; Sermoneta, Camilia, Zarfati, 61; Sermoneta, Emma, 2; Sermoneta, Eugenio, 58; Sermoneta, Franca, 5 months; Sermoneta, Giuseppe, 14; Sermoneta, Pacifico, 12; Sermoneta, Pellegrino, 62; Sermoneta, Prospero, 32; Sermoneta, Rosa, 69; Sermoneta, Rosa Fornari, 70; Sermoneta, Silvia, 47; Sessa, Virginia della Seta, 60; Sonnino, Adele, 64; Sonnino, Amedeo, 51; Sonnino, Amedeo, 19; Sonnino, Amedeo, 39; Sonnino, Celeste, 9; Sonnino, Cesira Maria, 3, Sonnino, Costanza, 34; Sonnino, Elisa, 27; Sonnino, Ester, 67; Sonnino, Ester, 20; Sonnino, Editta, 19; Sonnino, Fabrizio, 3; Sonnino, Gina, 19; Sonnino, Giuliana, 18; Sonnino, Giuseppe, 11; Sonnino, Grazia, 14; Sonnino, Grazia, 19; Sonnino, Ida, 24; Sonnino, Ida Fatucci, 53; Sonnino, Isacco, 60; Sonnino, Lalla, 54; Sonnino, Leone, 57; Sonnino, Mario, 2; Sonnino, Mario, 46; Sonnino, Margherita 59; Sonnino, Massimo, 11; Sonnino, Michele, 1; Sonnino, Mosè, 73; Sonnino, Rachele, 13; Sonnino, Rosa Della Torre, 56; Sonnino, Samuele Sandro, 5; Sonnino, Samuele, 35; Sonnino, Sara Perugia, 67; Sonnino, Sperenza Sciunnach, 39; Sonnino, Virginia Astrologo, 53; Sonnino, Vito, 62; Spagnoletto, Samuele, 57; Spagnoletto, Sofia Coen, 78; Spagnoletto, Virtuosa Piperno, 73; Spagnoletto, Virtuosa, 49; Spizzichino, Ada Calò, 28; Spizzichino, Ada, 29; Spizzichino, Adelaide Funaro, 45; Spizzichino, Alberto, 38; Spizzichino, Allegra Pavoncello, 49; Spizzichino, Costanza Astrologo, 61; Spizzichino, Enrica, 10; Spizzichino, Enrica*; Spizzichino, Enrica, 56; Spizzichino, Enrica Frascati, 46; Spizzichino, Enrichetta*; Spizzichino, Ester, 31; Spizzichino, Fiorina, 65; Spizzichino, Fortunata, 67; Spizzichino, Fortunata, 61; Spizzichino, Franca, 7; Spizzichino, Giacomo, 5; Spizzichino, Giuditta, 21; Spizzichino, Grazia, 57; Spizzichino, Ida*; Spizzichino, Ines, 44; Spizzichino, Letizia* Spizzichino, Luciana, 22; Spizzichino, Mario, 1; Spizzichino, Mario, 18; Spizzichino, Norina, 19; Spizzichino, Pacifico, 41; Spizzichino, Ricca di Tivoli,

* Age unknown.

50; Spizzichino, Rosa Limentani, 60; Spizzichino, Rosa del Monte, 43; Spizzichino, Stella Fatulli, 77; Spizzichino, Virginia, 7; Spizzichino, Vittorio Emanuele, 37; Tagliacozzo, Celeste Sabatello, 48; Tagliacozzo, Amedeo, 45; Tagliacozzo, Colomba, 59; Tagliacozzo, Enrica Sabatello, 31; Tagliacozzo, Ester di Segni, 33; Tagliacozzo, Ester Sed, 65; Tagliacozzo, Italia, 12; Tedeschi, Arrigo, 56; Tedeschi, Giuliana, 20; Tedeschi, Marco, 64; Tedeschi, Marisa, 16; Tedeschi, Sabato 75; Tedeschi, Giulia, 56; Terracina, Eleonora, 58; Terracina, Emma, 10; Terracina, Enrica, 43; Terracina, Franca, 18; Terracina, Giacomo, 28; Terracina, Giuditta Spizzichino, 30; Terracina, Leonello, 3; Terracina, Letizia, 43; Terracina, Marco, 1; Terracina, Mario, 34; Terracina, Mirella, 20; Terracina, Rosa Anticoli, 37; Terracina, Virginia, 1; Terracina, Vittorio Emanuele, 58; Toscano, Eleonora, 88; Toscano, Elisa, 28; Toscano, Mario Mosè, 66; Toscano, Rachele, Coen, 57; Toscano, Rebecca Piatelli, 63; Toscano, Rosina, 63; Treves, Amelia Segre, 76; Valabrega, Leone Italo, 53; Valabrega, Samuele, 62; Valabrega, Samuele, 51; Veneziani, Aida, 57; Veneziani, Aldo, 44; Veneziani, Donato, 60; Veneziani, Edoardo, 34; Veneziani, Evelina, Sonnino, 36; Veneziani, Guido, 9; Veneziani, Lea, 30; Veneziani, Marcella, 22; Veneziani, Margherita, 36, Veneziani, Mario, 42; Veneziani, Mosè, 69; Veneziani, Pellegrino, 66; Veneziani, Pierina Fiorentini, 52; Veneziani, Piero, 37; Veneziani, Vanda, 49; Vitale, Benedetta, 81; Vivanti, Amerigo, 1; Vivanti, Benedetto, 4; Vivanti, Celeste, 38; Vivanti, Celeste, 37; Vivanti, Diamantina di Capua, 56; Vivanti, Emma, 44; Vivanti, Emma, Sermoneta, 61; Vivanti, Eugenio, 13; Vivanti, Fortunata, 2; Vivanti, Laura, 8; Vivanti, Letizia, 11; Vivanti, Leone, 6; Vivanti, Pellegrino, 65; Vivanti, Rachele, 34; Vivanti, Raoul, 45; Volterra, Aldo, 46; Volterra, Elena, 34; Volterra, Mario, 52; Volterra, Oscar, 39; Volterra, Palmira, 76, Volterra, Ugo, 47; Volterra, Valentina*; Wachsberger, Regina*; Wachsberger, Clara, 5; Zarfati, Angelo*; Zarfati, Angelo, 67; Zarfati, Angelo, 45; Zarfati, Aurelia, 48; Zarfati, Bianca, 36; Zarfati, Debora, 14; Zarfati, Emma, 22; Zarfati, Enrica, 33; Zarfati, Enrica di Segni, 41; Zarfati, Ester del Monte, 45; Zarfati, Fausta, 44; Zarfati, Giuseppe, 17; Zarfati, Graziella, 20; Zarfati, Italia, 3; Zarfati, Italia, 12; Zarfati, Leo, 7; Zarfati, Leone*; Zarfati, Leone, 68; Zarfati, Leone, 26; Zarfati, Marco, 10; Zarfati, Rosita, 8; Zarfati, Settimio, 18; Zarfati, Vitale, 51; Zarfati, Zaira, 40.

* Age unknown.

APPENDIX II

The fifteen who came back[1]

Amati, Michele (b. 1926)	peddler, Rome
Anticoli, Lazzaro (b. 1910)	handyman, Rome
Camerino, Enzo (b. 1928)	Montreal
Camerino, Luciano (b. 1926) (d. 1966)*	
Di Segni, Cesare (b. 1899)	shopkeeper, Rome
Di Segni Lello (b. 1926)	shopkeeper, Rome
Efrati, Angelo (b. 1924)	peddler, Rome
Efrati, Cesare (b. 1927)	window washer, Rome
Finzi, Sabatino (b. 1927)	scrap metal dealer, Rome
Piperno, Mario (b. 1916)	shipping agent, Rome
Sabatello, Leone (b. 1927)	dealer in secondhand goods, Rome
Sermoneta, Angelo (b. 1913)	Rome
Sermoneta, Isacco (b. 1912)	traveling salesman, Rome
Spizzichino, Settimia (b. 1921)	postal employee, IBM operator, Rome
Wachsberger, Arminio (b. 1913)	chemical executive, Milan

* For the circumstances regarding Camerino's death, see page 307.

NOTES

(All translations of material taken directly from foreign language sources are by the author.)

Abbreviations used

Almansi report	D. Almansi, "Prima relazione al governo italiano circa le persecuzioni nazi-fasciste degli ebrei in Roma (settembre 1943-giugno 1944)," Aug. 15, 1944 (CDEC doc. Title C)
CDEC	Archives of the Centro di documentazione ebraica contemporanea, Milan, Italy
CRDE	Bound file of names and other data on the Jews of Italy deported 1943-1944; compiled by the Comitato ricerche deportati ebrei, the archives of which are deposited in CDEC
De Felice collection	A group of 37 documents published in R. De Felice, *Storia degli ebrei italiani sotto il fascismo,* Turin, 1961
Dosi collection	Documents of the Via tasso Gestapo headquarters captured and retained by G. Dosi (see p. 303)
Foà report-I	U. Foà, "Relazione del presidente della comunità israelitica di Roma Foà Ugo circa le misure razziali adottate in Roma dopo 18 settembre (data dell'armistizio Badoglio) a diretta opera delle autorità tedesche di occupazione,"

	Nov. 15, 1943, and June 20, 1944 (CDEC doc. Title C)
Foà report-II	U. Foà, "Appunti circa il salvataggio dalla rapina tedesca degli arredi sacri della comunità israelitica di Roma," Nov. 27, 1950 (CDEC doc. Title C)
Gestapo report	Telegraphed report signed by Kappler but probably written by Dannecker, Oct. 17, 1943, in Records of the Reichsführer SS (Himmler) in NA, Microcopy T-175, Roll 53, Frames 2567133-2567134
Inland II AB (Juden in Italien)	Documents of the German Foreign Ministry, 1920-1945, in NA, Microcopy T-120, Roll 4668 (miscatalogued as Roll 4662)
Inland II Geheim	Documents of the German Foreign Ministry, 1920-1945, in NA, Microcopy T-120, Roll 4353
IAD	Interview with Angelo De Fiore, a high Rome police official during the occupation, Rome, Jan. 13, 1968
IAK	Interview with Albrecht von Kessel, Bad Godesberg, June 9, 1967
IAW	Interview with Arminio Wachsberger, Milan, July 12, 1967
ICE	Interview with Cesare Efrati, Rome, Dec. 3, 1967
IEM	Interview with Eitel F. Möllhausen, Milan, June 13, 1967
IES	Interview with Elena Sonnino Finzi, Rome, Sept. 13, 1967
IET	Interview with Elio Toaff, present chief rabbi of Rome, Rome, Dec. 12, 1967
IGD	Interview with Giuseppe Dosi, Rome, Sept. 19, 1967
IGG	Interview with Gerhard Gumpert, Bologna, Jan. 16, 1968

IGT	Interview with Gianfranco Tedeschi, Rome, July 24, 1967
IHS	Interview with Hermine Speier, Rome, July 14, 1967
IIMA	Interviews with Michele Amati, Rome, Nov. 24 and 27, 1967
IISF	Interviews with Sabatino Finzi, Rome, Dec. 5 and 7, 1967
IISS	Interviews with Settimia Spizzichino, Rome, Dec. 28, 1967, and Jan. 10, 1968
ILA	Interview with Lazzaro Anticoli, Rome, Dec. 8, 1967
ILM	Interview with Luciano Morpurgo, Rome, May 16, 1967
ILP	Interview with Lello Perugia, Rome, Sept. 12, 1967
ILS	Interview with Leone Sabatello, Rome, Dec. 6, 1967
IMN	Interview with Maurice Neufeld, New York, April 7, 1967
IPF	Interview with Piero Foà, son of Ugo Foà, Rome, July 28, 1967
IQZ	Interview with Quirino Zazza, Rome, Nov. 28, 1967
IRL	Interview with Renzo Levi, Rome, July 10, 1967
ISS	Interview with Settimio Sorani, Florence, Sept. 1, 1967
JCR report	Undated and unsigned report of an official of the Jewish Community of Rome (CDEC doc. Title C-VI)
Kappler sentence	Final judgment handed down in THK, Jan. 10, 1954, by the Military Tribunal of Rome after several appeals (Doc. no. 600 3/45)
Karvat statement	Statement by David Karvat to Michael Tagliacozzo, Jan. 1946 (see fn. p. 275)

KT	Transcript of sworn testimony of Herbert Kappler in TAE, taken at the military prison at Gaeta, June 27, 1961
NA	National Archives, Washington, D.C.
Neufeld papers	Letters and other documentary material held by Maurice Neufeld (deposited also in the Library of Congress)
NGNI	Documents of the Nuremberg trials.
Sorani diary	R. Sorani, "Appunti personali di Rosina Sorani del periodo di occupazione tedesca in Roma" (YIVO document)
Sorani report	Report by Settimio Sorani on the activities of the DELASEM organization in Rome during the German occupation, May 16, 1944 (YIVO document)
Stahel war diary	Kriegstagebuch Deutsche Kommandant in Rome (Gen. Stahel), in NA, Microcopy T-501, Roll 331
Survivors depositions	Sworn depositions made between June and Oct. 1945 by the following survivors: Amati, Anticoli, C. Di Segni, L. Di Segni, A. Efrati, Finzi, Sabatello, A. Sermoneta, I. Sermoneta (CDEC docs. Title E-II)
Survivors recording	An interview recorded on discs with the following survivors: Anticoli, L. Camerino, C. Di Segni, L. Di Segni, Piperno, A. Sermoneta (CDEC doc.)
TAE	Trial of Adolf Eichmann
TEW	Trial of Ernst von Weizsäcker (Case no. 11, Nuremberg Trials of War Criminals)
THK	Trial of Herbert Kappler
Wachsberger report	Report prepared for author by Arminio Wachsberger, Oct. 8, 1967, and Jan. 1, 1968
Wachsberger statement	A. Wachsberger, "Les deportations des juifs italiens," Dec. 25, 1955 (CDEC doc. Title E-II)
YIVO	Archives of the YIVO Institute for Jewish Research, New York, N.Y.

Foreword

1. See R. Katz, *Death in Rome,* New York, 1967.
2. See H. Arendt, "The Formidable Dr. Robinson" in *The New York Review of Books,* Jan. 20, 1966, pp. 26-30.
3. A. L. Kubovy, "Criminal State vs. Moral Society" in *Yad Vashem Bulletin,* Jerusalem, Oct. 1963, p. 5.
4. H. Arendt, *Eichmann in Jerusalem,* New York, 1965 (rev. ed.), p. 117.
5. R. Hilberg, *The Destruction of the European Jews,* Chicago, 1967 (rev. ed.), p. v. (This edition carries the same pagination as the first, which was published in 1961)
6. *Sorani diary*; the expurgated version was published by the Jewish Community of Rome in a booklet entitled *Ottobre 1943 Cronaca di un'infamia,* Rome, 1961.
7. M. Mushkat, "Eichmann in New York" in *Yad Vashem Bulletin,* Jerusalem, Mar. 1964, pp. 4-5.
8. A. Eichmann, "Eichmann Tells His Own Damning Story" in *Life,* New York, Dec. 5, 1960, p. 146; cf. Hilberg, *op. cit.*, pp. 543-544.

Part One: The Gold of Rome

1. *Ketubot, iiia*; quoted in L. I. Newman, *A "Chief Rabbi" of Rome Becomes a Catholic,* New York, 1945, p. 23.

I

1. L. Morpurgo, *Caccia all'uomo,* Rome, 1946, p. 13.
2. The literature on these dramatic days is vast and still growing. See especially A. Garland and H. M. Smyth, *Sicily and the Surrender of Italy,* Washington, 1965; R. Zangrandi, *1943: 25 luglio-8 settembre,* Milan, 1964.
3. Quoted in J. Scrivener (pseud.), *Inside Rome with the Germans,* New York, 1945, pp. 8-9.
4. *Ibid.*, p. 9; cf. C. Trabucco, *La prigionia di Roma,* Rome, 1945, pp. 11-13.
5. *Ibid.*
6. Quoted in *ibid.*, p. 10.
7. Text of speech in F. Watts and N. Ausubel (eds.), *Voices of His-*

tory, New York, 1944, p. 343; see also L. Lochner (ed.), *The Goebbels Diaries,* Garden City, 1948, paperback ed., New York, nd., p. 508.

II

1. G. Debenedetti, "16 ottobre 1943" in *Mercurio,* Rome, Dec. 1944, pp. 76-77; cf. R. De Felice, *Storia degli ebrei italiani sotto il fascismo,* Turin, 1961, p. 523; *Foà report-I/A.*
2. *Ibid.*
3. *Ibid.*, p. 82.
4. Josephus, *Jewish War*; quoted in F. Gregorovius, *The Ghetto and the Jews of Rome* (M. Hada, trans.), New York, 1948, paperback ed., 1966, pp. 21-22. Gregorovius's essay was written in 1853 and remains one of the best on the Roman ghetto.
5. For a history of the ghetto see *ibid.*, H. Vogelstein, *Rome,* Philadelphia, 1940, and A. Milano, *Il ghetto di Roma,* Rome, 1964.
6. For a demographic survey of Italian Jewry during this period see De Felice, *op. cit.,* pp. 5-20; also *De Felice collection,* doc. 24.
7. See Gregorovius, *op. cit.*, pp. 85-105.
8. S. P. Dunn, "The Roman Jewish Community: a Study in Historical Causation" in *The Jewish Journal of Sociology,* London, Nov. 1960, pp. 185-201. During the 1950s, Dunn, a sociologist, and his father, L. C. Dunn, a geneticist, made a series of studies of the Jews of Rome, probably the only one of its kind. See also L. C. and S. P. Dunn, "The Jewish Community of Rome" in *Scientific American,* New York, March, 1957; S. P. Dunn, "An Outsider Visits the Roman Ghetto" in *Commentary,* New York, Feb. 1958, and the younger Dunn's doctoral dissertation, *The Influence of Ideology on Culture Change.*
9. *Ibid.*
10. *IET*; see also "Norme sulle communità israelitiche e sulla unione delle comunità medesime" Royal Decree no. 1731 of Oct. 30, 1930, in *De Felice collection*, doc. 2.
11. Cf. R. Segre, *Appunti sulle persecuzioni antisemitiche e sulla vita delle comunità israelitiche nell'Italia occupata,* Rome, 1964, p. 8; also A. Milano, *Storia degli ebrei in Italia,* Turin, 1963, p. 474, and De Felice, *op. cit.*, pp. 120-124.

III

1. Milano, *Storia . . . , op. cit.*, p. 394; for the text of the law see *De Felice collection*, doc. 2.
2. E. Zolli, *Before the Dawn,* New York, 1954, pp. 140-152; cf. *Foà report-I/A* and *Neufeld papers.*

3. *IRL* and *ISS*; cf. *Foà report-I.*
4. Zolli, *op. cit.*, p. 148.
5. Milano, *Storia . . . , op. cit.*, pp. 331 and 386.
6. *IPF.* Sources for biographical material on Foà include *IPF, Neufeld papers,* Newman, *op. cit.*
7. *Gli Israeliti Italiani nella guerra, 1915-18,* Turin, 1921, p. 221.
8. *IPF.*
9. *IRL, ISS, IET.*
10. *IPF, IRL, ISS.*
11. *Ibid.*
12. Zolli, *op. cit.*, p. 142.
13. *Ibid.*, p. 148.
14. *Ibid.*, pp. 149-150.
15. *Ibid.*; cf. *Neufeld papers.*
16. See *De Felice collection,* doc. 2.

IV

1. Zolli, *op. cit.*, p. 145-146.
2. *Ibid.*, p. 5.
3. G. Bertel, "The Case of Rabbi Zolli" in *The Congress Weekly,* New York, Mar. 2, 1945, pp. 11-12; see also A.S.E. Yahuda, "The Conversion of a 'Chief Rabbi' " in *The Churchman,* New York, Jan. 1, 1945, pp. 7-9, and *Neufeld papers.*
4. *IET.*
5. Zolli, *op. cit.*, p. 63.
6. *Ibid.*, pp. 119-120.
7. Bertel, *op. cit.*
8. *Ibid.*
9. Zolli, *op. cit.*, p. 72.
10. *Ibid.*, pp. 139-140.

V

1. E. Weizsäcker, *Memoirs,* Chicago, 1951, pp. 271-285.
2. Telegram from Weizsäcker to Berlin, July 5, 1943; text in S. Friedländer, *Pius XII and the Third Reich,* New York, 1966, pp. 179-180.
3. G. Reitlinger, *The Final Solution,* New York, 1953, paperback ed., 1961, p. 96.
4. Memorandum from Hans Luther to Ribbentrop, Oct. 6, 1942, submitted by Weizsäcker, NG-5086.
5. E. F. Möllhausen, *La carta perdente,* Rome, 1948, p. 56.
6. *IAK*; cf. A. Kessel's article in *Die Welt,* Hamburg, Apr. 6, 1963, later published as "The Pope and the Jews" in *The Storm Over*

the Deputy, New York, 1964, pp. 71-76. See also Kessel's testimony of June 21, 1948, in TEW, transcript, p. 9518.

7. *Ibid.*
8. *Ibid.*
9. *Ibid.;* cf. Kessel, *op. cit.,* pp. 73-74, and Kessel's testimony of June 22, 1948, in TEW, transcript, p. 9567.
10. Kessel, *op. cit.*, p. 74.

VI

1. Letter from Pius XII to Bishop Preysing, Apr. 30, 1943, in *Letters of Pius XII to the German Bishops,* Vatican City, 1966; quoted in *The New York Times,* Mar. 7, 1966, p. 12.
2. *Ibid.*; quoted in *ibid.*, Mar. 5, 1966, p. 1.
3. See documents in Friedländer, *op. cit.*, pp. 103-147.
4. G. B. Montini (Pope Paul VI), "Pius XII and the Jews" in *The Tablet,* London, June, 1963.
5. Telegram from Tittmann to Washington, Jan. 5, 1943; text in *Foreign Relations of the United States, 1943, Volume II, Europe,* Washington, U.S. Government Printing Office, 1964, pp. 911-912; see also Friedländer, *op. cit.*, 134-135.
6. Telegram from Weizsäcker to Ribbentrop quoting Cardinal Secretary of State Maglione, Sept. 23, 1943; text in Friedländer, *op. cit.*, p. 190.
7. Telegram from Weizsäcker to Berlin, Sept. 24, 1943; text in *ibid.*, p. 193.
8. Letter from Bishop Radonski to Pius XII, Feb. 15, 1943, in *The Holy See and the Religious Situation in Poland and in the Baltic Countries, 1939-45,* Vatican City, 1967; quoted in Associated Press dispatch of May 31, 1967.
9. R. Leiber, "Pio XII e gli ebrei di Roma, 1943-1944" in *La civiltà cattolica,* Rome, Mar. 4, 1961, pp. 451-453.
10. A. Giovannetti, *Roma città aperta,* Milano, 1962, p. 179.
11. Weizsäcker, *op. cit.,* pp. 289-290; see also affidavit of Bishop Hudal, Jan. 30, 1948, in TEW, *Weizsäcker Document Book 3,* doc. 103.
12. Keesing's Contemporary Archives, Vol. V, London, 1943-1946, p. 6166.

VII

1. De Felice, *op. cit.,* pp. 483 and 540; see also P. Lapide, *Three Popes and the Jews,* New York, 1967, pp. 136-137.
2. *IRL.*
3. *ISS.*
4. *Ibid.*

5. *Ibid.*
6. *Ibid.*; see also *Sorani report.*
7. *Sorani report.*
8. *Ibid., ISS.*
9. *ISS, IRL.*
10. *Foà report-I/A* and introductory section.
11. *IRL, ISS.*
12. *IRL.*

VIII

1. The sources for Wachsberger's role are *IAW, Wachsberger statement,* and *Wachsberger report.*
2. "Provvedimenti per la difesa della razza Italiana" Royal Decree no. 1728 of Nov. 17, 1938; text in *De Felice collection,* doc. 21.
3. *Wachsberger report.*

IX

1. Zolli, *op. cit.,* p. 151.
2. See Trabucco, *op. cit.,* pp. 16-22.
3. F. W. Deakin, *The Six Hundred Days of Mussolini,* New York, 1966, p. 40. (This is a rev. ed. of Part III of *The Brutal Friendship,* New York, 1962.)
4. De Felice, *op. cit.,* pp. 510-512; see also *De Felice collection,* doc. 33.
5. Zolli, *op. cit.,* p. 162.
6. *Ibid.,* p. 151.
7. *Ibid.,* pp. 141-142.
8. Sources for biographical material on Almansi include De Felice, *op. cit.,* and *Neufeld papers.*
9. G. Leto, *OVRA: Fascismo-antifascismo,* Bologna, 1951, p. 16.
10. *Neufeld papers.*
11. *Ibid., ISS.*
12. De Felice, *op. cit.,* pp. 478-481; cf. *Neufeld papers.*
13. *ISS.*
14. *Ibid.*
15. *Ibid.*; see also Milano, *Storia . . . op. cit.,* p. 401.
16. *Neufeld papers.*
17. Zolli, *op. cit.,* p. 151.
18. *Ibid.*
19. *Ibid.,* p. 152.
20. *Ibid.,* p. 153.
21. *Ibid.,* p. 154; cf. *Neufeld papers.* See also letter from Roberto Modigliani to Zolli, July 25, 1944, in *ibid.* p. 204. Zolli's advocacy of the destruction of the lists was later disputed by Foà, at least

by implication, in his denial that Zolli had suggested measures to protect the city's Jews (text in *ibid.*, p. 203). Checking the authenticity of Zolli's supporting evidence, *i.e.*, the letter from Modigliani, the author contacted Modigliani, now justice of the Civil and Penal Tribunal of Rome. In a letter to the author dated Oct. 23, 1967, Modigliani recalled meeting with the rabbi "some days" after the Germans occupied Rome. On that occasion, he believes, Zolli "expressed his intention to close the offices of the Jewish Community and destroy the lists of the members." Modigliani does not remember writing the letter in which he confirmed Zolli's version of the events, but, he wrote, "I am disposed to believe that it is a document written by me."

22. *De Felice collection*, doc. 2.
23. Zolli, *op. cit.*, p. 155.
24. *IET*; see also Debenedetti, *op. cit.*
25. *Il Giornale d'Italia*, Sept. 26, 1943, p. 1.
26. *ISS.*
27. Zolli, *op. cit.*, pp. 156-159.
28. See above, p. 300; also *JCR report.*

X

1. *IAK*, Kessel, *op. cit.*, p. 74.
2. *IHS.*
3. Kessel, *op. cit.*, p. 74.
4. *IAK.*
5. Kessel, *op. cit.*, p. 74.
6. *IAK.*
7. Kessel, *op. cit.*, p. 75.
8. *IHS.*
9. *Ibid.*; see also Kessel's testimony of June 22, 1948, in TEW, transcript, p. 9567.
10. P. Levi Cavaglione, *Guerriglia nei Castelli Romani*, Rome, 1945, p. 15.
11. *Ibid.*, p. 14.
12. E. Pisciatelli, *Storia della Resistenza romana,* Bari, 1965, pp. 62-65.
13. Levi Cavaglione, *op. cit.*, p. 15.
14. *Ibid.*

XI

1. KT.
2. Deakin, *op. cit.*, p. 25; see also Kappler's testimony of May 31, 1948, in THK.
3. KT.
4. M. Tagliacozzo, "La comunità di Roma sotto l'incubo della svas-

tica" in *Quaderni del Centro di documentazione ebraica contemporanea,* Milan, Nov. 1963, p. 9.
5. KT.
6. Kappler's testimony of June 1, 1948, in THK.
7. KT.
8. Sources for biographical material on Kappler include KT, THK (especially his testimony of May 31, 1948), Möllhausen, *op. cit.,* and S. Bertoldi, *I tedeschi in Italia,* Milan, 1964.
9. Kappler's testimony of May 31, 1948, in THK.
10. *Ibid.*
11. G. Stendardo, *Via Tasso,* Rome, 1965, pp. 7-116.
12. Möllhausen, *op. cit.,* p. 113.
13. Kappler's testimony of May 31, 1948, in THK.
14. *Ibid.*
15. KT.

XII

1. Deakin, *op. cit.,* pp. 43-49.
2. Cf. De Felice, *op. cit.,* p. 523, and *American Jewish Yearbook, 1939,* Philadelphia, 1940, p. 370; see also below, Chapter XVI.
3. D. Almansi, "La progettata espulsione" in *Israel,* Rome, Oct. 18, 1945, p. 3.
4. Quoted in De Felice, *op. cit.,* pp. 297-298.
5. *Ibid.,* p. 503; see also pp. 407-408 and *Neufeld papers.*
6. *ISS, Neufeld papers.*
7. *Neufeld papers.*
8. Quoted in Deakin, *op. cit.,* p. 104.
9. Mussolini's speech of Sept. 18, 1943; text in A. Tamaro, *Due anni di storia, 1943-1945,* 3 vols., Rome, 1948-1950, I, 590-593.

XIII

1. Möllhausen, *op. cit.,* p. 111.
2. KT.
3. Möllhausen, *op. cit.,* p. 111.
4. Tagliacozzo, *op. cit.,* p. 10.
5. Mölhausen, *op. cit.,* pp. 124-132.
6. *Ibid.,* pp. 128-130; see also P. Duclos, *Le Vatican et la seconde guerre mondiale,* Paris, 1955, p. 190.
7. *Osservatore della Domenica,* Vatican City, June 28, 1964, pp. 61 and 76; see also Duclos, *op. cit.,* p. 190.
8. Möllhausen, *op. cit.,* p. 131.
9. *Ibid.,* p. 130.
10. *Ibid.,* p. 108.
11. *Ibid.,* p. 112.

12. *Ibid., IEM.*
13. *IEM.*
14. *Ibid.*; cf. Möllhausen, *op. cit.*, p. 113.
15. *Ibid.*
16. *Ibid.* The sources for biographical material on Möllhausen include *IEM*, Möllhausen, *op. cit.*, and Bertoldi, *op. cit.*
17. *IEM.*
18. Bertoldi, *op. cit.*, p. 222.
19. Möllhausen, *op. cit.*, pp. 108-111.
20. *Ibid.*
21. *Ibid.*

XIV

1. *Ibid.*, pp. 113-114, *IEM.*
2. *Ibid.*, p. 114.
3. KT.
4. Möllhausen, *op. cit.*, p. 114.
5. *IEM*; cf. Möllhausen, *op. cit.*, p. 114.
6. *IEM*; cf. KT.
7. *Ibid.*; cf. Möllhausen, *op. cit.*, pp. 114-115.
8. *Ibid.*; cf. Möllhausen, *op. cit.*, p. 115.
9. Hilberg, *op. cit.*, p. 412.
10. *Ibid.*
11. Möllhausen, *op. cit.*, p. 115, *IEM.*
12. *IEM.*
13. Möllhausen, *op. cit.*, p. 115.
14. A. Kesselring, *A Soldier's Record*, New York, 1954; see also Möllhausen, *op. cit.*, p. 197.
15. *Ibid.*, p. 226.
16. *IEM*; cf. Möllhausen, *op. cit.*, p. 115.
17. *Ibid.*
18. Möllhausen, *op. cit.*, p. 115.
19. *Ibid.*, p. 116.
20. *Ibid., IEM.*

XV

1. KT; see also Tagliacozzo, *op. cit.*, p. 19.
2. *Ibid.*
3. Letter from Kappler to Kaltenbrunner; quoted in *Kappler sentence.*
4. *ISS.*
5. KT.
6. *Kappler sentence.*
7. *Foà report-I/A*; cf. *Almansi report.*

8. *Ibid.*
9. *Ibid.*
10. *Ibid.*; cf. *Almansi report.*
11. Kappler's testimony of June 11, 1948, in THK; also quoted in *Kappler sentence.*
12. *Foà report- I/A*; cf. *Almansi report* and Foà's testimony of June 11, 1948, and Kappler's of June 1, in THK.
13. *Kappler sentence.*
14. *Foà report-I/A;* cf. *Almansi report.*
15. *Ibid.*; cf. *Almansi report.*
16. *Almansi report.*
17. *Foà report-I/A*; cf. *Almansi report* and Foà's testimony of June 11, 1948, and Kappler's of June 1, in THK.
18. *Foà report-I/A.*
19. *Ibid.*
20. *Ibid.*; cf. *Almansi report.*
21. *Ibid.*; cf. *Almansi report.*
22. *Ibid.*; cf. *Almansi report.*
23. *Ibid.*; cf. *Almansi report.*
24. *Ibid.*; cf. *Almansi report.*
25. *Ibid.*
26. *Ibid.*
27. *Almansi report.*
28. On the state of mind of the leaders see Debenedetti, *op. cit.* (see II), "Perchè non si difesero" (an interview with Roman Jewish leaders) in *L'Espresso,* Rome, Dec. 3, 1961, p. 12, De Felice, *op. cit.*, pp. 523-528.
29. Renzo Levi in *L'Espresso, ibid.*; cf. *Almansi report.*
30. *Sorani diary,* entry for Sept. 27, 1943.

XVI

1. *Exodus* 25; 1-3, 23-24, 31-39.
2. Quoted in E. A. Synan, *The Popes and the Jews in the Middle Ages,* New York, 1965, p. 189.
3. *Ibid.*, p. 145.
4. United Nations War Crimes Commission, *History of the UNWCC,* London, 1948, pp. 189-190.
5. *Ibid.*
6. *Israel,* Rome, Dec. 12, 1935, p. 5.
7. Newman, *op. cit.*, p. 29.
8. De Felice, *op. cit.*, p. 493; see also G. Seldes, *Facts and Fascism,* New York, 1943, p. 44.
9. *Ibid.* pp. 79-85.
10. Speech by Mussolini, Dec. 1930.
11. *Israel,* Rome, Oct. 27, 1932.

12. *Ibid.*, Dec. 12, 1935, p. 5.
13. *Ibid.*
14. *Ibid.*
15. *Ibid.*, May 7-14, 1936, p. 1.
16. *American Jewish Yearbook, 1939, op. cit.*, p. 370.
17. *Israel,* Rome, May 7-14, 1936, p. 1.
18. *Ibid.*
19. Quoted in F. Chabod, *L'Italia contemporanea (1918–1948), Turin,* 1961, p. 96.
20. Quoted in De Felice, *op cit.*, p. 105.
21. On the Rosselli brothers see A. Garosci, *La vita di Carlo Rosselli,* Rome, 1946, 2 vols., and C. Delzell, *Mussolini's Enemies: The Italian Anti-Fascist Resistance,* Princeton, 1961.
22. "Protocol No. 217," Feb. 1, 1939, of the Union of Italian Jewish Communities; CDEC doc. Title B-II-4.
23. De Felice, *op. cit.*, pp. 216-218.
24. A. Bullock, *Hitler,* New York, 1953, paperback rev. ed., 1961, p. 304.
25. See A. Spinosa, "Le persecuzioni razziali in Italia," a book-length article in *Il Ponte,* Florence, July, Aug., and Nov. 1952, and July, 1953, pp. 1604-1617 (1952).
26. P. Orano, *Gli ebrei in Italia,* Rome, 1937; quoted in De Felice, *op. cit.*, p. 249.
27. De Felice, *op. cit.*, pp. 257-264.
28. *Ibid.*
29. See Spinosa, *op. cit.*, pp. 1604-1617 (1952); cf. De Felice, *op. cit.*, p. 250.
30. "Intorno alla questione del sionismo" in *La civiltà cattolica,* Rome, Mar. 27, 1938.
31. "La questione giudaica e il sionismo," in *ibid.*, June 19, 1937.
32. De Felice, *op. cit.*, p. 251.
33. Quoted in *ibid.*, p. 290.
34. *Ibid.*, pp. 260-270.
35. *Ibid.*
36. Text in A. Levi, *Noi ebrei,* Rome, 1937, pp. 46-48.
37. Text in *ibid.*, pp. 62-63.
38. Text of racial laws in *De Felice collection,* doc. 21.
39. Minutes of meeting of Nov. 15, 1938; CDEC doc. Title B-II-4.
40. Resolution of the Council, Oct. 12, 1938; quoted in De Felice, *op. cit.*, p. 38.
41. *Israel,* Rome, Aug. 11-18, 1938.
42. De Felice, *op. cit.*, pp. 382-383.
43. D. Prato, *Dal pergamo della comunità di Roma,* Rome, 1950, pp. xxiv-xxv.
44. "Protocol No. 217," Feb. 1, 1939, of the Union of Italian Jewish Communities; CDEC doc. Title B-II-4.

45. See De Felice, *op. cit.*, pp. 478-485.
46. *Ibid.*
47. *Ibid.*
48. *Ibid.*
49. E. Wiskemann, *The Rome-Berlin Axis,* rev. ed., London, 1966, pp. 331, and 342.
50. L. Poliakov, *La condition des juifs en France sous l'occupation Italienne,* Paris, 1946, pp. 42-43; see also De Felice, *op. cit.*, pp. 466-467.
51. Hilberg, *op. cit.*, p. 425.
52. G. Ciano, *Ciano's Hidden Diary, 1937-1938,* New York, 1952, p. 199.
53. L. Sturzo, *Church and State,* London, 1939, p. 524.

XVII

1. *IRL.*
2. Scrivener, *op. cit.*, p. 30.
3. *Sorani diary,* entry for Sept. 27, 1943.
4. *IRL*; see also Levi in *L'Espresso, op. cit.*, p. 12.
5. *Ibid.*; see also Debenedetti, *op. cit.*, pp. 78 and 83.
6. *Ibid.*
7. Debenedetti, *op. cit.*, p. 79; see also declaration of Miriam Zolli in Zolli, *op. cit.*, p. 208.
8. *IRL*; see also Levi in *L'Espresso, op. cit.*, p. 12.
9. See F. Ripa di Meana, *Roma clandestina,* Rome, 1944, p. 89; also G. Vento, "18 anni dopo (inchiesta sul 16 ottobre 1943)" in C. Lizzani, *L'Oro di Roma,* Bologna, 1961, pp. 161-180.
10. *Sorani diary,* entry for Sept. 27-28, 1943.
11. *IRL;* cf. Levi in *L'Espresso, op. cit.*, p. 12.
12. *Ibid.*
13. Debenedetti, *op. cit.*, p. 79; cf. *Foà report-I/A.*
14. *IRL.*
15. Debenedetti, *op. cit.*, p. 79.
16. *Foà report-I/A.*
17. Debenedetti, *op. cit.*, p. 79.
18. Vento, *op. cit.*, p. 173.
19. *IRL.*
20. Vento, *op. cit.*, pp. 161-162.
21. *Ibid.*, pp. 169 and 173.
22. *IIMA.*
23. Vento, *op. cit.*, p. 173.
24. *ILP.*
25. *Ibid.*
26. *ICE.*
27. *IES.*
28. Letter from Elena Sonnino Finzi to Zolli, July 2, 1944, in Zolli,

op. cit., p. 209. In *IES* Sonnino Finzi only vaguely recalled writing this letter, but said that "very likely" she had done so and that it corresponded to the facts stated therein.

29. Vento, *op. cit.*, pp. 170-171.
30. *IRL;* cf. Levi in *L'Espresso, op. cit.,* p. 12.
31. *Ibid.*
32. *Ibid.*
33. *Ibid.*; see also Giovannetti, *op. cit.*, p. 171.
34. Levi in *L'Espresso, op. cit.*, p. 12.
35. *IRL.*
36. *Foà report-I/A.*
37. Ripa di Meana, *op. cit.*, p. 90; see also Vento, *op. cit.*, p. 175.

XIX

1. Zolli, *op. cit.*, p. 160.
2. Katz, *op. cit.*, p. 140; see also *L'Unità*, Rome, July 28, 1967.
3. See Friedländer, *op. cit.*, pp. 199-204.
4. Zolli, *op. cit.*, p. 160.
5. *Ibid.*
6. *Ibid.*; see also letter from Giorgio Fiorentino to Zolli in *ibid.*, pp. 206-207.
7. Letter from Foà to Zolli, July 4, 1944, in *ibid.*, p. 203.
8. Resolution of the Board of the Jewish Community of Rome, April 2, 1944, in *ibid.*, pp. 201-202.
9. *Ibid.*
10. *Ibid.*
11. Declaration of Miriam Zolli in *ibid.*, p. 208.
12. Morpurgo, *op. cit.*, p. 97.
13. Debenedetti, *op. cit.*, p. 79.
14. *Ibid.*
15. De Felice appears to have been the first to learn that additional offerings were taken (see De Felice, *op. cit.*, p. 527). This was confirmed in *IET*. So secret was this tactic, not even Rosina Sorani appears to have known about it. (See *Sorani diary*, entry for Sept. 28, 1943.)
16. Debenedetti, *op. cit.*, pp. 79-80.
17. *Ibid.*
18. *Foà report-I/A.*
19. *Ibid.*
20. Morpurgo, *op. cit.*, p. 97.
21. "Prospetto riassuntivo delle sovvenzioni elargite dal governo fascista ai giornalisti, scrittori ed artisti nel decennio 1933-1943, prelevati dai fondi segreti del Ministero della Cultura Populare" in NA, Microcopy T-586, Roll 425, Frame 012634. (Captured documents of the Fascist government.)

22. L. Morpurgo, *Roma mussolinea,* Rome, 1932, p. vi.
23. Morpurgo, *Caccia . . . op. cit.*, pp. 47-49.
24. *Ibid.*, p. 97.
25. *Ibid.*, pp. 97-98.
26. *Ibid.*, p. 98.
27. *IET*; cf. De Felice, *op. cit.*, p. 527.
28. *Ibid.*; see also above, p. 313.
29. Debenedetti, *op. cit.*, p. 79.
30. *IRL*; for the amount of cash see *Foà report-I/B,* and *Sorani diary,* entry for Sept. 28, 1943.
31. Debenedetti, *op. cit.*, p. 79.

XX

1. *Foà report-I/A.*
2. *Ibid.*
3. *IRL.*
4. Debenedetti, *op. cit.*, p. 80.
5. *IET.*
6. *Foà report-I/A, Almansi report;* cf. Foà's testimony of June 11, 1948, in THK, *Kappler sentence,* and Debenedetti, *op. cit.*, p. 80.
7. *Ibid.*
8. *Ibid.*
9. *IRL.*
10. Debenedetti, *op. cit.*, p. 80.
11. *Foà report-I/A.*
12. Kappler's testimony of June 1, 1948, in THK.
13. Debenedetti, *op. cit.*, p. 80.

XXI

1. Levi Cavaglione, *op. cit.*, pp. 16-17.
2. *Ibid.*, p. 16.
3. *Ibid.*, p. 17.
4. *Ibid.*

XXII

1. See Ripa di Meana, *op. cit.*, p. 90, A. Troisio, *Roma sotto il terrore nazi-fascista,* Rome, 1944, p. 173, and Scrivener, *op. cit.*, p. 31.
2. See Vento, *op. cit.*, p. 175. For another view of the legend see O. Halecki, *Pius XII . . . Pope of Peace,* New York, 1951. Halecki, who was blessed by Pius XII for having written his book, says that the Pope made the gold available to the Jews of Rome "probably by melting down religious vessels" (p. 192).

3. Scrivener, *op. cit.*, p. 31.
4. M. de Wyss, *Rome Under the Terror,* London, 1945, pp. 139-140.
5. Möllhausen, *op. cit.*, p. 117.
6. *IAK.*
7. Möllhausen, *op. cit.*, p. 117.
8. *IEM.*
9. KT.

XXIII

1. *Kappler sentence.*
2. KT.
3. Letter from Kappler to Kaltenbrunner; quoted in *Kappler sentence.*
4. KT.
5. For biographical material on Kaltenbrunner see especially E. Davidson, *The Trial of the Germans,* New York, 1966, pp. 315-328.
6. *Kappler sentence.*

Part Two: The Books of Rome

1. Debenedetti, *op. cit.*, p. 77.

I

1. *Foà report-I/B.*
2. *Ibid.*; cf. *Almansi report* and Debenedetti, *op. cit.*, p. 81.
3. Tagliacozzo, *op. cit.,* p. 15.
4. *Foà report-I/B.*
5. *Ibid.*
6. *Sorani diary,* entry for Sept. 29, 1943.
7. *American Jewish Yearbook,* Philadelphia, 1944, vol. 46, p. 234.
8. *Foà report-I/B.*
9. *JCR report.*
10. *Foà report-I/B.*
11. *JCR report.*
12. *Ibid.*; see also *Foà report-II, Sorani diary,* and Tagliacozzo, *op. cit.*, p. 18.
13. *Foà report-I/B.*
14. Among the eyewitnesses were Regina Wachsberger (see *Wachsberger report* and *Wachsberger statement*) and Luciano Morpurgo (see Morpurgo, *Caccia . . . op. cit.*, p. 104.); see also Zolli, *op. cit.,* pp. 154-156, Debenedetti, *op. cit.,* p. 81, and especially above, pp. 301-303.

15. *Foà report-I/B and E.*
16. *Sorani diary,* entry for Sept. 29, 1943 (deleted from the version published by the community).
17. *Ibid.*

II

1. *Wachsberger report*; cf. *Wachsberger statement.*
2. *Ibid.*
3. *Ibid.*
4. R. P. Capano, *La Resistenza in Roma,* Naples, 1963, 2 vols., I, 448-462.
5. Ripa di Meana, *op. cit.*, p. 79.
6. Pisciatelli, *op. cit.*, pp. 150-151.
7. See, for example, Scrivener, *op. cit.*, p. 35.
8. *Ibid.*, p. 26.
9. *Wachsberger statement, Wachsberger report.*
10. *Ibid.*
11. *Wachsberger report.*

III

1. Eichmann, *op. cit.*, in *Life,* Nov. 28, 1960, p. 101.
2. *Ibid.*
3. *Ibid.*, in *Life,* Dec. 5, 1960, p. 146.
4. *Ibid.*; see also *ibid.*, Nov. 28, 1960, p. 106.
5. Quoted in Arendt, *op. cit.*, p. 114
6. Quoted in *ibid.*, p. 48.
7. Eichmann, *op. cit.*, in *Life,* Dec. 5, 1960, p. 152.
8. Arendt, *op. cit.*, pp. 49-50.
9. Quoted in *ibid.*
10. Memorandum from IV-B-4 to 16 SS officials, *et. al.*, Sept. 23, 1943; doc. NG-2652-H.
11. Quoted in Arendt, *op. cit.*, p. 49.
12. Minutes of the Wannsee Conference, Jan. 20, 1942; doc. NG-2586-G.
13. Hilberg, *op. cit.*, p. 425.
14. Memorandum from IV-B-4 to 16 SS officials, *et al.*, Sept. 23, 1943; doc. NG-2652-H.
15. Tagliacozzo, *op. cit.*, p. 9.
16. *Ibid.*, p. 19
17. For Dannecker's work in Paris, see Reitlinger, *op. cit.*, pp. 312-316, and Hilberg, *op. cit.*, pp. 402-408.
18. KT
19. Tagliacozzo, *op. cit.*, p. 19; see also KT and Kappler's testimony of June 1, 1948, in THK.

IV

1. *Sorani diary,* entry for Sept. 30, 1943.
2. Reitlinger, *op. cit.*, p. 289; see also Davidson, *op. cit.*, pp. 137-139.
3. Davidson, *op. cit.*, p. 138.
4. Quoted in *ibid.*
5. *Foà report-I/C, Sorani diary,* entry for Oct. 1, 1943.
6. *Ibid.*
7. *Foà report-I/C.*
8. *Ibid.*/D
9. *Ibid.*
10. *Ibid.*
11. *Ibid.*
12. *Sorani diary,* entry for Oct. 2, 1943.
13. See P. Secchia and F. Frascati, *Storia della Resistenza,* Rome, 1965, 2 vols., I, 229-238; for a bibliography on this episode, see also II, 1032.
14. Trabucco, *op. cit.*, p. 51.
15. See especially the memorandum of the Apostolic Delegation at Washington to the State Department, Aug. 20, 1943, in *Foreign Relations of the U.S., 1943, op. cit.*, pp. 945-946, and the letter from the Apostolic Deleg. at Wash. to the Secretary of State, Mar. 22, 1944, in *Foreign Relations of the U.S., 1944, Vol. IV, Europe,* Washington, 1966, pp. 1277-1278; also Katz, *op. cit.*, pp. 15-16.
16. Levi Cavaglione, *op. cit.*, p. 23; cf. L. D'Agostini and R. Forti, *Il sole e' sorto a Roma,* Rome, 1965, p. 134.
17. Scrivener, *op. cit.*, p. 35.
18. Telegram from Weizsäcker to Berlin, Oct. 14, 1943; text in Friedländer, *op. cit.*, p. 196 cf. Giovannetti, *op. cit.* p. 177.
19. Scrivener, *op. cit.*, p. 35.
20. *Ibid.*, p. 33.
21. Milano, *Storia . . . op cit.*, p. 402.
22. Debenedetti, *op. cit.*, p. 81; cf. *Foà report-I/C.*
23. *Sorani diary,* entry for Oct. 11, 1943.
24. *Ibid.*; cf. *Almansi report.*
25. *Ibid.*; cf. *Foà report-I/D.*
26. *Foà report-I/D, Almansi report.*
27. *Ibid.*
28. *Ibid.*
29. *JCR report*; see also *Foà report-II.*

V

1. KT.
2. *Ibid.*

3. Kappler's testimony of June 1, 1948, in THK.
4. *Ibid.*
5. KT.
6. Hilberg, *op. cit.*, p. 402.
7. Reitlinger, *op. cit.*, p. 317.
8. KT; cf. Kappler's testimony of June 1, 1948, in THK.
9. Kappler's testimony of June 1, 1948, in THK.
10. *Ibid.*, KT.
11. KT.
12. Reitlinger, *op. cit.*, p. 307.
13. Hilberg, *op. cit.*, pp. 483-484; cf. Arendt, *op. cit.*, pp. 186-188.
14. Reitlinger, *op. cit.*, p. 317; on Dannecker see also G. Wellers, *De Drancy à Auschwitz*, Paris, 1946.
15. Quoted in *ibid.*, p. 316.
16. Kappler's testimony of June 1, 1948, in THK, KT.
17. KT.
18. Tagliacozzo, *op. cit.*, p. 19.
19. *Ibid.*, p. 20; on Cappa see report of Rome police chief Morazzini, Aug. 11, 1944, in the transcript of the trial of Pietro Caruso (Sept. 1944) in Z. Algardi, ed., *Il Processo Caruso,* Rome, 1945.
20. *Ibid.*

VI

1. Levi Cavaglione, *op. cit.*, p. 19.
2. *Ibid.*, p. 18.
3. *Ibid.*, p. 19.
4. *Ibid.*, pp. 20-21.

VII

1. *IAK.*
2. *IEM.*
3. *IAK.*
4. *Ibid.*
5. See telegram from Möllhausen to Ribbentrop, Oct. 6, 1943, in *Inland II Geheim*, doc. E421525. This telegram has been published in various places and languages, including above, in my translation, p. 136.
6. *IAK.*
7. *Ibid.*
8. *IEM.*
9. Telegram from Möllhausen to Ribbentrop, Oct. 6, 1943, in *Inland II Geheim,* doc. E421525.
10. *IEM.*
11. *Ibid.*

12. Telegram from Möllhausen to Ribbentrop, Oct. 7, 1943, in *Inland II Geheim*, doc. E421524.
13. Möllhausen, *op. cit.*, p. 116.
14. *Ibid.*
15. *Ibid.*, p. 117.
16. *IEM.*
17. See letter from Rahn to Möllhausen, Oct. 19, 1943, in Möllhausen, *op. cit.*, p. 119.
18. *Ibid.*
20. Teletype to Büro RAM, Oct. 9, 1943, in *Inland II Geheim*, doc. E421522.
21. Telegram from Thadden to Möllhausen, Oct. 9, 1943, in *ibid.*, doc. E421521.
22. Telegram from Thadden to Möllhausen, Oct. 9, 1943, text in Tagliacozzo, *op. cit.*, pp. 16-17.
23. *IEM.*

VIII

1. Tagliacozzo, *op. cit.*, p. 17.
2. "Ordinanza N. 6," Oct. 2, 1943; reproduced in "Roma città aperta" a special issue of *Capitolium,* Rome, June, 1964, p. 330.
3. Tagliacozzo, *op. cit.*, p. 17.
4. *Keesing's Contemporary Archives, op. cit.*, V, 6023.
5. *Ibid.*
6. *Ibid.*
7. *Ibid.*
8. Tagliacozzo, *op. cit.*, pp. 17-18.
9. de Wyss, *op. cit.*, p. 144.
10. Cf. Tagliacozzo, *op. cit.*, p. 18; see also Morpurgo, *Caccia . . . op. cit.*, p. 104.
11. *IRL, ISS.*
12. Statements to author by many ghetto Jews, including *IIMA.*
13. *IPF, Sorani diary*, entry for Nov. 16, 1943.
14. *Sorani diary*, entry for Sept. 30, 1943, (deleted from the version published by the community).
15. Pisciatelli, *op. cit.*, p. 183.
16. For the role of the Carabinieri in the Roman Resistance see especially F. Caruso, *L'Arma dei Carabinieri in Roma durante L'occupazione tedesca*, Instituto Paligrafico dello Stato, Rome, 1949.
17. See Capano, *op. cit.*, vol. II, pp. 458-464.
18. Debenedetti, *op. cit.*, pp. 82-83.
19. *Ibid.*
20. *Ibid.*
21. *Ibid.*

22. *Almansi report.*
23. *Ibid.*
24. *Ibid.*
25. *Ibid.*
26. *Ibid.*
27. *Ibid.*
28. See *Sarani report,* De Felice, *op. cit.,* p. 542.
29. *Almansi report.*
30. *ISS.*

IX

1. *Sorani diary,* entry for Oct. 13, 1943.
2. *Foà report-I/D.*
3. See Deakin, *op. cit.,* pp. 101-105; also De Felice, *op. cit.,* pp. 502-522.
4. *Sorani diary,* entries for Oct. 13 and 14, 1943.
5. *JCR report.*
6. *Foà report-I/D.*
7. CDEC doc. Title C-VI-8.
8. *JCR report.*
9. *Foà report-II.*
10. *Foà report-I/D.*
11. *Sorani diary,* entry for Oct. 14, 1943.
12. *Foà report-I/D.*
13. *Ibid.*
14. Debenedetti, *op. cit.,* p. 82.
15. *Ibid.*
16. Trabucco, *op. cit.,* p. 77.

X

1. KT.
2. *IAD.*
3. See *Gestapo report* (full text printed above, pp. 222-223).
4. KT.
5. *Ibid.*
6. *Ibid.*
7. *Ibid.*
8. Text of instructions was published first in Debenedetti, *op. cit.,* p. 90. It appears also in *Sorani diary,* entry for Oct. 16, 1943, and below, in my translation, pp. 175-176.
9. See *Gestapo report.*
10. *Ibid.*
11. See *Stahel war diary,* frames 565-566.
12. KT.

13. *Stahel war diary,* frame 566.
14. *Ibid.*
15. *Ibid.*
16. *Ibid.*
17. Tagliacozzo, *op. cit.,* p. 21; see also *Gestapo report.*

XI

1. *JCR report.*
2. "Roma città aperta" in *Capitolium,* June 1964, *op. cit.,* p. 329.
3. Statements to author by several ghetto Jews, including *IIMA, IISS, ILS;* also *survivors recording /C. Di Segni.*
4. Debenedetti, *op cit.,* pp. 75-77.
5. *Ibid.,* p. 76.
6. *Ibid.*
7. *Ibid.*
8. *ILA.*
9. Levi Cavaglione, *op. cit.,* p. 23.
10. D'Agostini and Forti, *op. cit.,* p. 134.
11. Levi Cavaglione, *op. cit.,* pp. 20-23.
12. *Ibid.,* p. 23.
13. *Wachsberger report.*
14. Debenedetti, *op. cit.,* pp. 83-84; also *IISS, et al.,* and *survivors recording /L. Di Segni.*
15. *Ibid.,* p. 83.
16. *Ibid.,* p. 84.
17. *Ibid.*
18. The wall writing incident of the night of Oct. 15-16 is described in Scrivener, *op. cit.,* p. 38.

Part Three: The Jews of Rome

1. *JCR report.*

I

1. State Department memorandum by A. A. Berle, Oct. 16, 1943, in *Foreign Relations of the U.S., 1943, op. cit.,* p. 1021.
2. State Department memorandum by E. Stettinius, Oct. 16, 1943, in *ibid.,* p. 949.
3. *The New York Times,* Oct. 17, 1943, p. 44.

II

1. See Bertoldi, *op. cit.,* pp. 126-127.
2. *ILS.*

3. Debenedetti, *op. cit.*, p. 85.
4. *ILS.*
5. Debenedetti, *op. cit.*, p. 84.
6. *Gestapo report.*

III

1. *Sorani diary*, entry for Oct. 16, 1943.
2. *IAW.*
3. *Wachsberger report.*
4. *Ibid.*
5. Debenedetti, *op. cit.*, p. 86.
6. *IISS.*
7. *Ibid.*
8. *CRDE.*
9. *IISS.*
10. *Ibid.*

IV

1. Debenedetti, *op. cit.*, p. 87.
2. *Ibid.*
3. *IISS.*
4. *Ibid.*
5. *Ibid.*
6. *Ibid.*
7. *ILS.*
8. *Ibid.*
9. *Ibid.*
10. F. Odoardi, "Sabato 16 ottobre 1943" in Morpurgo, *Caccia . . . op. cit.*, pp. 106-108.
11. Quoted in Tagliacozzo, *op. cit.*, pp. 22-23.
12. Debenedetti, *op. cit.*, p. 88.
13. *ILA.*
14. Statement by Assunta Fratini in M. Alloisio, *et al.*, eds., *Mille volte no*!, Rome, 1965 (?), pp. 43-44.
15. *Wachsberger report, IAW.*

V

1. *Sorani diary*, entry for Oct. 16, 1943.
2. *Ibid.*
3. *Ibid.*
4. *IPF.*
5. *Foà report-I/E.*
6. *Ibid.*
7. *Sorani diary*, entry for Oct. 16, 1943.

8. *ISS.*
9. *Sorani diary,* entry for Oct. 16, 1943.
10. *Foà report-I/E.*
11. *Ibid./D.*
12. *Ibid*
13. *ILM.*
14. *Foà report-I/E.*
15. *ISS.*
16. Quoted in Zolli, *op. cit.,* p. 152.
17. *Foà report-I/E.*
18. *Wachsberger statement;* see also Morpurgo, *Caccia . . . op. cit.,* p. 141.
19. *IGT.*

VI

1. Quoted in Tagliacozzo, *op. cit.,* p. 24.
2. *ILP.*
3. *ICE.*
4. Quoted in Bertoldi, *op. cit.,* p. 127; see also *Foà report-I/E.*
5. Statement of Rev. Sbaffi in Tagliacozzo, *op. cit.,* pp. 23-24; see also *Foà report-I/E.*
6. Debenedetti, *op. cit.,* pp. 89-92.
7. Quoted in *Paese Sera,* Rome, Oct. 16, 1955.
8. Ripa di Meana, *op. cit.,* p. 88.
9. Debenedetti, *op. cit.,* p. 95.
10. *Ibid.,* p. 95.
11. Letter from Weizsäcker to Berlin, Oct. 28, 1943, in *Inland II Geheim,* doc. E421515.

VII

1. Möllhausen, *op. cit.,* p. 118.
2. *IEM.*
3. Möllhausen, *op. cit.,* p. 118.
4. *IGG.*
5. *Ibid.*
6. *Ibid.*
7. *Ibid.*
8. *Ibid.*
9. *Osservatore della Domenica,* Vatican City, June 28, 1964, p. 61.
10. Duclos, *op. cit.,* p. 190.
11. Affidavit of Bishop Hudal, Jan. 30, 1948, in TEW, *Weizsäcker Document Book 3,* doc. 103.
12. Kessel's testimony of June 21, 1948, in TEW, transcript, p. 9518.
13. *Osservatore della Domenica,* Vatican City, June 28, 1964, p. 61.

14. *IGG*
15. Text in telegram from Gumpert to Berlin, Oct. 16, 1943, in *Inland II Geheim,* doc. E421514. The genesis of this well-known letter has hitherto been unknown, the initiative having been always credited to the Vatican or Bishop Hudal. Something of its origin, however, seems to have been learned by the author of *The Deputy,* Rolf Hochhuth, from a source independent of mine (*IGG*). Without citing his source, he wrote, "Gumpert arranged with Kessel for Pancrazius Pfeiffer . . . to bring a letter to the German commandant of the city which threatened that . . . the Pope would issue an un-neutral statement." ("Sidelights on History" in *The Deputy,* New York, 1964, p. 326.) Gumpert in *IGG* expressed surprise that Hochhuth could have known of this arrangement, since he had never told anyone of his role, and most of the principals, except Kessel, are long dead. In any event, Hochhuth's further statement that Bishop Hudal signed this letter "without consulting his superiors" (p. 327) is not correct.
16. *IGG.*

VIII

1. Debenedetti, *op. cit.,* p. 94.
2. Morpurgo, *Caccia . . . op. cit.,* pp. 139-140.
3. Quoted in "Roma città aperta" in *Capitolium, op. cit.,* June 1964, p. 329.
4. *Il Messaggero,* Oct. 16, 1943.
5. *Il Giornale d'Italia,* Oct. 16, 1943.
6. Quoted in "Roma città aperta" in *op. cit.,* p. 329.
7. *Ibid.,* p. 339.

IX

1. *Wachsberger report*; see also *survivors depositions* and *survivors recording.*
2. *IISS.*
3. *Wachsberger statement.*
4. *Wachsberger report.*
5. *Wachsberger statement.*
6. *Wachsberger report.*
7. *Ibid.*
8. *Ibid.*
9. Tagliacozzo, *op. cit.,* p. 26.
10. *Gestapo report.*
11. Debenedetti, *op. cit.,* p. 96.
12. Tagliacozzo, *op. cit.,* pp. 26-27.
13. *ILA.*

14. Statements to author by several survivors, including *IIMA, IISS, ILA, ILS, et al.*, also *survivors depositions* and *survivors recording.*
15. *ILA.*
16. *ILS.*
17. *IISS.*
18. *Wachsberger statement.*
19. *Wachsberger report.*
20. Tagliacozzo, *op. cit.*, p. 27.
21. *Gestapo report.*
22. *Wachsberger statement.*
23. *Gestapo report.*
24. See Appendix I, note 1.

X

1. *IGG.*
2. *Ibid.;* see also Duclos, *op. cit.*, pp. 189-190.
3. *Ibid.*
4. *Ibid.*
5. Telegram from Gumpert to Berlin, Oct. 16, 1943, in *Inland II Geheim,* doc. E421514.
6. Telegram from Weizsäcker to Berlin, Oct. 17, 1943, in *Inland II Geheim,* doc. E421512.

XI

1. See Debenedetti, *op. cit.*, p. 96, Tagliacozzo, *op. cit.*, p. 27.
2. *ILS, IIMA, IISS.*
3. *Wachsberger report.*
4. *IAW.*
5. *Wachsberger report*; also statements to author by several survivors.
6. *Ibid.*
7. *IAW.*
8. *IIMA, ICE.*
9. *IAW, Wachsberger report.*
10. *Ibid.*

XII

1. *The New York Times,* Oct. 17, 1943, p. 1.
2. Trabucco, *op. cit.*, p. 76.
3. de Wyss, *op. cit.*, p. 144.
4. Scrivener, *op. cit.*, p. 39.
5. *L'Italia Libera,* Oct. 17, 1943; reprinted in Capano, *op. cit.*, II, 134-135.

6. *Gestapo report.*
7. *Ibid.*
8. *Stahel war diary,* frame 568.
9. *Gestapo report.*
10. *ILA*: see also Debenedetti, *op. cit.*, p. 96, who speaks of two such cases.

XIII

1. Debenedetti, *op. cit.*, p. 94.
2. *Almansi report.*
3. Morpurgo, *Caccia . . . op. cit.*, p. 104.
4. Levi Cavaglione, *op. cit.*, p. 24.
5. Quoted in Tagliacozzo, *op. cit.*, p. 34.
6. Quoted in Duclos, *op. cit.*, p. 190.
7. Quoted in *ibid.*
8. *Stahel's war diary,* frame 568, entry for 10:30 A.M., Oct. 17, 1943.
9. See, for example, Lapide, *op. cit.*, pp. 259-260. Lapide, a former Israeli diplomat, refers to the Himmler "order" and writes that Pius's intervention at Stahel's office was "a masterpiece of diplomatic subtlety" (p. 259).
10. *IRL, ISS.*
11. *Ibid.*
12. *ISS.*
13. *Ibid.*; see also S. Sorani, "Come sono riuscito ad imbrogliare la Gestapo," in Morpurgo, *Caccia . . . op. cit.*, pp. 248-258.
14. *ILA*; see also Debenedetti, *op. cit.*, p. 96.
15. Scrivener, *op. cit.*, p. 38.
16. Quoted in "Roma città aperta" in *op. cit.*, p. 329.

XIV

1. *IISS.*
2. *ICE.*
3. *IQZ.*
4. *ICE.*
5. Statements to author by survivors and *IQZ.*
6. Quoted in Bertoldi, *op. cit.*, p. 127.
7. *IISS.*
8. *Ibid.*

XV

1. *IQZ.*
2. Quoted in Debenedetti, *op. cit.*, p. 96.

3. *IQZ.*
4. *Ibid.*
5. *Ibid.*
6. Photocopy of letter from Alatri in CDEC.
7. *Ibid.*
8. *Sorani diary*, entry for Oct. 18, 1943 (deleted from version published by the community).

XVI

1. Statements to author by several survivors; also *Wachsberger report* and *survivor depositions/A. Efrati.*
2. *ILS.*
3. *IISS.*
4. *Wachsberger report, ILA.*
5. The makeup of the cars was described to author by several survivors; also *Wachsberger report.*
6. *Wachsberger report.*
7. *Ibid., IAW.*
8. *IAW.*
9. *Ibid.*
10. *Ibid.*
11. *IQZ.*
12. *Ibid.*
13. Debenedetti, *op. cit.*, p. 97.
14. *Ibid., IQZ.* Zazza in *IQZ* said he thought some prisoners actually succeeded in escaping at this point, but on the basis of statements to author by several survivors this does not appear likely.
15. *IQZ.*
16. *Ibid.*

XVII

1. Descriptions of conditions on board the train are from statements to author by several survivors; also *survivors depositions, survivors recording, Wachsberger statement,* and *Wachsberger report.*
2. *ILA.*
3. Statement by Mario Tagliati, Apr. 5, 1958; CDEC doc. Title E-III.
4. *Ibid.*
5. *Ibid.* (Photocopy of letter by Tedeschi, the text of which is not given by Tagliati, is in CDEC.)
6. *Ibid.*
7. *IISS, et al.*

XVIII

1. *IIMA.*
2. Diary of Lucia de Marchi, entry for Oct. 19, 1943; CDEC doc.
3. *IAW, Wachsberger report.*
4. *Ibid.*
5. *Ibid.*
6. *Ibid.*, see also *survivors depositions, survivors recording,* and Diary of Lucia De Marchi, entry for Oct. 19, 1943; CDEC doc.
7. Diary of Lucia De Marchi, entry for Oct. 19, 1943; CDEC doc.
8. *Ibid.*
9. *Wachsberger report, IAW.*
10. Photocopy of letter by Tedeschi in CDEC.
11. Photocopy of letter to Prima in CDEC.
12. *Wachsberger report, IAW.*
13. *IAW.*
14. *Ibid.*
15. *Wachsberger report, IAW.*
16. *ILS.*
17. *IIMA.*
18. *ICE.*
19. *Ibid.*

XIX

1. de Wyss, *op. cit.*, pp. 144-145.
2. Scrivener, *op. cit.*, p. 39.
3. Notes by Thadden, Oct. 19, 1943, in *Inland II Geheim,* docs. E421511 and E421513.
4. Möllhausen, *op. cit.*, p. 118.
5. *Ibid.*
6. *Ibid.*, pp. 118-119.
7. Text in *ibid.*, p. 119.
8. Giovannetti, *op. cit.*, p. 177.
9. Telegram from Tittmann to Secretary of State Hull, Oct. 19, 1943, in *Foreign Relations of the U.S., 1943, op. cit.*, p. 950.
10. Levi Cavaglione, *op. cit.*, p. 24.
11. *Ibid.*, p. 25.

XX

1. *IAW*; see also Tagliacozzo, *op. cit.*, p. 29.
2. *IAW, Wachsberger report;* cf. L. Camerino's statement in Bertoldi, *op. cit.*, p. 117.
3. *IAW, Wachsberger statement*; cf. Tagliacozzo, *op. cit.*, p. 35.

XXI

1. See *Karvat statement.*
2. See table of arrivals in F. Friedman, *This Was Oswiecim*, London, 1946, pp. 24-25.
3. *Karvat statement.*
4. *Ibid.*
5. *Wachsberger report.*

XXII

1. *Ibid.*
2. *IIMA.*
3. *IISS.*
4. *Ibid.*
5. *ILA.*
6. *Wachsberger report.*
7. *Ibid.*; also *survivors recording/C. Di Segni*, et al.
8. See Tagliacozzo, *op. cit.*, p. 29.
9. CRDE and Bertoldi, *op. cit.*, p. 116.
10. Tagliacozzo, *op. cit.*, p. 36.
11. *Ibid., Wachsberger report.*
12. *Wachsberger report.*

XXIII

1. *Ibid.*
2. *IISS.* For the arrival at Auschwitz see also *survivors depositions* and *survivors recording.*
3. *Wachsberger report.*
4. *Ibid.*, and statements to author by several survivors.
5. *IIMA.*
6. *Wachsberger report*, and statements to author by several survivors.
7. *IAW.*
8. *Wachsberger report.*
9. *IAW.*
10. *Wachsberger report.*
11. *Survivors depositions* and *IISS.*
12. *IISS.*
13. *Survivors recording/Anticoli.*
14. *Wachsberger report.*

XXIV

1. *Karvat statement.*
2. *Ibid.*

3. *Ibid.*
4. *Ibid.*
5. The virtually invariable procedure involved is reconstructed in O. Lengyel, *Hitler's Ovens* (paperback ed. of *Five Chimneys*), New York, 1947, p. 68. The author is an Auschwitz survivor from Hungary.
6. This was the common reaction; see Reitlinger, *op. cit.*, p. 151.
7. Hilberg, *op. cit.*, p. 627.
8. Seen by the author at the Auschwitz museum.
9. Lengyel, *op. cit.*, p. 69.
10. J. Sehn, *Le camp de concentration d'Oswiecim-Brzezinka*, Warsaw, 1961, p. 133.
11. *Karvat statement.*
12. This step is described in Reitlinger, *op. cit.*, p. 151; cf. Lengyel, *op. cit.*, pp. 70-71.
13. *Karvat statement.*
14. *Ibid.*
15. *Ibid.*
16. See Reitlinger, *op. cit.*, p. 151; cf. Lengyel, *op. cit.*, p. 71.
17. Memorandum from Thadden to Eichmann, Oct. 23, 1943, in *Inland II Geheim*, docs. E421509-E421510.
18. *Ibid.*
19. *Ibid.*
20. Eichmann's testimony of July 3, 1961, in TAE, transcript of session 84. I have used the French translation.
21. Eichmann, *op. cit.*, in *Life*, Dec. 5, 1960, p. 150.

XXV

1. Statements to author by several survivors; cf. *survivors depositions.*
2. *Wachsberger report.*
3. *IISS, IAW, et al.*
4. Statements to author by several survivors.
5. *Ibid., Wachsberger report*; cf. *survivors recording.*
6. *Wachsberger report.*
7. *Ibid.*
8. *Ibid.*
9. *Ibid.*
10. *Ibid.* and *IAW.*
11. *Ibid.*
12. *Ibid.*
13. *Ibid.*
14. *IAW.*
15. *Ibid.*
16. *Survivors recording/Anticoli* and *ILA.*

17. *IIMA.*
18. *IISS.*
19. *Wachsberger report.*
20. *Ibid.*

XXVI

1. Sorani, *op. cit.*, pp. 248-250.
2. *IPF.*
3. *ISS.*
4. Tagliacozzo, *op. cit.*, p. 37.
5. *L'Osservatore Romano,* Oct. 25-26, 1953.
6. Letter from Weizsäcker to Berlin, Oct. 28, 1943, in *Inland II Geheim*, docs. E421515-E421517.
7. *Ibid.*, doc. E421515.
8. Levi Cavaglione, *op. cit.*, p. 30.
9. *Ibid.*
10. *Ibid.*, p. 31.
11. *Ibid.*
12. *Ibid.*

Part Four: Epilogue

1. P. Weiss, *The Investigation* (Eng. vers. by J. Swan and U. Grosbard), New York, Atheneum, 1966, p. 109.

I

1. *IISS.*
2. *Ibid.*
3. "Ordine di polizia n. 5," of Nov. 30, 1943; text in De Felice, *op. cit.*, p. 503.
4. *Ibid.*, pp. 502-510.
5. For this interesting case, see Verbalnote of the Italian embassy in Berlin to the German Foreign Office, Nov. 8, 1943, in *Inland IIAB*, Frame 346049 and subsequent docs. in frames 346053-346061.
6. Report by Inland II chief Horst Wagner, Dec. 4, 1943, in *Inland II Geheim*, docs. E421505-E421506.
7. *Ibid.*
8. *Ibid.*
9. *Ibid.*
10. Cf. De Felice, *op. cit.*, pp. 518-522.
11. Letter from Consul Koester to Berlin, Dec. 7, 1943; text in Friedländer, *op. cit.*, pp. 209-211.

12. Möllhausen, *op. cit.*, pp. 162-165.
13. *Sorani diary*, entry for Feb. 2, 1944; regarding the Roman Jews arrested during this period see the documents of the Questura di Roma contained in the Wiener Library, London.
14. For the official figures see the Rome Jewish community's publication *Ottobre 1943 . . . op. cit.*, p. 29.
15. Katz, *op. cit.*, p. 168.
16. *Dosi collection* and CDEC.
17. Quoted in *L'Italia Libera*, Rome, Mar. 26, 1947, p. 2; see also G. Lombroso, "Pantera nera, la tragedia del ghetto alle Assise" in *Israel*, Rome, Mar. 13, 1947, p. 6.
18. *Ibid.*
19. *Dosi collection.*
20. Cf. De Felice, pp. 518-522; see the documents in this regard contained in the Wiener Library, London.
21. Letter from Eichmann to German Foreign Office, Nov. 15, 1943, reproduced in *Yad Vashem Bulletin*, Jerusalem, Apr. 1961, p. 13.
22. De Felice, *op. cit.*, p. 522; see also Hilberg, *op. cit.*, p. 432.
23. Cf. Segre, *op. cit.*, pp. 9-11.
24. *Ibid.*, pp. 11-12, De Felice, *op. cit.* p. 530. For a contemporary German report on this incident see *Inland II AB*, frame 346031.
25. Levi Cavaglione, *op. cit.*, p. 50.
26. D'Agostini and Forti, *op. cit.*, p. 225; see also dedication page of Levi Cavaglione, *op. cit.*
27. *Ibid.*, p. 209.
28. *ILP.*
29. De Felice, *op. cit.*, p. 546.
30. CRDE.

II

1. *Sorani diary*, entry for June 5, 1944 (deleted from version published by the community).
2. *Ibid.*
3. See *ibid.*, entry for July 12, 1944 (deleted from version published by the community) and *Neufeld papers.*
4. *Ibid.*
5. Signatories in A. Levi, *op. cit.*, p. 46.
6. *Neufeld papers.*
7. *The New York Times*, July 9, 1944, p. 18.
8. *Ibid.*
9. *Ibid.*
10. *Israel*, Rome, July, 1944.
11. Letter from Foà to Zolli, July 4, 1944, in Zolli, *op. cit.*, p. 203.
12. *Ibid.*, pp. 154-156, *Neufeld papers*; see also Newman, *op. cit.*, p. 132.

13. Tagliacozzo, *op. cit.*, pp. 20-21.
14. *Foà report-I/E.*
15. *Ottobre 1943 . . . op. cit.*, p. 28n.
16. *IMN.*
17. Debenedetti, *op. cit.*, p. 94.
18. *Foà report-I/B.*
19. *Ibid./E.*
20. *Sorani diary,* entry for Sept. 29, 1943 (deleted from version published by the community).
21. *Foà report-I/B.*
22. Disi's testimony of June 14, 1948, in THK.
23. *Ibid.*
24. *IGD.*
25. *Ibid.*
26. *Ibid.* Document signed by Piperno in *Dosi collection.*
27. *Ibid.*
28. *Ibid.*
29. *Neufeld papers.*
30. *Sorani diary,* entries from July 14, 1944 to final entry, Sept. 17, 1944 (all deleted from version published by the community).
31. *Neufeld papers.*
32. *Ibid.*
33. *IES* and letter from Roberto Modigliani to author, Oct. 23, 1967.
34. Zolli, *op. cit.*, pp. 182-183.
35. *Ibid.*, p. 184.
36. See especially Yahuda, *op. cit.*, pp. 7-9 and Leiber, *op. cit.*, pp. 457-458.
37. Zolli, *op. cit.*, p. 185.
38. *London Jewish Chronicle,* Feb. 23, 1945, p. 9.
39. *Israel,* Rome, Feb. 15, 1945, p. 4.
40. *Neufeld papers.*
41. *Ibid.*
42. Foà rose to a high position in the postwar Italian judiciary system; for a recent assessment of Almansi, see Milano, *Storia . . . op. cit.*, p. 401.
43. E. Zolli, *Antisemitismo,* Rome, 1945.
44. Zolli, *Before . . . op. cit.*
45. *Ibid.*, p. 198.

III

1. Statements to author by several survivors.
2. See *survivors depositions.*
3. *ILA.*
4. *IISS.*

5. See especially *Israel,* Rome, Oct. 24, 1963, pp. 1-2, reporting on the twentieth anniversary ceremonies.
6. Statement to author by eyewitness Eloisa Ravenna, executive secretary of CDEC; see also *La voce della comunità israelitica,* Rome, Dec. 1966, pp. 2-3.
7. *Medical World News,* New York, April 2, 1965, pp. 52-53.

IV

1. *Kappler sentence.*
2. *Ibid.*
3. *Ibid.*
4. *Ibid.*
5. *Ibid.*
6. *Ibid.*
7. Some of the documents and testimony in TEW were published in Eng. trans. in *Trials of War Criminals Before the Nuremberg Military Tribunals,* Washington, 1951-1952, 15 vols., vols. XII, XIV.
8. Letter from Pope Pius XII in TEW, *Weizsäcker Document Book 3*
9. Hudal affidavit in *ibid.*
10. Jedin affidavit, Apr. 2, 1948, in *ibid.*
11. Kessel's testimony of June 21 and 22, 1948, in TEW, transcript, pp. 9518 and 9567.
12. TEW, transcript of judgment, pp. 28293 and 28330.
13. *L'Osservatore Romano,* May 16-17, 1949.
14. Letter from Speier to Gen. John J. McCloy, July 13, 1949; copy given to author by Dr. Speier.
15. Weizsäcker, *op. cit.,* p. 280.
16. KT.
17. See especially *The Observer,* London, July 16, 1967, pp. 1-2.
18. Hilberg, *op. cit.,* p. 705. West German authorities maintain that Dannecker committed suicide in a prison cell at Bad Tölz, Dec. 10, 1945, and thus he has never been sought. There appears to be no evidence to support this claim, however, and most experts list him as missing.
19. See *The Observer,* London, July 16, 1967, pp. 1-2, and S. Wiesenthal, *The Murderers Among Us,* New York, McGraw-Hill, 1967.

V

1. Milano, *Storia . . . op. cit.,* pp. 413-415.
2. *IET*; cf. De Felice, *op. cit.,* p. 527.
3. *IET.*
4. Milano, *Storia . . . op. cit.,* p. 415.
5. *Israel,* Rome, Dec. 12, 1946, p. 4.
6. *Ottobre 1943 . . . op. cit.,* p. 5.

7. *Ibid.*, pp. 5-7.
8. *Ibid.*, p. 5.
9. Cf. *Ibid.*, pp. 35-43 with *Sorani diary*.
10. *IET*.

A Conclusion

1. N. Podhoretz, "Hannah Arendt on Eichmann, a Study in the Perversity of Brilliance" in *Commentary*, Sept. 1963, p. 205.
2. *Ibid.*, p. 207.
3. Kubovy, *op. cit.*, p. 6.
4. Hausner's summation in TAE; excerpt quoted in *Saturday Review*, July 2, 1966, p. 27.
5. J. Robinson, *And the Crooked Shall Be Made Straight*, New York, 1965.
6. *Ibid.*, p. 144.
7. *Ibid.*, p. 168.
8. *Ibid.*, p. 224.
9. *Ibid.*, p. 225.
10. *Ibid.*, p. 224.
11. *Ibid.*, p. 226.
12. Weiss, *op. cit.*, pp. 108-109.
13. Robinson, *op. cit.*, p. 224.
14. Hilberg, *op. cit.*, p. 32.
15. See F. Fischer, *Germany's Aims in the First World War*, New York, Norton, 1968.
16. A.J.P. Taylor, *The Origins of the Second World War*, London, Hamish Hamilton, 1961, paperback, rev. ed., 1965, p. 23.
17. Memorandum from H. Ewing to W. Swint, July 17, 1933, doc. NI-9784; quoted in Hilberg, *op. cit*, p. 58.
18. Quoted in *ibid.*, p. 122.
19. Memorandum from Murmelstein to S. Kolisch (director of the Vienna Jewish war invalids organization), Oct. 13-14, 1941 (YIVO doc.); quoted in *ibid.*, p. 279.
20. Speech to General Assembly of the Bialystok Judenrat by Vice Chairman Ephraim Barasz, Apr. 4, 1942; minutes published in N. Blumenthal, *Darko shel Judenrat*, Jerusalem, Yad Vashem, 1962 (in Yiddish and Hebrew), p. 160; quoted in Eng. trans. in Kubovy, *op. cit.*, pp. 7-8.
21. Speech to Plenary Assembly of the Bialystok Judenrat by Chairman Gedaliah Rozenman, Aug. 16, 1942, in *ibid.*, p. 237; quoted in Kubovy, *op. cit.*, p. 8.
22. See, for example, the report on the activities of organized French Jewry during the years 1941-1943 in J. Kaplan (acting grand rabbi of France) "French Jewry Under the Occupation" in *American Jewish Yearbook, op. cit.,* vol. 47, 1945-1946.

23. Quoted in H. Arendt, "Zionism Reconsidered" in *The Menorah Journal*, New York, Autumn, 1945, p. 180.
24. Quoted in Arendt, *Eichmann . . . op. cit.*, p. 59; see also Arendt, "Zionism . . ." *op. cit.*, pp. 162-196.
25. R. Kastner, *Der Kastner-Bericht über Eichmanns Menschenhandel in Ungarn*, Munich, Kindler, 1961, pp. 67-68; quoted in Robinson, *op. cit.*, p. 180.
26. Quoted in Arendt, *Eichmann . . . op. cit.*, p. 118.
27. A. Morse, *While Six Million Died*, New York, 1968.
28. Hochhuth, *op. cit.*, and Friedländer, *op. cit.*, G. Lewy, *The Catholic Church and Nazi Germany*, New York, 1964, C. Falconi, *Il silenzio di Pio XII*, Milan, 1965.
29. Weiss, *op. cit.*
30. J. Joll, "How Hitler Made It" in *The New York Review of Books*, Feb. 15, 1968, p. 14.

Appendix I

1. Until now there existed no list of the deportees of Oct. 16, 1943, their names being included in general lists of Italian Jews deported during the war. This list was compiled from CRDE, CDEC. Some 10-15 names of persons said to be among the October 16th group could not be confirmed at these sources and were not included, although there can be little doubt that they were in fact among these deportees, as were many who forever will remain unidentified. The unconfirmed names were not added to this list because in no case was it possible to obtain the full name and among those where the last name was known, they were already represented by several others bearing the same surname.

Appendix II

1. The sources for the names and details for this listing are CRDE, CDEC, and several of the survivors themselves.

ACKNOWLEDGMENTS

I WOULD LIKE to thank the many people who in one way or another contributed to the realization of this book, particularly the survivors of the October 16th deportation and other persons who were witnesses to the events described herein and who met with me to relive the past, often for many long and anguished hours. Some have been named in this book, others have not, and still others prefer to remain anonymous. To all of them I express my appreciation for their kindnesses.

I am thankful for the services rendered to me by the following research centers: the Centro di Documentazione Ebraica Contemporanea, Milan; the National Archives, Washington, D.C.; the New York Public Library; the Wiener Library, London; and the YIVO Institute for Jewish Research, New York.

Finally, I am especially grateful to the following persons: Alfonso Cascone, Beverly Katz, Peter Matson, Maurice F. Neufeld, Oscar Ochs, Eloisa Ravenna, Peter Ritner, Settimia Spizzichino, Michael Tagliacozzo, Massimo Adolfo Vitale, Simon Wiesenthal, and Arminio Wachsberger.

R.K.

BIBLIOGRAPHY

APART FROM THE published and unpublished primary documents (described in the "Notes" section of this book), a bibliography of the October 16th incident as such would be virtually complete with the listing of two articles: Giacomo Debenedetti's classic "16 ottobre 1943" and Michael Tagliacozzo's little known study, "La comunità di Roma sotto l'incubo della svastica." Both articles are of exceptional value and complement each other, but unfortunately almost everything that has been written about the deportation of the Jews of Rome can be traced to Debenedetti's. This is hardly surprising of course, since, for one thing, the Debenedetti piece was published nineteen years prior to Tagliacozzo's. But this fact, as well as the early availability of Foà's 1943 report, had the unintentional effect of "prewriting" many subsequent secondary sources.

Debenedetti, who was to become a literary figure of major importance in Italy, published his article in 1944 in the December issue of *Mercurio,* a short-lived periodical that appeared after the Allied liberation of Rome. His report was drawn entirely from eyewitness accounts, first-hand information of the events described, and his own superior knowledge of the Jews of Rome, of whom he was one. It was written at a time when Debenedetti, like most poeple, did not know what had happened to the deported Jews, and it breaks off shortly after their departure from the Tiburtina station. The 10,000-word article, which was not without the unavoidable errors that characterize early accounts of any event, was reprinted several times in booklet form and became the standard work on the subject.

Tagliacozzo, now an Israeli, was also a Roman Jew, who published his article in November 1963 in the infrequent and rather obscure journal of the Milan Jewish document center, Centro di Documentazione Ebraica Contemporanea. His quiet study of some thirty pages contains much original material and is of great interest. It is part of an as-yet-unpublished manuscipt dealing with the conditions of the

Jews of Rome under the occupation. Though he does not say so in the article, during the occupation of Rome Tagliacozzo had taken refuge in St. John in Lateran, a church protected under the Vatican's sanctuary agreement with the Germans. Among his fellow refugees were leading members of the Resistance, including a group of Italian spies in the service of the Allies. This intelligence operation had agents placed inside Kappler's Gestapo headquarters, and as a result Tagliacozzo obtained access to top secret documents, which were subsequently destroyed by the Nazis before falling into Allied hands. Tagliacozzo's article clarifies in many ways the various roles played by the Gestapo men in the October 16th affair and offers important confirmations of Kappler's testimony in connection with his own trial and Eichmann's.

For a critical understanding of the event, however, it is necessary to go beyond the specific documents. A valuable aid in doing so is the extensive bibliography on Italian Jewry since ancient Rome prepared by the historian Attilio Milano, *Bibliotheca historica italo-judaica*, Florence: Sansoni, 1954. A supplement to this annotated work was published in 1964 and covers the years 1954-1963, a decade when most of the important books on the Nazi-Fascist period appeared. A similar aid that deals with Jews under Nazism throughout Europe is: J. Robinson and P. Friedman, *Guide to Jewish History Under Nazi Impact*, New York: Yad Vashem-YIVO, 1960, although this is rapidly becoming outdated.

The following lists a selection of additional published works which I have found helpful in writing this book. Those that offer some details about one aspect or another of the October 16th incident, I have indicated with an asterisk; those that treat it to some extent are marked with two asterisks. I have also taken the liberty of commenting on some of this material.

Algardi, Z., *Processi ai fascisti*, Florence: Parenti, 1958.*

Arendt, H., *Eichmann in Jerusalem*, rev. ed., New York: The Viking Press, Inc. 1965.*

Artom, E., *Diari*, Milan: Centro di Documentazione Ebraica Contemporanea, 1966. (The diaries of an Italian Jewish partisan.)

Ascarelli, A., *Le fosse Ardeatine*, Bologna: Canesi, 1965.** (This edition of Ascarelli's 1945 report on the identification of the victims of the Ardeatine caves massacre contains the full text of the sentence in the Kappler trial.)

Battaglia, R., *Storia della Resistenza italiana*, rev. ed. Turin: Giulio Einaudi editore, 1964.* (Most books about the Italian Resistance make note of the fate of the Jews of Rome.)

Barkai, M., ed., *The Fighting Ghettoes*, Philadelphia: J. B. Lippincott Company, 1962.

Berenson, B., *Rumour and Reflection,* London: Constable & Co., Ltd., 1952.*

Bertoldi, S., *I tedeschi in Italia,* Milan: Rizzoli, 1964.**

Buonaiuti, E., *Pio XII,* Rome: Universale, 1946.

Caleffi, P., *Si fa presto a dire fame,* Milan: Edizioni Avanti, 1955.

Capano, R.P., *La Resistenza in Roma,* 2 vols., Naples: Gaetano Macchiaroli Editore, 1963.** (Vol. II contains a 70-page chapter on the anti-Jewish persecutions in Italy, with emphasis on Rome.)

Carter, B.B., *Italy Speaks,* London: Victor Gollancz, Ltd., 1947.*

Chabod, F., *L'Italia contemporanea,* Turin: Giulio Einaudi Editore, 1961.

Ciano, G., *Ciano's Hidden Diary, 1937-1938,* New York: E.P. Dutton & Co., Inc., 1953.

D'Agostini, L., and Forti, R., *Il sole è sorto a Roma,* Rome: Associazione Nazionale Partigiani d'Italia, 1965.**

Davidson, E., *The Trial of the Germans,* New York: The Macmillan Company, 1966.

Deakin, F.W., *The Brutal Friendship,* New York: Harper & Row, Publishers, 1962.

———, *The Six Hundred Days of Mussolini,* New York: Anchor Books, 1966. (A rev. ed. of Part III of *The Brutal Friendship.*)

De Felice, R., *Storia degli ebrei italiani sotto il fascismo,* Turin: Giulio Einaudi Editore, 1961.**

Delzell, C.F., *Mussolini's Enemies: The Italian Anti-Fascist Resistance,* Princeton: Princeton University Press, 1961.*

de Wyss, M., *Rome Under the Terror,* London: Robert Hale Ltd., 1945.**

Dollmann, E., *Roma nazista,* Milan: Longanesi, 1949.

Duclos, P., *Le Vatican et la seconde guerre mondiale,* Paris: Editions Pedone, 1955.**

Dunn, S.P., *The Influence of Ideology on Culture Change,* doctoral dissertation, Columbia University, New York, 1959. (See above, p. 347.)

Enciclopedia Italiana, Seconda Appendice, Vol. 2, Rome: Istituto della Enciclopedia Italiana, 1949.**

European Jewry 10 Years After the War, New York: Institute of Jewish Affairs, 1956.*

Fergnani, E., *Un' uomo e tre numeri,* Milan: Edizioni Avanti, 1945.

Friedländer, S., *Pius XII and the Third Reich,* New York: Alfred A. Knopf, Inc., 1966.**

Friedman, F., *This Was Oswiecim,* London: United Jewish Relief Appeal, 1946.*

Giovannetti, A., *Roma città aperta,* Milan: Editrice Ancora, 1962.** (The author is a Vatican diplomat who had access to the archives of the Holy See.)

Gregorovius, F., *The Ghetto and the Jews of Rome,* New York: Schocken Books, 1948. (See above, p. 347.)

Halecki, O., and Murray, J., *Pius XII: Eugenio Pacelli, Pope of Peace,* New York: Farrar, Strauss & Giroux, Inc., 1954.**

Hilberg, R., *Prologue to Annihilation,* doctoral dissertation, Columbia University, New York, 1955. (This became part of the author's well-known published work noted below, but it contains material of interest that was not included and remains unpublished.)

———, *The Destruction of the European Jews,* rev. ed., Chicago: Quadrangle Books, 1967.** (See above, p. 346.)

Hochhuth, R., *Sidelights on History* (Appendix to *The Deputy*), New York: Grove Press, Inc., 1964.**

Hughes, H.S., *The United States and Italy,* rev. ed., Cambridge: Harvard University Press, 1965.

Katz, R., *Death in Rome,* New York: The Macmillan Company, 1967.*

Kesselring, A., *A Soldier's Record,* New York: William Morrow & Company, Inc., 1954.

Kirkpatrick, I., *Mussolini: A Study in Power,* New York: Hawthorn Books, Inc., 1964.

Lapide, P., *Three Popes and the Jews,* New York: Hawthorn Books, Inc., 1967.**

Leto, G., *OVRA: Fascismo-antifascismo,* Bologna: Cappelli Editore, 1951.

Levi, A., ed., *Noi ebrei,* Rome: Pinciana, 1937. (Fascist Jewry's reply to Fascist anti-Semitism.)

Levi, P., *If This Be A Man,* New York: The Orion Press, Inc., 1959. (This is the Eng. trans. of *Se questo è un 'uomo,* the best known of several accounts by survivors of the deportations in northern Italy which followed the Rome episode.)

Levi Cavaglione, P., *Guerriglia nei Castelli Romani,* Rome: Giulio Einaudi Editore, 1945.**

Lewy, G., *The Catholic Church and Nazi Germany,* New York: McGraw-Hill, Inc., 1964.**

Lochner, L., ed., *The Goebbels Diaries,* Garden City: Doubleday Company, Inc., 1948.

Lizzani, C., *L'oro di Roma,* Bologna: Cappelli Editore, 1961.** (The screenplay of a film about the Jews of Rome during the occupation. Also contains the transcript of interviews by G. Vento; see above, p. 356.)

Mack Smith, D., *Italy, A Modern History,* Ann Arbor: University of Michigan Press, 1959.

Milano, A., *Il ghetto di Roma,* Rome: Staderni, 1964.

———, *Storia degli ebrei in Italia,* Turin: Giulio Einaudi Editore, 1963.**

Möllhausen, E.F., *La carta perdente,* Rome: Sestante, 1948.**

Momigliano, E., *Storia tragica e grottesca del razzismo fascista,* Milan: Arnaldo Mondadori Editore, 1946.

Monelli, P., *Roma, 1943,* rev. ed., Milan: Longanesi, 1963.*

Morpurgo, L., *Caccia all'uomo,* Rome: Casa Editrice Dalmatia, 1946.**

Newman, L.I., *A "Chief Rabbi" of Rome Becomes a Catholic,* New York: Renascence Press, 1945.** (Rabbi Newman's long attack on Rabbi Zolli.)

Orano, P., *Gli ebrei in Italia,* Rome: Pinciana, 1937. (An anti-Semitic tract which had profound effects in Italy.)

Ottobre 1943: Cronaca di un'infamia, Rome: Comunità Israelitica di Roma, 1961.** (See above, p. 313.)

Pellicani, A., *Il papa di tutti,* Milan: Sugar Editore, 1964.

Pisano', G., *Mussolini e gli ebrei,* Milan: Edizioni FPE, 1967.** (A neo-Fascist view of the Fascist persecution of Italian Jews.)

Piscitelli, E., *Storia della Resistenza romana,* Bari: Editori Laterza, 1965.**

Poliakov, L., *Harvest of Hate,* Syracuse: Syracuse University Press, 1954.*

———, *La condition des juifs en France sous l'occupation italienne,* Paris: Centre de Documenation Juive Contemporaine, 1946.

Rahn, R., *Ruheloses Leben,* Dusseldorf: Diedrichs Verlag, 1949.

Reitlinger, G., *The Final Solution,* New York: The Beechhurst Press, Inc., 1953.*

Ripa di Meana, F., *Roma clandestina,* Rome: O.E.T., 1944.**

Robinson, J., *And the Crooked Shall Be Made Straight,* New York: The Macmillan Company, 1965.*

Roma città aperta, Rome: Comune di Roma, 1964.** (Special issue of *Capitolium.*)

Roth, C., *The History of the Jews of Italy,* Philadelphia: Jewish Publication Society, 1946.

Salvatorelli, L., and Mira, G., *Storia d'Italia nel periodo fascista,* Turin: Giulio Einaudi Editore, 1956.*

Scrivener, J. (pseud.), *Inside Rome with the Germans,* New York: The Macmillan Company, 1945.**

Sehn, J., *Le camp de concentration d'Oswiecim-Brzezinka,* Warsaw: Wydawnictwo Prawnicze, 1961.

Seldes, G., *Facts and Fascism,* New York: In Fact, Inc., 1943.

Segre, R., *Appunti sulle persecuzioni antisemitiche e sulla vita delle comunità Israelitiche nell'Italia occupata,* Rome: Amministrazione Provinciale di Roma, 1964.* (Pamphlet.)

Stendardo, G., *Via Tasso,* Rome: privately printed, 1965.

Suhl, Y., ed., *They Fought Back,* New York: Crown Publishers, Inc., 1967.*

Szner, Z., ed., *Extermination and Resistance,* Vol. I, Haifa: Ghetto Fighters House, 1958.

Tamaro, A., *Due anni di storia, 1943-45,* 3 vols., Rome: Tosi, 1948-1950.** (A neo-Fascist account.)

Trabucco, C., *La prigionia di Roma,* Rome: S.E.L.I., 1945.**

Trials of War Criminals Before the Nuremberg Military Tribunals, Vols. XII-XIV, Washington: U.S. Government Printing Office, 1951-1952. (This partial transcript of the Weizsäcker trial does not contain the material relative to the Jews of Rome.)

Troisio, A., *Roma sotto il terrore nazi-fascista,* Rome: Mondini, 1944.**

United Nations War Crimes Commission, *History of the United Nations War Crimes Commission,* London: H.M. Stationery Office, 1948.

Valabrega, G., ed., *Gli ebrei in Italia durante il fascismo,* Milan: Centro di Documentazione Ebraica Contemporanea, 1963.** (Special issue of the *Quaderni* of CDEC. Contains the Tagliacozzo article.)

Vogelstein, H., *Rome,* Philadelphia: Jewish Publication Society, 1941. (A history of the Jews of Rome.)

Weizsäcker, E., *Memoirs,* Chicago: Henry Regnery Company, 1951.

Wiskemann, E., *The Rome-Berlin Axis,* rev. ed., London: The Fontana Library, 1966.

Zangrandi, R., *1943: 25 luglio-8 settembre,* Milan: Feltrinelli Editore, 1964.

Zolli, E., *Antisemitismo,* Rome: A.V.E., 1945.*

———, *Before the Dawn,* New York: Sheed & Ward, Inc., 1954.**

Articles

Arendt, H., "Zionism Reconsidered," in *Menorah Journal,* New York, Autumn, 1945.

Arvay, R., "The Italian People and the Jews," in *The Commonweal,* June 8, 1945.

Bertel, G., "The Case of Rabbi Zolli," in *The Congress Weekly,* New York, Mar. 2, 1945.

Collotti, E., "Documenti sull'attività del Sicherheitsdienst nell'Italia," in *Movimento di Liberazione in Italia,* Milan, Apr.-June, 1966.

"I rapporti italo-tedeschi dopo l'8 settembre." in *Studi Storici,* 1962, No. 4.

De Felice, R., "La Chiesa cattolica e il problema ebraico durante gli anni dell'antisemitismo fascista," in *La Rassegna Mensile di Israel,* Rome, Jan. 1957.

Dunn, L.C. and S.P., "The Jewish Community of Rome," in *Scientific American,* Mar. 1957.

Dunn, S.P., "An Outsider Visits the Roman Ghetto," in *Commentary,* Feb. 1958.

"The Roman Jewish Community: A Study in Historical Causation," in *Jewish Journal of Sociology*, London, Nov. 1960.

Eichmann, A., "Eichmann Tells His Own Damning Story," in *Life*, Nov. 28, and Dec. 5, 1960.

Kessel, A., "The Pope and the Jews," in Bentley, E., ed., *The Storm Over The Deputy*, New York: Grove Press, Inc., 1964.**

Kubovy, A.L., "Criminal State vs. Moral Society," in *Yad Vashem Bulletin*, Jerusalem, Oct. 1963.

Leiber, R., "Pio XII e gli ebrei di Roma," in *La Civiltà Cattolica*, Rome, Mar. 4. 1961.**

Michaelis, M., "Gli ebrei Italiani sotto il regime fascista," in *La Rassegna Mensile di Israel*, 1962.

"On the Jewish Question in Fascist Italy," in *Yad Vashem Studies*, Vol. IV, Jerusalem: Yad Vashem, 1960.

Mushkat, M., "Eichmann in New York," in *Yad Vashem Bulletin*, Mar. 1964.

Poliakov, L., "Pope Pius XII and the Nazis," in Bentley, E., ed., *The Storm Over The Deputy*, New York: Grove Press, Inc., 1964.

"The Vatican and the Jewish Question," in *Commentary*, Nov. 1950.

Romano, G., "Una testimonanza sul capitolò italiano al processo Eichmann," in *La Rassegna Mensile di Israel*, 1962, Nos. 3-4.*

Spinosa, A., "Le persecuzioni razziali in Italia," in *Il Ponte*, Florence, 1952, Nos. 7, 8, and 11; 1953, No. 7.

Volli, G., "Gli ebrei nella lotta antifascista," in *Emilia*, Bologna, Aug.-Sept. 1955.

Yahuda, A.S.E., "The Conversion of a 'Chief Rabbi'," in The Churchman, June 1, 1945.

Index

Index

JEWISH QUARTER OF ROME, 1943

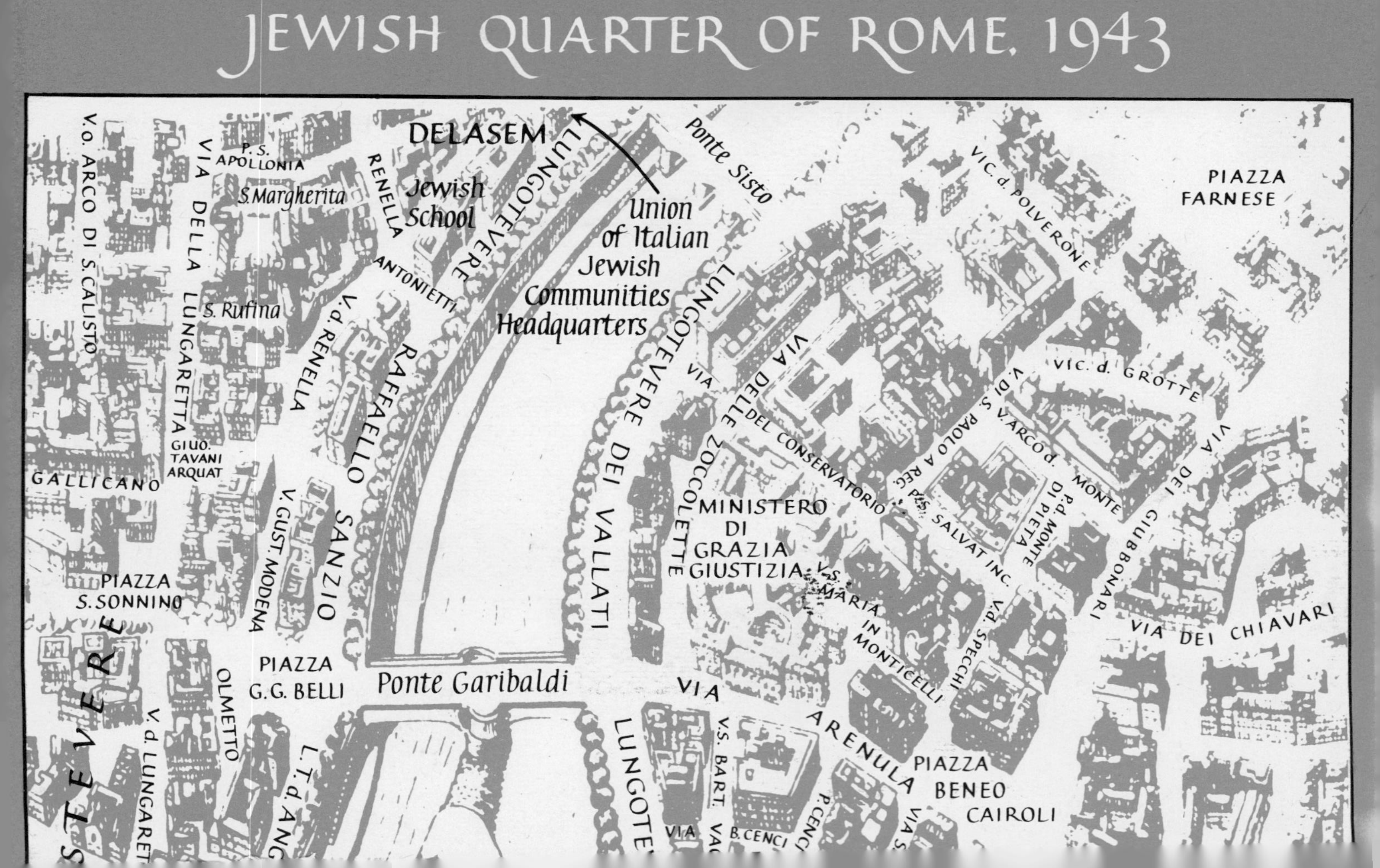